Strategy Formulation And Implementation

Tasks of the
General Manager

Strategy Formulation And Implementation

Tasks of the General Manager

Arthur A. Thompson, Jr.
A. J. Strickland III

both of
The University of Alabama

Fourth Edition

1989

**BPI
IRWIN**

Homewood, IL 60430
Boston, MA 02116

Sponsoring editor: William R. Bayer
Project editor: Paula M. Buschman
Production manager: Bette Ittersagen
Compositor: Graphic World, Inc.
Typeface: 10½/12 Times Roman
Printer: R.R. Donnelley & Sons Company

Library of Congress Cataloging-in-Publication Data

Thompson, Arthur A., 1940-
  Strategy formulation and implementation : tasks of the general
manager / Arthur A. Thompson, Jr., and A.J. Strickland, III.—4th
ed.
    p.   cm.
  Includes bibliographies and index.
  ISBN 0-256-06901-8 (pbk.)
  1. Strategic planning. I. Strickland, A. J. (Alonzo J.)
II. Title.
HD30.28.T54   1989
658.4′012—dc19

88–28599
CIP

Printed in the United States of America

      3 4 5 6 7 8 9 0 DO 6 5 4 3 2 1 0

Preface

This fourth edition of *Strategy Formulation and Implementation* represents a major revision and incorporates significant new features. We have reorganized the presentation into 10 chapters, improved the graphics, steamlined the presentations, broadened the coverage in several areas, created a four-chapter module on business-level situation analysis and a two-chapter section on strategic analysis in diversified companies, developed Analytical Checklists at the end of most chapters to highlight the key components of strategic thinking and strategic analysis, inserted nine new Illustration Capsules, and included six recent journal articles to form a text-readings package. Throughout, the content reflects new contributions to the strategic-management literature, a more straightforward conceptual framework, and a sharper focus on concepts, analytical techniques, and practitioner experiences.

WHAT'S NEW IN THE TEXT CHAPTERS

The rapid-fire development of the strategic-management literature dictates that major edition-to-edition refinements be made in the treatment given to concepts and analytical techniques. In our updating and adjusting, however, we have kept the focus of this edition strongly centered on the strategy-related tasks of managers and on the methods of strategic analysis. Senior managers (major department heads and on up) are cast firmly in the twin roles of chief strategy-maker and chief strategy-implementer, charged with presiding over insightful strategic analysis, formulating and reviewing strategic-action plans, and leading the process of strategy implementation and execution in their respective areas of responsibility. Every key aspect of strategic management is examined—defining the business, setting strategic objectives, conducting industry and competitive analysis, doing company situation analysis, evaluating diversified business portfolios, checking the various generic corporate and business-strategy options, probing for sustainable competitive advantage, building a capable organization, shaping the corporate culture, creating strategy-related administrative fits, and exerting strategic leadership.

We've made several changes worth calling to your attention:

- Chapter 1 has been thoroughly overhauled to lay out more sharply and more concisely just what strategy-making, strategy-implementing, and the strategic-planning process are all about. The separate roles of line managers, strategic planners, and boards of directors are spelled out.
- Chapter 2 zeros in on the direction-setting entrepreneurial tasks—defining

the business, establishing strategic objectives, and crafting a strategy. The layers of strategy and the strategy-making issues at each level of the managerial hierarchy are given special prominence.

- The treatment of business-level situation analysis has been divided into two chapters: one on the techniques of industry and competitive analysis (Chapter 3) and one on company situation analysis (Chapter 4).

- The chapter on industry and competitive analysis incorporates a conceptual approach applicable to any market situation. It draws together all the necessary tools—how to profile industry structure, identifying the drivers of industry change, Porter's model of competitive forces, the technique of strategic group mapping, the identification of key success factors, and the assessment of long-term industry attractiveness. The overall analytical model is appealingly simple and guides its users to thinking strategically about the answers to a few select questions.

- The role of experience curve economics in strategic analysis is given increased attention.

- The chapter on company situation analysis features diagnosing how well the present strategy is working, SWOT analysis, competitive strength assessments, strategic cost or value chain analysis, and identification of strategic issues confronting the company.

- A much revised chapter on competitive strategy and competitive advantage incorporates the trailblazing approach of Michael Porter in his two books, *Competitive Strategy* (1980) and *Competitive Advantage* (1985).

- Chapter 6, "Matching Strategy to the Situation," covers the major strategy alternatives in generic types of industry environments and company situations. Coverage of strategic issues and alternatives in globally competitive markets has been strengthened.

- We've continued our practice of covering strategic analysis for single-business situations ahead of corporate strategy and diversification issues, because the concepts and techniques of corporate strategy rely so heavily on a good grasp of business-strategy concepts. However, because of their stand-alone nature, instructors who prefer to do so can cover the material on corporate strategy (Chapters 7 and 8) ahead of the business-strategy chapter grouping (Chapters 3, 4, 5, and 6).

- One of the two chapters on strategic analysis in diversified companies explains the various corporate strategy alternatives with emphasis on building a diversified business portfolio and post-diversification portfolio management. The other chapter concentrates on the analytical tools for appraising diversified corporate portfolios; it features treatment of how to use diversification to create competitive advantage.

- The job of implementing strategy is seen as consisting of five key managerial tasks: building a capable organization, linking the budgeting process to the strategic plan, generating commitment to the chosen strategy up and down the organization, putting strategy-supportive policies and administrative practices into place, and exercising strategic leadership. Chapter 9 deals with the first two tasks and Chapter 10 with the last three.

- The importance of building a strategy-supportive corporate culture continues to get center-stage treatment as a key to successful strategy execution.
- Analytical checklist sections at the end of most chapters draw attention to key concepts, techniques, and questions to ask, in an effort to build the skill of thinking about "the big picture" in strategic terms.
- Shorter, crisper Illustration Capsules have been written to demonstrate real-world application of core concepts. Nine of the 20 capsules are new to this edition.

All in all, we are confident you will find the text portion of this edition better organized, more tightly written, comfortably mainstream, and as close to the cutting edge of both theory and practice as basic textbook discussions can be.

THE READINGS SELECTIONS

In the first two editions, we included readings to complement the text discussion; in the preceding third edition, we dropped readings. This fourth edition reverts to the inclusion of readings for three reasons: (1) to provide detailed treatment of several important, newly published topics; (2) to provide readers with modest exposure to the strategic management literature; (3) to respond to the requests of users who, as a regular practice, assign articles out of the current journals to their classes. However, in deference to length, we have chosen just six readings for this edition; all six are current and serve particular roles.

The first reading, by Henry Mintzberg on "Crafting Strategy," won a best article award in the *Harvard Business Review;* it stresses the very important point that strategy is more often crafted as events unfold than formulated by strict, preconceived design. It provides a marvelous insight into where strategy comes from and how it takes shape. The next reading explores the ever-relevant question of "What business are we in?"; William G. McGowan, the genius behind MCI, explains how MCI defines its business. These first two readings are grouped behind Chapters 1 and 2 and add both conceptually and pragmatically to the text discussion.

Reading 3, by Kevin Coyne, on sustainable competitive advantage (reprinted from a 1986 issue of *Business Horizons*) serves as a fitting conclusion to the four-chapter sequence on strategic analysis at the line-of-business level. Sustainable competitive advantage is the goal in crafting a successful business strategy; Coyne provides a clear view of what it takes to achieve this goal.

Michael Porter's article on "From Competitive Advantage to Corporate Strategy" accompanies the two-chapter module on strategic analysis in diversified companies. This article won the McKinsey award as the best *HBR* article during 1987. It presents significant research findings about the success and failure of corporate diversification strategies and provides some important prescriptions for making diversification work to greater advantage.

The last two readings deal with implementation of strategy and follow Chapters 9 and 10. One is by Jay Lorsch on the problems of managing culture to support shifts in strategic direction, and the other, by Randall Schuler and Susan Jackson, addresses the need to tightly link human resource practices and competitive strategy.

We think you will find these six readings well worth covering. Given the limited number we have included, they should not burden readers or cause them to get bogged down in excessive detail. All six articles are eminently readable and are well matched to the chapter discussions. We think you will find them a welcome feature of this fourth edition.

ADDITIONAL PEDAGOGICAL FEATURES

As in previous editions, all the chapters incorporate liberal use of examples and references to the strategic successes and failures of companies—what has worked, what hasn't, and why. The use of boxed Illustration Capsules to further highlight "strategy in action" was well received in earlier editions and has been continued. Together, the examples and the capsules keep the bridge between concept and actual practice always open, giving the reader a stronger feel for how strategic-analysis concepts and techniques are utilized in real-world management circumstances.

The Appendix gives students positive direction in case method pedagogy and offers suggestions for approaching case analysis. In our experience, many students are unsure about what they are to do in preparing a case, and they are certainly inexperienced in analyzing a company from a "big picture" or strategic point of view. The appendix discussion is intended to provide explicit guidance and to focus student attention on the traditional analytical sequence of (1) identify, (2) evaluate, and (3) recommend. To address the question of how to conduct a strategic analysis, we have included a comprehensive "what to look for" checklist to further supplement the chapter-end analytical checklists. This table, along with one on how to calculate and interpret key financial ratios, should satisfy the needs of students for pointers. Other features of the Appendix include a discussion of how to prepare a case for oral class discussion and guidelines for doing a written case analysis. All told, this material should be useful for students who (1) need assistance in making the transition from the lecture method to the case method of teaching or learning or both, and (2) want more guidance in figuring how to size up a company's strategic situation.

ACKNOWLEDGMENTS

We have benefited from the help of many people in the evolution of this book. Our intellectual debt to those academics, writers, and practicing managers upon whose works and experiences we have drawn will be obvious to any reader familiar with the literature of strategic management; we have endeavored to acknowledge their specific contributions in our many footnote references and in the list of suggested readings at the end of each chapter. Students, adopters of previous editions, and reviewers have kindly offered an untold number of insightful comments and helpful suggestions for improving the manuscript.

Naturally, as custom properly dictates, we are responsible for whatever errors of fact, deficiencies in coverage or in exposition, and oversights that remain. As always, we value your recommendations and thoughts about the book. Your comments regarding coverage and content will be most welcome, as will your calling our attention to specific errors. Please write us at P.O. Box 870223, Department of Management and Marketing, Tuscaloosa, Alabama 35487-0223.

Arthur A. Thompson, Jr.
A. J. Strickland III

Contents

Part Two **Strategic Analysis in Single-Business Companies 67**

3. Industry and Competitive Analysis 69

4. Company Situation Analysis 108

Illustration Capsule

5. Competitive Strategies and Competitive Advantage 122

The Three Generic Types of Competitive Strategy, 123 *Striving to Be the Low-Cost Producer. Differentiation Strategies. Focus and Specialization Strategies.* Building Competitive Advantage Via Low-Cost Leadership, 130 *Controlling the Cost Drivers. Revamping the Makeup of the Activity-Cost Chain. Cost-Cutting Strategies. Pitfalls in Pursuing a Cost Advantage.* Building Competitive Advantage Via Differentiation, 135 *Ways to Differentiate. Creating a Differentiation-Based Advantage. Real Value, Perceived Value, and Signals of Value. Keeping the Cost of Differentiation in Line. The Risks of Pursuing a Differentiation-Based Competitive Advantage.* Building Competitive Advantage Via Focusing, 139 *Choosing the Segment On Which to Focus. The Focuser's Advantage: Differentiation or Low Cost? Protecting a Focus-Based Competitive Advantage.* Using Offensive Strategies to Secure Competitive Advantage, 141 *Frontal Attacks on Competitors' Strengths. Attacks on Competitors' Weaknesses. Simultaneous Attack on Many Fronts. End-Run Offensives. Guerrilla Offensives. Preemptive Strategies. Choosing Whom to Attack.* Using Defensive Strategies to Protect Competitive Advantage, 148 *The Kinds of Defensive Tactics.* First-Mover Advantages and Disadvantages, 151 Analytical Checklist, 151

Illustration Capsules

6. Matching Strategy to the Situation 157

Strategies for Competing in Young, Emerging Industries, 157 Strategies for Competing During the Transition to Industry Maturity, 160 *Strategic Pitfalls.* Strategies for Firms in Mature or Declining Industries, 162 Strategies for Competing in Fragmented Industries, 163 Strategies for Competing in Global Industries, 166 *The Pros and Cons of a Globally Competitive Approach. Strategic Alternatives for Global Situations.* Strategies for Industry Leaders, 168 Strategies for Runner-Up Firms, 170 Strategies for Weak Businesses, 173 Turnaround Strategies for Distressed Businesses, 174 Analytical Checklist, 176 *Weighing the Different Alternatives.*

Reading

Part Four   Strategy Implementation: The Key Administrative Tasks   261

9. Implementing Strategy: Organization-Building, Budgets, and Work Assignments   263

A General Framework for Strategy Implementation,   264   *The Manager's Role in Leading the Implementation Process.* Building a Capable Organization,   266   *Matching Organization Structure to Strategy. How Structure Evolves as Strategy Evolves: The Stages Model. The Strategy-Related Pros and Cons of Alternative Organization Forms. Perspectives on Matching Strategy and Structure. Building a Distinctive Competence. Selecting People for Key Positions.* Linking the Budget With Strategy,   287 Linking Work Assignments to Performance Targets,   288   Analytical Checklist, 290

Illustration Capsule

10. Implementing Strategy: Commitment, Culture, Support Systems, and Leadership   292

Galvanizing Organizationwide Commitment to the Strategic Plan,   292 *Motivating People to Execute the Strategy. Building a Strategy-Supportive Corporate Culture. Creating a Results Orientation and a Spirit of High Performance. Linking Rewards to Performance.* Installing Internal Administrative Support Systems: Creating More Fits,   305   *Implementing Strategy-Supportive Policies and Procedures. Gathering Strategy-Critical Information—The MBWA Approach. Instituting Formal Reporting of Strategic Information.* Bonding the Administrative Fits: The Role of Shared Values and Beliefs,   309   Exerting Strategic Leadership,   310   *Fostering a Strategy-Supportive Climate and Culture. Keeping the Internal Organization Responsive and Innovative. Empowering Champions. Dealing with Company Politics. Leading the Process of Making Corrective Adjustments.* Analytical Checklist,   320

PART I

An Overview of Managing Strategy: Tasks, Concepts, and Process

1

1

The Manager as Strategy-Maker and Strategy-Implementer

"Cheshire Puss," she [Alice] began . . . "would you please tell me which way I ought to go from here?"
"That depends on where you want to get to," said the cat.
Lewis Carroll

My job is to make sure the company has a strategy and that everybody follows it.
Kenneth H. Olsen
CEO, Digital Equipment Corporation

If you want things to be better, you probably will have to change something.
George S. Odiorne

This book is about the managerial tasks of crafting and implementing organization strategy. As the term has come to be used in management circles, *an organization's strategy consists of the pattern of moves and approaches devised by management to produce successful organization performance.* In even simpler terms, strategy is *the managerial game plan.*

Strategy formulation and implementation are core management functions. Among all the varied things that managers have to deal with and act upon, few affect an organization's performance more lastingly than do the tasks of charting an organization's future course, figuring out what strategic moves and approaches to undertake, and then orchestrating execution of the chosen strategy as close to perfection as is managerially possible. How well an organization's management team performs the strategy-making and strategy-implementing functions is always a very big factor in determining whether the organization performs up to potential. Indeed, *good strategy and good implementation are the most trustworthy proof of good management.*

The reason why organizational performance is linked so tightly to the managerial tasks of formulating and implementing strategy is simple but telling. Any time an organization's managers develop a great strategic plan but then unwittingly misjudge (or foul up!) how it is implemented and executed, there's all kinds of room for the organization's performance to fall short of full potential. The reverse condition, that of choosing a subpar strategy but then implementing and executing it in a first-rate manner, is not conducive to producing top-flight organizational performance, either. An organization's best chance for achieving superior performance over the long-term occurs when managers do *both* a fine job of strategy formulation and a fine job of strategy implementation and execution. The better an organization's strategy and the more powerful the implementation approach, the less room there is for an organization to underperform its potential.

This is not to say doing a good job of strategy-making and strategy-implementing will *guarantee* that an organization's performance will be excellent every year, year after year. Organizations sometimes perform badly for a short while because of adverse external circumstances beyond management's ability to foresee or to control. But the bad luck of adverse events never excuses persistently weak performance. Over time, it is management's responsibility to take action to adjust to these adverse conditions—specifically, to devise and execute strategic moves and managerial approaches that will produce a par-for-the-course performance in spite of the obstacles that arise.

STRATEGY FORMULATION AND STRATEGY IMPLEMENTATION DEFINED

The term *strategy formulation* refers to *the entire management function of establishing organization direction, setting objectives, and devising a managerial game plan for the organization to pursue*. The strategy-formulating function has a *strongly entrepreneurial character,* in the sense that managers wind up having to choose among alternative business directions and to pursue approaches and moves that entail at least a small dose of venturesomeness and risk-taking. How boldly/cautiously managers push out in new directions and whether they install new or higher performance measures are often good indicators of their enterprising spirit. The entrepreneurial risk inherent in managerial strategy-making is becoming complacent or becoming smothered in analysis and hesitation. The entrepreneurial challenge is to keep the organization's strategy fresh, to maintain the organization's capacity for dealing with changing conditions, and to steer the organization into doing the right things at the right time.

The enterprising quality of strategy formulation extends deep into the managerial hierarchy. There is entrepreneurship in crafting a *narrow* strategy directed at boosting the productivity of office workers with strategic investments in computer-driven office information systems, just as there is entrepreneurship in devising of a *broad* business strategy aimed at driving a firm's overall costs so far below competitors' costs that it becomes feasible to undercut the prices charged by rivals, grab away some of their customers, build market share, and still make a good profit. As we will discuss shortly, the task of strategy-making falls upon the shoulders of managers up and down the organizational hierarchy, in functional departments and out in geographic operating units (plants and district offices) as well as at the top of the organizational pyramid.

By the term *strategy implementation* we mean *acting on what has to be done internally to put the chosen strategy into place and to actually achieve the targeted results*. Strategy implementation is primarily *an administrative task* that involves figuring out workable approaches to executing the strategy and then, during the course of day-to-day operations, getting people to accomplish their jobs in a strategy-supportive and results-achieving fashion. The cornerstones of strategy implementation are building an organization capable of carrying out the strategy successfully, steering adequate resources into those internal activities critical to strategic success, instituting a strategy-supportive set of policies and procedures, creating a strategy-supportive working environment, tying the reward structure tightly to achievement of target objectives, inducing people to redirect their energies and modify their work habits to meet the needs of strategic change, and then personally leading the implementation-execution of strategy as it applies to one's own area of managerial responsibility. Simply put, the strategy-implementing function consists of seeing what it will take to make the strategy work and then getting it done in a manner that produces the targeted performance on schedule—*the skill in managing strategy implementation comes in knowing how to achieve results*.

THE FIVE TASKS OF STRATEGY MANAGEMENT

The managerial job of forming a strategy and presiding over its implementation involves five distinguishable tasks:

1. *Developing a concept of the business and forming a vision of where the organization needs to be headed*—in effect, infusing the organization with a sense of purpose and direction and giving it a *mission*.
2. *Translating the mission into specific long-range and short-range performance objectives*.
3. *Crafting a strategy* that fits the organization's situation and that should produce the targeted performance.
4. *Implementing and executing the chosen strategy* efficiently and effectively.
5. *Evaluating performance, reviewing the situation, and initiating corrective adjustments* in mission, objectives, strategy, or implementation in light of actual experience, changing conditions, new ideas, and new opportunities.

Let's take a birds-eye look at each one (we'll expand this overview in later chapters).

Developing a Vision and a Mission

The most basic direction-setting question facing the senior managers of any enterprise is "What is our business and what will it be?" Developing a thoughtful answer to this question pushes managers to think through the scope and mix of organizational activities, to reflect on which specific customer needs and customer groups the organization ought to be trying to serve, to consider what the organization should be doing and not doing, and to develop a clearer vision of where the organization needs to be headed and why. Developing an answer to "What is our business and what will it be?" is a necessary first step in carving out a meaningful direction for the organization to take and for giving it an identity. Management's vision of what the organization seeks to do and to become over the long term is commonly referred to as the organization's *mission*. A mission statement broadly outlines the organization's future course and serves as a guiding concept. Some examples of *company mission statements* are presented in Illustration Capsule 1.

Setting Objectives

The act of setting formal performance objectives not only converts an organization's mission and direction into specific performance targets to be achieved but also helps protect against drift, confusion over what to accomplish, and a toleration of undemanding results. Both short-range and long-range objectives are needed. Short-range objectives draw attention to what immediate results to achieve, while long-range objectives put pressure on managers to consider *what to do now* to have the organization in position *to produce good results later*. Objective-setting involves *all managers;* each and every organization unit needs concrete, measurable performance targets that specify what the unit's contribution to strategic success will be. Objectives give an organization something to shoot for, something specific to achieve. When every organization unit has a set of objectives, when these objectives are coordinated across and down the organizational pyramid, and when managers are held accountable for achieving the objectives, the effect is to establish a results-oriented climate and to get the whole organization and its managers pointed in the desired direction.

Examples of organizational objectives are shown in Illustration Capsule 2.

Crafting a Strategy

This task brings into play the critical managerial issue of just *how* the targeted results are to be achieved, given the organization's situation. *Objectives* are the "ends" and *strategy* is the "means" of achieving them. The task of forming a strategy begins with an analysis of the organization's internal and external situation; managerial diagnosis of the situation then serves as the basis for devising a comprehensive set of moves and approaches calculated to produce the targeted short-run and long-run results. Conceptually, *strategy is a blueprint of all the important organizational moves and managerial approaches that are to be taken to achieve organizational objectives and to carry out the organization's mission.* One of the entrepreneurial objectives in devising a strategy is to achieve "goodness of fit" between strategy and all the relevant aspects of the organization's internal situation and external environment. In addition to seeking situational fit, strategy-making has to be aimed at moves/approaches that will (1) help secure competitive advantage and (2) elevate company performance.

From the perspective of the whole organization, the task of "strategizing" is never a one-time exercise.[1] While "the whats" of an organization's mission and

---

[1] Robert N. Anthony, *Planning and Control Systems: A Framework for Analysis* (Boston: Division of Research, Graduate School of Business Administration, Harvard University, 1965), pp. 38–39; and James B. Quinn, *Strategies for Change: Logical Incrementalism* (Homewood, Ill.: Richard D. Irwin, 1980), chap. 2, especially pp. 58–59.

ILLUSTRATION CAPSULE 1

Examples of How Companies Define Their Business

Presented below are verbatim quotations that illustrate how several firms have defined their business and strategic mission.

Hershey Foods Corporation

Hershey Foods Corporation's basic business mission is to become a major, diversified food company. The company uses four approaches in pursuit of this mission: (1) to capitalize on the considerable growth potential of the company's existing brands and products in current markets; (2) to introduce new products; (3) to expand the distribution of Hershey's long-established, well-known brands and new products into new markets—domestic and foreign; and (4) to make acquisitions and other types of alliances. These approaches are pursued within the context of maintaining the financial strength of the company.

A basic principle which Hershey will continue to embrace is to attract and hold consumers with products and services of consistently superior quality and value.

Polaroid

Polaroid manufactures and sells photographic products based on inventions of the company in the field of one-step instant photography and light-polarizing products, utilizing the company's inventions in the field of polarized light. The company considers itself to be engaged in one line of business.

MCI Communications, Inc.

MCI's mission is leadership in the global telecommunications services industry. Profitable growth is fundamental to that mission, so that we may serve the interests of our stockholders and our customers.

To maintain profitable growth, MCI will: Provide a full range of high-value services for customers who must communicate or move information electronically throughout the United States and the world; manage our business so as to be the low-cost provider of services; make quality synonymous with MCI to our growing customer base; set the pace in identifying and implementing cost-effective technologies and services as we expand our state-of-the-art communications network; continue to be an entrepreneurial company, built of people who can make things happen in a competitive marketplace.

Public Service Company of New Mexico

Our mission is to work for the success of the people we serve, by providing our CUSTOMERS reliable electric service, energy information, and energy options that best satisfy their needs.

ILLUSTRATION CAPSULE 2

Examples of Corporate Objectives: Nike and Lotus Development Corp.

Nike's 1987 Objectives

1. Protect and improve NIKE's position as the number one athletic brand in America, with particular attention to the company's existing core businesses in running, basketball, tennis, football, baseball, and kid's shoes and newer businesses with good potential like golf and soccer.
2. Build a strong momentum in the growing fitness market, beginning with walking, workout, and cycling.
3. Intensify the company's effort to develop products that women need and want.
4. Explore the market for products specifically designed for the requirements of maturing Americans.
5. Direct and manage the company's international business as it continues to develop.
6. Continue the drive for increased margins through proper inventory management and fewer, better products.

Lotus Development Corporation's 1986 Objectives

1. To provide customer-driven solutions to practical business and professional problems.
2. To advance the standards which our anchor products have set.
3. To introduce complementary and companion products which make our software more valuable to existing users and accessible to new users.
4. To create and acquire new products which offer data pathways into our existing software and which create entirely new categories of software.
5. To invest in new strategic initiatives which will improve long-term competitiveness.
6. To continue to improve our financial performance by continuing to strengthen our organization and deepen both our management and development teams.

SOURCE: Nike's 1986 annual report and Lotus Development Corporation's 1985 annual report.

long-term objectives, once chosen, may stay in place unchanged for several years, "the hows" of strategy are always evolving, partly out of a need for strategy to be responsive to changes in an organization's internal situation and external environment and partly out of managers being able to spot improved ways of doing things and seeing new windows of opportunity. Thus, a fresh move is made in one part of the organization; a different approach is initiated in another part of the organization. New ideas emerge on how to recast a piece of the strategy to make it work better. Still other modifications are forced when strategy comes off the drawing board and is put to test in the real world. As a consequence, refinements in and additions to this or that aspect of the strategic plan, coupled with an occasional major new strategy-shaping initiative, are normal occurrences.

The ongoing stream of new and revised strategic moves and approaches, some big in scope and some little, some applying to one part of the organization and some applying to another part, means that an organization's prevailing strategy is almost never the result of a single "strategizing" effort. Rather, the pattern of moves, approaches, and decisions that establishes an organization's strategy assumes its shape over a period of time. Of course, a major crisis can come along and force many big strategic moves to be made so very quickly that a brand new strategic pattern emerges almost overnight. But, other than these few occasions plus new company start-up situations, the current strategy is likely to have evolved gradually and to represent the handiwork of many managers—and not necessarily just those managers presently in office. As a general rule, therefore, one should not view strategy as some managerial grand design fully conceived "at the beginning."

As an example of what strategy is and how it works, read Illustration Capsule 3 on Beatrice Foods.

Strategy Implementation and Execution

Putting the strategy into place and getting individuals and organizational subunits to go all out in executing their part of the strategic plan successfully is, as stated earlier, essentially *an administrative task*. The specific elements of institutionalizing the strategy involve:

- Building an organization capable of carrying out the strategic plan.
- Developing strategy-supportive budgets and programs.
- Instilling a strong organizationwide commitment both to organizational objectives and to the chosen strategy.
- Linking the motivation and reward structure directly to achieving the targeted results.
- Creating an organization "culture" and a working environment that is in tune with strategy in every success-causing respect.
- Installing policies and procedures that facilitate strategy implementation.
- Developing an information and reporting system to track progress and monitor performance.
- Exerting the internal leadership needed to drive implementation forward and to keep improving on how the strategy is being executed.

Developing an *action agenda* for implementing and executing strategy involves managers at all levels, from headquarters on down to each operating department, deciding upon answers to the question "What is required for us to implement our part of the overall strategic plan and how can we best get it done?" Doing this task well means scrutinizing virtually every operating activity for ways to improve strategy execution and to institutionalize strategy-supportive practices and behavior. The process is one of moving incrementally and deliberately to consciously *fit* the "way we do things around here" to the requirements of first-rate strategy

ILLUSTRATION CAPSULE 3

Strategy at Beatrice Foods: From a Local Dairy to a Diversified Corporate Giant

Originally a butter and egg company serving a portion of Nebraska, Beatrice's corporate management launched an effort in the 1950s to reduce the company's dependence on local conditions. It started by acquiring small dairies in other midwestern locations. Only firms headed by independent-minded entrepreneurs were brought into the fold and the former owners were allowed wide latitude to continue to run their operations as they saw fit. Although Beatrice found that the dairy business had the disadvantage of low profit margins, it had the advantage of generating big cash flows (mainly because of low capital requirements and rapid inventory turnover). This allowed Beatrice the ability to finance its acquisitions mostly with cash, rather than debt or new stock. Over the years, Beatrice's management broadened the company's geographic scope, acquiring dairies coast to coast and growing into a $200 million dairy company.

Then the strategic focus at Beatrice shifted to diversification, and cash flows were used to purchase higher-margin food companies. LaChoy Food Products, a well-known producer of Chinese foods, was the first acquisition outside the dairy industry and, when it worked out well, Beatrice began to push into other food lines at an accelerating rate. Along the way, Beatrice decided to acquire some nonfood firms and, by the 1970s, owned several different kinds of manufacturing operations, a warehousing division, and an insurance company. The major acquisitions were Samsonite (luggage), Dannon (yogurt), Clark (candy bars), Eckrich (meats), Gebhardt's (chili and tamales), and LaChoy (Chinese foods).

Beatrice's diversification strategy followed some strict guidelines. Commodity-oriented firms were excluded, because of the unpredictable price swings. Companies in head-on competition with such powerhouses as Kellogg and Campbell Soup were avoided. In the nonfood areas, Beatrice shied away from labor-intensive companies, because of the risks of sharply rising labor costs. Industries like steel and chemicals were avoided, because of their heavy capital demands.

The basic acquisition strategy was to go after companies with at least five years of sales and profit increases and to eliminate from consideration any firm so large that failure could seriously damage Beatrice's overall profitability. While Beatrice sought companies with a growth rate higher than its own, management's financial strategy called for a purchase price keyed to a price-earnings multiple about one third below Beatrice's own current price-earnings ratio. Beatrice was generally successful in buying firms it wanted at a "discount," because the Beatrice stock it was offering in return had performed so very well over the years.

Once acquired, the new businesses were managed under a decentralized structure; the general managers of each unit were given broad-ranging authority and turned loose to formulate and implement their own strategies, thereby permitting each business to be operated in tune with the specifics of its own market and competitive environment.

SOURCE: Linda Grant Martin, "How Beatrice Foods Sneaked Up on $5 Billion," *Fortune*, April 1976, pp. 118–29.

execution. Implementation is soon defeated if the ingrained attitudes and habits of managers and employees are hostile or at cross-purposes with the needs of strategy and if their customary ways of doing things block strategy implementation instead of facilitating it. The most important fits are:

GOTHAM

RANK IN IMPORTANCE

- • Between strategy and the internal organizational structure. 3
- • Between strategy and the allocation of budgets and staff size. 4
- • Between strategy and the organization's systems of rewards and incentives. 5
- • Between strategy and internal policies, practices, and procedures. 2
- • Between strategy and the internal organizational atmosphere (as determined by the values and beliefs shared by managers and employees, the philosophies and decision-making style of senior managers, and other such factors that make up the organization's personality and culture).

The stronger these fits, the more strategy-supportive an organization's ways of doing things.

Both the sequence of actions and the speed of the implementation process are important aspects of uniting the entire organization in behind strategy accomplishment. The strategy-implementing challenge is to generate an *organizationwide crusade* on the part of employees to carry out the chosen strategy efficiently and effectively.

Evaluating Performance, Reviewing the Situation, and Initiating Corrective Adjustments

None of the previous four tasks are one-time exercises. Circumstances are always cropping up that make corrective adjustments desirable. Long-term direction may need to be altered, the business redefined, and management's vision of the organization's future course narrowed or broadened. Performance targets may need raising or lowering in light of past experience and future prospects. Strategy may need to be modified, because it is not working well or because changing conditions make fine tuning (or even major overhaul) necessary. Even a good strategy can be improved; and it requires no great argument to see that changes in industry and competitive conditions, the emergence of new opportunities or threats, the appointment of new executive officers, and a host of other circumstances can prompt the use of a different strategy.

So also is it with strategy implementation. There will be times when one or another aspect of implementation does not go as well as planned and ways are seen to improve things. Testing new ideas and learning what works and what doesn't through trial and error is normal management practice. Hence, progress in putting strategy in place occurs unevenly, going faster in some areas and slower in others, with some things getting done easily and other facets proving to be quite nettlesome. Implementation comes through the pooling effect of many administrative decisions about how to do things and of gradual adjustments in the actions and behavior of both managerial subordinates and employees. Normally, the bigger the degree of strategic change, the more time it takes to achieve full-scale implementation. Some strategies literally take years to implement and bear fruit.

The Cycle of Strategy Management

Because each one of the five tasks of strategy management requires constant attention and judgment about whether to continue with things as they are or to make changes, *the process of managing strategy is ongoing*—nothing is final and all prior actions and decisions are subject to future modification. Changes in the organization's situation, coming either from the inside or the outside, or both, are constant drivers of strategic adjustments. The process of cycling through these five ever-present tasks is shown in Figure 1–1.

Once an organization's managers have worked their way through the first three components, a *strategic plan* exists—in effect, management will have charted a course for the organization to follow and have established a blueprint for managing the organization. While some companies prepare elaborate written strategic plans, in others the strategic plan consists largely of oral understandings among managers, along with any number of unspoken thoughts and ideas. Organizational objectives are the part of the strategic plan that most often ends up in writing and that gets the widest circulation among managers and employees.

The fourth component is easily the most complicated and time-consuming part of managing strategy, because it involves not only deciding what internal administrative actions to take but also supervising all the details of implementation and pushing the organization hard to convert the strategic plan into actual results. The fifth component, evaluating performance and initiating corrective adjustments, is both the end and the beginning of the strategic-management cycle. The march of external and internal events guarantees that revisions in the four previous components will sooner or later be in order. It is always incumbent on management to push for better performance and to find ways to improve the existing strategy

FIGURE 1–1
The Five Ever-Present Tasks of Strategy Management

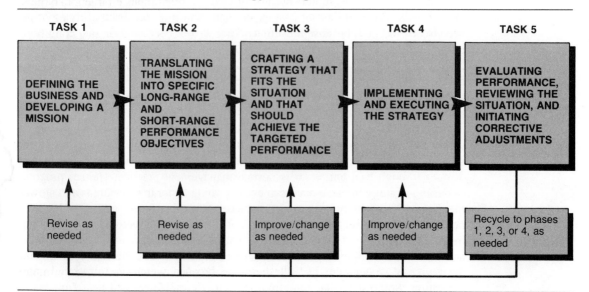

TASK 1	TASK 2	TASK 3	TASK 4	TASK 5
DEFINING THE BUSINESS AND DEVELOPING A MISSION	TRANSLATING THE MISSION INTO SPECIFIC LONG-RANGE AND SHORT-RANGE PERFORMANCE OBJECTIVES	CRAFTING A STRATEGY THAT FITS THE SITUATION AND THAT SHOULD ACHIEVE THE TARGETED PERFORMANCE	IMPLEMENTING AND EXECUTING THE STRATEGY	EVALUATING PERFORMANCE, REVIEWING THE SITUATION, AND INITIATING CORRECTIVE ADJUSTMENTS
Revise as needed	Revise as needed	Improve/change as needed	Improve/change as needed	Recycle to phases 1, 2, 3, or 4, as needed

and the manner in which it is being executed. Changing external conditions add further impetus to the need for periodic revisions in a company's mission, performance objectives, strategy, and approaches to strategy execution. Most of the time, the adjustments involve fine tuning, but occasions for major overhaul do arise—sometimes because of significant external developments and sometimes because of sharply sliding financial performance.

Characteristics of the Process. While developing a mission, setting objectives, forming a strategy, implementing and executing the strategic plan, and evaluating performance accurately conceptualize the elements of managing strategy, the tasks themselves are not so cleanly divided and neatly sequenced in actual practice. To begin with, there is back and forth interplay between the elements. For example, consideration of what strategic actions to take almost always provokes discussions of whether and how the strategy can be satisfactorily implemented. Deciding on a company mission shades into setting objectives for the organization to achieve (both involve directional priorities). Establishing reasonable performance targets requires looking both at the strategies it will take to achieve them and at the organization's recent performance track record. Deciding upon a strategy gets entangled with decisions about long-term direction and discussions about whether objectives have been set too high or too low.

It is important, also, to remember that the tasks involved in managing strategy have to be done in the midst of a managerial schedule that is fragmented with assorted other special assignments, civic duties, meetings, paperwork deadlines, people problems, and unexpected crises. Thus, while the job of managing strategy may well be the most important function an organization's management team performs insofar as an organization's future success or failure is concerned, it by no means constitutes the whole of what managers have to do or be concerned about. Moreover, the demands that strategy management put on a manager's time are irregular. Strategic issues and decisions take up big chunks of management time some weeks and months and not so much in others; the big day in, day out strategic challenge comes in pushing for peak strategy execution and trying to get the best strategy-supportive performance out of every individual.

WHO ARE THE STRATEGY-MANAGERS?

An organization's chief executive officer is the most visible and most important *strategy-manager*. The CEO, as captain of the ship, bears full responsibility for leading the tasks of formulating and implementing the strategic plans of the organization as a whole, irrespective of the fact that others have a hand in the process. The CEO functions as chief direction-setter, chief objective-setter, chief strategy-maker, and chief strategy-implementer for the total enterprise. What the CEO thinks is important usually moves to the top of every manager's priority list, and the CEO has the final word on big decisions.

Vice presidents for such functions as sales, marketing, production, finance, and personnel nearly always have important strategy-formulating and strategy-implementing responsibilities as well—it usually is their role to devise and execute functional support strategies to flesh out the broader overall organizational game plan. Plus they usually are involved in proposing and developing key elements of the overall strategy, working closely with the CEO to hammer out a consensus, and to make certain parts of the strategy more effective. Only rarely is an organization's overall strategy almost wholly fashioned by the CEO personally.

But managerial positions with strategy-making and strategy-implementing responsibility are by no means restricted to these few senior executives; in very real ways, *every manager is a strategy-maker and strategy-implementer for the area he or she has authority over and supervises.* This is because every part of a company—be it a business unit, division, operating department, plant, or district office—has a strategic role to carry out; and the manager in charge of that unit, with guidance from superiors, is the person who needs to carry the burden for proposing an appropriate strategy and for implementing whatever strategic choices are made—see Figure 1–2. Obviously, though, managers who are deeper down in the managerial hierarchy have a narrower, more specific strategy-making/strategy-implementing role than managers closer to the top of the pyramid.

The larger and more complex an organization is, the more impractical it is for a few senior executives to handle all of the strategic planning that needs to be done. The typical solution is to delegate some of the strategy-making responsibility to those lower-level managers who head the very organizational subunits where specific strategic results must be achieved. Delegating a lead strategy-making role to those middle-level managers who will be deeply involved in carrying out the strategy in their assigned areas fixes accountability for strategic success or failure

FIGURE 1–2
The Levels of Strategy-Making

LEVEL 1: **Corporate strategy** – Formulated by the chief executive officer and other corporate executives

LEVEL 2: **Line of business strategy** – Formulated by business division heads/product line managers

LEVEL 3: **Functional area support strategy** – Formulated by functional area heads/heads of major departments

LEVEL 4: **Operating-level/strategy** – Formulated by heads of operating departments, geographic field units, and production facilities.

directly on those who are in charge of the results-producing organizational units—when the manager who implements the strategy is also the architect of the strategy, it is hard for the manager in charge to shift the blame or to make excuses if the target results are not achieved. A large multi-industry, multibusiness company usually has four distinct levels of strategy managers:

- *The chief executive officer and other senior corporate-level executives* who have primary responsibility and personal authority for big strategic decisions affecting the total enterprise.
- *Managers who have profit-and-loss responsibility for subsidiary business units* and who are expected to exercise a major leadership role in formulating and implementing strategy at the business-unit level.
- *Functional area managers within a given business unit* who have direct authority over a major piece of the business (manufacturing, marketing and sales, finance, R&D, personnel) and, therefore, must support the business unit's overall strategy with strategic actions in their own areas.
- *Managers of major operating departments and geographic field units* who have front-line responsibility for putting together the details of strategic efforts in their areas and for carrying out their pieces of the overall strategic plan at the grassroots level.

A single-business enterprise typically has no more than three of these levels—business-level strategy-managers, functional-area strategy-managers, and operating-level strategy-managers; together, they form a management team with responsibility for directing the strategic efforts of the total enterprise in that one business. Proprietorships, partnerships, and small owner-managed enterprises, of course, typically have only one or two strategy-managers since the whole strategy-making/strategy-implementing function can be handled by just a few key people.

Managerial jobs involving strategy formulation and implementation abound in not-for-profit organizations as well. For example, a multicampus state university has four strategy-managing levels: (1) the president of the whole university system is a strategy-manager with broad direction-setting responsibility and strategic decision-making authority over all the campuses; (2) the chancellor for each campus customarily has strategy-making/strategy-implementing authority over all academic, student, athletic, and alumni matters, plus budgetary, programmatic and coordinative responsibilities for the whole campus; (3) the academic deans of the various colleges or schools have lead responsibility for charting future direction at the college level, steering resources into some programs and out of others, and otherwise devising a collegewide plan to fulfill the college's teaching-research-service mission; and (4) the heads of the various academic departments within a college or school are strategy-managers with first-line strategy-making/strategy-implementing responsibility for the department's undergraduate and graduate program offerings, faculty research efforts, and all other activities relating to the department's mission, objectives, and future direction.

In federal and state government, and heads of local, district, and regional offices function as strategy-managers in their efforts to be responsive to the specific needs and situation of the particular geographical area their office serves (a district-manager in Portland may need a slightly different strategy than does the district-manager in Orlando). In municipal government, the heads of the police department, the fire department, the water and sewer department, the parks and recreation department, the health department, and so on are strategy-managers because they have line authority for the operations of their department and, thus, are in position to put their personal stamp on departmental objectives, on the formation of a strategy to achieve these objectives, and on how the strategy is implemented.

Managerial jobs with strategy-making/strategy-implementing roles, thus, are commonplace. The ins and outs of strategy formulation and implementation are a *basic* aspect of managing, *not* just something for top-level managers to deal with.[2]

The Role and Tasks of Strategic Planners

If senior and middle managers have the lead role for whatever strategy-making and strategy-implementing that needs doing in their areas of responsibility, then what should strategic planners do? Is there a legitimate place in big companies for a strategic planning department staffed with specialists in planning and strategic analysis? The answer is yes; but its role and tasks should consist chiefly of helping to gather and organize data and information that strategy-managers need, establishing and administering an annual strategy review cycle whereby all strategy-managers go through the exercise of reconsidering and refining their strategic plans, and then coordinating the process of reviewing and approving the strategic plans developed in various parts of the company. The value added by strategic planners comes in their facilitating and coordinating the strategic planning efforts of line-managers, helping managers at all levels crystalize the strategic issues that ought to be addressed, providing information, helping with the analysis of industry and competitive conditions if asked, and generating information on the company's strategic performance. But they should not be charged with making strategic decisions, preparing detailed strategic plans (for someone else to implement), or making strategic action recommendations that usurp the strategy-making responsibilities of managers in charge of major operating units.

When strategic planners are asked to go beyond the function of providing specialized staff assistance and to prepare a comprehensive strategic plan for top management's consideration, either of two adverse consequences may result. One, some managers will gladly toss the tough strategic problems in their areas onto the desks of strategic planners to let them do their strategic thinking for them. The planners, not knowing as much about the situation as the managers themselves ought to know, are in a weaker position to design a workable action plan, and, in any event, they cannot be held responsible for implementing what they recommend. Putting responsibility for strategy-making into the hands of planners and respon-

---

[2]Since the scope of a manager's strategy-making/strategy-implementing role varies according to the manager's position in the organizational hierarchy, our use of the word *organization* will include whatever kind of organizational unit the strategy-manager is in charge of—whether it be an entire company or not-for-profit organization, a business unit within a diversified company, a major geographic division, an important functional area unit within a business, or an operating department or field unit reporting up to a specific functional area head. This will permit us to avoid having to use the awkward phrase "the organization or organizational subunit" to indicate the range or scope of a manager's strategy-making/strategy-implementing responsibilities. We think it will be clear from the context of the discussion whether the subject applies only to the total enterprise or whether it applies at most or all management levels.

sibility for implementation into the hands of line-managers not only makes it hard to fix accountability for unacceptably poor strategic results but it also deludes senior managers into thinking they really don't have to be deeply and personally involved in leading the organization down a clear-cut path and crafting a strategy capable of generating above-average results. The hard truth is that strategy-making is simply not a staff function, nor is it something that can be handed off to an advisory committee of lower-ranking managers.

Two, when strategic planners end up having to take a lead strategy-making role, then senior and middle managers, lacking a personal stake or real emotional commitment to the strategic agenda proposed by the planners, may well give lip service acceptance to the strategic plan, make a few token implementation efforts, then quickly get back to "business as usual," knowing full well that the formal written plan concocted in the plan-developers' offices does not represent their own "real" managerial agenda. The strategic plan, thus, becomes a paper document collecting dust on managers' shelves—few managers take the work product of the strategic-planning staff seriously enough to pursue wholehearted implementation.

Either of these two consequences renders formal strategic-planning efforts ineffective and opens the door for a strategy-making vacuum conducive to organizational drift or to fragmented, uncoordinated strategic decisions. The odds are then heightened that the organization will have no strong strategic rudder and insufficient top-down direction. The lesson here is clear: When the "ownership" of the proposed strategy is taken out of the hands of the line-managers who must take responsibility for carrying out the recommended strategy, the formal strategy-making process is likely to become a ceremonial exercise and real strategic leadership is likely to be missing.

The flaws in having staffers or advisory committees formulating strategies for areas they do not have responsibility for managing are (1) that they cannot be held strictly accountable if their recommendations don't produce the desired results (since they don't have authority for directing implementation) and (2) that what is recommended won't be well accepted or enthusiastically implemented by those who "have to sing the song the planners have written." But when managers are expected to be the chief strategy-maker and chief strategy-implementer for the areas they head, then it is their own strategy and their own implementation approach that is being put to the test of workability—in which case they are likely to be more committed to making the plan work (given that their future careers with the organization are at more risk!) and they certainly can be held strictly accountable for achieving the target results in their area.

The Strategic Function of the Board of Directors

If it is the duty of senior and middle managers to craft and implement strategy, then it is necessarily the responsibility of an organization's board of directors to see that the overall task of managing strategy is adequately done.[3] It is the norm for the board to review important strategic moves and to put their stamp of approval

---

[3]Kenneth R. Andrews, *The Concept of Corporate Strategy,* 3rd ed. (Homewood, Ill.: Richard D. Irwin, 1987), p. 123.

on strategic plans—a procedure which makes the board ultimately responsible for the strategic actions that are taken. But directors rarely can or should play a direct role in formulating the strategy they must approve. The immediate task of directors in ratifying strategy and new direction-setting moves is to ensure that the proposals presented to them have been adequately analyzed and thought through and that the proposed strategy can be defended as superior to available alternatives; flawed proposals are customarily withdrawn for revision by management.[4] The longer-range task of directors is to evaluate the caliber of senior managers' strategy-making and strategy-implementing skills. Here it is necessary to determine whether the current CEO is doing a good job of strategic management (as a basis for awarding salary increases and bonuses and deciding on retention or removal) and, also, to evaluate the strategic skills of other senior executives in line to succeed the current CEO.

THE BENEFITS OF A "STRATEGIC APPROACH" TO MANAGING

The message of this book is that doing a good job of managing inherently requires doing a good job of managing strategy. Looking at the management function through strategic eyes and seeing how strategy formulation and strategy implementation impact performance will show why the fundamentals of strategic management need to drive the whole approach to managing organizations.[5] The chief executive officer of one successful company put it well when he said:

> In the main, our competitors are acquainted with the same fundamental concepts and techniques and approaches that we follow, and they are as free to pursue them as we are. More often than not, the difference between their level of success and ours lies in the relative thoroughness and self-discipline with which we and they develop and execute our strategies for the future.

The advantages of first-rate strategic thinking and conscious strategy manage-

---

[4]Ibid.

[5]For a representative sample of studies on the impact of strategic planning and strategic thinking on performance, see Stanley Thune and Robert House, "Where Long-Range Planning Pays Off," *Business Horizons* 13, no. 4 (August 1970), pp. 81–87; Joseph O. Eastlack and Phillip R. McDonald, "CEO's Role in Corporate Growth," *Harvard Business Review* 48, no. 3 (May–June 1970), pp. 150–63; David M. Herold, "Long-Range Planning and Organizational Performance: A Cross-Validation Study," *Academy of Management Journal* 15, no. 1 (March 1972), pp. 91–102; Dan Schendel, G. R. Patton, and James Riggs, "Corporate Turnaround Strategies," *Journal of General Management* 3, no. 3 (Spring 1976), pp. 3–11; S. Schoeffler, Robert Buzzell, and Donald Heany, "Impact of Strategic Planning on Profit Performance," *Harvard Business Review* 52, no. 2 (March–April 1974), pp. 137–45; Donald W. Beard and Gregory G. Dess, "Corporate-Level Strategy, Business-Level Strategy, and Firm Performance," *Academy of Management Journal* 24, no. 4 (December 1981), pp. 663–88; Michael E. Porter, *Competitive Strategy* (New York: Free Press, 1980); Joel Ross and Michael Cami, *Corporate Management in Crisis: Why the Mighty Fall* (Englewood Cliffs, N.J.: Prentice-Hall, 1973); Alfred D. Chandler, *The Visible Hand* (Cambridge, Mass.: Harvard University Press, 1977); William K. Hall, "Survival Strategies in a Hostile Environment," *Harvard Business Review* 58, no. 5 (September–October 1980), pp. 75–85; Thomas J. Peters and Robert H. Waterman, Jr., *In Search of Excellence: Lessons from America's Best-Run Companies* (New York: Harper & Row, 1982); and V. Ramanujam and N. Venkatraman, "Planning and Performance: A New Look at an Old Question," *Business Horizons* 30, no. 3 (May–June 1987), pp. 19–25. See also Henry Mintzberg, "The Strategy Concept: Another Look at Why Organizations Need Strategies," *California Management Review* 30, no. 1 (Fall 1987), pp. 25–32.

ment (as opposed to freewheeling improvisation, gut feel, and drifting along) include (1) providing better guidance to the entire organization on the crucial point of just "What it is we are trying to do and to achieve?"; (2) enhancing managerial alertness to the winds of change, new opportunities, and threatening developments; (3) providing managers with a much-needed rationale for evaluating competing budget requests for investment capital and new staff—a rationale that argues strongly for steering resources into strategy-supportive, results-producing areas; (4) helping to unify the numerous strategy-related decisions by managers all across the organization; and (5) creating a more *proactive* management posture and counteracting any tendencies for decisions to be mostly reactive and defensive.[6]

The fifth advantage of being proactive, rather than merely reactive, frequently enhances long-term performance. Business history shows that high-performing enterprises like to *initiate* and *lead,* not just *react* and *defend.* They see strategy as a tool for securing a sustainable competitive advantage and for pushing performance to superior levels. Ideally, devising and executing a powerful, opportunistic strategy will propel a firm to a leadership position so above and apart from industry rivals that not only will earnings prosper but also its products / services will become *the* standard for industry comparison.

A Recap of Important Terms

Let's conclude this introductory overview of the managerial tasks of formulating and implementing strategy by reiterating the meaning of key terms that will be used again and again in the chapters to come:

Organization mission—represents management's customized answer to the question "What is our business and what will it be?" A mission statement broadly outlines the organization's future direction and serves as a guiding concept for what the organization is to do and to become.

Performance objectives—are the organization's targets for achievement.
Long-range objectives—the achievement levels to be reached within the next few years.
Short-range objectives—the near-term performance targets; they establish the pace and interim milestones in reaching the long-range objectives.

Strategy—is the managerial game plan for achieving the chosen objectives; strategy is mirrored in the *pattern* of moves and approaches devised by management to produce the desired performance. Strategy is the *how* of pursuing the mission and reaching target objectives.

Strategic plan—a comprehensive statement about the organization's mission and future direction, near-term and long-term performance targets, and how management intends to produce the desired results and fulfill the mission, given the organization's overall situation.

Strategy formulation—refers to the entire direction-setting management function

---

[6]Kenneth R. Andrews, *The Concept of Corporate Strategy,* rev. ed. (Homewood, Ill.: Richard D. Irwin, 1980), pp. 15–16, 46, 123–29; and Seymour Tilles, "How to Evaluate Corporate Strategy," *Harvard Business Review* 41, no. 4 (July–August 1963), p. 116.

of concepting an organization's mission, setting specific performance objectives, and forming a strategy. The end product of strategy formulation is a strategic plan.

Strategy implementation—includes the full range of managerial activities associated with putting the chosen strategy into place, supervising its pursuit, and achieving the targeted results.

In the chapters and readings to come, we will zero in more intensively on the strategy-related tasks of managers and on the methods of strategic analysis. When you get to the end of the book we think you will see why the two things that usually separate the best-managed organizations from the rest are:

1. Superior strategy-making and entrepreneurship.
2. Competent implementation and execution of the chosen strategy.

An organization's management team, whether it devises and implements new strategies or whether it is preoccupied with implementing prior strategies in better ways or whether it does nothing overt to change either strategy or the organization's basic manner of doing things, is still the organization's chief strategy-maker and chief strategy-implementer. There is no escaping the significant impact that the quality of managerial strategy-making and strategy-implementing has on an organization's performance. A company that has no clear-cut direction, or vague or undemanding objectives, or a muddled or flawed strategy, is much more likely to drift, to tolerate subpar performance, and to lose its competitiveness.

SUGGESTED READINGS

Andrews, Kenneth R. *The Concept of Corporate Strategy*. 3rd ed. Homewood, Ill.: Richard D. Irwin, 1987, chap. 1.

Drucker, Peter F. *Management: Tasks, Responsibilities, Practices*. New York: Harper & Row, 1974, chaps. 2, 4, 30, 31, and 50.

Gluck, Frederick W. "A Fresh Look at Strategic Management." *Journal of Business Strategy* 6, no. 2 (Fall 1985), pp. 4–21.

Katz, Robert L. "Skills of an Effective Administrator." *Harvard Business Review* 33, no. 1, (January–February 1955), pp. 33–42.

Kelley, C. Aaron. "The Three Planning Questions: A Fable." *Business Horizons* 26, no. 2 (March–April 1983), pp. 46–48.

Kotter, John P. *The General Managers*. New York: Free Press, 1982.

Levinson, Harry, and Stuart Rosenthal. *CEO: Corporate Leadership in Action*. New York: Basic Books, 1987.

Livingston, J. Sterling. "Myth of the Well-Educated Manager." *Harvard Business Review* 49, no. 1 (January–February 1971), pp. 79–87.

Mintzberg, Henry. "The Strategy Concept: Five Ps for Strategy." *California Management Review* 30, no. 1 (Fall 1987), pp. 11–24.

————. "The Strategy Concept: Another Look at Why Organizations Need Strategies." *California Management Review* 30, no. 1 (Fall 1987), pp. 25–32.

Peters, Thomas J., and Robert H. Waterman. *In Search of Excellence: Lessons from America's Best-Run Companies*. New York: Harper & Row, 1982.

Peters, Thomas J., and Nancy Austin. *A Passion for Excellence: The Leadership Difference.* New York: Random House, 1985, chaps. 16–21.

Quinn, James B. *Strategies for Change: Logical Incrementalism.* Homewood, Ill.: Richard D. Irwin, 1980, chaps. 2 and 3.

Ramanujam, V., and N. Venkatraman. "Planning and Performance: A New Look at an Old Question." *Business Horizons* 30, no. 3 (May–June 1987), pp. 19–25.

Ross, Joel, and Michael Kami. *Corporate Management in Crisis: Why the Mighty Fall.* Englewood Cliffs, N.J.: Prentice-Hall, 1973.

Yip, George S. "Who Needs Strategic Planning?" *Journal of Business Strategy* 6, no. 2 (Fall 1985), pp. 22–29.

2

The Three Strategy-Making Tasks: Developing a Mission, Setting Objectives, and Forming a Strategy

> Without a strategy the organization is like a ship without a rudder, going around in circles. It's like a tramp; it has no place to go.
>
> *Joel Ross and Michael Kami*

> You've got to come up with a plan. You can't wish things will get better.
>
> *John F. Welch*

This chapter provides a more in-depth look at each of the three strategy-making tasks: defining the business and developing a mission, setting performance objectives, and forming a strategy to produce the desired results. We will examine the nature of strategy-making at each managerial level in the organizational hierarchy and also present four generic approaches managers can take in performing the strategy-making task.

DEVELOPING A MISSION: THE FIRST DIRECTION-SETTING TASK

The starting point in organizational direction setting is always with a vision of what the future course and path of development should be like. As one CEO put it so lucidly:

Management's job is not to see the company as it is . . . but as it can become.

To frame the issue of future direction, a strategy-manager needs to pose three questions about the organization he or she heads:

- What will performance be like in three to five years if the organization stays on its present track doing the same basic things, only doing them better?

- Where does the organization need to head in the next 5 to 10 years to be a strong performer?
- What changes in business makeup and direction will it take to get the organization from where it is now to where it needs to be?

To come up with thoughtful and persuasive answers to these three questions, a manager is forced to think deeply about the implications of acting as "caretaker of the status quo" and continuing to lead the organization down the same road it is already on. While most days the answer to the ever-present question "Are we doing the right things and are we headed in the right direction?" comes back "Yes," there will be days when the answer is "No, it's time to make some changes." Hence, it behooves a manager to review periodically the scope and mix of the activities being managed, to scrutinize whether to stop doing some things and to start doing others, and to confirm whether the organization is on the right track. Concepting an answer to "What is our business and what will it be?" is a necessary first step in charting a course for the organization to follow. Without a vision of where to head and how to shape what the organization does and doesn't do, a manager is in no position to function effectively as either leader or strategy-maker.

Management's vision of what the organization is trying to do and to become over the long term is commonly referred to as the organization's *mission*. A *mission statement* specifies what activities the organization intends to pursue and what course management has charted for the future. It is a concise organizational outline of "who we are, what we do, and where we are headed." Mission statements are, thus, personalized in the sense that they give an organization its own special identity, character, and path for development. Normally, decisions about mission are a function of an organization's history and past experiences, the specifics of its present situation, its prospects if it continues to do just what it is presently doing, opportunities and threats on the horizon, the personal aspirations key managers have for the organization, and managerial conclusions about the organization's best long-term course.

Defining the Business

Generally, the best way to conceptualize an organization's mission comes from looking at what the organization has to do "to create a customer." According to Peter Drucker, a widely respected authority on managing:[1]

> A business is not defined by the company's name, statutes, or articles of incorporation. It is defined by the want the customer satisfies when he buys a product or a service. To satisfy the customer is the mission and purpose of every business. The question "What is our business?" can, therefore, be answered only by looking at the business from the outside, from the point of view of customer and market. What the customer sees, thinks, believes, and wants, at any given time, must be accepted by management as an objective fact. . . .

---

[1]Peter F. Drucker, *Management: Tasks, Responsibilities, Practices* (New York: Harper & Row, 1974), pp. 79–80.

. . . to the customer, no product or service, and certainly no company, is of much importance. . . . The customer only wants to know what the product or service will do for him tomorrow. All he is interested in are his own values, his own wants, his own reality. For this reason alone, any serious attempt to state "what our business is" must start with the customer, his realities, his situation, his behavior, his expectations, and his values.

Derek Abell has taken Drucker's perceptive point two steps further, arguing that the mission of a company is defined along three dimensions: (1) customer needs, or *what* is being satisfied; (2) customer groups, or *who* is being satisfied; and (3) technologies, or *how* customer needs are satisfied.[2] According to Abell, a company's product/service represents the application of a particular technology to the satisfaction of a particular function or need for a particular customer group. A company's business, therefore, is defined by its choices about whom to satisfy, what to satisfy, and how to produce the satisfaction; hence, it is the specific combination of all three choices that spell out the answer to "What is our business?" and that say the most about a business's mission.[3] Illustration Capsule 4 describes the ways companies can use to define their business.

Where Entrepreneurship Comes in

Sooner or later, today's mission and directional path becomes obsolete. Thus, it is incumbent on managers to keep looking beyond the present definition of the business—always checking for whether it's time to steer a new course and adjust the mission. The key question here is "What new directions should we be moving in *now* to get ready for the changes that we believe may occur later?" Redirecting the enterprise in the anticipation of change reduces the chances of getting caught in the wrong position or doing the wrong things at the wrong time.

Good entrepreneurship and good strategic leadership always require managerial attention to such direction-setting issues as: What customer wants and needs are presently going unsatisfied? How will the needs and requirements of present customers change? Which new product ideas and new technological potentials now in the wings look like good opportunities to pursue? What customer needs and customer groups should the organization be getting in position to serve? What should the organization continue doing and what should it plan to abandon? What new directions, if pursued now, hold the prospect for big payoffs down the road? Sorting through the various possible answers to all these questions ultimately means making entrepreneurial judgments about which of the several forks in the road to

---

[2]Derek F. Abell, *Defining the Business: The Starting Point of Strategic Planning* (Englewood Cliffs, N.J.: Prentice-Hall, 1980), p. 169.

[3]Note how thoroughly the approach to defining the business is grounded in *external* considerations, as opposed to *internal* considerations. While there is some temptation to view a company's mission and ultimate purpose as one of "making a profit," this typifies all profit-seeking enterprises and, thus, fails to distinguish one enterprise from another (the mission of a bank is plainly different from that of a manufacturer of shoes, even though both may endeavor to earn a profit in what they do). Profit objectives are properly viewed as a *result* of doing something. It is the answer to the question "Make a profit doing what and for whom?" that is the real definition of an organization's business.

ILLUSTRATION CAPSULE 4

Eight Ways to Define a Business

Managers can frame an answer to the question of "What is our business?" in at least eight different ways:

- *In terms of the products or services being provided.* Thus, a pecan grower may define its business simply as one of producing pecans; a microwave manufacturer may see itself as being in the convenience cooking business; and a local fire department may view its business as fire fighting and fire prevention.
- *In terms of the principal ingredient in a line of products.* Paper companies, for example, can use the same paper machines to turn out newsprint, stationery, notebook paper, and slick printing papers; yet they see themselves as being in the paper business, rather than in the newsprint business or the stationery business or the notebook paper business, because they have some flexibility to shift production and sales from one end-use segment to another as market conditions warrant.
- *In terms of the technology that spawns the product(s).* General Electric owes its name and a big portion of its revenues to its broad, deep exploitation of the technology of electricity, coming up with the process with literally thousands of useful electricity-related products. 3M Corporation's lineup of some 50,000 products has emerged from the company's distinctive expertise in finding new applications for chemical coating and bonding technology.
- *In terms of the customer groups being served.* General Motors has long seen itself as being a full-line car manufacturer, with models to fit every purse and lifestyle. Personal computers sold to corporations and business professionals define a business/market segment that is quite distinct from home computers sold to individuals through mass-merchandise retail chain stores. Likewise, the business of a neighborhood convenience food store entails a narrower product line for a narrower customer group than does the business of a large supermarket.
- *In terms of the customer needs and wants being met.* The business of small appliance manufacturers is hinged on offering a variety of effort-saving and timesaving conveniences to household members. The educational program offerings of a two-year community college are intended to meet a different set of student needs than are the programs of a major, multicampus state university.
- *In terms of the scope of activities within an industry.* At one end of the spectrum, organizations can be highly *specialized,* with a mission of performing a limited service or function to fill a particular industry niche; an example would be an oil service firm that engaged exclusively in supplying parts and equipment to well drillers and well operators. At the other end of the spectrum, firms may seek to be *fully integrated,* participating in every aspect of the industry's production chain; such is the case of leading international oil companies, all of which engage in leasing sites to drill on, drilling their own wells, pumping crude oil out of the wells, transporting their own crude oil in their own ships and through their own pipelines to their own refineries, and selling gasoline and

---

ILLUSTRATION CAPSULE 4 *(concluded)*

other refined products at wholesale and retail through their own networks of branded distributors and service station outlets. In between these two extremes of industry scope, firms can stake out *partially integrated* positions, participating only in selected stages of the industry.

- *In terms of creating a diversified enterprise that engages in a group of related businesses.* The "related" aspect can be based on a core skill, a core technology, complementary relationships among products, common channels of distribution, common customer groups, or overlapping customer functions and applications. Procter & Gamble's lineup of products, for instance, includes Jif peanut butter, Duncan Hines cake mixes, Folger's coffee, Tide laundry detergent, Crest toothpaste, Head and Shoulders shampoo, Crisco vegetable oil and shortening, Charmin toilet tissue, and Ivory soap—all different businesses with different competitors, different manufacturing techniques, and so on. But what ties them together into a package of related diversification is that they are all marketed through a common distribution system to be sold in retail food outlets to customers everywhere; much the same core consumer marketing skills and merchandising know-how come into play for all of P&G's products.
- *In terms of creating a multi-industry portfolio of unrelated businesses.* Here the answer to "What is our business?" can be based on any of several considerations: opportunism, a preference for not putting all of the firm's eggs in one basket, attempts to stabilize earnings over the cycle of economic ups and downs, the fun of making a profit by shifting and shuffling the assets of several companies, a belief in growth via diversification, or even "getting into any business where we can make good money." In companies built around unrelated diversification, there is *no* conceptual theme that links different businesses in customer needs/customer groups/technology terms.

---

take. It is a manager's job to peer far down each side of the forks, evaluate the prospects of success of heading down each fork, accept some risk, and make whatever direction-setting decisions are needed to try to position the enterprise to be a successful performer over the years ahead.

A Broad or Narrow Mission?

In concepting an organization's mission and trying to articulate it down the line to other managers and employees, there is value in using both broad and narrow terminology. Missions can be broad, in the sense of embracing several distinct types of products, industries, customer groups, technologies, and needs to be served. Yet, at the same time, they have to be narrow enough to confine organizational activities to an understandable, meaningful arena. Consider the following definitions of scope:

Broad Definition	Narrow Definition
Home entertainment	Compact disk players
Furniture	Upholstered chair manufacturing
Travel and tourism	Luxury hotel
Air transportation	Commuter airline
Publishing	Publishing college textbooks in business administration

Broad/narrow distinctions are relative, of course. Home entertainment is probably too broad a definition for a company that makes only compact disk players, but it can be quite apropos for a multiproduct firm that manufacturers TV sets, stereo equipment, radios, and VCRs.

While overly narrow business definitions raise the risk of tunnel vision and increase the chance that managers will overlook important strategic opportunities or threats nearby, the bigger danger comes in stating the mission so broadly and all-inclusively that it reveals nothing about what the organization's business makeup and future course really is. A catchall concept, like "Our business is to serve the food needs of the nation," offers neither clear direction nor organizational identity—it can mean the organization's business is anything from growing wheat to operating a vegetable cannery to manufacturing farm machinery to running a supermarket chain to being a McDonald's franchisee. Both the U.S. Postal Service and Federal Express are in the "mail business," but this hides their sharply different business concepts and organizational missions. The foggier the language managers use to define an organization's business and future direction, the less guidance the mission statement gives subordinate managers in making decisions consistent with overall organizational direction, and the less helpful it is in conveying a sense of direction and organizational purpose to employees. In the absence of a strong sense of direction and a clarity about the kinds of change management is trying to promote, organizations tend to become reactive, lethargic, and bureaucratic—just drifting aimlessly along. Confusion abounds among employees and subordinate managers over where the organization is headed. Illustration Capsule 5 provides an example of how one company characterized the direction it was headed.

On the other hand, a precisely worded mission statement that projects a vision and a clear organizational direction has real managerial value. The benefits of a well-said mission statement include (1) crystallizing top management's own view about the firm's long-term direction and makeup, (2) cluing lower-level managers into what sorts of direction-related actions they need to be taking in their areas of responsibility, (3) communicating an organizational identity, and (4) giving all employees a sense of purpose in their work. A well-conceived answer to "What is our business and what will it be?" helps managers avoid the trap of trying to march in too many directions at once, and its counterpart, the trap of being unclear about when or where to march at all. When senior managers have a well-thought-out vision of what the organization is trying to do and to become, they are better able to train their decisions and actions on how to move on down the chosen path.

ILLUSTRATION CAPSULE 5

A & P's Statement of Company Direction

In 1987, The Great Atlantic & Pacific Tea Company presented the following summary of its directional course in five different areas:

	Where We Were	Where We Are	Where We're Going
Our People	Strategic reorganization. Performance-based bonus plans. Quality of Work Life Program tested by Super Fresh.	81,500 employees, more sophisticated and skilled. Quality of Work Life now expanded to 243 stores.	Better training programs and participatory management. Productivity results that surpass the industry standard.
Our Stores	1983—beginning of remodelling; Kohl's. 1984—birth of the Futurestore and Sav-A-Center. 1985—Dominion. 1986—Shopwell and Waldbaum.	Gourmet stores (Food Emporium), superstores (Futurestore, Sav-A-Center), upgraded supermarkets (A&P, Super Fresh, Kohl's Waldbaum, Dominion).	Complete three-year, $450 million plan to open 120 new stores and modernize 300 others by 1988. Larger stores to accommodate more service areas.
Our Operations	Disciplined cost controls instituted to pull the company back into profitability. Initial development of new store operating systems and procedures.	Three-year financial control program currently ahead of schedule. Store operations systems and procedures now fully implemented.	Further development of store checkout scanning capabilities. State-of-the-art computer applications on both corporate and store levels.
Our Merchandising	Smaller stores offering little product assortment or distinction; appeal was solely to the "traditional" family.	Store formats and products that more closely match regional demographics. Many service areas under one roof. Expanded perishables.	Even greater variety to keep pace with the specialized needs of consumer groups. Improved marketing and merchandising concepts.
Our Customers	Mass-market retailing. Majority of shoppers fit into median demographics for age, income, education, and lifestyle.	A keen eye to emerging consumer groups—working women, men, singles, and teenagers—all of whom are increasingly sophisticated. Renewed employee pride.	Increased customer service and helpfulness. Overriding goal: Keep looking for better ways to serve our customers.

SOURCE: 1986–1987 annual report.

Communicating the Mission

The task of communicating the mission to subordinate managers and employees is almost as important a task as that of developing the mission. If senior management couches the organization's mission in foggy language and platitudes, then the resulting hollow ring leaves lower-level managers and employees cold and uninspired; complaints will soon be voiced that there is "a lack of direction from top management." Similarly, if senior executives fail to communicate the mission in ways which convey a sense of urgency and purpose, or if they don't provide a convincing rationale for why the organization has to move in new directions, then the mission statement does little to induce changes in the attitudes, thinking, and behavior of employees—an outcome that makes it much harder to move the organization in new directions. The skill in wording a mission statement comes in choosing simple, concise terminology that speaks loudly and clearly to all concerned and that leaves no doubt about the future course management has charted. Then it needs to be articulated to the organization in convincing fashion. The effect of a well-worded, well-articulated mission is to turn heads in the intended direction and to begin a new organizational march. The first step in organizational direction-setting has then been taken.

ESTABLISHING LONG-RANGE AND SHORT-RANGE OBJECTIVES: THE SECOND DIRECTION-SETTING TASK

The act of establishing objectives not only converts the mission and directional course into specific performance targets to be achieved but it also begins the necessary process of training the energies of *each part* of the organization on what they need to accomplish. Objectives are needed for each and every *key result* that managers deem really important to success.[4] From an organizationwide perspective, objectives need to be set for such key results areas as: annual growth in revenues and earnings, return on investment, annual dividend increases, market share gains expected each year, reputation for product quality and/or technological leadership, recognition as a blue-chip company, ability to ride out ups and downs in the economy, degree of diversification, financial strength, product innovation, and the like. For example, a company might establish the following objectives:

- A 15 percent growth in earnings per share every year.
- A 30 percent pretax return on invested assets.
- Market-share leadership, with gains in market share expected every year.
- Dividend increases of 10 percent annually.
- Being the unquestioned technological leader in the industry.
- Providing truly superior customer service.

Both long-range and short-range objectives are needed. Long-range objectives serve two purposes. One, they raise the issue of what actions to take *now* to be able to reach the targeted long-range performance *later* (a manager seldom enjoys

---

[4]The literature of management is filled with references to *goals* and *objectives*. These terms are used in a variety of ways, many of them conflicting. Some writers use the term *goals* to refer to the *long-run* results an organization seeks to achieve and use the term *objectives* to refer to immediate, *short-run* performance targets. Other writers reverse the usage, referring to objectives as the desired long-run results and goals as the desired short-run results. Still other writers use the terms interchangeably, as synonyms. And still others use the term *goals* to refer to *general* organizationwide performance targets and the term *objectives* to mean the specific targets set by subordinate managers in response to the broader, more inclusive goals of the whole organization. In our view, there's little point in getting bogged down in semantic distinctions between the terms *goals* and *objectives;* the important thing is to recognize that the results an enterprise seeks to attain vary both in scope and in time perspective. In nearly every instance, organizations need long-range and short-range performance targets. It is managerially irrelevant which targets are called "goals" and which are called "objectives." To avoid creating any more of a semantic jungle of terms than is necessary, we have chosen to use the single term *objectives* to refer to the performance targets and results an organization seeks to attain. We will use the adjectives *long-range* (or *long-run*) and *short-range* (or *short-run*) to identify the relevant time frame, and we will endeavor to describe objectives in such a way as to indicate their intended scope and level in the organization.

the luxury of being able to wait until the end of year 4 to begin working on what needs to be achieved in year 5!). Two, having long-range objectives pushes managers to weigh the impact of today's decisions on longer-range performance. Without the pressure to meet ongoing or long-range performance targets, managers will invariably base decisions on what is most expedient in the near term.

Short-range objectives spell out the immediate and near-term results to be achieved. They indicate the *speed* at which the organization needs to move along its charted path as well as the *level of performance* which is being aimed for. They represent a commitment by managers to produce specified results in a specified time frame—this means they must spell out *how much by when*. Short-range objectives can be the same as long-range objectives when an organization is already performing at the target long-range level; for instance, if a company has a long-range or ongoing objective of 15 percent profit growth every year and is currently achieving this objective, then the company's long-range and short-range profit objectives coincide. The most important situation where short-range objectives differ from long-range objectives is when managers are trying to elevate organizational performance and cannot reach the long-range/ongoing target in just one year; short-range objectives then set the pace for reaching the ultimate target.

The Value of Performance Objectives

Unless an organization's mission and direction are translated into *measurable* performance targets, and until real pressure is put on managers to show progress in reaching these targets, there is every likelihood that the organization's mission statement will end up being nothing more than a set of nice words, good intentions, and unrealized dreams of accomplishment. The hard knocks of experience tell a powerful story about why results-oriented objective-setting is a critical task in the strategic-management process: *Companies whose managers do a good job of setting objectives for each key result area and then consciously pursue actions calculated to achieve their strategic targets are strong candidates to outperform the companies whose managers have "other considerations" in deciding what actions to take.* Spelling out strategic targets in specific, measurable terms and then holding managers accountable for reaching their assigned targets (1) acts to substitute purposeful, strategic decision making for aimless actions and confusion over what to accomplish and (2) provides a set of benchmarks for judging just how good the organization's actual strategic performance turns out to be.

It is essential that performance objectives be stated in *quantifiable* or measurable terms and that they contain a *deadline for achievement*. Illustration Capsule 6 discusses how to state objectives "correctly" and the importance of avoiding fuzzy targets like "maximize profits," "reduce costs," "become more efficient," or "increase sales."

The "Challenging but Achievable" Test

Objectives should never be based on whatever levels of achievement management decides would be "nice." Pie-in-the-sky wishful thinking has no place in objective-setting. For objectives to serve as a tool for *stretching* an organization to reach

ILLUSTRATION CAPSULE 6

Stating Objectives: "Good" versus "Bad" Examples

For the direction-setting purpose of objectives to be fulfilled, objectives need to meet five specifications:

1. An objective should relate to a single, specific topic.
2. An objective should relate to a result not to an activity to be performed. (The objective is the result of the activity, not the performing of the activity.)
3. An objective should be measurable (stated in quantitative terms).
4. An objective should contain a time deadline for its achievement.
5. An objective should be challenging but achievable.

Consider the following examples:

- *Poor:* Our objective is to maximize profits.
  Remarks: How much is "maximum"? The statement is not subject to measurement. What criterion or yardstick will management use to determine if and when actual profits are equal to maximum profits? No deadline is specified.
  Better: Our total profit target in 1988 is $1 million.
- *Poor:* Our objective is to increase sales revenue and unit volume.
  Remarks: How much? Also, because the statement relates to two topics, it may be inconsistent. Increasing unit volume may require a price cut; and if demand is price inelastic, sales revenue would fall as unit volume rises. No time frame for achievement is indicated.
  Better: Our objective this calendar year is to increase sales revenues from $30 million to $35 million; we expect this to be accomplished by selling 1 million units at an average price of $35.
- *Poor:* Our objective in 1989 is to boost advertising expenditures by 15 percent.
  Remarks: Advertising is an activity, not a result. The real objective is what result the extra advertising is intended to produce.
  Better: Our objective is to boost our market share from 8 percent to 10 percent in 1989 with the help of a 15 percent increase in advertising expenditures.
- *Poor:* Our objective is to be a pioneer in research and development and become the technological leader in the industry.
  Remarks: Very sweeping and ambitious especially if the industry is one with a wide range of technological frontiers.
  Better: During the 1980s our objective is to continue as a leader in introducing new technologies and new devices that will allow buyers of electrically powered equipment to conserve on electric energy usage.
- *Poor:* Our objective is to be the most profitable company in our industry.
  Remarks: Not specific enough; by what measures of profit—total dollars or earnings per share or unit profit margin or return on equity investment, or all of these? Also, because the objective concerns how well other companies will perform, the objective, while challenging, may not be achievable.
  Better: We will strive to lead the industry in rate of return on equity investment by earning a 25 percent aftertax return on equity investment in 1989.

its full potential, they must meet the criterion of being *challenging but achievable*. Satisfying this criterion means setting objectives in the light of several important "inside-outside" considerations:

- What performance levels will industry and competitive conditions realistically allow?
- What financial performance does the organization need to achieve to (1) please investors and the financial community and (2) have the financial resources to execute management's strategy and make other needed moves?
- What performance is the organization capable of *when pushed?*

In effect, therefore, setting challenging but achievable objectives requires managers to judge what performance is possible in light of external conditions against what performance the organization is really capable of achieving. The tasks of objective-setting and strategy-making often become intertwined at this point. Whereas strategy is management's tool for achieving strategic targets, the choice of a strategy has to be hinged upon the organization's financial performance objectives being set high enough to generate the funds needed for successful strategy execution.

The Need for Objectives at All Management Levels

For strategic thinking and strategy-driven direction-setting to penetrate either deeply or meaningfully into the organizational hierarchy, performance targets must be established not only for the organization as a whole but also for each of the organization's separate businesses and product lines and then on down to each functional area and department within the business-unit/product-line structure.[5] Only when every manager, from the chief executive officer on down to the lowest strategy manager, is held accountable for achieving specific results in the units they head, is the objective-setting process complete enough to be sure that the whole organization is pointed down the chosen trail and that each part of the organization knows what it needs to accomplish. Thus, organizational objectives act as a unifying force to channel efforts in particular directions and to elevate performance standards. Individually, objectives point to a key-result area; collectively, they influence the way people spend their time.

An example will clarify how strategic objectives at one managerial level drive the objectives and strategies of the next level down. Suppose the senior executives of a diversified corporation establish a corporate profit objective of $5 million for next year. Suppose further, after discussion between corporate management and the general managers of the firm's five different businesses, that each business is given the challenging but achievable profit objective of $1 million (the plan being that, if the five business divisions can contribute $1 million each in profit, the corporation as a whole can reach its $5 million profit objective). Observe so far, with respect to profit only, that corporate executives have set a priority of $5 million in total profit for the year and that the general managers of each business division have been assigned responsibility for $1 million in profit by year end. A

---

[5]Drucker, *Management*, p. 100. See also, Charles H. Granger, "The Hierarchy of Objectives," *Harvard Business Review* 42, no. 3 (May–June 1963), pp. 63–74.

concrete result, thus, has been agreed on and translated into measurable action commitments to achieve something at two levels in the managerial hierarchy. Next, suppose the general manager of business unit X, after some analytical calculations and discussions with functional area managers, concludes that reaching the $1 million profit objective will require selling 100,000 units at an average price of $50 and producing them at an average cost of $40 (the $10 profit margin multiplied by 100,000 units yields a $1 million profit). Consequently, the general manager and the manufacturing manager may settle on manufacturing objectives of producing 100,000 units at a unit cost of $40; and the general manager and the marketing manager may agree on a sales objective of 100,000 units and an average target selling price of $50. In turn, the marketing manager may break the sales objective of 100,000 units down into unit sales targets for each salesperson, for each sales territory, for each customer type, or for each item in the product line. In similar fashion, objectives can be agreed on for every other key result area of concern and priority to management.

The key thing to understand from this example is that the top-down process of establishing performance targets for each manager and organizational subunit to shoot for leads to a clearer definition of what results are expected and who is responsible for achieving them. If done right, *objective-setting energizes the organization,* points managers in the right direction, creates a *results-oriented* organizational climate, and brings more unity and cohesion to the decisions and actions being taken in different parts of the organization.

CRAFTING A STRATEGY: THE THIRD DIRECTION-SETTING TASK

Managers nearly always have some discretion in choosing *how* to achieve target objectives—as the old saying goes, "There's more than one way to skin a cat." Whereas objectives represent the "ends," strategy represents management's "means" of accomplishing its objectives. In definitional terms, *strategy is the pattern of approaches and moves crafted by management to produce successful performance.* Because every organization's situation contains unique aspects, management has to *customize* its strategic moves and approaches to fit the relevant internal and external circumstances. Because every organization's situation changes over time, its strategy is continually *evolving* as managers modify the approaches they take and initiate new moves to respond to changing conditions. Illustration Capsule 7 provides examples of the close link between objectives and strategy.

General Electric, a pioneer of strategic-management practices, once defined strategy as "a statement of how what resources are going to be used to take advantage of which opportunities to minimize which threats to produce a desired result." This definition points toward the cross-section of issues that strategy-making must address:

1. How to respond to changing external conditions.
2. How to compete and what kind of competitive advantage to try to secure.
3. What approaches and actions to take in each major functional department and operating unit to complement and flesh out the details of the overall strategy.
4. What moves to take in dealing with the company's own particular strategic issues and operating problems.

ILLUSTRATION CAPSULE 7

Strategy as a Means of Achieving Company Objectives

In the business world, it is common for companies to establish objectives and then set forth broad strategies to achieve them. Consider the following two examples:

Mattel Corporation

Our objective in 1987 is to increase worldwide market share and regain acceptable levels of profitability. To achieve this, Mattel will continue to focus on:

- Improving margins and reducing overhead expenses as a percentage of sales.
- Broadening our base of business by expanding our product categories to include activity, science, and educational toys; enhancing our presence in the preschool market; and capitalizing on the strength of our international operations.
- Fostering creative design and encouraging entrepreneurial risk-taking based on sound market research.
- Introducing, shipping, and promoting new lines and products throughout the year.
- Executing innovative marketing and sales programs that include advertising, consumer and trade promotion, public relations, and retail merchandising.

National Cash Register (NCR)

Our objective continues to be the achievement of revenue growth rates higher than the industry average while maintaining above-average profitability and a conservative balance sheet.

We see major opportunities for our products in two areas of large revenue potential: transaction processing and office information systems. Our approach to these market opportunities emphasizes creating value for shareholders by providing products of increasing value to customers.

Our marketing strategy is to sell products in large volumes and address all types of customers and prospects for whom our products are suitable. This requires developing NCR products based upon leading-edge technologies.

Our technology strategy calls for NCR products to be based on a minimal number of common microprocessor platforms. This increases our yield from development spending and helps to reduce manufacturing costs through volume production.

Selective use of industry standards is another key component of our technology strategy. This "open systems" concept provides flexibility to our customers and complements our strategy of offering advanced communications capabilities to link NCR systems in heterogeneous networks.

SOURCES: Company annual reports.

The Levels of Managerial Strategy-Making

As we emphasized in the opening chapter, strategy-making is not a task that only senior executives have to do. In large, diversified enterprises, decisions about what approaches to take and what new moves to initiate involve senior executives in the corporate office, the heads of business units and of product divisions, the functional department heads (manufacturing, marketing and sales, finance, human resources, and the like) within business units and divisions, and the managers of departmental subunits, plants, districts, and other geographic units. Table 2–1

TABLE 2–1
The Strategy-Making Hierarchy: Who Has Primary Responsibility for What Kinds of Strategic Actions

Strategy Level	Primary Strategy Development Responsibility	Strategy-Making Functions and Areas of Focus
Corporate strategy	CEO, other key executives. (Decisions are typically reviewed/approved by board of directors.)	• Choosing *how* to build and manage a high-performing portfolio of business units (making acquisitions, initiating divestitures, strengthening existing business positions). • Coordinating the strategies and activities of related business units in an effort to produce a corporate-level competitive advantage. • Reviewing/revising/approving the major strategic approaches and moves proposed by business-unit managers. • Steering corporate investments into businesses with the most attractive strategic opportunities.
Line-of-business strategies	General manager/head of business unit. (Decisions are typically reviewed/approved by senior corporate executives, usually CEO.)	• Choosing how to compete and what kind of competitive advantage to build. • Developing responses to changing industry and competitive conditions. • Coordinating major moves/approaches of key functional areas/operating. • Taking action to address other strategy-related problems and issues facing the business.
Functional area support strategies	Functional area/department heads. (Decisions are typically reviewed/approved by business-unit head.)	• Crafting specific approaches and moves to support business strategy (support strategies are needed in every functional area/major department). • Reviewing/revising/approving strategy-related moves and approaches proposed by lower-level managers and operating units.
Operating-level strategies	Field-unit heads/lower-level managers within functional areas. (Decisions are often made after consultations with lateral peers in closely related areas and are reviewed/approved by functional-area head/department head.)	• Crafting still narrower and more specific approaches and moves aimed at achieving performance objectives set for field units and departmental subunits and at supporting functional and business strategies.

shows how the strategy-making task tends to be divided up among managers at different levels in the organizational hierarchy.

Figure 2–1 shows the networking of objectives and strategies down through the managerial hierarchy. The key point to be gotten from this figure is that, while there needs to be a strategic game plan at each managerial level to achieve the objectives set at that level, there are also vertical linkages in both objectives and strategy that can serve to *unify* the objective-setting and strategy-making activities of many managers into a coherent, coordinated pattern. Creating *tight* linkages in the objectives and strategies of each organizational unit is what prevents each unit

FIGURE 2–1

The Networking of Objectives and Strategies down through the Managerial Hierarchy

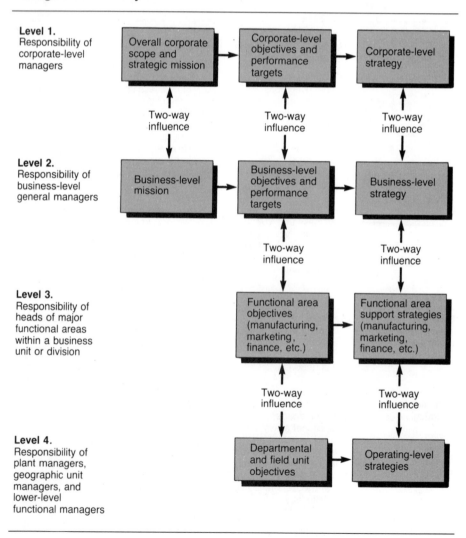

from marching off in its own direction. Generally, organizationwide objectives and strategy need to be established first, so they can drive the objective-setting and strategy-making of lower-level organizational units; without a top-down objective-setting/strategizing approach, one cannot expect lower-level organization units to formulate objectives and strategies that are in step with and contribute to those of the total enterprise.

Corporate Strategy.   The term *corporate strategy* refers to the overall managerial game plan for directing and running a diversified company. Corporate strategy is mirrored in the pattern of moves and approaches crafted by senior executives to achieve overall corporate performance targets. The top-management task of developing a corporate strategy for a diversified company has three pieces:

1.   Choosing How to Build and to Manage the Business-Unit Portfolio.   The first concern in a diversified company is what the portfolio of diversified business units should consist of—specifically, what new business units to add, which existing business units to dispose of, and how to strengthen the competitive positions of those business units top management wishes to keep in the corporate portfolio. This piece of corporate strategy establishes how far the scope of diversification will extend and what the structural mix of business units will be, at least for the time being. As the makeup of the corporate portfolio takes shape, there emerges the added issue of how to manage the business-unit portfolio, both individually and as a group, to meet corporate performance objectives. Normally, some business units are more important than others, because of their size or their more attractive growth opportunities or their industry standing or their contributions to profit and cash flow. The portfolio management plan, thus, is likely to involve selecting a general strategic posture (aggressive expansion, maintain current position, revamp and overhaul, or fix up in preparation to sell out) for each business in the portfolio. Sometimes, it may also involve designating a common strategic theme for all business units to pursue (such as always going after the high-quality end of the market or attempting to be the technological leader or providing truly superior customer service); such themes serve the purpose of building a specific image and reputation for the whole corporation.

2.   Coordinating the Strategies and Activities of Related Business Units in an Effort to Produce Corporate-Level Competitive Advantage.   Coordination of interrelated activities allows a diversified corporation to enhance the competitive strength of its business units and makes overall corporate strategy *more* than just a collection of the action plans of its independent business units. Several issues have to be addressed here: Is there cost-reduction potential in sharing technological know-how, R&D efforts, sales forces, distribution facilities, and so on across any business units? Do other cross-fertilization opportunities exist? Are the benefits worth capturing? What coordination is needed? Will such actions bolster the competitive positions and competitive strengths of the company's various business divisions?

3.   Establishing Investment Priorities and Allocating Corporate Resources Across Business Units.   Decisions about which organizational unit shall get how much of the corporate investment budget and actions to *control the pattern* of corporate resource allocation not only commit the firm to pursue some opportunities aggressively and to hold back on others but also serve to channel resources out of areas where earnings potentials are lower into areas where they are higher.

The decisions of corporate officers about how to build and manage the portfolio of business units are strategically important because they determine the organization's business positions in each of the industries where it competes. The first priority is usually to diversify into businesses that, for the most part, are in *attractive* industries. Then, the corporate-level strategic concern shifts to maintaining, if not substantially improving, the positions of the company's business units in each of these industries. The task of strengthening existing business positions can involve undertaking *offensive* moves to capture a bigger or more solidly held market share and launching *defensive* moves to protect existing positions against emerging threats. When a company is unable to win an adequately profitable business position in an industry, the best strategy may be to divest the business and reallocate funds either to other business units or to new diversification opportunities. The portfolio management strategy, therefore, is concentrated on trying to boost overall corporate performance by, one, improving on the *composition* of the portfolio itself and, two, by strengthening the performance of existing business units.

The second element of corporate strategy, coordinating strategic plans *across* business units, is an important corporate headquarters task because it is through coordination of the interrelated activities of the corporation's different business units that a *corporate-level competitive advantage* can be created.[6] Horizontal coordination of divisional strategies can (1) enhance cross-fertilization of skills, proprietary know-how, and technological capability; (2) prompt business units with closely related activities to undertake them jointly to reduce overall costs; and (3) strengthen differentiation of the firm's products and overall reputation—all of which can add up to a bigger net competitive advantage for divisional business units and increased corporate profitability. Indeed, one of the biggest advantages of diversification comes in achieving some sort of useful *strategic fit* among business units, so their combined performance as part of the same company is *greater* than the business units would be able to achieve as independent operations. The essence of strategic fit is, thus, a $2 + 2 = 5$ effect. When corporate-managers are able to assemble a business portfolio with lots of strategic fit among the business units, then corporate performance is boosted by the $2 + 2 = 5$ effect and additional gains in shareholder value can be realized.

The third element of corporate-level strategy—controlling the pattern of corporate resource allocation—is crucial because the number of "worthy projects" and "can't miss" opportunities put forward for funding by all the business units may entail capital requirements that exceed the available dollars. Ultimately, the pot of corporate monies and resources limits what strategies can be supported. With limited resources, it makes sense to (1) channel investment capital in behind those strategic moves with the highest expected profitability and (2) to deploy corporate resources in close alignment with the success requirements of each line of business the corporation is in.

---

[6]The desirability of explicit horizontal strategy coordination in diversified firms is incisively exposed in Michael E. Porter, *Competitive Advantage* (New York: Free Press, 1985), chaps. 9 and 10. Porter's work blazes a new trail in corporate strategy analysis and in building corporate-level competitive advantage.

Strategy-making at the corporate level, thus, is normally focused on "big picture" strategic choices and making sure that each business unit in the corporate portfolio adds something to overall performance. The challenge is one of how to get sustained high performance out of a multi-industry mix of business activities, some or many of which have nothing in common. When single-business enterprises start to contemplate diversification, then they, too, must confront how to build and manage a portfolio of diversified business units.

The spokes on the "corporate strategy wheel" in Figure 2–2 indicate what to consider in looking at a diversified company from the outside and trying to piece together what its corporate strategy is. However, observing what a company has done and is doing and reading what company officials say the strategy is doesn't always reveal the whole picture. At least part of the game plan, and sometimes the most interesting part, is always hidden from view in the mind of key executives and in their private discussions.

Some of the specific strategy-making considerations that the corporate-level managers in diversified companies have to wrestle with include:

- Choosing *how* to build a strong position in industries that the firm wants to enter (the strategic options here include buying a weak company and trying to turn it into a stronger contender, acquiring a company which

FIGURE 2–2
Identifying the Overall Corporate Strategy of a Diversified Company

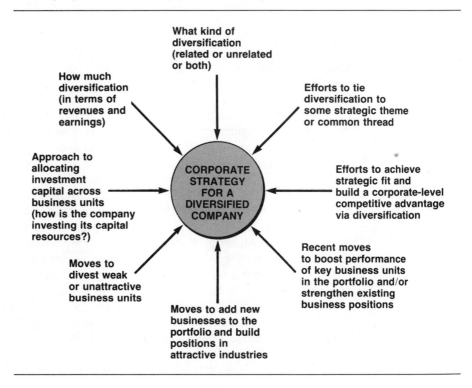

already has a leading position, or launching one's own new start-up company and building it from the ground up).

- Selecting moves to strengthen the market positions of existing business units (perhaps by merger with a smaller competitor or through investment in a new large-scale plant with state-of-the-art technology).
- Deciding what moves to take to restructure the makeup of the company's portfolio of business units (divesting some, merging others, and acquiring some altogether new businesses).
- Deciding *how* to divest a particular business (whether to sell it, spin it off as an independent company, or shut it down entirely and liquidate the assets).
- Choosing an offensive move to pursue a potentially lucrative new opportunity.
- Deciding on defensive actions to protect the existing positions of business units against threatening new developments.
- Maintaining a capacity to intervene should a business unit's performance unexpectedly turn sharply downward.
- Reviewing and approving the major strategic approaches and moves recommended by business-unit managers.
- Striving to coordinate the strategies and activities of related business units.

Business Strategy. The term *business strategy* (or *business-level strategy*) refers to the managerial game plan for directing and running a particular business unit. It is mirrored in the pattern of approaches and moves crafted by management to produce successful performance in that *one specific line of business*. Business strategy deals explicitly with (1) how to compete successfully and what kind of competitive advantage to try to secure; (2) what basic approaches to take in each key functional area of the business (production, marketing, finance, human resources, R&D) to undergird and flesh out the overall business-level game plan; (3) how to respond to changes underway in the industry, the economy at large, the political and regulatory arenas, and other relevant areas; and (4) what actions to take regarding any other strategic issues and operating problems confronting the business. Figure 2–3 shows some of the things to be alert for in trying to piece together what a business unit's overall strategy is.

As an example of line of business strategy, consider the moves and approaches Kellogg Company's management has employed in ready-to-eat cereals. Since 1906, when Will Keith Kellogg formed the company after accidentally discovering a way to make ready-to-eat cereal, Kellogg's objective has been to be the dominant leader in the industry. Kellogg's strategy has been grounded on product differentiation and market segmentation. The company's product line has featured a diverse number of brands, differentiated according to grain, shape, form, flavor, color, and taste—a something-for-everyone approach. Competing on the basis of low price has been slighted in favor of nonprice approaches keyed to extensive product variety, regular product innovation, substantial TV advertising, periodic promotional offers and prizes, and getting more space on the grocery shelf than rivals. Much of Kellogg's sales efforts have been targeted at the under-25 age group (the

FIGURE 2–3
Identifying Strategy in a Single-Business Enterprise

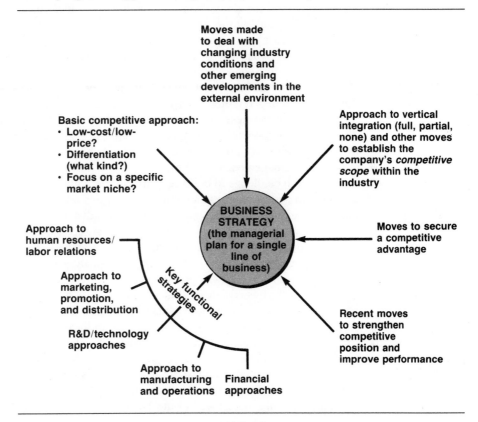

biggest cereal eaters with an average annual consumption of 11 pounds per capita), with the presweetened brands being promoted almost totally through TV advertising to children. The company has tried to offset industry maturity and product saturation with introductions of "new" types of cereals ("presweetened" cereals in the 1940, "nutritional" cereals in the 1950s, "natural" and "health-conscious" cereals in the 1960s and 1970s, and "adult" cereals in the late 1970s), and also by promoting a variety of other times and places for eating cereals than at the morning breakfast table. To maintain a fresh appearance in its product line, from time to time Kellogg introduced new cereal versions that differed only slightly from existing versions (flaked versus shredded, plain versus sugar-frosted, puffed versus cocoa-flavored). In 1979, Kellogg introduced five new adult cereals as part of a stepped-up effort to attract consumers in the 25–50 age group (where consumption levels were only half those of the younger age groups). Kellogg also was endeavoring to strengthen its international base; cereals had been introduced in four additional countries in South America and the Middle East using campaigns that featured free samples, demonstration booths in food stores, and heavy local advertising to promote the use of ready-to-eat cereals as a substitute for traditional breakfast foods of those areas of the world. Kellogg had upped its research budget (already the industry's most extensive) by 15 percent annually in an effort to develop more nutritional, health-conscious cereals and breakfast foods for the older-consumer segment. Overall, Kellogg's strategic performance targets were: (1) an increased market share, (2) sales increases of 5 percent annually (compared to an industry growth of 2 percent) and (3) year-to-year increases in cereal consumption per capita.

For a stand-alone and single-business company, corporate strategy and business strategy are one and the same, since there is only one business for which to form a strategy. But in diversified enterprises, where there is a different business strategy for each line of business the company is in, the term *corporate strategy* serves to distinguish the approaches of senior executives to managing the whole portfolio of business units from the more specific line-of-business strategies being pursued at the next management level down.

The central challenge in crafting a strategy for a given business is *how to secure a competitive advantage,* then capitalizing on this edge to achieve above-average profitability. Building a sustainable competitive advantage entails considering what sort of competitive edge to strive for, how to attract customers away from competitors, how to "position" the business in the marketplace vis-à-vis rivals, what product/service attributes to emphasize in appealing to customers for their patronage, and how to defend against the competitive moves of rivals.

Internally, the business-level strategy-making task must resolve how the different functional pieces of the business (manufacturing, marketing, finance, R&D, and so on) will be managed and made responsive to those market factors upon which the sought-after competitive advantage depends. The role of functional strategies is to *support* the overall business strategy; for this to happen, they have to be crafted *after* the overall business strategy outline is formed, and then the business-unit manager must review each functional strategy in sufficient detail to make sure that they not only add power to the business strategy but that they also are coordinated with each other.

It scarcely needs arguing or explaining that business strategy needs to lay out an action plan for dealing with significant changes that are underway in the industry, the economy, the political and regulatory arenas, and elsewhere. Likewise, strategy must map out an action plan for resolving any special strategic problems or issues confronting the business (such as whether to add new capacity or to replace an obsolete plant or to pour funds into R&D for a promising technology or to raise additional capital, or whatever). As previously discussed, managers must always custom-tailor strategy to fit the specifics of a company's own situation.

The manager in charge of a business has four, sometimes five, roles to play in discharging his or her strategy-making responsibilities:

- Serving as the chief strategist and leading the process of assessing the business's strategic situation, evaluating alternative strategies, and making strategic choices.
- Seeing that supporting strategies in each of the major functional areas of the business are well conceived and consistent with each other.
- Making sure that the chosen strategy stands a good chance of producing the desired results.

- Getting major strategic moves approved by higher authority (the board of directors and corporate-level officers) if needed, and also keeping them informed of important new developments, deviations from plan, and potential strategy revisions.
- In diversified companies, business-unit heads have the additional obligation of making sure that the chosen business strategy adequately supports the achievement of corporate objectives and is consistent with corporate strategy themes.

Functional Area Strategy. The term *functional area strategy* refers to the functional specific approaches and moves crafted by management in support of the overall business strategy. Functional area support strategies are needed for every major subpart of a business—production, marketing and sales, distribution, finance, human resources, information systems, and the like. Functional strategies flesh out the business game plan, adding more detail and specifying how functional activities will be conducted in furtherance of the overall business strategy and of functional area performance objectives. Thus, functional strategy in the production/manufacturing area consists of the managerial game plan for *how* manufacturing activities will be conducted to achieve manufacturing objectives and to support business strategy. Functional strategy in the finance area consists of the array of financial moves and approaches that are planned to achieve specific financial objectives and to support business strategy. And so also is it in the other functional areas. Illustration Capsule 8 provides a detailed look at a sample functional area strategy—the approach IBM employed in pricing and marketing mainframe computers.

Lead responsibility for functional area strategy-making is normally delegated to the functional manager unless, for some reason, the business-unit head decides to personally exercise a strong strategy-making influence. Functional managers usually work in concert with key subordinates, other functional area heads, and the business head in coming up with functional approaches and moves to recommend for final review and approval. The review of each functional area head's strategy proposals presents the business-level general manager with opportunity to unify the several functional strategies and make certain they are supportive of business strategy and conducive to the achievement of functional and business objectives. When all of the principal functional activities within a business are mutually reinforcing, the whole business strategy obtains added power.

Operating Strategy. *Operating strategy* refers to the even narrower and more detailed approaches and moves devised by departmental-subunit managers and geographic-unit managers to achieve the strategy-supporting performance objectives established in their areas of responsibility. Operating strategy, while of obviously lesser scope than the higher levels of strategy-making, is still important from the standpoint of strategic completeness. Even the smallest organizational units, if they are important enough to exist, are important enough to have performance targets of some kind to achieve. The managers of these units, thus, will need to devise approaches and make moves to achieve these objectives, thereby putting them into the role of strategy-makers. For instance, the manager of the eastern region is obligated to develop a strategy customized to the particular sit-

ILLUSTRATION CAPSULE 8

IBM's Marketing Approach—A Sample Functional Area Strategy*

IBM's strategic approach to marketing during the 1967–1972 period is considered by industry observers to be a prime reason for the firm's success in capturing about a 65 to 70 percent share of the computer systems market. At the heart of the IBM approach was the "systems selling" concept whereby IBM salespeople were encouraged to sell customers a complete data processing system. The IBM package included a central processing unit, peripheral equipment (tape storage, disk storage, high-speed printers, card readers, keypunch machines), software, maintenance, emergency repairs, applications support, and consulting services to train the customer's personnel. By offering a total system, IBM attempted to supply the full range of a customer's data processing needs.

IBM encouraged customers to lease, rather than purchase, its products. The advantage to the customer of a leasing arrangement was protection against rapid technological obsolescence. As new equipment was introduced and/or as customer requirements changed, the old system could be turned in for a bigger, better (albeit, generally more costly) new system. In introducing new systems, IBM priced the new equipment *lower* than the older system on a performance/price basis; thus, for a given set of jobs, the new system represented a savings to the customer over the old system. However, because the customer's usage of the new system expanded to cover more tasks and applications, the upgrading to the new system produced higher rentals for IBM.

Initially, IBM charged rentals for hardware and provided service, software, and consulting free to its customers—a pricing strategy which motivated customers to accept the total IBM package (to the exclusion of rivals who offerd only a partial package—just service or just hardware and software). When IBM was charged by the Justice Department in the late 1960s with monopolizing and attempting to monopolize the computer market (one complaint being the "one-price" rental system), IBM's marketing strategy shifted to one of pricing its equipment rental and services separately. IBM began using a standard base contract for all equipment, which provided for a monthly rental and required a 30-day notice for cancellation (a feature which facilitated upgrading of customers as new products were introduced). The base rental fee covered the use of equipment for a specified number of hours per week; usage beyond this amount (usually 40 to 50 hours) resulted in "additional use" rental fees of up to 40 percent of the base rental. All rented equipment was serviced by IBM under a separate service contract, with the amount of the service fee being pegged to equipment usage.

However, when IBM's competitors began to introduce attractively priced peripheral equipment (printers, tapes, disks, and memories) that were compatible with IBM central processing units, IBM adopted a fixed-term plan (FTP) leasing approach for its tape, disk, and printer products. Under the FTP, customers were allowed an 8 percent discount on one-year leases, a 16 percent discount on two-year leases, and all extra use charges were eliminated; the penalty for canceling an FTP was two and a half times the monthly rental for one-year contracts and five times the monthly rental for two-year contracts. The FTP not only made IBM products more price-competitive but it also shielded IBM's leased products from

ILLUSTRATION CAPSULE 8 *(concluded)*

competition for a longer period. To make up for the lost revenues under the FTP price discounts, IBM raised its prices for products not covered by the FTP and also raised prices for maintenance and services. The net effect was that, while most customers ended up paying IBM about the same total amount as before FTP, they paid less for those IBM products which faced active competition.

When the peripheral equipment manufacturers responded to the FTP with price cuts of their own, IBM initiated a second round of price cuts, along with product design changes. IBM's basic marketing strategy continued to be to induce customers to trade up to progressively higher performance computers.

*The content of this capsule has been extracted and synthesized from Derek F. Abell, *Defining the Business: The Starting Point of Strategic Planning* (Englewood Cliffs, N.J.: Prentice-Hall, 1980), pp. 32–48.

uation of that region; the southern regional manager needs a strategy for achieving this region's performance targets and for addressing whatever strategic issues and problems are unique to the southern region; the manager of plant X needs a strategy for accomplishing plant X's objectives, carrying out plant X's role in the overall manufacturing game plan, and dealing with whatever strategic problems exist of plant X. So it goes for all the managers of key operating units.

To further indicate the nature of operating strategy, consider the following instances of how departmental and other operating managers devise plans to carry out the finer details of higher-level strategies:

- A company with a low-price, high-volume business strategy and a need to achieve very low manufacturing costs launches a companywide effort to boost worker productivity by 10 percent. To contribute to the productivity-boosting objective: (1) the hiring director develops a new employee recruiting program to screen out all but the most highly motivated, best-qualified job applicants; (2) the director of information systems devises a way to use office technology to boost the productivity of office workers; (3) the employee benefits director devises an improved incentive compensation plan to reward increased output by manufacturing employees; and (4) the purchasing director launches a search for time-saving tools and equipment.

- A distributor of plumbing equipment emphasizes quick delivery and accurate order filling as keystones of its customer service approach. To support this strategy, the warehouse manager (1) develops an inventory stocking strategy that allows 99 percent of all orders to be completely filled without back ordering any item and (2) has a warehouse staffing strategy of maintaining a work force capability to ship any order within 24 hours.

Coordinating Strategy-Making Decisions. It is only when the managers of all strategy-critical operating units have clear-cut objectives and strategies to achieve them that management's direction-setting and strategy-making tasks have been thoroughly done. Furthermore, the managerial process of reviewing and approving performance objectives and strategies level by level allows for harmonizing and coordinating otherwise inconsistent and conflicting efforts. To get an idea what happens to an organization when senior managers fail to exercise strong *top-down* direction-setting and strategic *leadership,* imagine what would happen to a football team's offensive performance if the quarterback decided not to exercise leadership in calling a play for the team, but instead, instructed each individual player to choose whatever play he thought would work best and then run it when the center decided to snap the ball.

As a consequence, an oganization's strategy is not well formulated until the separate pieces and layers of strategy-making mesh together well—much like the pieces of a picture puzzle. The power of business strategy is enhanced when functional area and operating-level strategies form a unified, reinforcing pattern of approaches and moves—plainly enough, manufacturing strategy, marketing strategy, financial strategy, and so on should not be working at cross-purposes or marching off in separate directions. Getting all the pieces of business strategy pulling together neutralizes some of the effects of organizational politics and acts to keep the sometimes myopic views and loyalties of functional departments from blunting the priorities of what is best for the total enterprise.[7] Likewise, in a multibusiness enterprise, welding diverse business-level strategies together in some coherent fashion improves the power of corporate strategy. Thus, it is useful to view the links between the pieces and levels of strategy as (1) the conceptual glue that binds an organization's activities together and (2) the merging force of what makes a strategy well formulated.[8]

Figure 2–4 depicts a hypothetical composite strategy and the several levels of directional approaches and moves requisite for having a complete strategic plan. Note the logical flow from corporate strategy to business strategy to functional support strategies to operating-level strategies. It should be evident from an examination of this figure that an organization's strategic plan is the sum total of the directional actions and decisions it must make in trying to accomplish its objectives—in effect, *a strategic plan is a collection of strategies.*

APPROACHES TO PERFORMING THE STRATEGY-MAKING TASK

Companies and managers perform the strategy-making task differently. In small owner-managed companies, strategy-making is developed informally, often never being reduced to writing but existing mainly in the entrepreneur's own mind and in oral understandings with key subordinates. The largest firms, however, tend to develop their plans via an annual strategic-planning cycle (complete with prescribed procedures, forms, and timetables) that includes broad management participation, lots of studies, and multiple meetings to probe and question. The larger and more

---

[7]Functional area managers can sometimes be more interested in doing what is best for their own areas, in building their own empire, and in consolidating their personal power and organizational influence than they are in cooperating with other functional managers to unify behind the overall business strategy. As a consequence, it is easy for functional area support strategies to get at cross-purposes, thereby forcing the business-level general manager to expend time and energy refereeing functional strategy conflicts and building support for a more unified approach.

[8]Vancil, "Strategy Formulation in Complex Organizations," p. 18.

FIGURE 2–4
The Levels of Strategy for a Hypothetical Petroleum Company

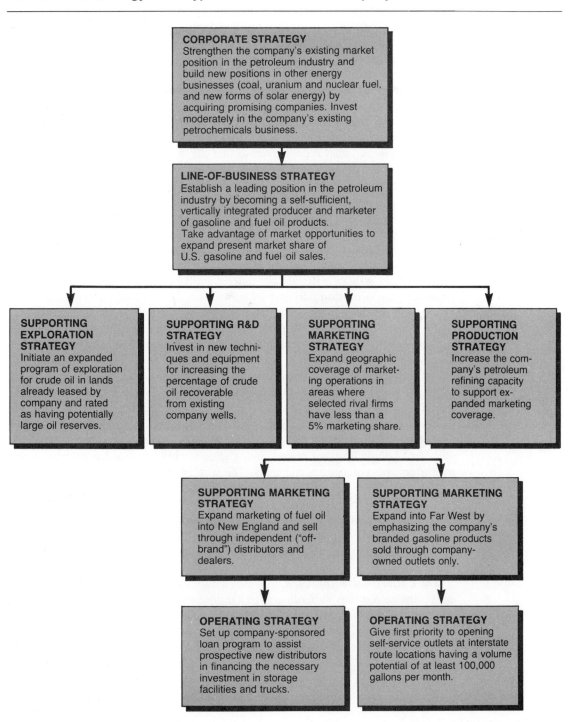

diverse an enterprise, the more that managers feel it is better to have a structured process that is done annually, involves written plans, and requires management scrutiny and official approval at each level.

Along with variations in the organizational process of formulating strategy come variations in the way the manager, as chief entrepreneur and organizational leader, personally participates in the actual work of strategic analysis and strategic choice. The four basic-strategy-making styles used by managers are:[9]

The Master Strategist Approach. Here the manager personally functions as chief strategist and chief entrepreneur, exercising *strong* influence over the kinds and amount of analysis conducted, over the strategy alternatives to be explored, and over the details of strategy. This does not mean that the manager personally does all the work; what it does mean is that the manager personally becomes the chief architect of strategy and wields a proactive hand in shaping some or all of the major pieces of strategy. The manager acts as strategy commander and has a big ownership stake in the chosen strategy.

The Delegate It to Others Approach. Here the manager in charge delegates the exercise of strategy-making to others, perhaps a strategic-planning staff or a task force of trusted subordinates. The manager then personally stays off to the side, keeps in touch with how things are progressing via reports and oral conversations, offers guidance if need be, quietly smiles or frowns as trial-balloon recommendations are informally run by him or her for reaction, then puts a stamp of approval on the "strategic plan" after it has been formally presented, discussed, and a consensus emerges. But the manager rarely has much ownership in the recommendations and, privately, may not see much urgency in pushing *truly hard* to implement some or much of what has been stated in writing in the company's "official strategic plan." Also, it is generally understood that "of course, we may have to proceed a bit differently if conditions change"—which gives the manager flexibility to go slowly or ignore those approaches/moves that "on further reflection may not be the thing to do at this time." This strategy-making style has the advantage of letting the manager pick and choose from the smorgasbord of strategic ideas that bubble up from below, and it allows room for broad participation and input from many managers and areas. The weakness is that a manager can end up so detached from the process of formal strategy-making that no real strategic leadership is exercised—indeed, the impression that subordinates get is that, all the lip service to the contrary, strategic planning is not an activity worth a big claim on the boss's personal time and attention. The stage is then set for rudderless direction-setting; often the strategy-making that does occur is short-run oriented and reactive.

The Collaborative Approach. This is a middle approach, whereby the manager enlists the help of key subordinates in hammering out a consensus strategy which all "the key players" will back and do their best to implement successfully. The biggest strength of this style of managing the formulation process is that those who are charged with strategy formulation are also those who are charged with

---

[9]The following list and discussion is based on David R. Brodwin and L. J. Bourgeois, "Five Steps to Strategic Action," in *Strategy and Organization: A West Coast Perspective*, ed. Carroll and Vogel, especially pp. 168-78.

implementing the chosen strategy. Giving subordinate managers a clear-cut ownership stake in the strategy they subsequently must implement not only enhances commitment to successful execution but also, when subordinates have had a hand in proposing their part of the overall strategy, they can be held accountable for making it work—the "I told you it was a bad idea" alibi won't fly.

The Champion Approach. In this style of presiding over strategy formulation, the manager is interested neither in a big personal stake in the details of strategy nor in the time-consuming tedium of leading others through participative brainstorming or a collaborative "group wisdom" exercise. Rather, the idea is to encourage subordinate-managers to develop, champion, and implement sound strategies. Here strategy moves upward from the "doers" and the "fast-trackers." The executive serves as a judge, evaluating the strategy proposals reaching his desk. This approach is especially well suited for large diversified corporations where it is impossible for the CEO to be on top of all the strategic and operating problems facing each of many business divisions. Therefore, if the CEO is to exploit the fact that there are many people in the enterprise who can see strategic opportunities that he cannot, then he must give up some control over strategic direction in order to foster strategic opportunities and new strategic initiatives. The CEO may well articulate general strategic themes as organizationwide guidelines for strategic thinking, but the real skill is stimulating and rewarding new strategy proposals put forth by a champion who believes in the opportunity and badly wants the blessing to go after it. With this approach, the total "strategy" is strongly influenced by the sum of the championed initiatives that get approved.

These four basic managerial approaches to forming a strategy bring to light several aspects about how a strategy comes into being. In situations where the manager in charge personally functions as the chief architect of strategy, the choice of what strategic course to steer is often influenced by his/her own vision of how to position the enterprise and by the manager's ambitions, values, business philosophies, and sense of what moves to make next. As Professor Andrews has noted in explaining the relevance of personal factors in shaping the choice of strategy, "Somebody has to have his heart in it."[10] Some master strategists exhibit a strong preference for being pioneers and exhibiting innovation leadership; others are cautious and risk-averse, being inclined toward "safe" strategies where the downside risk appears minimal, profits seem secure, and conservative financial approaches can be used. Still others attach high value to superior product quality or technological leadership or rapid growth or superb customer service. A strong manager-leader usually sees to it that such values and beliefs are embodied in the strategy.

The primary weakness of the master strategist approach is that the caliber of the strategy depends so heavily on the strategy-making skills of the individual functioning as strategy-commander. Highly centralized strategy-making can work fine when the manager in charge has a powerful, insightful vision of what needs to be done and how to do it; but it can break down in a large complex organization where many strategic initiatives are needed and the CEO's grasp of the situation

---

[10]Kenneth R. Andrews, *The Concept of Corporate Strategy,* rev. ed. (Homewood, Ill.: Richard D. Irwin, 1980), p. 85.

ILLUSTRATION CAPSULE 9

The L. L. Bean Tradition of Customer Satisfaction: An Example of How Values and Philosophy Shape Strategy

"THE GOLDEN RULE OF L.L. BEAN"

"Sell good merchandise at a reasonable profit, treat your customers like human beings and they'll always come back for more."

Leon Leonwood Bean started a company 74 years ago based on this simply stated business philosophy. We call it L.L.'s Golden Rule and today we still practice it.

Everything we sell is backed by a 100% unconditional guarantee. We do not want you to have anything from L.L. Bean that is not completely satisfactory. Return anything you buy from us at any time for any reason if it proves otherwise.

L.L. Bean pays all regular postage and handling charges on orders shipped within the United States. This means that the price listed is the only amount that you pay. There are no additional costs.

Send for our FREE fully illustrated 1986 catalogs. They feature a full range of quality products for men and women who enjoy the outdoors. Active and casual apparel and footwear, winter sports equipment, luggage, bedding and furnishings for home or camp. Practical and functional gift ideas. All fully illustrated and honestly described.

Order anytime 24 hours a day, 365 days a year by mail or with our convenient TOLL FREE phone number. Our Customer Service and Telephone Representatives are always here to serve you. We maintain large inventories and ship promptly.

☐ Please send FREE 1986 L.L. Bean Catalogs!

Name_____
Address_____
City_____
State_____ Zip_____

L.L. Bean, Inc., 7255 Alder St., Freeport, ME 04033

L.L.Bean®

ends up being stretched thinly over many isues and problems. Illustration Capsule 9 on L. L. Bean illustrates how the strongly held values and business philosophies of a manager-leader have a big influence on strategy.

On the other hand, when the manager in charge delegates much of the strategy-making task to others, the resulting strategy will seldom bear his/her personal stamp. Often, the strategy that emerges will then be shaped by influential subordinates, by powerful functional departments, or by political coalitions that have a strong interest in promoting their particular version of what the strategy ought to be. "Politics" and the exercise of power are most likely to come into play in situations where there is no strong consensus on what strategy to adopt; this opens the door for a political solution to emerge. The collaborative approach is conducive to political strategy formation as well, since powerful departments and individuals have ample opportunity to try to build a consensus for their favored strategic approach.

The strength of the champion approach is also its weakness. The value of championing is that it encourages innovative ideas to bubble up from below. Individuals with attractive strategic proposals are given room and resources to try them out. Such an approach can serve as an excellent vehicle for keeping strategy fresh and for developing an organization's capacity for renewed innovation. On the other hand, the weakness is that the overall strategy may become no more than an uncoordinated collection of championed strategy approaches and plans. A manager must work conscientiously to ensure that what is championed fits into the overall organization strategy; otherwise, strategic initiatives may be launched in many directions, with no integrating pattern or overarching rationale. The value of top-down strategy-making influence is to ensure enough cohesion and unity in the strategy-making being done throughout the lower eschelons of the managerial hierarchy.

ANALYTICAL CHECKLIST

To instill clear direction into an organization's activities, a manager has to perform three tasks: developing a mission, setting objectives, and forming a strategy. The starting point in the direction-setting process is for managers to form a vision of where to lead the organization and to conceptualize an answer to "What is our business and what will it be?" An organization's mission statement specifies what activities the organization is to pursue and what course management has charted for organization to follow.

The second direction-setting step is to establish short-range and long-range objectives for the organization to achieve. These serve to translate the mission statement into specific performance targets. The agreed-upon objectives need to be challenging but achievable, and they need to spell out precisely how much by when—in other words, objectives should be measurable and should involve deadlines for achievement. Objectives are needed at all organizational levels.

The third direction-setting step entails forming strategies to achieve the objectives set in each area of the organization. A corporate strategy is needed to achieve corporate-level objectives; business strategies are needed to achieve business-unit performance objectives; functional strategies are needed to achieve the performance targets set in each major functional department of the enterprise; and operating-level strategies are needed to achieve the objectives set in each operating and geographic unit. In effect, an organization's strategic plan is a collection of strategies that are unified and that interlock like the pieces of a puzzle. As shown in Table 2–1, different strategic issues are addressed at each level of managerial strategy-making. Typically, the strategy-making task is more top-down than bottom-up since the role of lower-level strategy is to support and complement higher-level strategic thrusts and to contribute to the achievement of higher-level companywide objectives.

There are essentially four basic ways to manage the strategy-formation process in an organization: the master strategist approach where the manager in charge personally functions as chief architect of strategy, the delegate-it-to-others approach, the collaborative approach, and the champion approach. All four have strengths and weaknesses. All four can succeed or fail depending on how well the approach is managed and depending on the strategy-making skills and judgments of the individuals involved.

SUGGESTED READINGS

Andrews, Kenneth R. *The Concept of Corporate Strategy*. Rev. ed. Homewood, Ill.: Dow Jones-Irwin, 1980, chaps. 2, 3, 4, and 5.

Ansoff, H. Igor. *Corporate Strategy*. New York: McGraw-Hill, 1965, chap 6.

Drucker, Peter. *Management: Tasks, Responsibilities, Practices*. New York: Harper & Row, 1974, chaps. 6 and 7.

Foster, Lawrence W. "From Darwin to Now: The Evolution of Organizational Strategies." *Journal of Business Strategy* 5, no. 4 (Spring 1985), pp. 94–98.

Granger, Charles H. "The Hierarchy of Objectives." *Harvard Business Review* 42, no. 3 (May–June 1964), pp. 63–74.

Hofer, Charles W., and Dan Schendel. *Strategy Formulation: Analytical Concepts*. St. Paul, Minn.: West Publishing, 1978, chap. 2.

McLellan, R., and G. Kelly. "Business Policy Formulation: Understanding the Process." *Journal of General Management* 6, no. 1 (Autumn 1980), pp. 38–47.

Mintzberg, Henry. "Crafting Strategy." *Harvard Business Review* 65, no. 4 (July–August 1987), pp. 66–77.

Morris, Elinor. "Vision and Strategy: A Focus for the Future." *Journal of Business Strategy* 8, no. 2 (Fall 1987), pp. 51–58.

Quinn, James Brian. *Strategies for Change: Logical Incrementalism*. Homewood, Ill.: Richard D. Irwin, 1980, chaps 2 and 4.

Vancil, Richard F. "Strategy Formulation in Complex Organizations." *Sloan Management Review* 17, no. 2 (Winter 1976), pp. 1–18.

Reading 1

CRAFTING STRATEGY

Henry Mintzberg

Imagine someone planning strategy. What likely springs to mind is an image of orderly thinking: a senior manager, or a group of them, sitting in an office formulating courses of action that everyone else will implement on schedule. The keynote is reason—rational control, the systematic analysis of competitors and markets, of company strengths and weaknesses, the combination of these analyses producing clear, explicit, full-blown strategies.

Now imagine someone *crafting* strategy. A wholly different image likely results, as different from planning as craft is from mechanization. Craft evokes traditional skill, dedication, perfection through the mastery of detail. What springs to mind is not so much thinking and reason as involvement, a feeling of intimacy and harmony with the materials at hand, developed through long experience and commitment. Formulation and implementation merge into a fluid process of learning through which creative strategies evolve.

My thesis is simple: the crafting image better captures the process by which effective strategies come to be. The planning image, long popular in the literature, distorts these processes and thereby misguides organizations that embrace it unreservedly.

In developing this thesis, I shall draw on the experiences of a single craftsman, a potter, and compare them with the results of a research project that tracked the strategies of a number of corporations across several decades. Because the two contexts are so obviously different, my metaphor, like my assertion, may seem farfetched at first. Yet if we think of a craftsman as an organization of one, we can see

that he or she must also resolve one of the great challenges the corporate strategist faces: knowing the organization's capabilities well enough to think deeply enough about its strategic direction. By considering strategy-making from the perspective of one person, free of all the paraphernalia of what has been called the strategy industry, we can learn something about the formation of strategy in the corporation. For much as our potter has to manage her craft, so too managers have to craft their strategy.

At work, the potter sits before a lump of clay on the wheel. Her mind is on the clay, but she is also aware of sitting between her past experiences and her future prospects. She knows exactly what has and has not worked for her in the past. She has an intimate knowledge of her work, her capabilities, and her markets. As a craftsman, she senses rather than analyzes these things; her knowledge is "tacit." All these things are working in her mind as her hands are working the clay. The product that emerges on the wheel is likely to be in the tradition of her past work, but she may break away and embark on a new direction. Even so, the past is no less present, projecting itself into the future.

In my metaphor, managers are craftsmen and strategy is their clay. Like the potter, they sit between a past of corporate capabilities and a future of market opportunities. And if they are truly craftsmen, they bring to their work an equally intimate knowledge of the materials at hand. That is the essence of crafting strategy.

In the pages that follow, we will explore this metaphor by looking at how strategies get made. Throughout, I will be drawing on the two sets of experiences I've mentioned. One . . . is a research project on patterns in strategy formation that has been going on at McGill University under my direction since 1971. The second is the stream of work of a successful potter, my wife, who began her craft in 1967.

Ask almost anyone what strategy is, and they will define it as a plan of some sort, an explicit guide to future behavior. Then ask them what strategy a competitor or a government or even they themselves have actually pursued. Chances are they will describe consistency in *past* behavior—a pattern in action over time. Strategy, it turns out, is one of those words that people define in one way and often use in another, without realizing the difference.

The reason for this is simple. Strategy's formal definition and its Greek military origins notwithstanding, we need the word as much to explain past actions as to describe intended behavior. After all, if strategies can be planned and intended, they can also be pursued and realized (or not realized, as the case may be). And pattern in action, or what we call realized strategy, explains that pursuit. Moreover, just as a plan need not produce a pattern (some strategies that are intended are simply not realized), so, too, a pattern need not result from a plan. An organization can have a pattern (or realized strategy) without knowing it, let alone making it explicit.

Patterns, like beauty, are in the mind of the beholder, of course. But anyone reviewing a chronological lineup of our craftsman's work would have little trouble discerning clear patterns, at least in certain periods. Until 1974, for example, she made small, decorative ceramic animals and objects of various kinds. Then this "knickknack strategy" stopped abruptly, and eventually new patterns formed around waferlike sculptures and ceramic bowls, highly textured and unglazed.

Finding equivalent patterns in action for organizations isn't that much more difficult. Indeed, for such large companies as Volkswagenwerk and Air Canada, in our research, it proved simpler! (As well it should. A craftsman, after all, can change what she does in a studio a lot more easily than a Volkswagenwerk can retool its assembly lines.) Mapping the product models at Volkswagenwerk from the late 1940s to the late 1970s, for example, uncovers a clear pattern of concentration on the Beetle, followed in the late 1960s by a frantic search for replacements through acquisitions and internally developed new

models, to a strategic reorientation around more stylish, water-cooled, front-wheel-drive vehicles in the mid-1970s.

But what about intended strategies, those formal plans and pronouncements we think of when we use the term *strategy?* Ironically, here we run into all kinds of problems. Even with a single craftsman, how can we know what her intended strategies really were? If we could go back, would we find expressions of intention? And if we could, would we be able to trust them? We often fool ourselves, as well as others, by denying our subconscious motives. And remember that intentions are cheap, at least when compared with realizations.

Reading the Organization's Mind

If you believe all this has more to do with the Freudian recesses of a craftsman's mind than with the practical realities of producing automobiles, then think again. For who knows what the intended strategies of a Volkswagenwerk really mean, let alone what they are? Can we simply assume in this collective context that the company's intended strategies are represented by its formal plans or by other statements emanating from the executive suite? Might these be just vain hopes or rationalizations or ploys to fool the competition? And even if expressed intentions exist, to what extent do others in the organization share them? How do we read the collective mind? Who is the strategist anyway?

The traditional view of strategic management resolves these problems quite simply, by what organizational theorists call attribution. You see it all the time in the business press. When General Motors acts, it's because Roger Smith has made a strategy. Given realization, there must have been intention, and that is automatically attributed to the chief.

In a short magazine article, this assumption is understandable. Journalists don't have a lot of time to uncover the origins of strategy, and GM is a large, complicated organization. But just consider all the complexity and confusion that gets tucked under this assumption—all the meetings and debates, the many people, the dead ends, the folding and unfolding of ideas. Now imagine trying to build a formal strategy-making system around that assumption. Is it any wonder that formal strategic planning is often such a resounding failure?

To unravel some of the confusion—and move away from the artificial complexity we have piled around the strategy-making process—we need to get back to some basic concepts. The most basic of all is the intimate connection between thought and action. That is the key to craft, and so also to the crafting of strategy.

Virtually everything that has been written about strategy making depicts it as a deliberate process. First we think, then we act. We formulate, then we implement. The progression seems so perfectly sensible. Why would anybody want to proceed differently?

Our potter is in the studio, rolling the clay to make a waferlike sculpture. The clay sticks to the rolling pin, and a round form appears. Why not make a cylindrical vase? One idea leads to another, until a new pattern forms. Action has driven thinking: a strategy has emerged.

Out in the field, a salesman visits a customer. The product isn't quite right, and together they work out some modifications. The salesman returns to his company and puts the changes through; after two or three more rounds, they finally get it right. A new product emerges, which eventually opens up a new market. The company has changed strategic course.

In fact, most salespeople are less fortunate than this one or than our craftsman. In an organization of one, the implementor is the formulator, so innovations can be incorporated into strategy quickly and easily. In a large organization, the innovator may be 10 levels removed from the leader who is supposed to dictate strategy and may also have to sell the idea to dozens of peers doing the same job.

Some salespeople, of course, can proceed on their own, modifying products to suit their customers and convincing skunkworks in the factory to produce them. In effect, they pursue their own strategies. Maybe no one else notices or cares. Sometimes, however, their innovations do get noticed, perhaps years later, when the company's prevalent strategies have broken down and its leaders are groping for something new. Then the salesperson's strategy may

be allowed to pervade the system, to become organizational.

Is this story farfetched? Certainly not. We've all heard stories like it. But since we tend to see only what we believe, if we believe that strategies have to be planned, we're unlikely to see the real meaning such stories hold.

Consider how the National Film Board of Canada (NFB) came to adopt a feature-film strategy. The NFB is a federal government agency, famous for its creativity and expert in the production of short documentaries. Some years back, it funded a filmmaker on a project that unexpectedly ran long. To distribute his film, the NFB turned to theaters and so inadvertently gained experience in marketing feature-length films. Other filmmakers caught onto the idea, and eventually the NFB found itself pursuing a feature-film strategy—a pattern of producing such films.

My point is simple, deceptively simple: strategies can *form* as well as be *formulated*. A realized strategy can emerge in response to an evolving situation, or it can be brought about deliberately, through a process of formulation followed by implementation. But when these planned intentions do not produce the desired actions, organizations are left with unrealized strategies.

Today we hear a great deal about unrealized strategies, almost always in concert with the claim that implementation has failed. Management has been lax, controls have been loose, people haven't been committed. Excuses abound. At times, indeed, they may be valid. But often these explanations prove too easy. So some people look beyond implementation to formulation. The strategists haven't been smart enough.

While it is certainly true that many intended strategies are ill conceived, I believe that the problem often lies one step beyond, in the distinction we make between formulation and implementation, the common assumption that thought must be independent of (and precede) action. Sure, people could be smarter—but not only by conceiving more clever strategies. Sometimes they can be smarter by allowing their strategies to develop gradually, through the organization's actions and experiences. Smart strategists appreciate that they cannot always be smart enough to think through everything in advance.

Hands & Minds

No craftsman thinks some days and works others. The craftsman's mind is going constantly, in tandem with her hands. Yet large organizations try to separate the work of minds and hands. In so doing, they often sever the vital feedback link between the two. The salesperson who finds a customer with an unmet need may possess the most strategic bit of information in the entire organization. But that information is useless if he or she cannot create a strategy in response to it or else convey the information to someone who can—because the channels are blocked or because the formulators have simply finished formulating. The notion that strategy is something that should happen way up there, far removed from the details of running an organization on a daily basis, is one of the great fallacies of conventional strategic management. And it explains a good many of the most dramatic failures in business and public policy today.

We at McGill call strategies like the NFB's that appear without clear intentions—or in spite of them—emergent strategies. Actions simply converge into patterns. They may become deliberate, of course, if the pattern is recognized and then legitimated by senior management. But that's after the fact.

All this may sound rather strange, I know. Strategies that emerge? Managers who acknowledge strategies already formed? Over the years, our research group at McGill has met with a good deal of resistance from people upset by what they perceive to be our passive definition of a word so bound up with proactive behavior and free will. After all, strategy means control—the ancient Greeks used it to describe the art of the army general.

Strategic Learning

But we have persisted in this use for one reason: learning. Purely deliberate strategy precludes learning once the strategy is formulated; emergent strat-

egy fosters it. People take actions one by one and respond to them, so that patterns eventually form.

Our craftsman tries to make a freestanding sculptural form. It doesn't work, so she rounds it a bit here, flattens it a bit there. The result looks better, but still isn't quite right. She makes another and another and another. Eventually, after days or months or years, she finally has what she wants. She is off on a new strategy.

In practice, of course, all strategy-making walks on two feet, one deliberate, the other emergent. For just as purely deliberate strategy-making precludes learning, so purely emergent strategy-making precludes control. Pushed to the limit, neither approach makes much sense. Learning must be coupled with control. That is why the McGill research group uses the word *strategy* for both emergent and deliberate behavior.

Likewise, there is no such thing as a purely deliberate strategy or a purely emergent one. No organization—not even the ones commanded by those ancient Greek generals—knows enough to work everything out in advance, to ignore learning en route. And no one—not even a solitary potter—can be flexible enough to leave everything to happenstance, to give up all control. Craft requires control just as it requires responsiveness to the material at hand. Thus, deliberate and emergent strategy form the end points of a continuum along which the strategies that are crafted in the real world may be found. Some strategies may approach either end, but many more fall at intermediate points.

Effective strategies can show up in the strangest places and develop through the most unexpected means. There is no one best way to make strategy.

The form for a cat collapses on the wheel, and our potter sees a bull taking shape. Clay sticks to a rolling pin, and a line of cylinders results. Wafers come into being because of a shortage of clay and limited kiln space in a studio in France. Thus, errors become opportunities, and limitations stimulate creativity. The natural propensity to experiment, even boredom, likewise stimulate stategic change.

Organizations that craft their strategies have similar experiences. Recall the National Film Board with its inadvertently long film. Or consider its experiences with experimental films, which made special use of animation and sound. For 20 years, the NFB produced a bare but steady trickle of such films. In fact, every film but one in that trickle was produced by a single person, Norman McLaren, the NFB's most celebrated filmmaker. McLaren pursued a *personal strategy* of experimentation, deliberate for him perhaps (though who can know whether he had the whole stream in mind or simply planned one film at a time?) but not for the organization. Then 20 years later, others followed his lead and the trickle widened, his personal strategy becoming more broadly organizational.

Conversely, in 1952, when television came to Canada, a *consensus strategy* quickly emerged at the NFB. Senior management was not keen on producing films for the new medium. But while the arguments raged, one filmmaker quietly went off and made a single series for TV. That precedent set, one by one his colleagues leapt in, and within months the NFB—and its management—found themselves committed for several years to a new strategy with an intensity unmatched before or since. This consensus strategy arose spontaneously, as a result of many independent decisions made by the filmmakers about the films they wished to make. Can we call this strategy deliberate? For the filmmakers perhaps; for senior management certainly not. But for the organization? It all depends on your perspective, on how you choose to read the organization's mind.

While the NFB may seem like an extreme case, it highlights behavior that can be found, albeit in muted form, in all organizations. Those who doubt this might read Richard Pascale's account of how Honda stumbled into its enormous success in the American motorcycle market. Brilliant as its strategy may have looked after the fact, Honda's managers made almost every conceivable mistake until the market finally hit them over the head with the right formula. The Honda managers on site in America, driving their products themselves (and, thus, inadvertently picking up market reaction), did only one thing right: they learned, firsthand.[1]

Grass-Roots Strategy-Making

These strategies all reflect, in whole or part, what we like to call a grass-roots approach to strategic management. Strategies grow like weeds in a garden. They take root in all kinds of places, wherever people have the capacity to learn (because they are in touch with the situation) and the resources to support that capacity. These strategies become organizational when they become collective, that is, when they proliferate to guide the behavior of the organization at large.

Of course, this view is overstated. But it is no less extreme than the conventional view of strategic management, which might be labeled the *hot-house approach*. Neither is right. Reality falls between the two. Some of the most effective strategies we uncovered in our research combined deliberation and control with flexibility and organizational learning.

Consider first what we call the *umbrella strategy*. Here senior management sets our broad guidelines (say, to produce only high-margin products at the cutting edge of technology or to favor products using bonding technology) and leaves the specifics (such as what these products will be) to others lower down in the organization. This strategy is not only deliberate (in its guidelines) and emergent (in its specifics), but it is also deliberately emergent in that the process is consciously managed to allow strategies to emerge en route. IBM used the umbrella strategy in the early 1960s with the impending 360 series, when its senior management approved a set of broad criteria for the design of a family of computers later developed in detail throughout the organization.[2]

Deliberately emergent, too, is what we call the *process strategy*. Here management controls the process of strategy formation—concerning itself with the design of the structure, its staffing, procedures, and so on—while leaving the actual content to others.

Both process and umbrella strategies seem to be especially prevalent in businesses that require great

---

[1] Richard T. Pascale, "Perspective on Strategy: The Real Story Behind Honda's Success," *California Management Review,* May–June 1984, p. 47.

[2] James Brian Quinn, IBM (A) case, in James Brian Quinn, Henry Mintzberg, and Robert M. James, *The Strategy Process: Concepts, Contexts, Cases* (Englewood Cliffs, N.J.: Prentice-Hall, forthcoming).

expertise and creativity—a 3M, a Hewlett-Packard, a National Film Board. Such organizations can be effective only if their implementors are allowed to be formulators, because it is people way down in the hierarchy who are in touch with the situation at hand and have the requisite technical expertise. In a sense, these are organizations peopled with craftsmen, all of whom must be strategists.

The conventional view of strategic management, especially in the planning literature, claims that change must be continuous: the organization should be adapting all the time. Yet this view proves to be ironic, because the very concept of strategy is rooted in stability, not change. As this same literature makes clear, organizations pursue strategies to set direction, to lay out courses of action, and to elicit cooperation from their members around common, established guidelines. By any definition, strategy imposes stability on an organization. No stability means no strategy (no course to the future, no pattern from the past). Indeed, the very fact of having a strategy, and especially of making it explicit (as the conventional literature implores managers to do), creates resistance to strategic change!

What the conventional view fails to come to grips with, then, is how and when to promote change. A fundamental dilemma of strategy-making is the need to reconcile the forces for stability and for change—to focus efforts and gain operating efficiencies on the one hand, yet adapt and maintain currency with a changing external environment on the other.

Quantum Leaps

Our own research and that of colleagues suggest that organizations resolve these opposing forces by attending first to one and then to the other. Clear periods of stability and change can usually be distinguished in any organization: While it is true that particular strategies may always be changing marginally, it seems equally true that major shifts in strategic orientation occur only rarely.

In our study of Steinberg, Inc., a large Quebec supermarket chain headquartered in Montreal, we found only two important reorientations in the 60 years from its founding to the mid-1970s: a shift to self-service in 1933 and the introduction of shopping centers and public financing in 1953. At Volkswagenwerk, we saw only one between the late 1940s and the 1970s, the tumultuous shift from the traditional Beetle to the Audi-type design mentioned earlier. And at Air Canada, we found none over the airline's first four decades, following its initial positioning.

Our colleagues at McGill, Danny Miller and Peter Friesen, found this pattern of change so common in their studies of large numbers of companies (especially the high-performance ones) that they built a theory around it, which they labeled the *quantum theory of strategic change*.[3] Their basic point is that organizations adopt two distinctly different modes of behavior at different times.

Most of the time they pursue a given strategic orientation. Change may seem continuous, but it occurs in the context of that orientation (perfecting a given retailing formula, for example) and usually amounts to doing more of the same, perhaps better as well. Most organizations favor these periods of stability because they achieve success not by changing strategies but by exploiting the ones they have. They, like craftsmen, seek continuous improvement by using their distinctive competencies in established courses.

While this goes on, however, the world continues to change, sometimes slowly, occasionally in dramatic shifts. Thus, gradually or suddenly, the organization's strategic orientation moves out of sync with its environment. Then what Miller and Friesen call a *strategic revolution* must take place. That long period of evolutionary change is suddenly punctuated by a brief bout of revolutionary turmoil in which the organization quickly alters many of its established patterns. In effect, it tries to leap to a new stability quickly to reestablish an integrated posture among a new set of strategies, structures, and culture.

But what about those emergent strategies, growing like weeds around the organization? What the quantum theory suggests is that the really novel ones are generally held in check in some corner of the organization until a strategic revolution becomes necessary. Then as an alternative to having to develop

---

[3]See Danny Miller and Peter H. Friesen, *Organizations: A Quantum View* (Englewood Cliffs, N.J.: Prentice-Hall, 1984).

new strategies from scratch or having to import generic strategies from competitors, the organization can turn to its own emerging patterns to find its new orientation. As the old, established strategy disintegrates, the seeds of the new one begin to spread.

This quantum theory of change seems to apply particularly well to large, established, mass-production companies. Because they are especially reliant on standardized procedures, their resistance to strategic reorientation tends to be especially fierce. So we find long periods of stability broken by short disruptive periods of revolutionary change.

Volkswagenwerk is a case in point. Long enamored of the Beetle and armed with a tightly integrated set of strategies, the company ignored fundamental changes in its market throughout the late 1950s and 1960s. The bureaucratic momentum of its mass-production organization combined with the psychological momentum of its leader, who institutionalized the strategies in the first place. When change finally did come, it was tumultuous: the company groped its way through a hodgepodge of products before it settled on a new set of vehicles championed by a new leader. Strategic reorientations really are cultural revolutions.

Cycles of Change

In more creative organizations, we see a somewhat different pattern of change and stability, one that's more balanced. Companies in the business of producing novel outputs apparently need to fly off in all directions from time to time to sustain their creativity. Yet they also need to settle down after such periods to find some order in the resulting chaos.

The National Film Board's tendency to move in and out of focus through remarkably balanced periods of convergence and divergence is a case in point. Concentrated production of films to aid the war effort in the 1940s gave way to great divergence after the war as the organization sought a new raison d'être. Then the advent of television brought back a very sharp focus in the early 1950s, as noted earlier. But in the late 1950s, this dissipated almost as quickly as it began, giving rise to another creative period of exploration. Then the social changes in the

early 1960s evoked a new period of convergence around experimental films and social issues.

We use the label *adhocracy* for organizations, like the National Film Board, that produce individual, or custom-made, products (or designs) in an innovative way, on a project basis.[4] Our craftsman is an adhocracy of sorts, too, since each of her ceramic sculptures is unique. And her pattern of strategic change was much like that of the NFB's, with evident cycles of convergence and divergence: a focus on knickknacks from 1967 to 1972; then a period of exploration to about 1976, which resulted in a refocus on ceramic sculptures; that continued to about 1981, to be followed by a period of searching for new directions. More recently, a focus on ceramic murals seems to be emerging.

Whether through quantum revolutions or cycles of convergence and divergence, however, organizations seem to need to separate in time the basic forces for change and stability, reconciling them by attending to each in turn. Many strategic failures can be attributed either to mixing the two or to an obsession with one of these forces at the expense of the other.

The problems are evident in the work of many craftsmen. On the one hand, there are those who seize on the perfection of a single theme and never change. Eventually the creativity disappears from their work and the world passes them by—much as it did Volkswagenwerk until the company was shocked into its strategic revolution. And then there are those who are always changing, who flit from one idea to another and never settle down. Because no theme or strategy ever emerges in their work, they cannot exploit or even develop any distinctive competence. And because their work lacks definition, identity crises are likely to develop, with neither the craftsmen nor their clientele knowing what to make of it. Miller and Friesen found this behavior in conventional business too; they label it *the impulsive firm running blind.*[5] How often have we

[4]See my article "Organization Design: Fashion or Fit?" HBR January–February 1981, p. 103; also see my book *Structure in Fives: Designing Effective Organizations* (Englewood Cliffs, N.J.: Prentice-Hall, 1983).

The term *adhocracy* was coined by Warren G. Bennis and Philip E. Slater in *The Temporary Society* (New York: Harper & Row, 1964).

[5]Danny Miller and Peter H. Friesen, "Archetypes of Strategy Formulation," *Management Science*, May 1978, p. 921.

seen it in companies that go on acquisition sprees?

The popular view sees the strategist as a planner or as a visionary, someone sitting on a pedestal dictating brilliant strategies for everyone else to implement. While recognizing the importance of thinking ahead and especially of the need for creative vision in this pedantic world, I wish to propose an additional view of the strategist—as a pattern recognizer, a learner if you will—who manages a process in which strategies (and visions) can emerge as well as be deliberately conceived. I also wish to redefine that strategist, to extend that someone into the collective entity made up of the many actors whose interplay speaks an organization's mind. This strategist *finds* strategies no less than creates them, often in patterns that form inadvertently in its own behavior.

What, then, does it mean to craft strategy? Let us return to the words associated with craft: dedication, experience, involvement with the material, the personal touch, mastery of detail, a sense of harmony and integration. Managers who craft strategy do not spend much time in executive suites reading MIS reports or industry analyses. They are involved, responsive to their materials, learning about their organizations and industries through personal touch. They are also sensitive to experience, recognizing that, while individual vision may be important, other factors must help determine strategy as well.

Manage Stability

Managing strategy is mostly managing stability, not change. Indeed, most of the time senior managers should not be formulating strategy at all; they should be getting on with making their organizations as effective as possible in pursuing the strategies they already have. Like distinguished craftsmen, organizations become distinguished because they master the details.

To manage strategy, then, at least in the first instance, is not so much to promote change as to know *when* to do so. Advocates of strategic planning often urge managers to plan for perpetual instability in the environment (for example, by rolling over five-year plans annually). But this obsession with change is dysfunctional. Organizations that reassess their strategies continuously are like individuals who reassess

their jobs or their marriages continuously—in both cases, people will drive themselves crazy or else reduce themselves to inaction. The formal planning process repeats itself so often and so mechanically that it desensitizes the organization to real change, programs it more and more deeply into set patterns, and thereby encourages it to make only minor adaptations.

So-called strategic planning must be recognized for what it is: a means, not to create strategy, but to program a strategy already created—to work out its implications formally. It is essentially analytic in nature, based on decomposition, while strategy creation is essentially a process of synthesis. That is why trying to create strategies through formal planning most often leads to extrapolating existing ones or copying those of competitors.

This is not to say that planners have no role to play in strategy formation. In addition to programming strategies created by other means, they can feed ad hoc analyses into the strategy-making process at the front end to be sure that the hard data are taken into consideration. They can also stimulate others to think strategically. And of course people called planners can be strategists, too, so long as they are creative thinkers who are in touch with what is relevant. But that has nothing to do with the technology of formal planning.

Detect Discontinuity

Environments do not change on any regular or orderly basis. And they seldom undergo continuous dramatic change, claims about our "age of discontinuity" and environmental "turbulence" notwithstanding. (Go tell people who lived through the Great Depression or survivors of the siege of Leningrad during World War II that ours are turbulent times.) Much of the time, change is minor and even temporary and requires no strategic response. Once in a while there is a truly significant discontinuity, or even less often, a gestalt shift in the environment, where everything important seems to change at once. But these events, while critical, are also easy to recognize.

The real challenge in crafting strategy lies in detecting the subtle discontinuities that may undermine a business in the future. And for that, there is no technique, no program, just a sharp mind in touch with the situation. Such discontinuities are unexpected and irregular, essentially unprecedented. They can be dealt with only by minds that are attuned to existing patterns yet able to perceive important breaks in them. Unfortunately, this form of strategic thinking tends to atrophy during the long periods of stability that most organizations experience (just as it did at Volkswagenwerk during the 1950s and 1960s). So the trick is to manage within a given strategic orientation most of the time yet to be able to pick out the occasional discontinuity that really matters.

The Steinberg chain was built and run for more than half a century by a man named Sam Steinberg. For 20 years, the company concentrated on perfecting a self-service retailing formula introduced in 1933. Installing fluorescent lighting and figuring out how to package meat in cellophane wrapping were the "strategic" issues of the day. Then in 1952, with the arrival of the first shopping center in Montreal, Steinberg realized he had to redefine his business almost overnight. He knew he needed to control those shopping centers and that control would require public financing and other major changes. So he reoriented his business. The ability to make that kind of switch in thinking is the essence of strategic management. And it has more to do with vision and involvement than it does with analytic technique.

Know the Business

Sam Steinberg was the epitome of the entrepreneur, a man intimately involved with all the details of his business, who spent Saturday mornings visiting his stores. As he told us in discussing his company's competitive advantage:

"Nobody knew the grocery business like we did. Everything has to do with your knowledge. I knew merchandise, I knew cost, I knew selling, I knew customers. I knew everything, and I passed on all my knowledge; I kept teaching my people. That's the advantage we had. Our competitors couldn't touch us."

Note the kind of knowledge involved: not intellectual knowledge, not analytical reports or abstracted facts and figures (though these can certainly help), but personal knowledge, intimate understand-

ing, equivalent to the craftsman's feel for the clay. Facts are available to anyone; this kind of knowledge is not. Wisdom is the word that captures it best. But wisdom is a word that has been lost in the bureaucracies we have built for ourselves, systems designed to distance leaders from operating details. Show me managers who think they can rely on formal planning to create their strategies, and I'll show you managers who lack intimate knowledge of their businesses or the creativity to do something with it.

Craftsmen have to train themselves to see, to pick up things other people miss. The same holds true for managers of strategy. It is those with a kind of peripheral vision who are best able to detect and take advantage of events as they unfold.

Manage Patterns

Whether in an executive suite in Manhattan or a pottery studio in Montreal, a key to managing strategy is the ability to detect emerging patterns and help them take shape. The job of the manager is not just to preconceive specific strategies but also to recognize their emergence elsewhere in the organization and intervene when appropriate.

Like weeds that appear unexpectedly in a garden, some emergent strategies may need to be uprooted immediately. But management cannot be too quick to cut off the unexpected, for tomorrow's vision may grow out of today's aberration. (Europeans, after all, enjoy salads made from the leaves of the dandelion, America's most notorious weed.) Thus, some patterns are worth watching until their effects have more clearly manifested themselves. Then those that prove useful can be made deliberate and be incorporated into the formal strategy, even if that means shifting the strategic umbrella to cover them.

To manage in this context, then, is to create the climate within which a wide variety of strategies can grow. In more complex organizations, this may mean building flexible structures, hiring creative people, defining broad umbrella strategies, and watching for the patterns that emerge.

Reconcile Change and Continuity

Finally, managers considering radical departures need to keep the quantum theory of change in mind. As Ecclesiastes reminds us, there is a time to sow and a time to reap. Some new patterns must be held in check until the organization is ready for a strategic revolution, or at least a period of divergence. Managers who are obsessed with either change or stability are bound eventually to harm their organizations. As pattern-recognizers, the manager has to be able to sense when to exploit an established crop of strategies and when to encourage new strains to displace the old.

While strategy is a word that is usually associated with the future, its link to the past is no less central.

As Kierkegaard once observed, life is lived forward but understood backward. Managers may have to live strategy in the future, but they must understand it through the past.

Like potters at the wheel, organizations must make sense of the past if they hope to manage the future. Only by coming to understand the patterns that form in their own behavior do they get to know their capabilities and their potential. Thus crafting strategy, like managing craft, requires a natural synthesis of the future, present, and past.

Reading 2

WHAT BUSINESS ARE WE REALLY IN? THE QUESTION REVISITED

William G. McGowan

In 1960, Theodore Levitt, then a lecturer in business administration at the Harvard Business School, published an article entitled "Marketing Myopia" in the *Harvard Business Review*. The article (July–August 1960) was a seminal event in business review history. For years afterward, it was widely quoted and anthologized; the *Review* sold hundreds of thousands of reprints; and Levitt himself went on to fame and glory as an educator and business philosopher.

Levitt's message was simple. One key to any company's survival and growth—perhaps *the* key— is how senior-managers answer a fateful question: "What business are we really in?"

Many businesses stop growing, then decline and fail, because they define their mission too narrowly, Levitt observed. The railroads, for example, which thrived for years, stopped growing primarily because their managers imagined themselves to be in the

railroad business, rather than the *transportation* business. Similarly, Hollywood was nearly ruined during television's early days because the Hollywood moguls believed themselves to be in the movie business, rather than the entertainment business.

Levitt's thesis actually had three parts. First, the greatest danger for managers lies in defining their mission too narrowly. Second, it is crucial to ask Levitt's Question—"What business are we really in?" And third, the key to answering the question well lies in being market-oriented, rather than product-oriented. Managers should ask not only, "How can we do what we're doing better?" but a more outward-looking question as well: "How should we be changing in response to the needs of today's (and tomorrow's) consumers?"

This three-part thesis set a generation of business school whizzes wondering, at meetings and to themselves, what business they were really in. These managers were determined to avoid, at all costs, the fate of those classic dunces described by Levitt: the buggy-whip manufacturers, who focused obses-

Reprinted with permission from the *Sloan Management Review* 28, no. 1 (Fall 1986), pp. 59–62. Copyright © 1986 by the Sloan Management Review Association. All rights reserved.

sively on producing more and better buggy whips, instead of shifting to automotive products as consumers turned to cars.

A World of Faster Change

Today, roughly a quarter of a century after he introduced it, Levitt's Question is even more crucial. For change is even swifter now than at the turn of the century, when the internal combustion engine revolutionized transportation; swifter than in the early 1950s, when television fundamentally changed the leisure habits of American families.

In recent years a quiet revolution has swept the business world, precipitating basic changes in the way organizations operate. The driving forces behind this revolution are the information technologies—the synergistic combination of advanced data processing, telecommunications, and online information systems. These technologies have vastly diminished the obstacles of geography and time; they have redefined the level of customer service; and they have changed the structure of entire industries by eliminating barriers to entry, thus encouraging organizations to intrude on others' traditional turf.

In such a world, it is still important for managers to ask themselves Levitt's Question—"What business are we really in?"—and to ask it more often and more seriously. It is even more important than it was in 1960 to answer the question with imagination and agility.

But even this may not be enough. We may need to reexamine and amplify Levitt's thesis somewhat, applying what modestly might be termed McGowan's Variant.

The Dangers of Expansiveness

First of all, defining one's business mission too narrowly is not the only way for a manager to stumble. A generation of megamergers, hostile takeovers, and acquisition mania suggests that there is also great danger in defining one's business mission too broadly.

For example, American Express in the 1970s might have answered Levitt's Question this way: "We are in the information and leisure business."

Didn't American Express have a vast, up-to-date electronic network for processing information swiftly? And was it not the foremost power in the credit card and travel industries?

This self-assessment led the corporation to attempt acquisitions of McGraw-Hill, a publishing company, and the Disney companies—takeover attempts which, had they succeeded, would almost surely have enmeshed the firm in businesses for which it had little aptitude and whose relationship to one another was tenuous at best.

Fortunately, American Express rethought its definition of itself, narrowing its strategic vision somewhat in the process. Senior management decided that they were in the business of providing financial services, especially to affluent clients who travel frequently for business and for pleasure. And subsequently American Express's strategic moves—acquisitions of investment banking and brokerage businesses and a diversified financial services company, to name three—have been coherent and have promoted the company's growth.

Too narrow a definition of mission, then, is dangerous. But so is too broad a definition. All of us know of conglomerates whose self-definitions are so sweeping as to be meaningless or even nonexistent: the conglomerate, for example, that manufactures suitcases as well as yogurt. Most companies that attempt such feats are courting disaster. They may prosper for a time, but in the end they will sag into confusion, low morale, and decline, because they attempt too much without a carefully defined vision of themselves.

What Other Businesses Are We in?

The second part of Levitt's thesis also needs updating.

At MCI, the company I know best, we have done a pretty good job over the years of answering Levitt's original question. In the beginning, we would have answered by saying, "We are in the communications business, providing a transportation system for information, whether expressed by voice, video, or data."

That answer, however, would never have been enough to ensure MCI's survival and growth. Why? Because in order to pursue our main business, we faced challenges that made it necessary to ask what *other* businesses we had to master in order to succeed in the communications field.

First, we had to learn the venture capital business. As a fledgling, capital-starved company in a capital-intensive industry, we had to raise enough money to convince the regulatory community that we really could construct and operate a long-distance network.

Later, we moved into a second business: lobbying. The industry in which we hoped to succeed was heavily regulated by the Federal Communications Commission, subject to Congressional oversight, and dominated by AT&T, then a monopoly with enormous clout in Washington. If we were to gain even a modest foothold in the market, we had to become as much a lobbying firm as we were a communications firm. It was precisely for this reason that we established our headquarters in Washington, D.C. A communications company with less-pressing political concerns could have settled, just as logically, anywhere else.

Our next business was approaching the financial markets to raise the money necessary to *build* a communications system. We were fortunate. We were able to raise $100 million without having generated one penny of revenue. At the time, this represented the largest start-up financing in Wall Street history.

Our fourth business was litigation. We challenged AT&T's domination of the long-distance telephone industry in court with such fervor that someone once described MCI as "a law firm with an antenna on top." Besides our private antitrust case against AT&T, which involved millions of pages of documents and two lawsuits, our most important litigation was with the Federal Communications Commission over what types of service we could provide (called the *Execunet* case).

We won. And so it was only in the early 1980s that MCI, founded in 1968, was able to focus completely on our original mission. By then marketplace changes and technological advancements had transformed the industry. Today, we answer the question "What business are we in?" by saying, "We are an integral part of the information technologies business. We help our customers make the most of these technologies."

My basic point is this: Given the multiple challenges of today's business world, limiting yourself to any one business, however carefully and generously defined, may get you into trouble. Levitt's original question is an important one, but it needs to be followed by McGowan's Variant: "What other businesses do we need to be in?"

Some readers may argue that MCI wasn't *really* in all these other businesses along the way, that we were merely dabbling in them. I disagree. We were indeed completely involved in these other businesses. They engaged the primary energies of our senior managers; consumed a large chunk of our human and financial resources; and were the principal focus of our efforts each day.

Consider the litigation with AT&T. I was the first witness to testify, and I attended the entire four-month trial. Before the trial I sat through a 17-day deposition by AT&T lawyers. Our legal strategy and progress were frequent subjects of discussion among MCI senior management.

And MCI is not unique. Today the major airlines must adjust to a whole new set of challenges. They still fly planes, but almost everything else is different. Having grown accustomed to life as a cartel, protected from rigorous competition by a fortress of federal regulation, the airlines must learn to compete in a new, deregulated environment.

Along the way they will find it is not enough simply to answer Levitt's original question—to say, "We're in the airline business," or even, "We're in the transportation business." Such a simple answer won't be enough, because the major airlines, if they are to survive, must literally master several new businesses, including merchandising (for example, bundling flights, hotel rooms, and rental cars into an attractive package) and cost cutting. These are businesses in which they once dabbled, but which they must now attack relentlessly.

Because technology is advancing so rapidly (one expert has likened keeping up with its pace to trying to change tires on a moving car) and blurring the distinction between industries, managers need to go one step further and ask: "Who are my competitors now, and who might soon be my competitors?"

Merrill Lynch had a lot of information and knowledge about how people invest their money. In 1977, its executives asked, "Why don't we use this skill to go into banking?" This question gave rise to the Cash Management Account (CMA). In its first 12 months of operation the Merrill Lynch CMA brought in $5 billion; today the company has CMA accounts with balances of $130 billion.

Sears Roebuck used the technological systems it had in place, which told the company how its customers spent their money, to offer financial services and insurance. More recently the giant retailer again used all its knowledge about buying habits to launch its Discover card.

Who would have thought a few years ago that we would have a securities firm in competition with a bank in competition with a retailer in competition with a credit card company?

As I follow General Motors's exploits with EDS and Hughes Aircraft, which have given the company an enormous base of telecommunications technology, I have to ask myself: "Roger Smith, are you my customer, or a potential competitor?"

Is Marketing Enough?

Finally, I think we need to enlarge on the third part of Levitt's thesis: his admonition to avoid what he called "marketing myopia" by being customer-oriented as well as product-oriented.

Of course, Levitt was right in 1960, and his point still holds: The buggy-whip manufacturers, by discerning early enough the inevitable shift of the population from buggies to cars, might have avoided disaster. The railroad men, by focusing on the needs of the public and the direction of technology, might have been able to reinvent themselves as transportation men. A business which does not discern and act upon shifts in consumer preference is a business under a death sentence.

However, Levitt's admonition to be sensitive to customer needs is the beginning of wisdom, not the end. To be customer-oriented today is necessary but by no means sufficient, a fact which Levitt now recognizes.

For today's business leaders and tomorrow's, the most difficult challenge—and the most creative role—will lie in exploiting technology to create and market *products and services of which consumers have not yet dreamed.*

The swift *pace* of technological change has two results: It multiplies the opportunities for innovation and creativity, and it often necessitates creating a market for products and services which consumers may not know they need.

The personal computer is an example of such creativity and innovation. The Cash Management Account, automated teller machines, electronic mail, and desk-top publishing are others. In each case new technology did more than simply improve an old product or service; it made possible something decidedly new.

Tomorrow's Leaders

Tomorrow's business geniuses will be those who exploit the swift pace of technology to create new goods and services. They will be adept not only at anticipating and responding to consumer demand; they also will be expert marketers who lead customers to try, then embrace, what is new.

A period of unprecedented change has brought us to a moment that makes Levitt's original thesis, taken alone, too simple. Managers face a more complicated set of requirements than even the perceptive Ted Levitt could see in 1960. They need to ask not only "What business are we in?" but "What other businesses do we need to be in?" They need to anticipate changing consumer preferences, but they also need, now as never before, to lead the consumer in wholly new directions as the ever-quickening pace of technological change creates new possibilities.

These requirements are what make business so difficult today. They are also what make it so exciting.

PART 2

Strategic Analysis in Single-Business Companies

3

Industry and Competitive Analysis

Analysis is the critical starting point of strategic thinking.
Kenichi Ohmae

Awareness of the environment is not a special project to
be undertaken only when warning of change becomes
deafening.
Kenneth R. Andrews

Crafting a strategy is an analysis-driven task, not an exercise where managers can
depend solely upon their creativity to come up with something clever or unique.
Judgments about what strategy to choose ideally need to be based on a probing
managerial assessment of the strategy-critical factors shaping a company's overall
situation. Unless strategy is well matched to the full range of situational considerations, its suitability is suspect.

The biggest situational considerations underlying the choice of strategy are (1)
industry and competitive conditions and (2) a company's own internal situation
and competitive position. Not all industries offer equally attractive prospects for
long-term profitability—some industries are beset with more problems and tougher
competitive conditions than others.[1] However, a firm in a very attractive industry
may not do well if it is in a poor competitive position; conversely, a firm in a
strong competitive position may be in such an unattractive industry that its performance is weak. But today's situation is always subject to a turn of events.
Industry conditions may improve or worsen and competitive positions of companies
may shift as the battle among rival firms unfolds. Openings are always being
created for companies to make a strategic move that either alters the industry
situation even further or that improves their competitive position. While a company's strategy must be kept responsive to changing industry and competitive
conditions, it can also aim at shaping them in a firm's favor.[2] This is what we
mean when we say strategy must *fit the situation;* achieving strong situational fit

---

[1]Michael E. Porter, *Competitive Advantage* (New York: Free Press, 1985), pp. 1–2.
[2]Ibid, p. 2.

requires business strategists to have analytical command of the overall industry situation, the competitive position of their company in relation to rivals, and the strategic opportunities presented by the situation at hand.

This chapter examines the manner and means of conducting a full-scale industry and competitive situation analysis; Chapter 4 presents the tools of company situation analysis.

THE ROLE OF SITUATION ANALYSIS IN FORMING A STRATEGY

From a strategy-making standpoint, *the purpose of situation analysis is to draw out those features in a company's internal/external environment which most directly frame its strategic window of options and opportunities*. Thus, conducting a situation analysis does *not* involve collecting reams of information about anything and everything the analyst can find, then preparing a lengthy treatise of facts and figures. Rather, managerial attention needs to be trained on a few, critical issues and these need to be examined primarily from a strategy-making perspective.

Figure 3–1 presents the framework of situation analysis, indicating both the analytical steps involved and the connection to strategy formulation. Note the logical flow from analysis of the situation to evaluation of alternatives to choice of strategy. It is this flow which makes situation analysis the starting point in the process of forming a strategic plan—indeed, as we shall see in the rest of this chapter and in Chapter 4, situation analysis is an essential precondition to doing a good job of establishing a mission, setting objectives, and crafting a strategy.

INDUSTRY AND COMPETITIVE SITUATION ANALYSIS

Industries differ widely in their business makeup, economic characteristics, competitive situations, and future outlooks. Some are full of growth potential and new business opportunities, whereas others are stagnant and beset with adversity. In some industries, rival firms compete against one another globally, whereas in others the market arena is national or regional or just local. Competitive forces vary across industries, both as to source and to strength, creating substantially stronger competitive pressures in some than in others. Industry and competitive situations differ so much that leading companies in "unattractive" industries may be very hard-pressed to earn respectable profits while in attractive industries even weak companies can turn in good performances.

The goal of industry and competitive analysis is to fully reveal the strategically relevant features of an industry's overall situation by probing into such specifics as the dominant economic characteristics of the industry, the drivers of change in the industry, the nature and strength of competitive forces, the positions of key competitors and the moves they are likely to make next, the key factors influencing competitive success, and the reasons why an industry is relatively attractive or unattractive. The following questions constitute the framework of industry and competitive situation analysis:

1. What are the chief business and economic characteristics of the industry environment?
2. What forces are driving change in the industry and how important will these changes be?

FIGURE 3–1
From Situation Analysis to Strategic Choices

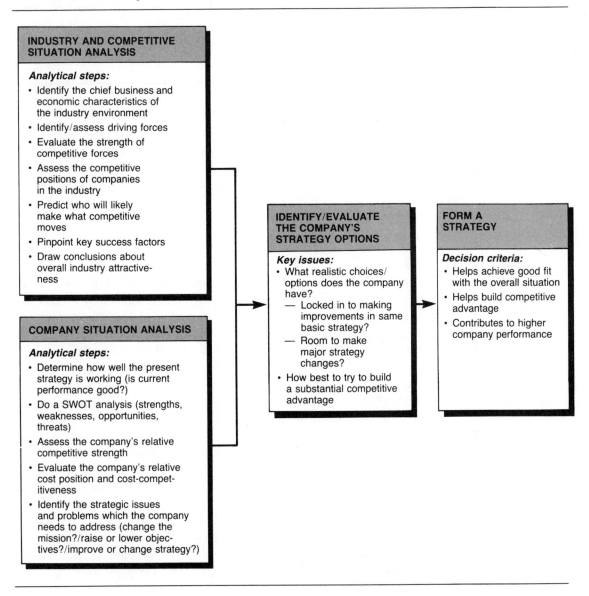

INDUSTRY AND COMPETITIVE SITUATION ANALYSIS

Analytical steps:

- Identify the chief business and economic characteristics of the industry environment
- Identify/assess driving forces
- Evaluate the strength of competitive forces
- Assess the competitive positions of companies in the industry
- Predict who will likely make what competitive moves
- Pinpoint key success factors
- Draw conclusions about overall industry attractiveness

COMPANY SITUATION ANALYSIS

Analytical steps:

- Determine how well the present strategy is working (is current performance good?)
- Do a SWOT analysis (strengths, weaknesses, opportunities, threats)
- Assess the company's relative competitive strength
- Evaluate the company's relative cost position and cost-competitiveness
- Identify the strategic issues and problems which the company needs to address (change the mission?/raise or lower objectives?/improve or change strategy?)

IDENTIFY/EVALUATE THE COMPANY'S STRATEGY OPTIONS

Key issues:

- What realistic choices/options does the company have?
  — Locked in to making improvements in same basic strategy?
  — Room to make major strategy changes?
- How best to try to build a substantial competitive advantage

FORM A STRATEGY

Decision criteria:

- Helps achieve good fit with the overall situation
- Helps build competitive advantage
- Contributes to higher company performance

3. What competitive forces are at work in the industry and how strong are they?
4. Which companies are in the strongest/weakest competitive positions and why?
5. Who will likely make what competitive moves next?
6. What are the keys to future competitive success?
7. All things considered, how attractive is the industry and how good are the prospects for above-average profitability?

With solid answers to these questions, a business strategist is in position to judge where an industry is headed and why, to predict what the industry's structure and competitive forces will be like in the next one to three years, and to spot interesting new strategic-move opportunities.

Let's turn now to the specific analytical steps of industry and competitive analysis to see exactly what is involved in each one and what analytical tools can be used.

Profiling the Strategically Relevant Features of the Industry Environment

The first step in industry and competitive situation analysis is to examine the chief economic and business characteristics of the industry. As a working definition, we shall use the word *industry* to mean a group of firms whose products have so many of the same attributes that they are drawn into close competitive rivalry to serve much the same buyers. The things to look for in profiling the industry environment are fairly standard:

- Market size.
- Scope of competitive rivalry (local, regional, national, or global).
- Market growth rate—where is the industry in the evolutionary or life-cycle stages (early development, rapid growth and takeoff, early maturity, late maturity and saturation, stagnant and aging, decline and decay?) and are there any clues regarding how long will it be to the next stage?
- Number of rivals and their relative sizes—is the industry fragmented with many small companies or concentrated and dominated by a few large companies?
- The structure of the buying side of the market (the number of buyers and their relative sizes).
- The prevalence of backward and forward integration within the industry.
- Ease of entry and exit.
- The pace of technological change as concerns both production process innovation and new-product introductions.
- Whether the product(s)/service(s) of rival firms are highly differentiated, weakly differentiated, or essentially identical.
- The extent to which economies of scale are present in manufacturing, transportation, or mass marketing and, if so, whether they give larger-scale firms an *important* cost advantage over smaller-scale firms.
- The extent to which high rates of capacity utilization are crucial to achieving low-cost production efficiency.
- Whether such a strong learning and experience curve exists in the industry that average unit cost declines as *cumulative* output (and thus, the experience of "learning by doing") builds up.
- Size of capital requirements and the degree of capital intensity.
- Whether industry profitability is above/below par.

For an illustration of what a profile of strategically relevant of an industry might look like, see the sample in Table 3–1.

The profile that emerges from an examination of an industry's business and economic characteristics provides some clues about what kinds of strategic moves and approaches to consider and to avoid. For example, when an industry entails heavy capital investment in plant and equipment, a firm can escape some of the resulting high fixed-cost burden by pursuing a strategy which promotes high fixed-asset utilization and generates more revenue per dollar of fixed-asset investment; thus, commercial airlines try to boost the revenue productivity of their expensive jet aircraft fleets with strategies that aim at cutting ground time at airport gates to an efficient minimum (to get in more flights/day with the same plane) and at reducing the number of empty seats on each flight. In consumer goods industries— like beer, fast food, tires, and home appliances—where there are often sizable scale economies in having extensive dealer networks and then using national advertising to pull products through the in-place dealer channels, companies employ strategies calculated to produce good distribution access, and they try to capture a market share big enough to support spending tens of millions annually on advertising.

TABLE 3–1
A Sample Profile of an Industry's Chief Business and Economic Characteristics

Market Size: $400–$500 million annual revenues; 4 million tons, total volume.

Scope of Competitive Rivalry: Primarily regional; producers rarely sell outside a 250-mile radius of plant due to high cost of shipping long distances.

Market Growth Rate: 2–3 percent annually.

Stage in Life-Cycle: Mature.

Number of Companies in Industry: About 30 companies with 110 plant locations and capacity of 4.5 million tons. Market shares range from a low of 3 percent to a high of 21 percent.

Customers: About 2,000 buyers; most are industrial chemical firms.

Degree of Vertical Integration: Mixed; 5 of the 10 largest companies are integrated backward into mining operations and also forward in that sister industrial chemicals divisions buy over 50 percent of the output of their plants; all other companies are engaged solely in manufacturing.

Ease of Entry/Exit: Moderate entry barriers exist in the form of capital requirements to construct a new plant of minimum efficient size (cost equals $10 million) and ability to build a customer base inside a 250-mile radius of plant.

Technology/Innovation: Production technology is standard and changes have been slow; biggest changes are occurring in products—about 1–2 newly formulated specialty chemicals products are being introduced annually, accounting for nearly all of industry growth.

Product Characteristics: Highly standardized; the brands of different producers are essentially identical (buyers perceive little real difference from seller to seller).

Scale Economies: Moderate; all companies have virtually equal manufacturing costs but scale economies exist in shipping in multiple carloads to same customer and in purchasing large quantities of raw materials.

Experience Curve Effects: Not a factor in this industry.

Capacity Utilization: Manufacturing efficiency is highest between 90–100 percent of rated capacity; below 90 percent utilization, unit costs run significantly higher.

Industry Profitability: Subpar to average; the commodity nature of the industry's product results in intense price-cutting when demand slackens, but prices firm up during periods of strong demand. Profits track the strength of demand for the industry's products.

In fast-paced high-technology industries where product advances are announced regularly, competitors have no other strategic option than to invest enough time and money in R&D to keep their technical skills and innovative capability abreast of competitors—a product innovation strategy becomes a condition of survival. As a final example, suppose in semiconductor manufacturing there is a *learning/ experience* curve effect such that unit costs decline by 20 percent each time *cumulative* production volume doubles. This would mean that, if the first 1 million chips cost $1 each, by a production volume of 2 million the unit cost would be $0.80 (80 percent of $1), by a production volume of 4 million the unit cost would be $0.64 (80 percent of $0.80), by a production volume of 8 million the unit cost would be 51.2 cents (80 percent of $0.64), and so on. With such an experience curve effect, a company that moved first to initiate production of a new-style chip and then developed a strategy to capture the largest market share would win the competitive advantage of being the low-cost producer. The bigger the experience curve effect, the bigger the cost advantage of the company with the largest *cumulative* production volume, as shown in Figure 3–2.

FIGURE 3–2
Comparison of Experience Curve Effects for 10 Percent, 20 Percent, and 30 Percent Cost Reductions for Each Doubling of Production Volume

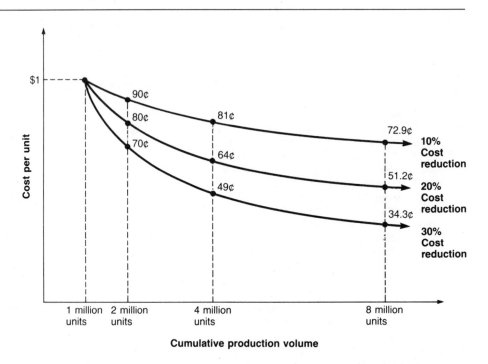

TABLE 3–2
Examples of the Strategic Importance of an Industry's Key Business and Economic Characteristics

Factor/Characteristic	*Strategic Importance*
● Market size	● Small markets don't tend to attract big/new competitors; large markets often draw the interest of corporations looking to acquire companies with established competitive positions in attractive industries.
● Market growth rate	● Fast growth breeds new entry; growth slowdowns spawn increased rivalry and a shakeout of weak competitors.
● Capacity surpluses or shortages	● Surpluses push prices and profit margins down; shortages pull them up.
● Industry profitability	● High-profit industries attract new entrants; depressed conditions encourage exit.
● Entry/exit barriers	● High barriers protect positions and profits of existing firms; low barriers make existing firms vulnerable to entry.
● Product is a big-ticket item for buyers	● More buyers will shop for lowest price.
● Standardized products	● Buyers have more power because it is easier to switch from seller to seller.
● Rapid technological change	● Raises risk factor; investments in technology facilities/equipment may become obsolete before they wear out.
● Capital requirements	● Big requirements make investment decisions critical; timing becomes important; creates a barrier to entry and exit.
● Vertical integration	● Raises capital requirements; often creates competitive differences and cost differences among fully versus partially versus nonintegrated firms.
● Economies of scale	● Affects volume and market share needed to be cost competitive.
● Rapid product innovation	● Shortens product life cycle; more risk because of opportunities for leapfrogging.

Table 3–2 presents some additional indications of how an industry's business and economic characteristics are relevant to managerial strategy-making.

The Concept of Driving Forces: Why Industries Change

An industry's business and economic characteristics tell only part of the story about industry conditions. Almost every industry stays in a state of flux—forces of change are constantly at work and new ones are usually building up steam just offstage. The popular hypothesis about industries going through evolutionary phases or life-cycle stages helps explain industry change but is, at best, incomplete. The life-cycle stages are strongly keyed to the overall industry growth rate (which is why such terms as *rapid growth, early maturity, saturation,* and *decline* are used to describe the stage; yet, there are more causes of industry change than whether industry growth is on the upswing or downswing. Moreover, the life-cycle approach suffers from uncertainty about the length of each phase. An industry can experience rapid growth for a few years or a few decades; maturity can go on and on and on, without real decline and decay setting in (who can predict when, if ever, decline and decay will hit the soft drink industry?). Sometimes growth reappears after a period of decay, as occurred in the radio broadcasting, bicycle, and motorcycle industries.[3] Sometimes the growth phase of the cycle can be lengthened by renewed product innovation.[4] Sometimes the paths of different industries collide, causing them to reform and merge as one industry (as is now occurring among banks, savings and loan associations, and brokerage firms—all of which used to be in distinctly separate industries but which now are reforming into a single financial services industry).

Hence, while it is worthwhile to consider where an industry is in the life cycle, there is more analytical value in identifying the specific forces giving rise to industry change. Industry conditions change *because forces are in motion that create incentives or pressures for change*.[5] The most dominant of these forces are called *driving forces* because they have the biggest influences on what kind of changes will take place in the industry's structure and environment.

The Kinds of Driving Forces and How They Work. There are at least 12 basic types of driving forces with power to produce important changes in industry conditions and overall industry attractiveness:[6]

- *Changes in the long-term industry growth rate.* Increases or decreases in industry growth are a powerful variable in the investment decisions of existing firms to expand capacity. A strong upsurge in long-term demand frequently attracts new firms to enter the market, and a shrinking market often causes some firms to exit the industry. Shifts in industry growth up or down are, thus, a force for industry change, because they affect the balance between industry supply and buyer demand, entry and exit, and how hard it will be for a firm to capture additional sales.

- *Changes in who buys the product and how they use it.* Shifts in the type and mix of buyers, along with the emergence of new ways to use the product, have potential for forcing adjustments in customer service offerings (credit, technical assistance, maintenance and repair), creating a need to market the industry's product through a different mix of dealers and retail outlets, prompting producers to broaden/narrow their product lines, increasing/decreasing capital requirements, and changing sales and promotion approaches. The hand calculator industry became a different market requiring different strategies when students and households began to use them as well as engineers and scientists. The mainframe computer industry has been transformed by the surge of buyers for personal and midsize computers. Consumer interest in cordless telephones and mobile telephones for use in cars and trucks has opened a major new buyer segment for

---

[3]For a more extended discussion of the problems with the life-cycle hypothesis, see Michael E. Porter, *Competitive Strategy: Techniques for Analyzing Industries and Competitors* (New York: Free Press, 1980), pp. 157–62.

[4]For a discussion on how firms can accomplish this, see Theodore Levitt, "Exploit the Product Life Cycle," *Harvard Business Review* 43, no. 6 (November–December 1965), pp. 81–94.

[5]Porter, *Competitive Strategy*, p. 162.

[6]What follows is a much condensed summary of the discussion in Porter, *Competitive Strategy*, pp. 164–83.

telephone equipment manufacturers. Trying to ascertain the kinds of industry change to expect should, therefore, include an assessment of changing buyer demographics and potential emergence of new buyer segments.

- *Product innovation.* Product innovation can broaden the customer base, rejuvenate industry growth, and widen the degree of product differentiation among rival sellers. Successful new-product introductions strengthen the market position of the innovating companies, usually at the market share expense of companies who either stick with their old products or are slow to follow in bringing out their own versions of the new product. Industries where product innovation has been a key driving force include copying equipment, cameras and photographic equipment, computers, electronic video games, toys, prescription drugs, soft drinks (sugar-free and caffeine-free), beer (low-calorie), cigarettes (low-tar, low-nicotine), and personal computer software.

- *Process innovation.* Frequent and important technological advances in manufacturing methods can dramatically alter unit costs, capital requirements, minimum-efficient plant sizes, the desirability of vertical integration, and learning or experience curve effects. All of these are capable of producing important changes in how large a firm needs to be, how many efficient-sized firms the market can support, and who has how big a manufacturing cost advantage.

- *Marketing innovation.* When firms initiate novel or clever ways to market their products, they can spark a burst of buyer interest, widen industry demand, increase product differentiation, and lower unit costs—any or all of which can precipitate changes in the competitive positions of rival firms and force strategy revisions.

- *Entry or exit of major firms.* When an established firm from another industry attempts entry either by acquisition or by starting its own new venture, it usually does so with the intent of applying its skills and resources in some innovative fashion; the outcome can be a new ball game with not only an important new player but also new rules for competing. Similarly, exit of a major firm changes industry structure by reducing the number of market leaders (perhaps increasing the dominance of the leaders who remain) and causing a rush to capture the business once had by the exiting firm.

- *Diffusion of proprietary knowledge.* As knowledge about a particular technique or production process spreads through the conduits of scientific journals, trade publications, suppliers, distributors, and customers, the advantage held by firms with proprietary technical know-how erodes. Other interested companies gradually accumulate the information and skills to initiate their own use, reducing entry barriers for new competitors, and also paving the way for suppliers or customers to integrate vertically into the industry. Except where strong patent protection effectively blockades the diffusion of an important technology, it is likely that rapid diffusion of proprietary knowledge will heighten competition and narrow or even eliminate the edge once held by the technological pioneers.

- *Changes in cost and efficiency.* In industries where new economies of scale are emerging or where strong learning curve effects are allowing firms with the most production experience to undercut the prices charged by rivals, large firm size becomes such a distinct advantage that all firms are driven to adopt volume-building strategies—a "race for growth" dominates the industry landscape. Likewise, sharply rising costs for a key input (either raw materials or necessary labor skills) can cause a scramble to either *(a)* line up reliable supplies of the input at affordable prices or else *(b)* search out lower-cost substitute inputs. Anytime important changes in cost or efficiency are taking place in an industry, the door is open for the positions of rival firms to change radically as concerns who has how big a cost advantage.

- *Emerging buyer preferences for a differentiated instead of a commodity product (or for a more standardized product instead of strongly differentiated products).* Sometimes growing numbers of buyers begin to decide that a standard "one-size-fits-all" product with a bargain price meets their requirements just about as effectively as do premium-priced brands offering a broad choice of features and options. Such a swing in buyer demand can drive industry change, shifting patronage away from sellers of more expensive differentiated products to sellers of cheaper commodity products and creating a very price-competitive market environment—a development that can so dominate the marketplace that it limits the strategic freedom of industry producers to do much other than compete hard on price. On the other hand, a shift away from standardized products occurs when sellers are able to win a bigger and more loyal following of buyers by bringing out new performance features, making style changes, offering options and accessories, and creating image differences via advertising and packaging; then the driver of change is the struggle among rivals to out-differentiate one another. Industries evolve differently depending on whether the forces in motion are acting to increase or decrease the emphasis on product differentiation.

- *Regulatory influences and government policy changes.* Regulatory and governmental actions can often force significant changes in industry practices and strategic approaches. Medicare/Medicaid provisions affect hospital and nursing home operations. The decisions of government regulators weigh heavily on the natural gas, telephone, and electric utility industries. Deregulation has been a big driving force in airlines and banking. Changes in defense spending affect the defense contracting business. Drunk driving laws and drinking age legislation recently became driving forces in the alcoholic beverage industry.

- *Changing societal priorities and lifestyles.* Emerging social issues and changing attitudes and lifestyles can be powerful instigators of industry change. Consumer concerns about salt, sugar, and chemical additives have forced the food industry to reexamine food-processing techniques, redirect R&D efforts into whole new areas, and introduce scores of new products.

Safety concerns have been major drivers of change in the automobile industry, the toy industry, and the outdoor power equipment industry, to mention a few. Increased interest in physical fitness has produced whole new industries to supply exercise equipment, jogging clothes and shoes, and medically supervised diet control programs. Social concerns about air and water pollution have been major forces in industries which discharge waste products into the air and water.

• *Reductions in uncertainty and business risk.* A young, emerging industry is typically characterized by much uncertainty over potential market size, technological bugs, an unproven cost structure, what to do about product development, how to distribute the products and access potential buyers, and what competitive strategy to employ. The risks of failure can be high, despite the fact that rapid expansion of the market may for a time allow firms the luxury of employing widely divergent strategies and market approaches (each representing a different "bet" about the future road ahead). Over time, however, the uncertainties get resolved and the poor strategies are abandoned while the successful ones are imitated and improved—an evolutionary process that tends to stiffen competitive pressures. Meanwhile, as uncertainty about the industry's viability and prospects dissipates, new firms may be enticed to enter the industry. Often, the new entrants are larger, established firms with a preference for going into lower-risk ventures where industry growth potential is large and where it is a good bet that the existing hurdles can be overcome. As uncertainty and business risk are reduced, those firms which have grown up with the industry must prepare to defend against the potential entry of bigger rivals and to modify competitive strategy (as earlier judgments about how best to try to compete become obsolete).

The foregoing list of factors that can serve as *potential* driving forces in an industry should indicate why an industry can suddenly switch gears and head off in a new direction and why it is too simplistic to view industry change only in terms of the life-cycle model.

However, it is important to understand that while there may well be *many* forces of change at work in a given industry, no more than three or four are likely to qualify as *driving* forces in the sense that they will be *the major determinants* of future industry direction and industry conditions. Thus, strategic analysts must resist the temptation to include as driving forces anything and everything they see changing; the analytical task is to evaluate the forces of industry change carefully enough to be able to separate the major factors from the minor factors.

The concept of driving forces has practical strategy-making value. *First,* the driving forces in an industry indicate to managers what factors will have the greatest impact on the company's business over the next one to three years. *Second,* if a company is to be positioned to deal with these forces, then management must specifically assess the implications of each driving force. *Third,* strategy-makers will obviously have to craft a strategy that explicitly takes the driving forces into account and prepares the company for the anticipated changes in the industry.

Environmental Scanning Techniques. One way to get a jump on what driving forces are likely to emerge is to utilize environmental scanning techniques as an early warning detector of "new straws in the wind." *Environmental scanning* is a term used to describe a broad-ranging, mind-stretching effort to monitor and interpret social, political, economic, ecological, and technological events in an attempt to spot budding trends and conditions that could eventually impact the industry. Environmental scanning involves time frames well beyond the next one to three years—for example, it could involve developing judgments about the demand for energy in the year 2000 or what kinds of household appliances will be needed in the "house of the future," or what people will be doing with computers 20 years from now, or what will happen to our forests if the demand for paper continues to grow at its present rate. Environmental scanning, thus, attempts to look very broadly at "first of its kind" happenings, what kinds of new ideas and approaches are "catching on," and extrapolate their possible implications 5 to 20 years into the future. The purpose and value of environmental scanning is to stimulate the thinking of managers about potential developments that could have an important impact on industry conditions and company opportunities and threats.

Environmental scanning can be accomplished using such techniques as systematic monitoring and study of current events of all kinds, futures research, scenarios, and the Delphi method (a technique for finding consensus among a group of "knowledgeable experts"); the methods of environmental scanning are highly qualitative and subjective. Companies that undertake formal environmental scanning on a fairly continuous and comprehensive level include General Electric, AT&T, Coca-Cola, Ford, General Motors, Du Pont, and Shell Oil. The appeal of environmental scanning to these companies is that it helps managers increase their planning horizon, assists them in translating a vague inkling of a future opportunity or threat into a clearer strategic issue (for which they can begin to develop a strategic answer), and helps them prepare for change.[7]

Evaluating the Strength of Competitive Forces

The next analytical step is to dig deeply into the industry's competitive process—the main sources of competitive pressure and how strong these pressures are. This phase of industry and competitive analysis is particularly essential, because managers cannot expect to devise a competitively successful strategy without first having good insight into the industry's own unique set of competitive characteristics and "rules of the game."

Even though the competitive pressures in one industry are never precisely the same as in another industry, there are enough similarities in how competition works from industry to industry to use a common analytical framework in gauging the

---

[7]For further discussion of the nature and use of environmental scanning, see Roy Amara and Andrew J. Lipinski, *Business Planning for an Uncertain Future: Scenarios and Strategies* (New York: Pergamon Press, 1983); Harold E. Klein and Robert U. Linneman, "Environmental Assessment: An International Study of Corporate Practice," *Journal of Business Strategy* V, no. 1 (Summer 1984), pp. 55–75; and Ian H. Wilson, *Environment/Public Policy: 1979 Conference Papers* (St. Louis: American Assembly of Collegiate Schools of Business, 1980), pp. 159–63.

nature and intensity of competition. Indeed, as a general rule, *competition in an industry is a composite of five competitive forces:*

1. The rivalry among competing sellers in the industry.
2. The market attempts of companies in other industries to win customers over to their own *substitute* products.
3. The potential entry of more competitors.
4. The bargaining power and leverage exercisable by suppliers of inputs.
5. The bargaining power and leverage exercisable by buyers of the product.

The *five-forces model* of competition, as shown in Figure 3–3, is a valuable conceptual tool for diagnosing the principal competitive pressures in a market and assessing how strong and important each one is. Five-forces analysis has been developed by Professor Michael E. Porter of the Harvard Business School (which is why Figure 3–3 is often referred to as *the Porter model*).[8] Since its appearance in 1980, the five-forces model has become the most widely used technique of competition analysis; it is unequivocally the best single analytical approach for discerning how competition works, plus it is uncommonly straightforward to use.

The Competitive Force of Interfirm Rivalry.   The most powerful of the five competitive forces is *usually* the competitive maneuvering of rival firms.[9] Indeed the vigor with which sellers use the competitive weapons at their disposal to jockey for a stronger market position and win a competitive edge over rivals is a solid measure of the strength of this competitive force. *Competitive strategy* is the narrower portion of business strategy dealing with management's *competitive approaches for achieving market success, its offensive moves to secure a competitive edge over rival firms, and its defensive moves to protect its competitive position.*[10] The profit incentive of competitors to develop a "winning" competitive strategy produces a competitive interplay with the following characteristics:

1. Rival firms are more or less constantly jockeying for improved market position. The struggle for better position manifests in an independent striving for patronage, whereby rivals formulate and reformulate their own competitive strategies in an ongoing struggle to outmaneuver one another and secure a more profitable market share.
2. The competitive strategies that rival firms may devise and the ways they may seek out new openings to compete are diverse, limited mainly by their imagination, by what will work in the marketplace (i.e., the constraints and reactions of buyers), and by what is legally permissible (based on antitrust legislation and definitions of "fair competitive practices").

---

[8] For a thoroughgoing treatment of the five-forces model by its originator, see Michael F. Porter, *Competitive Strategy: Techniques for Analyzing Industries and Competitors* (New York: Free Press, 1980), chap. 1.

[9] Parts of this section are based on the discussion in Arthur A. Thompson, "Competition as a Strategic Process," *Antitrust Bulletin* 25, no. 4 (Winter 1980), pp. 777–803.

[10] The distinction between *competitive strategy* and *business strategy* is useful here. As we defined it in Chapter 2, business strategy not only addresses squarely the issue of how to compete but it also embraces all of the functional-area support strategies, how management plans to respond to changing industry conditions of all kinds (not just those that are competition-related), and how management intends to address the full range of strategic issues confronting the business. Competitive strategy, however, is narrower in scope and zeros in on the firm's competitive approach, the competitive edge strived for, and specific moves to outmaneuver rival companies.

FIGURE 3–3
The "Five-Forces" Model of Competition: A Key Analytical Tool

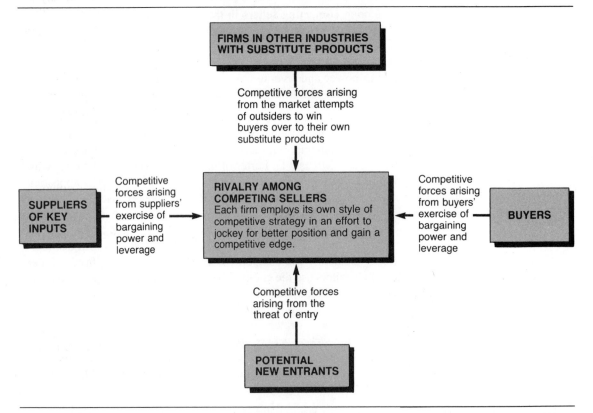

Source: Adapted from Michael E. Porter, "How Competitive Forces Shape Strategy," *Harvard Business Review,* 57, no. 2 (March–April 1979), pp. 137–45.

3. Fresh competitive pressures can be activated any time that one or more competitors initiates a new "offensive" strategic move to improve its position or launches a new "defensive" move to protect the position it already has. How long a firm goes without fine tuning its strategy or subjecting it to major overhaul is a function of its market success (or failures) and the durability of its competitive approach in withstanding strategic challenges from rival firms. When a firm realizes that its competitive strategy has been stalemated or defeated by rivals' strategies, then it is challenged to seek a better strategy not as easily defeated or else remain content with the stalemate it has encountered.

4. In considering which of several optional moves to make, *there is good reason for a firm to choose a competitive strategy that is neither easily imitated nor easily thwarted.* Offering buyers something that competitors cannot duplicate easily or cheaply gives a firm not only a market edge but also a unique competitive capability—outcomes that can be translated into above-average profitability.

The challenge in crafting a winning competitive strategy, of course, is *how to gain an edge over rivals*. The big complication is that the success of any one firm's strategy hinges on what strategies its rivals employ, in conjunction with the resources rivals are willing and able to put behind their strategies. What is the "best" strategy for one firm in its maneuvering for competitive advantage depends, in other words, on the competitive strength and competitive strategies of rival companies. And whenever a firm makes a strategic move, rivals may well elect to retaliate with offensive or defensive countermoves. Thus, competitive rivalry turns out to be a game of strategy, of move and countermove, played under "warlike" conditions according to the rules of business competition.

It follows that rivalry among competing sellers can assume many forms and shades of intensity. The weapons used for competing include price, quality, performance features offered, services offered, warranties and guarantees, advertising, better networks of wholesale distributors and retail dealers, ability to innovate, and so on. The use of these weapons can change over time, as emphasis shifts from one to another competitive weapon and as competitors make various offensive and defensive moves. Rivalry, thus, is dynamic; the current scene is always modified as companies inititate new moves and countermoves. But the two things to really appreciate from this discussion are (1) that the deployment of a powerful competitive strategy on the part of one or more companies intensifies the competitive pressures on the remaining companies and (2) that the particular competitive weapons being used by rivals to try to outmaneuver one another shape "the rules of competition" in the industry and the requirements for competitive success.

Strategic analysts, once the specific rules of interfirm rivalry in the industry are understood, then need to evaluate just how strong this particular competitive force is. There are several factors which, industry after industry, seem to influence the *strength* of rivalry among competing sellers:[11]

1. *Rivalry tends to intensify as the number of competitors increases and as they become more equal in size and capability.* Up to some point, the greater the number of competitors the greater the probability for fresh, creative strategic initiatives; in addition, greater numbers reduce the effects of any one rival's actions upon the others, thereby lessening somewhat the probability of direct retaliation. When rivals are more equal in size and capability, the chances are better that they will compete on a fairly even footing, a feature which makes it harder for one or two firms to "win" the competitive battle and then dominate the market on more or less their own terms.

2. *Rivalry is usually stronger when demand for the product is growing slowly.* In a rapidly expanding market, there tends to be enough business for everybody to grow; indeed, it may take all of a firm's financial and managerial resources just to keep abreast of the growth in buyer demand, much less devoting efforts to stealing away the customers of rivals. But when growth slows, expansion-minded firms and/or firms with excess capacity often initiate price cuts and thereby ignite a battle for market share that can result in a shakeout of the weak

---

[11]These indicators of what to look for in evaluating the intensity of interfirm rivalry are based upon Porter, "How Competitive Forces Shape Strategy," pp. 142–43 and Porter, *Competitive Strategy*, pp. 17–21.

and less-efficient firms—the industry "consolidates" to consist of a smaller, but individually stronger, group of sellers. Anytime market share is a key driver of profitability and maybe even survival, firms have a strong incentive to try to boost their own market shares at the expense of their rivals.

3. *Rivalry is more intense when competitors are tempted by industry conditions to use price cuts or other competitive weapons to boost unit volume.* Whenever fixed costs are high and marginal costs are low, firms are under strong economic pressure to produce at or very near full capacity. Hence, if market demand weakens and capacity utilization begins to fall off, rival firms frequently resort to secret price concessions, special discounts, rebates, and other sales-increasing tactics. A similar situation arises when a product is perishable or seasonal or is costly or difficult to store or hold in inventory.

4. *Rivalry is stronger when the products/services of competitors are not so strongly differentiated that customers become locked in by the high costs of switching from one brand to another.* Product differentiation per se is not a deterrent to competition; indeed, it has the capacity for enlivening rivalry by forcing firms to seek creative new ways of improving their price/quality/ service/performance offering. The strategic moves of one firm to differentiate its products may well call forth important countermoves from rivals. However, when the nature of product differentiation begins to result in layers of insulation from rivalry—as occurs when switching becomes costly or otherwise difficult—then a firm may gain protection from raids on its customers by its rivals. Should this occur, competitive intensity is obviously lessened.

5. *Rivalry increases in proportion to the size of the payoff from a successful strategic move.* The greater the potential reward the more likely some firm will give in to the temptation of a particular strategic move. How big the strategic payoff is varies partly with the speed of retaliation. When competitors can be expected to respond slowly (or maybe even not at all), the initiator of a fresh competitive strategy can reap the benefits in the intervening period and perhaps gain a first-mover advantage which is not easily surmounted; the greater the benefits of moving first the more likely that some firm will accept the risk of pioneering along with the consequences of eventual retaliation.

6. *Rivalry tends to be more vigorous when it costs more to get out of a business than to stay in and compete.* The higher the exit barriers (and, thus, the more costly it is to abandon a market) the stronger the incentive for firms to remain and compete as best they can, even though they may be earning low profits or even incurring a loss.

7. *Rivalry becomes more volatile and unpredictable the more diverse competitors are in terms of their strategies, personalities, corporate priorities, resources, and countries of origin.* A diverse range of views and approaches enhances the probability that one or more firms will behave as "mavericks" and employ strategies that produce more market flux and uncertainty than would otherwise occur.

8. *Rivalry is increased when strong companies outside the industry acquire weak firms in the industry and launch aggressive, well-funded moves to transform the newly acquired competitors into major market contenders.* A classic example of this occurred when Philip Morris, a leading cigarette firm with excellent

marketing know-how, shook up the whole beer industry's approach to marketing by its acquisition of stodgy Miller Brewing Company in the late 1960s. In short order, Philip Morris revamped the marketing of Miller High Life and pushed it to the number 2 best-selling brand; PM also pioneered low-calorie beers with the introduction of Miller Lite—a move which made light beer the fast-growing segment in the beer industry.

From the standpoint of assessing the nature and strength of interfirm rivalry, the important understanding is that fresh strategic moves are likely from time to time and that these stir competitive pressures. Because the jockeying for position among competitors varies from industry to industry and from time to time within the same industry, it is always the strategist's job to identify what the current weapons of competitive rivalry are, to discern how the game is being played, and to judge how strong the pressures of competitive rivalry are.

The Competitive Force of Potential Entry.   New entrants to a market bring new production capacity, the desire to establish a secure place in the market, and sometimes substantial resources with which to compete.[12] Just how serious the competitive threat of entry is into a particular market depends on two classes of factors: *barriers to entry* and the *expected reaction of firms to new entry*. A barrier to entry exists whenever it is hard for a newcomer to break into the market and if the economics of the business put a potential entrant at a price/cost disadvantage relative to its competitors. There are several major sources of entry barriers:[13]

- *Economies of scale*. The presence of important scale economies deters entry because it forces the potential entrant to commit to entering on a large-scale basis (a costly and perhaps risky move) or else to accept a cost disadvantage (and, consequently, lower profitability). Large-scale entry could result in chronic overcapacity in the industry and/or it could so threaten the market shares of existing firms that they are pushed into aggressive competitive retaliation (in the form of price cuts, increased advertising and sales promotion, and similar such steps) to maintain their position; either way, the entrant's outlook is for lower profits. Scale-related barriers may be encountered not just in production but in advertising, marketing and distribution, financing, after-sale customer service, raw-materials purchasing, and R&D as well.

- *The existence of learning and experience curve effects*. When achieving lower unit costs is partly or mostly a function of experience in producing the product and other learning curve benefits, a new entrant is put at a disadvantage in competing with older established firms with more accumulated know-how (see Illustration Capsule 10 for a more extensive discussion of the strategic implications of experience curve economics).

- *Brand preferences and customer loyalty*. When the products of rival sellers are differentiated, buyers usually have some degree of attachment to existing brands. This means that a potential entrant must be prepared to spend

---

[12]Porter, "How Competitive Forces Shape Strategy," p. 138.
[13]Porter, *Competitive Strategy,* pp. 7–17.

ILLUSTRATION CAPSULE 10

Experience Curve Economics: Its Implications for Industry Situation Analysis

The Boston Consulting Group (BCG), one of the premier strategy consulting firms, has made a big impact on industry analysis with a concept called *the experience curve.* The origins of the experience curve reside with studies in the 1930s showing that a doubling of the cumulative production of airframes was accompanied by a 20 percent reduction in unit labor costs. This phenomenon, termed *the learning curve,* was attributed to (1) the ability of workers to get better at doing a repetitive task the more times they did it and (2) the discovery of more efficient ways to perform the task.

In the late 1960s, Bruce Henderson, BCG's founder and president, noticed a recurring theme that kept running through the cost studies being done for client companies: the declining cost principle underlying the learning curve went beyond just labor costs and seemed to apply to the total value-added costs (all costs except purchased materials and components) measured in constant dollars. Further analysis of the empirical evidence BCG had accumulated showed that each time the cumulative number of units manufactured doubled, the deflated value-added cost per unit declined by a fixed percentage. In integrated circuits and cement, a doubling of cumulative production volume entailed about a 30 percent unit-cost reduction, in air conditioners and power tools the deflated unit-cost declines ran about 20 percent, and in primary magnesium and industrial trucks the declines averaged 10 percent. Deflating the actual historical cost data was necessary to correct for the effects of inflation (when the cost data were not expressed in constant dollars, inflationary factors tended to obscure the true size of the cost savings being realized). The decline in unit cost with each doubling of cumulative production experience was attributed to the combined effects of:

- Learning associated with the repetitive performance of labor tasks.
- Cost-effective improvements in product design.
- Incremental gains associated with "debugging" the production technology.
- The making of bit-by-bit improvements in the whole operating process (better use of materials, more efficient inventory handling, more efficient distribution methods, and computerization and automation of assorted production, sales, and clerical tasks).
- An increased scale of operation that yielded access to new operating economies.
- Enriched know-how in managing and operating the business.

BCG plotted the declines in unit cost against cumulative production volume on a graph—the resulting graphical relationship was labeled the *experience curve.*

The significance of the experience curve effect for a given *industry* depends not only on the percentage decline (whether it is 15 percent or 30 percent), but also on the rate at which experience accumulates, reflected by the annual rate of market growth. The table below shows the potential for annual cost reductions for different combinations of experience curve effects and market growth:

ILLUSTRATION CAPSULE 10 *(continued)*

Experience Curve Effect	*Annual Cost Reduction Based on a Rate of Market Growth of*				
	2%	5%	10%	20%	30%
90%	0.3%	0.7%	1.4%	2.7%	4.1%
80%	0.6	1.6	3.2	6.4	9.6
70%	1.0	2.5	5.0	10.0	15.0
60%	1.4	3.5	7.0	14.0	21.0

A firm can achieve even bigger annual cost reductions than the industry averages shown above if its market share of industry volume is increasing (this is because the firm's rate of growth in production volume is bigger than the overall industry rate, allowing the firm to accumulate production experience faster than the industry as a whole). As a consequence, the stronger the experience curve effect in an industry the greater the strategic importance of a firm's market share in determining its ability to remain cost-competitive and achieve above-average profitability.

Strategic Implications

Bruce Henderson and BCG argued that the presence of a strong experience curve produced the following cause-effect chain:

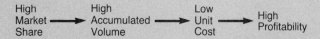

The implications of this chain can be seen by looking at the graph below, which shows the relative position of three competing firms on an industry's experience curve. Firm A, with the largest cumulative volume, has a commanding cost ad-

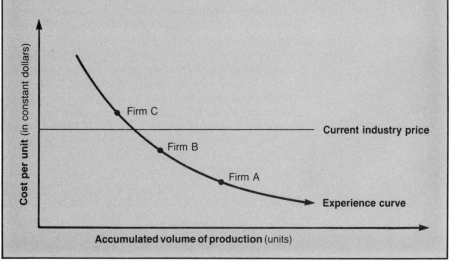

ILLUSTRATION CAPSULE 10 *(continued)*

vantage over firms B and C. At the current industry price, firm C is losing money; to become profitable, it has little choice but to move aggressively to increase its market share and, thereby, move down the experience curve quickly enough to get its costs below the industry price level. Firm B, though able to survive, must live with subpar profitability (in comparison to the leader). Plainly, as long as firm A maintains greater cumulative experience than competitors, it can sustain its cost advantage.

When an industry is characterized by a fairly strong experience curve effect, competitors with less than one quarter of the market share of the largest firm are hard pressed to survive. A shakeout of the low-share firms is virtually inevitable, barring some unusual external constraint or control on competition. As firms exit, the remaining competitors have to grow faster than the industry at large just to maintain their relative positions; if runner-up firms want to gain on the leader, then they have to use the exit of weak firms as their opportunity to add volume faster than the leader and move down the experience curve closer to the leader's position. If they fail to capture enough volume to approach the leader's experience curve position, very likely their profits will remain subpar or negative; the best long-run choice then may be to cash out their investment in the industry and reinvest elsewhere.

Estimates of the experience curve effect can be used to forecast costs. Such forecasts become the basis for setting realistic cost-reduction goals and for setting prices based on anticipated costs, rather than current or historical costs. Lowering prices at the same rate at which costs decline may well discourage the entry of competing firms into the industry.

Some Added Complexities

There are some subtleties in diagnosing experience curve economics in an industry:

- Occasionally, experience effects are lumpy and uneven, causing the curve to decline not at a smooth, uniform rate but rather at rates that change at somewhat unpredictable intervals—the experience curve becomes flatter, then steeper, then flatter again.
- A new entrant firm with improved technology and/or smart followership abilities may be able to ride its own experience curve down more quickly and achieve a cost position significantly closer to the low-cost leaders than would be the case if it was forced to operate on the same experience curve as established competitors.
- There can be different experience curve effects in each part of the industry chain: R&D, design engineering, manufacturing of parts and components, assembly of the final product, marketing, wholesale distribution, and retailing. While the accumulation of experience may result in cost reductions in all stages, seldom will the sizes of the reductions be the same. In like fashion, if a firm produces a whole line of different models, experience will accrue faster for the best-selling models and their costs may fall faster than for slower-selling models.

ILLUSTRATION CAPSULE 10 *(continued)*

Applications of Experience Curve Techniques by BCG Clients

One of BCG's first efforts at applying experience curve theory was with the Norton Company of Worcester, Massachusetts. Norton was having trouble profitably penetrating the market for pressure-sensitive tape—a market dominated by 3M. Norton had successfully cut production costs and lowered prices but still was unable to make a dent in increasing its market share. BCG's experience curve analysis showed that Norton, in effect, was chasing 3M down the cost curve, and that, so long as 3M followed pricing and growth strategies to maximize market share, it was a fruitless struggle for Norton. Subsequently, Norton concluded it could not compete successfully against 3M by trying to produce a broad range of products sold in a large number of markets; rather, the company decided it was better off concentrating in selected areas. In BCG's view, the Norton situation illustrated an important experience curve commandment: If you cannot get enough market share to be cost-competitive, then get out of the business.

Another instance where the same lesson applied was the effort of Allis-Chalmers Company to compete against General Electric and Westinghouse in steam turbine engines. Between 1946 and 1963, Allis-Chalmers' market share was too small for it to be competitive on cost (and, therefore, on price) with large-volume manufacturers; thus, Allis-Chalmers' best decision was to withdraw from the industry.

Black & Decker, Texas Instruments, and Weyerhaeuser have all applied experience curve analysis at one time or another. In 1973, Texas Instruments described its strategy in semiconductors in strong experience curve language: "Follow an aggressive pricing policy, focus on continuing cost reduction and productivity improvement, build on shared experience gained in making related products, and keep capacity growing ahead of demand."

Some Cautions

Three warnings about the experience curve are in order.

One, experience curve effects do not exist in all industries; the size of the experience curve effect can range from tiny (or inconsequential) to large, and it is the analyst's task to appraise how important experience is in cost determination.

Two, even where a fairly strong experience curve exists, the cost reduction benefits do not occur automatically—a concerted effort has to be made to capitalize on the cost-reduction opportunities.

Three, an overly strong emphasis on driving costs down the experience curve can produce some unwanted strategic consequences. Selecting a strategy based on sustained cost reduction associated with growing experience means putting cost-price-efficiency considerations ahead of differentiation-market-effectiveness considerations. For an "efficiency" or low-cost leadership strategy to succeed, significant numbers of customers must want low price, as opposed to differentiating features (quality, service, product innovation, specialized use). Moreover, once a firm decides to pursue a low-cost leadership strategy, it has to guard against losing its ability to respond to product-technology-customer changes. Strategies based on tight adherence to experience curve effects frequently result in narrow skills-building, rigid task performance, and relatively inflexible facilities and technologies.

ILLUSTRATION CAPSULE 10 *(concluded)*

As a consequence, aggressive attempts to ride down the experience curve rapidly can sometimes entail great difficulty in (1) responding to changes in customer needs and product uses, (2) matching or surpassing the product innovations of rival firms, (3) accommodating major changes in process technology and implementing technological breakthroughs, and (4) initiating these changes to drive the market in new directions.

SOURCES: "Selling Business a Theory of Economics," *Business Week,* September 8, 1973, pp. 85–90; Derek F. Abell and John S. Hammond, *Strategic Market Planning* (Englewood Cliffs, N.J.: Prentice-Hall, 1979), pp. 106–21; Arnaldo C. Hay and Nicolas S. Majluf, *Strategic Management: An Integrative Perspective* (Englewood Cliffs, N.J.: Prentice-Hall, 1984), chap. 6; David A. Aaker, *Developing Business Strategies* (New York: John Wiley & Sons, 1984), chap. 10; and Pankaj Ghemawat, "Building Strategy on the Experience Curve," *Harvard Business Reivew* 63, no. 2 (March–April 1985), pp. 143–49.

enough money on advertising and sales promotion to overcome customer loyalties and build its own clientele. Substantial time, as well as money, can be involved. Not only may a new entrant have to budget more funds for marketing than existing firms (which gives existing firms a cost advantage) but also the capital invested in establishing a new brand (unlike the capital invested in facilities and equipment) has no resale or recoverable value, which makes such expenditures a riskier "investment." In addition, product differentiation can entail costs to buyers of switching brands, in which case the new entrant must persuade buyers that the changeover or *switching costs* are worth incurring; this may require lower prices or better quality or better service or better performance features (the results of which may be lower expected profit margins for new entrants—something that is a significant barrier for new start-up companies dependent on sizable early profits to support their new investment).

- *Capital requirements.* The larger the total dollar investment needed to enter the market successfully, the more limited is the pool of potential entrants. The most obvious capital requirements are associated with manufacturing plant and equipment, working capital to finance inventories and customer credit, introductory advertising and sales promotion to establish a clientele, and bearing start-up losses.

- *Cost disadvantages independent of size.* Existing firms may have cost advantages not available to potential entrants, regardless of the entrant's size. These advantages relate to access to the best and cheapest raw materials, possession of patents and proprietary technological know-how, the benefits of any learning and experience curve effects, having purchased fixed assets at preinflation prices, favorable locations, and ability to access financial capital at a lower cost.

- *Access to distribution channels.* Where a product is distributed through established market channels, a potential entrant may face the barrier of gaining adequate distribution access. Some distributors may be reluctant to take on a product that lacks buyer recognition. The more limited the number of wholesale and retail outlets and the more that existing producers have these tied up, the tougher entry will be. Potential entrants, to overcome this barrier, may have to "buy" distribution access by offering better margins to dealers and distributors or by giving advertising allowances and other promotional incentives, with the result that the potential entrant's profits may be squeezed unless and until its product gains such good market acceptance that distributors and retailers want to carry it because of its popularity.

- *Government actions and policies.* Government agencies can limit or even bar entry by instituting controls over licenses and permits. Regulated industries—like trucking, radio and television stations, liquor retailing, and railroads—all feature government-controlled entry. Entry can also be restricted, and certainly made more expensive, by stringent government-mandated safety regulations and environmental pollution standards.

Even if a potential entrant is willing to tackle the problems of entry barriers, it may be dissuaded by its expectations about how existing firms will react to new entry.[14] Will incumbent firms move over grudgingly and let the new entrant take a viable share of the market, or will they launch a vigorous "survival-of-the-fittest" defense of their market positions—including prices cuts, increased advertising, new product improvements, and whatever else is calculated to give a new entrant (as well as other rivals) a hard time? A firm is likely to have second thoughts about entry:

- When incumbent firms have previously been aggressive in defending their market positions against entry.
- When incumbent firms possess substantial financial resources with which to defend against new entry.
- When incumbent firms are in a position to use leverage with distributors and customers to keep their business.
- When incumbent firms are able and willing to cut prices to preserve their market shares.
- When product demand is expanding slowly, thus limiting the market's ability to absorb and accommodate the new entrant without adversely affecting the profit performance of all the participant firms.
- When it is more costly for existing firms to leave the market than to fight to the death (because the costs of exists are very high, owing to heavy investment in specialized technology and equipment, union agreements that contain high severance costs, or important shared relationships with other products).

One additional point needs to be made about the threat of entry as a competitive force: The threat of entry changes as economic and market conditions change. For example, the expiration of a key patent can greatly increase the threat

---

[14]Porter, "How Competitive Forces Shape Strategy," p. 140, and Porter, *Competitive Strategy,* pp. 14–15.

of entry. New technological discovery can create a big scale economy where none existed before. New actions by incumbent firms to increase advertising or strengthen distributor-dealer relations or step up R&D or improve product quality can erect higher roadblocks to entry.

The Competitive Force of Substitute Products. Firms in one industry are, quite often, in close competition with firms in another industry because their respective products are good substitutes. Soft-drink producers to some extent are in competition with the sellers of fruit juices, milk, coffee, tea, powdered-mix drinks, and perhaps some alcoholic beverages (wine and beer). The producers of wood stoves are in competition with the producers of kerosene heaters and portable electric heaters. Sugar producers are in competition with the companies that produce artificial sweeteners. The producers of plastic containers are in competition with the makers of glass bottles and jars, the manufacturers of paperboard cartons, and the producers of tin cans and aluminum cans. The producers of rival brands of aspirin are in competition with the makers of other pain relievers and headache remedies.

The competitive force of closely related substitute products impacts sellers in several ways. First, the price and availability of acceptable substitutes for an item places a ceiling on the prices that the producers of that item can charge (and to some extent, therefore, places a limit on the profit they can earn).[15] Second, unless sellers can upgrade quality, reduce prices via cost reduction, or otherwise differentiate their product from its substitutes, they risk a low growth rate in sales and profits owing to the market inroads that substitutes may make. The more sensitive a product's sales volume is to changes in the prices of substitutes, the stronger is the competitive influence of the substitutes.

Third, the strength of competition from substitutes is affected by the ease with which buyers can change over to the substitute. The ease of changing over to a substitute is usually governed by the buyer's *switching costs*—the one-time costs facing the buyer of switching from use of one good over to a substitute.[16] Typical switching costs include employee retraining costs, the cost to purchase additional equipment that will also be needed, payments for technical help in making the changeover, the time and cost in testing the quality and reliability of the substitute, and the psychic costs of severing old supplier relationships and establishing new ones. If buyers' switching costs are high, then the sellers of substitutes must offer a major cost or performance benefit to steal the industry's customers away. When switching costs are low, it is easier for sellers of substitutes to hurdle the barrier of convincing buyers to change over to their product.

As a rule, then, the lower the price of substitutes the higher their quality and performance; and the lower the user's switching costs the more intense are the competitive pressures posed by substitute products. One very telling indicator of the strength of competitive pressures emanating from the producers of substitutes is their growth rate in sales; other indicators are their plans for expansion of capacity and the profits they are earning.

---

[15]Porter, "How Competitive Forces Shape Strategy," p. 142, and Porter, *Competitive Strategy*, pp. 23–24.

[16]Porter, *Competitive Strategy*, p. 10.

The Economic Power of Suppliers. The competitive impact suppliers can have on an industry is chiefly a function of how significant the input they supply is to the buyer.[17] When the input of a particular group of suppliers makes up a sizable proportion of total costs, or is crucial to the buyer's production process, or else significantly affects quality of the industry's product, then suppliers' *potential* bargaining power and influence over firms in the buying industry is enhanced. The extent to which this potential impact is realized depends upon a number of factors; in general, a group of supplier firms has more bargaining leverage over an industry's producers:

- When the input is, in one way or another, important to the user industry.
- When the supplier industry is dominated by a few large producers that enjoy reasonably secure market positions and that are not beleaguered by intensely competitive conditions.
- When suppliers' respective products are differentiated to such an extent that it is difficult or costly for users to switch from one supplier to another.
- When the buying firms are *not* important customers of the suppliers. In such instances, suppliers are not constrained by the fact that their own well being is tied to the industry they are supplying; hence, they have no overriding incentive to protect the customer industry via reasonable prices, improved quality, or new products which might well enhance the buying industry's sales and profits.
- When the suppliers of an input do *not* have to compete with the substitute inputs of suppliers in other industries. (For instance, the power of the suppliers of glass bottles to the soft-drink bottlers is checked by the ability of the soft-drink firms to use aluminum cans and plastic bottles.)
- When one or more suppliers pose a credible threat of forward integration into the business of the buyer industry (attracted, perhaps, by the prospect of higher profits than it can earn in its own market).
- When the buying firms display no inclination toward backward integration into the suppliers' business.

The power of suppliers can be an important economic factor in the marketplace because of the impact they can have on their customers' profits. Powerful suppliers can squeeze the profits of a customer industry via price increases which the latter is unable to pass on fully to the buyers of its own products. An industry's suppliers can also jeopardize industry profits via reductions in the quality of what is being supplied—for example, to the extent that semiconductor manufacturers supply lower-quality components to the makers of hand calculators, they can so increase the warranty and defective goods costs of the calculator firms that the latter's profits and reputation are seriously impaired (a force with obviously negative competitive impact).

The Economic Power of Buyers. Just as powerful suppliers can exert a competitive influence over an industry, so also can powerful customers.[18] The

---

[17]Porter, *Competitive Strategy,* pp. 27–28.
[18]Ibid., pp. 24–27.

bargaining power and leverage which buyers are able to exercise tends to be relatively greater:

- When customers are large and few in number and when they purchase in large quantities (often large customers are successful in using their volume-buying leverage to obtain important price concessions and other favorable terms and conditions of sale).
- When customers' purchases are a sizable percentage of the selling industry's total sales (the actions of the very biggest customers usually carry a lot of clout; and, the bigger customers are, the more clout they have in negotiating with sellers).
- When the supplying industry is comprised of large numbers of relatively small sellers (a few big buyers are often able to dominate a bunch of smaller suppliers).
- When the item being purchased is sufficiently standardized among sellers that not only can customers find alternative sellers but also they can switch suppliers at virtually zero cost.
- When customers pose a credible threat of backward integration, being attracted by the prospects of earning greater profits or by the benefits of reliable prices and reliable delivery.
- When sellers pose little threat of forward integration into the product market of their customers.
- When the item being bought is *not* an important input.
- When it is economically feasible for customers to follow the practice of purchasing the input from several suppliers rather than one.
- When the product/service being bought does not save the customer money.

A firm can enhance its profitability and market standing by seeking out customers who are in a comparatively weak position to exercise adverse power. Rarely are all buyer groups in a position to exercise equal degrees of bargaining power, and some may be less sensitive to price or quality of service than others. An example is the automobile tire industry, where the major tire manufacturers on the one hand confront very significant customer power in selling original equipment tires to the automobile manufacturers and, on the other hand, find themselves in a position to get much better prices selling replacement tires to individual car owners through their own retail dealer networks.

The Strategic Implications of the Five Competitive Forces. The unique analytical contribution of Figure 3–3 is the systematic way it exposes the makeup of competitive forces. *Analysis of the competitive environment requires that the strength of each one of the five competitive forces be assessed.* The collective impact of these forces determines what competition is like in a given market. As a rule, the stronger the competitive forces are the lower is the collective profitability of participant firms. The sternest and most brutally competitive condition is where the five forces combine to create pressures so oppressive that the industry outlook is for prolonged subpar profitability or even losses for most or all firms. However, when an industry offers the prospect of superior long-term profit performance, it can be inferred that competitive forces are not unduly strong and that the competitive structure of the industry is favorable and attractive.

In trying to cope with the five competitive forces, it makes sense for a firm to search out a market position and competitive approach that will (1) insulate it as much as possible from the forces of competition, (2) influence the industry's competitive rules in its favor, and (3) give it a strong position from which to play the game of competition as it unfolds in the industry. Doing this requires analysis-based judgments about what the competitive pressures are and will be, where they are coming from, and how they can be defended against or otherwise lived with.

Assessing the Competitive Positions of Rival Companies

Important as the analysis of competitive forces is, it is the first but not the only step in putting together a complete picture of an industry's competitive situation. The second step is to examine the respective competitive positions of companies in the industry. The newest and most revealing technique for examining the competitive positions of industry participants is *strategic group mapping.*[19] This analytical tool is useful whenever an industry is populated with several distinct *groups* of competitors, each occupying a distinguishably different position in the overall market and having a distinguishably different appeal to buyers. *A strategic group consists of those rival firms with similar competitive approaches and positions in the market.*[20] Companies in the same strategic group can resemble one another in several ways: having comparable product-line breadth, utilizing the same kinds of distribution channels, being vertically integrated to much the same degree, offering buyers similar services and technical assistance, appealing to similar types of buyers, trying to satisfy buyer needs with the same product attributes, making extensive use of mass-media advertising, depending on identical technological approaches, and selling in the same price/quality range.

An industry contains only *one* strategic group when all sellers approach the market with essentially identical strategies; and, at the other extreme, there are as many strategic groups as there are competitors when each rival pursues a distinctively different competitive approach and occupies a substantially different competitive position in the marketplace. The major home appliance industry, for example, contains three identifiable strategic groups. One cluster (composed of General Electric and Whirlpool) produces a full line of home appliances (refrigerators, freezers, clothes washers and dryers, dishwashers, cooking appliances, garbage disposals, and microwaves), employs heavy national advertising, is vertically integrated, and has established a national network of distributors and dealers. Another cluster consists of premium-quality, specialist firms (like Amana in refrigerators and freezers, Maytag in washers and dryers, Kitchen Aid in dishwashers, and Jenn-Air in cooking tops) that focus on high-price market segments and have selective distribution. A third cluster—consisting of firms like Roper, Design and

---

[19]Porter, *Competitive Strategy*, chap. 7.
[20]Ibid., pp. 129–30.

Manufacturing, and Hardwick—concentrates on supplying private-label retailers (like the Kenmore brand sold by Sears) and budget-priced basic models for the low end of the market.

A *strategic group map* is constructed by plotting the market positions of the industry's strategic groups on a two-dimensional map using two strategic variables as axes—see the retail jewelry industry example in Figure 3–4. The map serves

FIGURE 3–4
A Strategic Group Map of Retail Jewelry Competitors

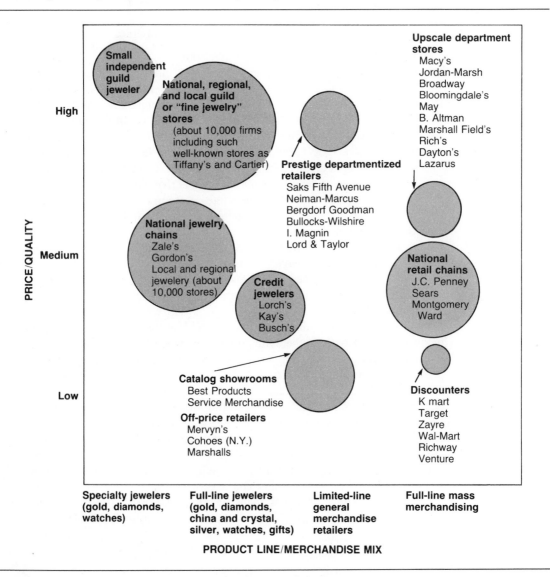

Note: The sizes of the circles are roughly proportional to the market shares of each group of competitors

as a convenient bridge between looking at the industry as a whole and considering the standing of each firm separately. There are five important guidelines to observe in trying to map the relative competitive positions of firms in the industry's overall "strategy space."[21]

First: The two variables selected as axes for the map should *not* be highly correlated; if they are, the circles on the map will fall along a diagonal and the map tells nothing more about the relative positions of competitors than would considering one of the variables by itself. For instance, if companies with broad product lines use multiple distribution channels while companies with narrow lines use a single distribution channel, then one of the variables is redundant—since one learns just as much about who is positioned how by looking at broad versus narrow product lines as by adding in consideration of single versus multiple distribution channels.

Second: The market-related variables to choose as axes for the map are those that best expose big differences in how rivals have positioned themselves to compete against one another in the marketplace. This, of course, requires identifying the characteristics that differentiate rival firms from one another and then using these differences as variables for the axes on the map and as the basis for deciding which firm belongs in which strategic group.

Third: The variables used as axes don't have to be either quantitative or continuous; rather, they can be discrete variables or defined in terms of distinct classes and combinations (as turned out to be the case in Figure 3–4).

Fourth: Drawing the sizes of the circles on the map proportional to the combined sales of the firms in each strategic group allows the map to reflect the relative sizes of each strategic group.

Fifth: If more than two good competitive variables can be used as axes for the map, then several maps can be drawn to give different exposures to the competitive positioning relationships present in the industry's structure. Because there need not be one best map for portraying how competing firms are positioned in the market, it is advisable to experiment with different pairs of competitive variables.

The method for constructing a strategic group map and deciding which firms belong in which strategic group can be summarized thus:

- Identify the competitive characteristics that differentiate firms in the industry from one another—typical variables are price/quality range (high, medium, low), geographic coverage (local, regional, national, global), degree of vertical integration (none, partial, full), product-line breadth (wide, narrow), use of distribution channels (one, some, all), and degree of service offered (no frills, limited, full-service).
- Plot the firms on a two-variable map using pairs of these differentiating characteristics.
- Assign firms that fall in about the same strategy space to the same strategic group.
- Draw circles around each strategic group, making the circles proportional to the size of the group's respective share of total industry sales revenues.

---

[21]Ibid., pp. 152–154.

Strategic group analysis adds to the picture of interfirm rivalry in an industry. There are five important things to recognize about strategic groups:[22]

1. Changing market conditions often have different implications for different strategic groups. Sometimes the direction of market changes closes off the viability of one or more strategic groups, prompting competitors in the affected groups to shift to a more favorably situated group. Sometimes changes act to raise/lower the entry barriers into a group, causing competitive pressures in the group to increase/decrease.

2. The profit potential of different strategic groups often varies because of strengths and weaknesses in each group's market position.

3. Entry barriers vary according to the particular strategic group that an entrant seeks to join—entry into some strategic groups is easier than into others.

4. Firms in different strategic groups often enjoy differing degrees of bargaining leverage with suppliers or with customers, or both, and they may also face differing degrees of exposure to competition from substitute products outside the industry.

5. Greater numbers of strategic groups generally intensify industry rivalry, because firms have to compete both within their group and across groups. However, firms in the same strategic group tend to be close rivals, whereas firms in strategic groups that are *far apart* on the map may compete hardly at all. For instance, Tiffany's and K mart both sell jewelry, but they are not competitors to any real degree; in the same way, Timex is not much of a competitive threat to Rolex and Chevrolet is not a close competitor of Lincoln or Mercedes-Benz.

If there are strong indications that certain strategic groups (or specific firms) are trying to change their positions in the strategy space on the map, then attaching arrows to the circles showing the targeted direction adds to the picture of competitive jockeying for position.

Competitor Analysis: Predicting What Moves Which Rivals Are Likely to Make Next

Competitor analysis is important for two reasons. First, without a perceptive understanding of rivals' strategies, the would-be strategist is flying blind. It is foolish to expect to outmaneuver rival companies without knowing a good bit about what strategies various rivals are using, why some rivals have been more successful in the marketplace than others, and what moves which rival firms are likely to make next. Second, because rivals' strategies are highly interdependent (the strategic moves of one rival directly impact the others and may prompt counterstrategies), the positions and success of competitors have direct relevance to choosing one's own best strategy.

As a way of cutting into the task of profiling the strategies of rivals, consider that there are three basic approaches a firm can pursue with respect to *market share:*

---

[22]Ibid., pp. 130, 132–38, and 154–55.

- *Grow and build*—capture a bigger market share by growing *faster* than the industry as a whole; be aggressive in investing in more production capacity so as to support rapid sales increases.
- *Hold and maintain*—protect market share, grow at a rate *equal* to industry average.
- *Surrender share,* with or without a strong fight (maybe in preparation to withdraw from the market later).

And, when it comes to the issue of how to compete there are three generic types of *competitive strategies:*[23]

- Striving to be the low-cost producer (a *cost-leadership strategy*).
- Seeking to differentiate one's product offering in one way or another from the offerings of rivals (a *differentiation strategy*).
- Concentrating on catering to a narrower group of buyers and a limited part of the market, rather than going after the whole market with a something-for-everyone approach (a *focus strategy*).

In analyzing competitor's strategies and trying to anticipate rivals' next moves, one needs to watch for:

- What degree of success each rival is enjoying with its strategy.
- Which competitors are likely to be hurt the most by the impact of industry's driving forces and which ones, if any, may be helped.
- Which competitors are gaining ground, which ones are losing ground, and why.
- Which competitors are locked into continuing with their present strategy and which ones have flexibility to make important strategy changes and new moves.

Doing a thorough job of diagnosing what competitors are up to and predicting what moves they may make next has more aspects, however: (1) finding out whether a rival is under pressure to improve its performance; (2) listening to what rival managers are saying about what they think is going to happen in the industry and about what it will take to be successful; (3) studying the backgrounds and experiences of rival managers for clues about what moves they may be inclined to make; and (4) appraising the rivals' competitive capabilities (their strengths and weaknesses, what they can and can't do).[24]

A Rival's Priorities and Performance Objectives. Doing the detective work to uncover how a competitor's current performance compares with its target performance objectives has several payoffs. It can reveal whether the rival is satisfied with its current performance and, thus, with its current strategy. It can aid in assessing both the likelihood of a shift in strategy and the vigor with which the

---

[23]Porter, *Competitive Strategy,* chap. 2.

[24]The following discussion of these aspects of competitor analysis is based on Porter, *Competitive Strategy,* chap. 3.

rival might respond to new driving forces or strategic moves by other competitors. Some particulars to be alert for include:

1. Is the rival's financial performance satisfactory or is it in trouble? Is it trying to achieve some important new market objective? Does it aspire to industry leadership in pricing or technological innovation or market share or product quality or some other aspect?
2. Is the competitor a subsidiary of a larger corporate parent? If so, is the subsidiary under pressure to contribute more in terms of profitability, growth, and cash flow? Does the parent view this industry as one of its main strategic interests (in which case, it will fight hard to protect/improve its position), or is it comparatively unimportant? To what extent does the parent give its subsidiary financial support?
3. Can the rival meet its profit and other objectives without doing anything different or without launching a major strategic offensive? Can the rival afford to be happy or content with its current performance?

The Rival's Beliefs about the Industry and about Competitive Success. Every firm's management operates on assumptions and beliefs about the industry and about how the business ought to be run. How the managers see their own firm and its situation is often a good barometer of their strategic thinking. The relevant areas to probe here include: What do rival managers believe (based on speeches, advertising claims, what salespeople are telling customers, and so on) about their firm's standing in the marketplace. Is the rival's reputation tightly identified with some competitive aspect (superior service, quality of manufacture, product innovation, breadth of product line, or focus on particular products or market segments) and, if so, will it fight to keep its reputation intact? What are the rival's managers saying about industry trends and future competitive conditions? What views do they have about the strengths and weaknesses of other firms in the industry? Do they use certain consultants, advertising agencies, banks, or other advisors that are known for particular techniques and approaches?

The Backgrounds, Experiences, and Styles of the Senior Managers of Rival Companies. Sometimes important clues about the behavior and strategies of a firm can be gleaned from the personal experiences, philosophies, and styles of its senior-level managers. Hence, while the information may be hard to come by, it is worth exerting an effort to get. The most important areas of inquiry include:

1. What are the work backgrounds of the key managers (accounting, finance, sales, production, R&D) and how likely is it that they lean toward strategies emphasizing their own areas of expertise and experiences?
2. Have the current chief executives of rival companies held their positions for a long time (which may suggest continuation of the same basic strategy)? Do any rivals have new senior-level managers that have been recently brought in from outside the company (which may suggest some changes can be expected)?
3. Is there reason to believe that the actions decided upon by rival managers will be conditioned by some previous major event in their background or experience (a sharp recession, having managed a rapid-growth business, or success in

turning other companies around), or do they hold strongly to some managerial approach or philosophy that is likely to shape what actions they will take?

A Rival's Ability to Compete Effectively.   One of the things that matters most about a rival is the competitive edge it may have and its capacity for competing effectively in the marketplace. Its strengths and weaknesses regarding product line, marketing and selling, dealer distribution network, R&D, engineering, manufacturing, cost and efficiency, financial condition, and managerial competence determine its ability to respond to competitive moves or to deal with industry driving forces. In assessing a rival's competitive advantages and overall strength, attention has to be paid to what it is best and worst at doing, what flexibility it has to adapt to a change in competitive conditions, and why it is doing better/worse than other rivals. Most important, though, is an appraisal of the degree to which it is likely to be a major factor in the marketplace over the long haul and why its market standing is likely to increase or decrease.

Predicting a Competitor's Next Moves—The Payoff of Competitor Analysis.   Gaining useful answers to the kinds of questions and issues posed above is not a simple, short-run task. Compiling a profile of a rival's true competitive strength and resources is a task where the relevant information comes in bits and pieces, and it takes both time and hard work to get a real "feel" for both a competitor's situation and how its management thinks. But if the task is done systematically, the result can be a good ability to predict:

- How a rival will respond to changes in market trends or economic conditions.
- How satisfied a rival is with its present market position and profitability and, thus, whether it is likely to initiate a fresh strategic move.
- The most likley moves a rival will make, given its strategic objectives, its management approach, and its competitive strengths and weaknesses.
- How vulnerable a rival is to new strategic moves by other industry participants.
- How much a rival can be pushed before it will be provoked into retaliation.
- The meaning and intent of a rival's new strategic move and how seriously it should be taken.

Such predictive ability is immensely valuable in drawing conclusions about the next round of competitive moves, who is vulnerable to attack and who is not, and one's own best time, place, and method for fighting it out with competitors.

Pinpointing the Key Factors for Competitive Success

Key success factors (KSFs) consist of the *three* or *four* really major determinants of financial and competitive success in a particular industry. Key success factors have to do with the things all firms in the industry must concentrate on doing well, the specific kinds of skills and competence needed to compete successfully, and which functional-area aspects (for example, technical expertise, manufacturing efficiency, advertising cleverness, and product-innovation skills) are the most crucial and why.

Identification of key success factors is a top-priority industry and competitive analysis consideration. At the very least, management needs to know the industry well enough to pinpoint what the key factors for competitive success are; at the most, KSFs can serve as *the cornerstones* upon which business strategy is built—frequently, a company can win a competitive advantage by concentrating on being distinctively better than rivals when it comes to one or more of the industry's key success factors.

While it would be nice to be able to generalize about what an industry's key success factors are, the truth is that they vary from industry to industry and even from time to time within the same industry as economic characteristics, driving forces, and competitive conditions change. And even where two industries may have some of the same general kinds of key success factors, the specifics attached to each factor can differ greatly, as well as can their rank in overall importance. One or two key success factors may well be more important than the rest—there's nothing that says all three or four key success factors have to be equally important, only that, as a group, they are more important than other competitive considerations.

To see the variability of key success factors across industries consider the following examples. In beer, the keys are utilization of brewing capacity (to keep manufacturing costs low), a strong network of wholesale distributors (to gain access to as many retail outlets as possible), and clever advertising (to induce beer drinkers to buy a particular brand and thereby pull beer sales through the established wholesale/retail channels). In apparel manufacturing, the keys are fashion design (to create buyer appeal) and manufacturing efficiency (to keep selling prices competitive). In industries where the cost of shipping manufactured goods is relatively high, the keys are having plants located close to end-use customers and having the ability to market plant output within economical shipping distances (regional market share proves far more crucial than national share).

Table 3–3 provides a shopping list of the most common types of key success factors. However, rarely are there more than three or four key success factors in any one industry at any one time. Strategic analysts, therefore, have to resist the temptation to include factors that have only minor importance on their list of key success factors—the purpose of identifying key success factors is to make judgments about what things are relatively more important to competitive success and what things are of less importance. To compile a list of everything that matters even a little bit defeats the purpose of training management's eyes on the very things that are truly crucial to long-term competitive success.

Drawing Conclusions about Overall Industry Attractiveness

While each of the preceding analytical steps has added something new to the picture of the industry and competitive environment, the role of this final step is to review the overall situation and develop reasoned conclusions above the relative attractiveness or unattractiveness of the industry, both nearterm and longterm. An assessment that the industry is very attractive typically calls for some kind of an

TABLE 3–3
An Illustrative List of Possible Key Success Factors

Technology-Related KSFs
- Scientific research expertise (important in such fields as pharmaceuticals, medicine, space exploration, telecommunications, energy, computers, and other high-tech industries).
- Production process innovation capability.
- Product innovation capability.
- Recognition by customers as a technological leader.

Manufacturing-Related KSFs
- Ability to achieve lower-cost operating efficiencies.
- Ability to improve quality of manufacture (fewer defects, product failures, need for repairs).
- High utilization of fixed assets (important in capital intensive / high fixed-cost industries).
- Cheap access to key raw material inputs.
- Low-cost plant locations (in areas where labor costs are low or in areas where shipping costs can be held to a minimum).
- Access to adequate supplies of skilled labor.
- Ability to use nonunion labor.
- Being able to capture manufacturing economies of scale.
- Being able to capitalize on learning curve / experience curve effects.
- Recruiting very qualified, highly productive employees.
- Being vertically integrated backward into the production of important raw material / component inputs.
- Low-cost product design and engineering.

Distribution-Related KSFs
- Building a strong network of wholesale distributors.
- Gaining ample space on retailer shelves and displays.
- Retaining the loyalty of distributors / dealers.
- Having company-owned retail outlets.
- Having low forward channel distribution costs.

Marketing-Related KSFs
- Having a well-trained, highly effective sales force.
- Offering excellent after-the sale service.
- Providing technical assistance to buyers.
- Prompt delivery.
- Accurate filling of buyer orders (few back orders or mistakes).
- Clever advertising.
- Reputation for quality.
- Ability to come up with product innovations (something new or better, extra features, more options).
- Breadth of product line and product selection.
- Merchandising skills.
- A reputation for being customer-oriented and attentive to customer needs and preferences.
- Attractive styling / packaging.
- Customer guarantees and warranties.

Other Types of KSFs
- Favorable image / reputation with buyers.
- Recognition as a leader.
- Convenient locations (especially important in many retailing businesses).
- Pleasant, courteous employees.
- Access to financial capital (important in newly emerging industries with high degrees of business risk and in capital intensive industries).
- Patent protection.
- Overall low cost (not just in manufacturing).

aggressive, expansion-oriented strategic approach, whereas if the industry and competitive situation is judged relatively unattractive many companies will have to consider strategies to protect their profitability and the weakest companies may seriously have to consider exit from the industry.

The factors to be especially alert for in drawing conclusions about industry attractiveness are:

- The industry's growth potential.
- Whether the industry will be favorably or unfavorably impacted by the prevailing driving forces.
- Potential for the entry/exit of major firms (probable entry reduces attractiveness to existing firms; the exit of a major firm or several weak firms opens up market share growth opportunities for the remaining firms).
- The stability/dependability of demand (as affected by seasonality, the business cycle, the volatility of consumer preferences, inroads from substitutes, and the like).
- Whether competitive forces will become stronger or weaker.
- Which strategic groups are most/least favorably situated and the kinds of strategic moves likely to be forthcoming from industry participants.
- The severity of problems/issues confronting the industry as a whole.
- The degrees of risk and uncertainty in the industry's future.
- Whether the industry's overall profit prospects are favorable or unfavorable.

Aside from these industrywide considerations, it is important to realize that an industry that is relatively unattractive overall can still be very attractive to a particular company, especially one that is already favorably situated in the industry or to an outsider with the resources to acquire an existing company and turn it into a major industry contender. Appraising industry attractiveness from the standpoint of a particular company in the industry means looking at the following *additional aspects:*

- The company's competitive position in the industry and whether its position is likely to grow stronger or weaker (being a well-entrenched leader in an otherwise lackluster industry can still produce good profitability).
- The company's potential to capitalize on the vulnerabilities of weaker rivals (thereby converting an unattractive *industry* situation into a potentially interesting *company* opportunity).
- Whether the company is somewhat insulated from, or else able to defend against, the factors that make the industry as a whole unattractive.
- Whether continued participation in this industry adds importantly to the firm's ability to be successful in other industries in which it has business interests.

The conclusions drawn about the attractiveness of the industry and competitive situation should, obviously enough, have a major bearing on a company's strategic options and ultimate choice of strategy.

INDUSTRY AND COMPETITIVE ANALYSIS CHECKLIST

Table 3–4, provides a blank *format* for conducting industry and competitive analysis. It incorporates the analytical steps we have covered in this chapter and, if completed consciously, provides a readily digested bottom-line analysis of the industry and competitive environment.

Two things need to be kept in mind in doing industry and competitive analysis. First, the task of analyzing an industry's overall situation cannot be reduced to a mechanical, formula-like process in which facts and data are plugged in and definitive conclusions come pouring out. There can be several appealing scenarios about how the industry will evolve and what future competitive conditions will be like. For this reason, strategic analysis always leaves room for differences of opinion about "how all the factors add up" and "how industry and competitive conditions will evolve." However, while no strategy analysis methodology can guarantee a single diagnosis and strategy prescription, it doesn't make sense to discard strategic analysis and depend solely on a gut feeling and an ability to react later if need be. Managers become better strategists when they know what analytical questions to pose, how to hunt for answers with the aid of the available situation analysis techniques, and are skilled in reading the clues about which way the winds of industry and competitive change are blowing. It is because each industry situation produces its own set of analytical conclusions that we have concentrated in this chapter on explaining concepts and analytical techniques, describing the important kinds of considerations, and suggesting the right questions to ask.

The second perspective to keep in mind about business-level strategy analysis is that, in real-word practice, the process is incremental and ongoing, the result of gradually accumulated understanding and continuous rethinking and retesting of how all the relevant factors "add up." Sweeping industry and competitive analyses need to be done periodically but, in the interim, there is a need to update and reexamine the picture as events unfold. Managerial sizeups of a situation and the path leading to strategic decisions are usually the products of a *gradual* buildup of clues and signals that important changes in the external and internal environments are occurring, a *gradual* documentation and understanding of these changes and their implications, and gradually made conclusions about what strategic path to take.

SUGGESTED READINGS

Ghemawat, Pankaj. "Building Strategy on the Experience Curve." *Harvard Business Review* 64, no. 2 (March–April 1985), pp. 143–49

Linneman, Robert E., and Harold E. Klein. "Using Scenarios in Strategic Decision Making." *Business Horizons* 28, no. 1 (January–February 1985), pp. 64–74.

Ohmae, Kenichi. *The Mind of the Strategist.* New York: Penguin, 1983, chap. 3, 6, 7, and 13.

Porter, Michael E. "How Competitive Forces Shape Strategy." *Harvard Business Review* 57, no. 2 (March–April 1979), pp. 137–45.

———*Competitive Strategy: Techniques for Analyzing Industries and Competitors.* New York: Free Press, 1980.

———*Competitive Advantage.* New York: Free Press, 1985, chap. 2.

South, Stephen E. "Competitive Advantage: The Cornerstone of Strategic Thinking." *Journal of Business Strategy* 1, no. 4 (Spring 1981), pp. 15–25.

TABLE 3-4
Industry and Competitive Analysis Summary Profile

1. **CHIEF BUSINESS AND ECONOMIC CHARACTERISTICS OF THE INDUSTRY ENVIRONMENT** (market growth, geographic scope, industry structure, scale economies, experience curve effects, capital requirements, and so on)

2. **DRIVING FORCES**

3. **COMPETITION ANALYSIS**
   - **Rivalry among competing sellers** (a strong, moderate, or weak force/weapons of competition)

   - **Threat of potential entry** (a strong, moderate, or weak force/assessment of entry barriers)

   - **Competition from substitutes** (a strong, moderate, or weak force/why)

   - **Power of suppliers** (a strong, moderate, or weak force/why)

   - **Power of customers** (a strong, moderate, or weak force/why)

4. **COMPETITIVE POSITION OF MAJOR COMPANIES/STRATEGIC GROUPS**
   - **Favorably positioned/why**

   - **Unfavorably positioned/why**

5. **COMPETITOR ANALYSIS**
   - **Strategic approaches/predicted moves of key competitors**

   - **Who to watch and why**

6. **KEY SUCCESS FACTORS**

7. **INDUSTRY PROSPECTS AND OVERALL ATTRACTIVENESS**
   - **Factors making the industry attractive**

   - **Factors making the industry unattractive**

   - **Special industry issues/problems**

   - **Profit outlook (favorable/unfavorable)**

4

Company Situation Analysis

The secret of success is to be ready for opportunity when it comes.

Disraeli

The distinctive competence of an organization is more than what it can do; it is what it can do particularly well.

Kenneth R. Andrews

In the last chapter, we explored the elements of industry and competitive analysis; the purpose was to introduce analytical approaches that exposed those features of a company's *external* environment bearing most heavily on what strategy to follow. In this chapter, we present techniques for diagnosing a company's situation and how the particulars of its situation affect its best choice of a strategy.

THE ELEMENTS OF COMPANY SITUATION ANALYSIS

Analyzing a company's overall situation from a strategy-making perspective has five elements:

1. Assessing how well the present strategy is working (as indicated by the company's recent strategic performance) and how well it matches the anticipated industry and competitive environment.
2. A SWOT analysis—an appraisal of the firm's internal strengths and weaknesses, the market opportunities it has, and the external threats it faces.
3. An examination of the firm's cost position relative to rival companies.
4. An assessment of the firm's competitive position and competitive strength (probing especially into reasons why the firm is gaining ground, losing ground, or holding its own) and how the firm matches up against rivals on each of the industry's key success factors.
5. A determination of the particular strategic issues and problems which the company needs to address.

Let's look at these elements one by one in some detail, concentrating on the techniques of analysis and on the implications of the results for choosing a strategy.

How Well the Present Strategy Is Working

In evaluating how well a company's present strategy is working, one needs to start with an identification of just what the strategy is. Figure 2–3 in Chapter 2 pinpoints the key components of business strategy. The most important business strategy component is how the company is trying to compete (whether it is striving for low-cost leadership, trying to differentiate itself from rivals in some particular way, or focusing narrowly on certain specific customer groups and market niches). The company's basic competitive approach is undergirded by specific functional-area support strategies in production, marketing, finance, human resources, and so on; these need to be identified and understood as well. In addition, the company may have initiated some recent strategic moves (for instance, a price cut or stepped-up advertising or entry into a new geographic area or merger with a competitor) that are integral to its strategy and that aim at securing a particular competitive advantage or improved competitive position, or both.

It is not enough, though, to merely identify the different parts of a company's strategy. One must *understand what the rationale is* for each piece of the strategy— for each move and each strategic approach. And then the analyst must see whether and how the different parts of business strategy fit together. Normally, a strategy doesn't work well, or at least as well as it might, unless its parts are mutually reinforcing and unless functional strategies are strongly supportive of the overall business-level strategy.

While it is valuable to evaluate the logical consistency of a strategy, to make judgments about how well-formulated a strategy is, and to render opinions about whether this or that part of the strategy is flawed, the best evidence of just how well a company is working comes from looking at a company's recent strategic performance. The most obvious indicators of strategic performance include (1) whether the firm's market share is rising or falling, (2) whether the firm's profit margins are increasing or decreasing and how big the company's profit margins are relative to rival firms, (3) trends in the firm's net profits and its return on investment, (4) whether the firm's sales are growing faster or slower than the market as a whole, and (5) whether the firm's competitive position is improving or slipping.

The signs of past strategic success or failure are fairly easy to spot. What is usually not so obvious is how well the present strategy is matched to the expected future industry and competitive environment. There are several things to consider:

- Whether the present strategy is responsive to the industry's driving forces and the strategic issues confronting the industry.
- How closely the present strategy is geared to the industry's *future* key success factors.
- How good a defense the present strategy offers against the five competitive forces—the future ones, not so much the past or present ones.
- Whether the firm's functional area support strategies appear adequate for the road ahead.

While these inquiries open the door on where a company currently stands, a broader and deeper probe into its situation is needed.

SWOT Analysis

SWOT is an acronym for a company's **S**trengths, **W**eaknesses, **O**pportunities, and **T**hreats. A SWOT analysis consists of compiling and sizing up a firm's internal strengths and weaknesses and its external opportunities and threats. It is an easy-to-use tool for quickly coming up with an *overview* of a firm's strategic situation. A SWOT analysis introduces the basic point that strategy must produce a strong fit between a company's internal capability (its strengths and weaknesses) and its external situation (reflected, in part, by its opportunities and threats).

Identifying Strengths and Weaknesses. Figure 4–1 provides a list of things to look for in identifying a company's internal strengths and weaknesses. A *strength* is something a company is good at doing or a characteristic the company has that gives it an important capability—in other words, a strength can be a skill, a competence, a particular organizational resource or asset, or something the company has done which puts it in a position of market advantage (like having a better product, stronger name recognition, superior technology, or better customer service). A *weakness* is something a company lacks or does poorly (in comparison to others) or a condition that puts it at a disadvantage.

Once a company's internal strengths and weaknesses have been identified, then the two lists have to be carefully evaluated. Some strengths are more important

FIGURE 4–1
SWOT Analysis—What to Look for

Potential Internal Strengths	*Potential Internal Weaknesses*
A distinctive competence.	No clear strategic direction.
Adequate financial resources.	Obsolete facilities.
Good competitive skills.	Subpar profitability because . . . .
Well thought of by buyers.	Lack of managerial depth and talent.
An acknowledged market leader.	Missing some key skills or competences.
Well-conceived functional area strategies.	Poor track record in implementing strategy.
Access to economies of scale.	Plagued with internal operating problems.
Insulated (at least somewhat) from strong competitive pressures.	Falling behind in R & D.
	Too narrow a product line.
Proprietary technology.	Weak market image.
Cost advantages.	Weak distribution network.
Better advertising campaigns.	Below-average marketing skills.
Product innovation skills.	Unable to finance needed changes in strategy.
Proven management.	Higher overall unit costs relative to key competitors.
Ahead on experience curve.	Other?
Other?	
Potential External Opportunities	*Potential External Threats*
Serve additional customer groups.	Likely entry of new competitors.
Enter new markets or segments.	Rising sales of substitute products.
Expand product line to meet broader range of customer needs.	Slower market growth.
	Adverse government policies.
Diversify into related products.	Growing competitive pressures.
Add complementary products.	Vulnerability to recession and business cycle.
Vertical integration.	Growing bargaining power of customers or suppliers.
Ability to move to better strategic group.	Changing buyer needs and tastes.
Complacency among rival firms.	Adverse demographic changes.
Faster market growth.	Other?
Other?	

than others, because they count for more in determining performance, in forming a strategy, and in competing successfully. Likewise, some weaknesses can prove fatal, while others might not matter much or can be easily remedied.

From a strategy-making perspective, a company's strengths are important, because they can serve as the cornerstones on which strategy and competitive advantage can be built; there's something to be said for grounding strategy on a company's strongest skills, competence, and resources. If a company doesn't have the strengths it needs to craft an attractive strategy, then management must move quickly to build the required capabilities. At the same time, a good strategy necessarily needs to aim at correcting those weaknesses that make a company vulnerable or that disqualify it from pursuing an attractive opportunity. The point here is simple: *An organization's strategy must be well suited to what it is capable of doing.* Achieving this condition means determining a company's strengths and weaknesses and then deciding what strategic actions need to be taken to achieve an effective match with strategy.

Because of the strategy-making relevance of organizational strengths, weaknesses, and resource capabilities, it makes sense to consider whether a company has or can build a distinctive competence. A distinctive competence is something a company does especially well in comparison to its competitors. In practice, there are many possible types of distinctive competence: excelling in the manufacture of a quality product, offering customers superior service after the sale, finding innovative ways to achieve low-cost production efficiency and then offering customers the attractiveness of a lower price, being better at developing innovative new products that buyers consider a step ahead of the performance of rivals' products, designing more clever advertising and sales promotion techniques, having the best technological expertise, being better at working with customers on new applications and uses of the product, having the best network of dealers and distributors, and so on. *The importance of distinctive competence to strategy formation rests with (1) the unique capability it gives an organization in going after a particular market opportunity, (2) the competitive edge it may give a firm in the marketplace, and (3) the potential for using the distinctive competence as the cornerstone of strategy.* It is always easier to develop competitive advantage in a market when a firm has a distinctive competence in one of the key requirements for market success, where rival companies do not have offsetting competence, and where rivals are not able to match the competence without the expenditure of much time and money.

Identifying Opportunities and Threats. Figure 4–1 also displays some of the things to be alert for in identifying a company's external opportunities and threats. Market opportunity is virtually certain to be a big factor in shaping a company's strategy. Unless a company is positioned to pursue a given opportunity, and unless the opportunity is interesting enough to pursue, it usually makes more sense to choose some other strategic course. However, there is an important distinction between *industry opportunities* and *company opportunities*. Not every company in an industry is as well positioned to pursue each opportunity that exists in the industry—some are always better situated than others and some may be hopelessly out of contention altogether. *The prevailing and emerging industry opportunities that are likely to be most relevant to a particular company are those* *where the company in question will be able to enjoy some kind of competitive advantage.*

Very often, certain factors in a company's external environment pose *threats* to its well-being. These externally imposed threats may stem from the emergence of cheaper technologies, the advent of new substitute products, adverse economic trends, restrictive government action, changing consumer values and lifestyles, projections of natural resource depletion, unfavorable demographic shifts, new sources of strong competition, and the like (see Figure 4–1). Identifying threats is important, not only because they affect the attractiveness of a company's situation but also because they drive the forming of business-level strategy. If strategy is to be adequately matched to a company's situation, then it must (1) be aimed at pursuing those opportunities best suited to the company's capabilities and (2) provide a defense against external threats.

All this says unequivocally that SWOT analysis is more than an exercise in making four lists. It is essential to evaluate the strength, weakness, opportunity, and threat listings in terms of what conclusions can be drawn about the company's situation and what the implications are for strategy. Some of the pertinent questions to consider, once the SWOT listings have been compiled, are:

- Does the company have any internal strengths around which an attractive strategy can be built? In particular, does the company have a distinctive competence that can produce a competitive edge?

- Do the company's weaknesses make it competitively vulnerable and do they disqualify the company from pursuing certain opportunities? Which weaknesses does strategy need to be aimed at correcting?

- Which opportunities does the company have the skills and resources to pursue with a real chance of success? *Remember:* Opportunity without the means to capture it is an illusion. An organization's strengths and weaknesses make it better suited to going after some opportunities and not after others. An objective appraisal of what a firm can do and what it shouldn't try to do always needs to guide the choice of strategy.

- What threats should management be worried most about and what strategic moves does management need to consider in formulating a good defense?

Strategic-Cost Analysis and Activity-Cost Chains: Tools for Assessing a Company's Relative-Cost Position

One of the most telling signs of a company's situation is its cost position relative to competitors. Cost comparisons are especially critical in a commodity-product industry where price competition typically dominates and lower-cost companies have the upper hand over higher-cost companies. But even in industries where products are differentiated and competition is based on something besides price, competing companies have to keep costs *in line with* rivals or else risk putting their competitive position in jeopardy.

Competitors do not necessarily, or even usually, incur the same costs in supplying their products to end-users. The disparities in costs among rival producers can stem from:

- Differences in the prices paid for raw materials, components parts, energy, and other items purchased from suppliers.
- Differences in basic technology and in the age of plants and equipment. Because rival companies have usually invested in plants and key pieces of equipment at different points in time, they enter into competition with facilities having somewhat different technological efficiencies and different fixed costs. Older facilities built when technology was less developed are typically less efficient; but if they were constructed in a time when it took less money to put them in place or if they were acquired used at bargain prices, they *may* still be reasonably cost competitive with modern facilities costing more to build. Whether older plants having lower fixed-investment costs are, overall, cost competitive with newer plants having higher fixed-investment costs depends on the trade-off between the lower depreciation and other fixed costs of older plants and the increased operating efficiency of newer plants.
- Differences in internal operating costs, owing to the economies of scale associated with different size plants, learning and experience curve effects, different wage rates, different productivity levels, different administrative overhead expenses, different tax rates, and the like.
- Differences in rival firms' exposure to rates of inflation and changes in foreign exchange rates (as can occur in global industries, where competitors have plants located in different nations).
- Differences in marketing costs, sales and promotion expenditures, and advertising expenses.
- Differences in inbound transportation costs and outbound shipping costs.
- Differences in forward channel distribution costs (the costs and markups added on by distributors, wholesalers, and retailers in performing their function of getting the product from the point of manufacture into the hands of end-users).

Plainly enough, for a company to be competitively successful, its costs must be in line with those of rival producers, after taking into account, of course, that product differentiation creates justification for some cost disparity. The need to be cost competitive is not so stringent as to *require* the costs of every firm in the industry to be *equal* but, as a rule, the more a firm's costs are above those of the low-cost producers the more vulnerable its market position becomes. Given the numerous opportunities for cost disparities among competing companies, a company must be alert to how its costs compare with rivals' costs. This is where *strategic-cost analysis* comes in.

Strategic-cost analysis focuses on a firm's relative-cost position vis-à-vis its rivals. The primary analytical tool of strategic-cost analysis is the construction of a multistage *activity-cost chain* showing the makeup of costs all the way from raw materials purchase to the end price paid by ultimate customers.[1] The activity-cost

---

[1]The ins and outs of strategic-cost analysis are discussed at greater length in Michael E. Porter, *Competitive Advantage* (New York: Free Press, 1985), chap. 2. What follows is a distilled adaptation of the approach pioneered by Porter.

chain, thus, goes beyond a company's own internal-cost structure and includes the build up of cost (and, thus, the "value-added") at each stage in the whole industry chain of producing the product and distributing it to final-users, as shown in Figure 4–2. Constructing an activity-cost chain for all of an industry's principal stages is especially revealing to a manufacturing firm, because its overall ability to furnish end-users with its product at a competitive price can easily depend on cost factors originating either *backward* in the suppliers' portion of the activity-cost chain or *forward* in the distribution channel portion of the chain.

The task of constructing an activity-cost chain is not easy. It requires breaking a firm's own historical cost-accounting data out into several principal-cost categories and also developing cost estimates for the backward and forward channel portions of getting the product to the end-user as well. In addition, it requires estimating the same cost elements for one's rivals and estimating their cost chains—an advanced art in competitive intelligence in itself. But despite the tediousness of the task and the imprecision of some of the estimates, the payoff in exposing the cost competitiveness of one's position and the attendant strategic alternatives makes it a valuable analytical tool. Illustration Capsule 11 shows a simplified activity-cost chain comparison of the cost competitiveness of U.S. steel producers and Japanese steel producers over a 20-year period. The shifts in the several cost components over the period are dramatic. Some resulted from relative shifts in inputs prices, which built up gradually over time, but technological changes in input requirements and labor productivity were also at work.

While the example in Illustration Capsule 11 shows the relative-cost position of firms in one country versus those in another, the most important application of the activity-cost technique is to expose how a particular firm's cost position compares with those of its rivals. What is needed is company-versus-company cost estimates for a given product. Plainly, the size of a company's cost advantage/disadvantage can vary from item to item in the product line, from customer group to customer group (if different distribution channels are used), and from plant to plant (if plants employ different technologies or if plants are located in widely different geographic locations—different countries, for example).

Looking again at Figure 4–2, observe there are three main areas in the cost chain where important differences in the *relative* costs of competing firms can occur: in suppliers' part of the cost chain, in their own respective activity segments, or in the forward channel portion of the chain. To the extent that the reasons for a firm's lack of cost competitiveness lie either in the backward or forward sections of the cost chain, then its job of reestablishing cost competitiveness may well have to extend beyond its own in-house operations. When a firm's cost disadvantage lies principally in the backward end of the activity-cost chain, four strategic options quickly emerge for consideration:

- Negotiate more-favorable prices with suppliers.
- Integrate backward to gain control over material costs.
- Try to use lower-priced substitute inputs.
- Search out sources of savings in inbound shipping and materials logistics costs.

FIGURE 4–2
Generic Activity-Cost Chain for a Representative Industry Situation

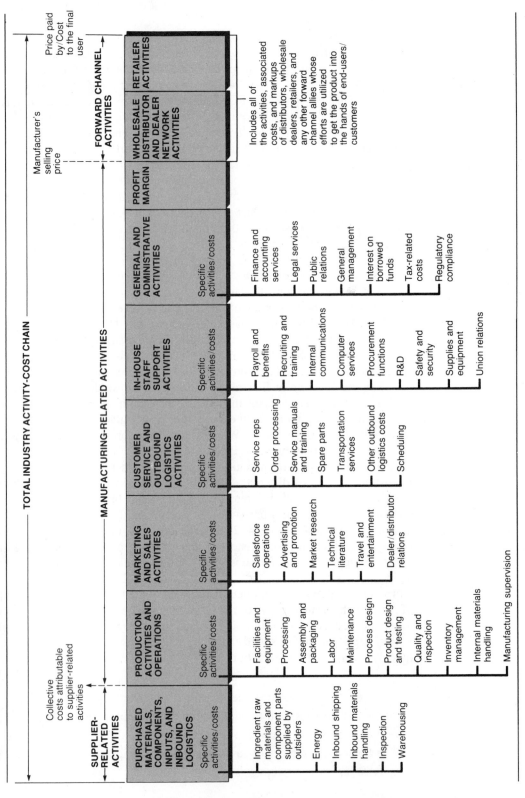

ILLUSTRATION CAPSULE 11

Activity-Cost Chains for U.S. Steel Producers versus Japanese Steel Producers, 1956 and 1976

Cost Chain Elements	Per Ton Cost for Cold-Rolled Sheet Steel, 1956		Net Cost Advantage 1956	ACTIVITIES	Net Cost Advantage 1976	Per Ton Cost for Cold-Rolled Sheet Steel, 1976		Cost Chain Elements
	Typical U.S. Producer	Typical Japanese Producer				Typical U.S. Producer	Typical Japanese Producer	
Coking coal	$ 12.02	$ 19.90	$ 7.88 (U.S.)	**Purchased inputs and basic materials**	$10.70 (Japan)	$ 52.15	$ 41.45	Coking coal
Other energy	9.65	12.35	2.70 (U.S.)		8.76 (Japan)	30.25	21.49	Other energy
Scrap steel	17.80	34.75	16.95 (U.S.)		0.95 (U.S.)	20.80	21.75	Scrap steel
Iron ore	16.70	26.17	9.47 (U.S.)		20.30 (Japan)	47.90	27.60	Iron ore
Subtotal	$ 56.17	$ 93.17	$37.00 (U.S.)		$38.81 (Japan)	$151.10	$112.29	Subtotal
Manufacturing labor	$ 54.07	$ 28.80	$25.27 (Japan)	**Manufacturing operations and administrative support**	$90.66 (Japan)	$142.93	$ 52.25	Manufacturing labor
Capital charges for facilities and all other operating costs	9.80	31.17	21.37 (U.S.)		7.93 (U.S.)	55.95	63.88	Capital charges for facilities and all other operating costs
Profit margin	5.00	4.00	1.00 (Japan)		1.40 (Japan)	4.90	3.50	Profit margin
Subtotal	$ 68.87	$ 63.97	$ 4.90 (Japan)		$84.15 (Japan)	$203.78	$119.63	Subtotal
Transocean shipping import duties	0	$ 35.69	$35.69 (U.S.)	**Distribution and forward channel activities**	$36.36 (U.S.)	0	$ 36.36	Transocean shipping import duties
Price paid by U.S. end-user	$125.04	$192.83	$67.79 (U.S.)		$86.60 (Japan)	$354.88	$268.28	Price paid by U.S. end-user

SOURCES: Compiled by the author from data in U.S. Federal Trade Commission, *The United States Steel Industry and Its International Rivals: Trends and Factors Determining International Competitiveness* (Washington, D.C.: U.S. Government Printing Office, 1978).; and Robert W. Crandall, *The U.S. Steel Industry in Recurrent Crisis* (Washington, D.C.: Brookings Institution, 1981).

115

- Try to make up the difference by initiating cost savings elsewhere in the overall cost chain.

When a firm's cost disadvantage occurs in the forward end of the cost chain, there are three corrective options:

- Push for more favorable terms with distributors and other forward channel allies.
- Change to a more economical distribution strategy, including the possibility of forward integration.
- Try to make up the difference by initiating cost savings earlier in the cost chain.

When the source of relative-cost disadvantage is internal, five options for restoring cost parity emerge:

- Initiate internal budget-tightening measures aimed at using less inputs to generate the desired output (cost-cutting retrenchment).
- Invest in cost-saving technological improvements.
- Innovate around the troublesome cost components as new investments are made in plant and equipment.
- Redesign the product to achieve cost reduction.
- Try to make up the internal-cost disadvantage by achieving cost savings in the backward and forward portions of the cost chain.

The construction of activity-cost chains is a valuable tool in company situation analysis because of what is revealed about a firm's cost competitiveness. Examining the makeup of a company's own activity-cost chain and comparing it against the chains of important rival firms indicates who has how much of a cost advantage/disadvantage and pinpoints which cost components are the source of the cost advantage or disadvantage. Such information then becomes the basis for forming strategy.

Competitive Position Assessment

In addition to the cost-competitiveness diagnosis that activity-cost chain analysis provides, a more broad-based assessment needs to be made of a company's overall competitive position and competitive strength. Particular elements to single out for evaluation are (1) how strongly the firm holds its present competitive position, (2) whether the firm's position can be expected to improve or deteriorate if the present strategy is continued (allowing for fine tuning), (3) how the firm ranks *relative to key rivals* on each important measure of competitive strength and industry key success factor (ratings of stronger, weaker, or equal may be adequate), (4) the net competitive advantage(s) the firm has, and (5) the firm's ability to defend its position in light of industry driving forces, competitive pressures, and the anticipated moves of rivals.

Figure 4–3 contains a checklist of factors that often come into play in determining whether a firm's competitive position is improving or slipping. Again,

FIGURE 4–3
Assessing a Company's Competitive Position

*(INPUT
OUTPUT
REWARDS)*

Signs of Competitive Strength	Signs of Competitive Weakness
• Important distinctive competences.	• No really good competitive advantage.
• Strong market share (or a leading market share).	• Losing ground to rival firms.
• A pacesetting or distinctive strategy.	• Below-average growth in revenues.
• Growing customer base and customer loyalty.	• Short on financial resources.
	• A slipping reputation with customers.
• Above-average market visibility.	• Trailing in product development.
• In a favorably situated strategic group.	• In a strategic group that is destined to lose ground.
• Concentrating on fastest-growing market segments.	• Weak in areas where there is the most market potential.
• Strongly differentiated products.	• Weaker distribution access.
• Cost advantages.	• A higher-cost producer.
• Above-average profit margins.	• Too small to be a major factor in the marketplace.
• Above-average marketing skills.	• No real distinctive competences.
• Above-average technological and innovational capability.	• Not in good position to deal with emerging threats.
• A creative, entrepreneurially alert management.	• Weak product quality.
• In position to capitalize on opportunities.	

more is needed than just a listing of the signs of improvement and slippage. The important thing is to assess just how strong the company's position is, what is causing it to change, and to begin to think through what strategic actions it will take to improve the company's position.

The really telling part of this aspect of company situation analysis, however, comes in formally appraising the firm's competitive strength versus key rivals on each key success factor and important competitive variable. Much of the information for this piece of company analysis comes from what has been done before. Industry analysis reveals the key success factors. Competitor analysis provides a basis for judging the strengths and capabilities of key rivals. *Step one* is to make a list of key success factors and any other relevant measure of competitive strength. *Step two* is to rate the firm and its key rivals on each factor; rating scales from 1 to 5 or 1 to 10 can be used (or ratings of stronger $(+)$, weaker $(-)$, and about equal $(=)$ may suffice, especially if the information base is thin). *Step three* is to judge the company's overall competitive strength, noting specifically where the company is strongest and weakest and determining how much of a competitive edge, if any, the company has.

Table 4–1 provides two examples of competitive strength assessments. The first one employs an unweighted rating scale; with unweighted ratings, each key success factor/competitive strength measure is assumed to be equally important. The sum of the ratings assigned on each measure give an overall strength rating. However, it is conceptually stronger to use a weighted rating system in recognition of the fact that the different measures are not likely to be *equally* important determinants of competitive strength. In a commodity-product industry, for instance, being the low-cost supplier is far and away the biggest determinant of competitive strength whereas in an industry with strong product differentiation, the most significant

TABLE 4–1
Illustrations of Unweighted and Weighted Competitive Strength Assessments

A. Sample of an Unweighted Competitive Strength Assessment

Key Success Factor/Strength Measure	ABC Co.	Rival 1	Rival 2	Rival 3	Rival 4
Quality/product performance	8	5	9	5	6
Reputation/image	8	7	10	5	6
Raw material access/cost	5	5	6	3	4
Technological skills	8	5	5	3	4
Advertising effectiveness	9	7	10	5	6
Marketing/distribution	9	7	9	5	6
Financial resources	5	4	7	3	4
Relative-cost position	5	9	6	3	4
Ability to compete on price	5	9	7	3	4
Unweighted overall strength rating	62	58	69	35	44

Rating scale: 1 = weakest; 10 = strongest.

B. Sample of a Weighted Competitive Strength Assessment

Key Success Factor/Strength Measure	Weight	ABC Co.	Rival 1	Rival 2	Rival 3	Rival 4
Quality/product performance	0.10	8/0.80	5/0.50	9/0.90	5/0.50	6/0.60
Reputation/image	0.10	8/0.80	7/0.70	10/1.00	5/0.50	6/0.60
Raw material access/cost	0.05	5/0.25	5/0.25	6/0.30	3/0.15	4/0.20
Technological skills	0.05	8/0.40	5/0.25	5/0.25	3/0.15	4/0.20
Manufacturing capability	0.05	9/0.45	7/0.35	10/0.50	5/0.25	6/0.30
Marketing/distribution	0.05	9/0.45	7/0.35	9/0.45	5/0.25	6/0.30
Financial strength	0.10	5/0.50	4/0.40	7/0.70	3/0.30	4/0.40
Relative-cost position	0.25	5/1.25	9/2.25	6/1.50	3/0.75	4/1.00
Ability to compete on price	0.25	5/1.25	9/2.25	7/1.75	3/0.75	4/1.00
Sum of weights	1.00					
Weighted overall strength rating		6.15	7.30	7.35	3.60	4.60

Rating scale: 1 = weakest; 10 = strongest.

measures of competitive strength may be brand awareness, amount of advertising, reputation for quality, and distribution capability.

The procedure for using a weighted rating system involves assigning each relevant measure of competitive strength a weight based on its perceived importance in influencing who wins and who loses in the industry's competitive arena. The largest weight could be as high as 0.75 (maybe even higher) in situations where one particular competitive variable is overwhelmingly decisive in determining a company's ability to be competitively successful. Lesser competitive-strength indicators can carry weights of 0.05 or 0.10. However the weights are distributed across the competitive-strength measures on which the companies are being rated, *the sum of the weights must add up to 1.0*. Weighted-strength ratings are then calculated by deciding how a company stacks up on each strength measure (using the 1 to 5 or 1 to 10 rating scale) and then multiplying the assigned rating by the assigned weight (a rating score of 4 times a weight of 0.20 gives a weighted rating of 0.80). The sum of the weighted ratings on each strength measure gives the company's overall-strength rating. Comparisons of the weighted-strength scores indicates how well the company stacks up against its competitors.

The bottom half of Table 4–1 shows a sample competitive-strength assessment for ABC Company using a weighted rating system. (Note that in the two examples in Table 4–1 the use of weights resulted in a different ordering of the companies as compared with when no weights were used. In both examples, all companies were assigned the same scores on the rating scale of 1 to 10; yet, when weights were used, ABC Company dropped from second to third in strength and Rival 1 jumped from third into a virtual tie for first—all because Rival 1 was strong on the two factors that counted the most.) The use of weights can make a significant difference in the outcome of the assessment and, thus, in the conclusions drawn about a company's competitive strength relative to its rivals.

The competitive-strength assessment provides valuable insight into a company's competitive situation. The ratings show how a company stacks up against its rivals, factor by factor or measure by measure, thereby revealing where the company is strongest and weakest and against whom. Moreover, comparisons of the overall competitive-strength scores indicate whether the company is at a net competitive advantage or disadvantage against each rival. The company with the largest overall competitive-strength rating can be said to have a net competitive advantage over each rival, with the size of the advantage being reflected in the amount by which its competitive-strength score exceeds those of the other companies being rated. The net competitive advantage/disadvantage of the other companies is indicated by how much their overall competitive-strength scores come out above/below the scores of each other rival.

Where a company is competitively strong and weak has direct implications in crafting a strategy to improve the company's competitive position. As a general rule, a company should endeavor to capitalize on its competitive strengths and to shore up or else protect against its competitive weaknesses. In other words, it should consider building its strategy on its competitive strengths, and it should look at making strategic moves which will alleviate its competitive weaknesses. At the same time, the competitive-strength ratings done for rival companies provide clear indications of which rivals may be vulnerable to competitive attack and the areas where they are weakest. When a company has important competitive strengths in the very areas where certain rivals are comparatively weak, then it may make sense to design offensive moves to exploit the advantage.

Determining the Company's Strategic Issues and Problems

The final step of company situation analysis is to identify all of the important strategic issues and problems which management needs to address in forming an overall game plan for the company. This is, of course, a case-by-case exercise; the listing that emerges is necessarily peculiar to the company and the particulars of its situation. However, most of the issues and problems should have been revealed in the four preceding steps of the company situation analysis; others may be apparent from the industry and competitive situation confronting the firm; and still others may emerge from difficulties in implementing the prevailing strategy

FIGURE 4–4
Company Situation Analysis

1. STRATEGIC PERFORMANCE INDICATORS

Performance Indicator	19—	19—	19—	19—	19—
Market share	____	____	____	____	____
Sales growth	____	____	____	____	____
Net profit margin	____	____	____	____	____
Return on equity investment	____	____	____	____	____
Other ?	____	____	____	____	____

2. INTERNAL STRENGTHS

INTERNAL WEAKNESSES

EXTERNAL OPPORTUNITIES

EXTERNAL THREATS

3. COMPETITIVE STRENGTH ASSESSMENT
Rating Scale: 1 = Weakest; 10 = Strongest

Key Success Factor/ Competitive Variable	Weight	Firm A	Firm B	Firm C	Firm D	Firm E
Quality/product performance	____	____	____	____	____	____
Reputation/image	____	____	____	____	____	____
Raw material access/cost	____	____	____	____	____	____
Technological skills	____	____	____	____	____	____
Manufacturing capability	____	____	____	____	____	____
Marketing/distribution	____	____	____	____	____	____
Financial strength	____	____	____	____	____	____
Relative cost position	____	____	____	____	____	____
Other ?	====	====	====	====	====	====
Overall strength rating	____	____	____	____	____	____

4. CONCLUSIONS CONCERNING COMPETITIVE POSITION
(improving/slipping? Competitive advantages/disadvantages?)

5. MAJOR STRATEGIC ISSUES/PROBLEMS THE COMPANY MUST ADDRESS

effectively and operating problems which the company is experiencing. The list of problems and issues should include all the things that need to go on the strategy-making agenda and be resolved by the strategy that is chosen.

ANALYTICAL CHECKLIST

There are five steps to conducting a company situation analysis:

1. Identifying the current strategy and evaluating how well it is working.
2. Doing a SWOT analysis.
3. Evaluating the company's cost position relative to competitors (using the concepts of strategic-cost analysis and activity-cost chains if appropriate).
4. Assessing the company's competitive position and competitive strength.
5. Determining the strategic issues and problems which the company needs to address.

Figure 4–4 contains a generic format for doing a company situation analysis. The format covers all of the steps and many of the points discussed in this chapter and, if followed conscientiously, it will help analysts draw insightful conclusions about the strategy-critical character of a company's present situation. Such is the purpose of company situation analysis.

SUGGESTED READINGS

Andrews, Kenneth R. *The Concept of Corporate Strategy.* 3rd ed. Homewood, Ill.: Richard D. Irwin, 1987, chap. 3.

Hax, Arnoldo C., and Nicolas S. Majluf. *Strategic Management: An Integrative Perspective.* Englewood Cliffs, N.J.: Prentice-Hall, 1984, chap. 15.

Henry, Harold W. "Appraising a Company's Strengths and Weaknesses." *Managerial Planning,* July–August 1980, pp. 31–36.

Stevenson, Howard H. "Defining Corporate Strengths and Weaknesses." *Sloan Management Review* 17, no. 2 (Winter 1976), pp. 1–18.

5

Competitive Strategies and Competitive Advantage

Competing in the marketplace is like war. You have injuries and casualties, and the best strategy wins.

John Collins

Competitive advantage is at the heart of a firm's performance in competitive markets.

Michael E. Porter

The strategist seeks opportunities to upset industry equilibrium, pursuing strategies that will allow a business to disrupt the "normal" course of industry events and to forge new industry conditions to the disadvantage of the competitors.

Ian C. MacMillan

Any business strategy, to be capable of sustained success, must be grounded in competitive advantage. Competitive advantage is gained when a company moves into a position where it has an edge in coping with competitive forces and in attracting buyers. Many different positioning advantages exist: making the highest-quality product on the market, providing customer service that is superior to rivals, being the biggest and best-known firm in the market, recognition as a low-price seller, being in the best geographic location, having a product that does the best job in performing a particular function, making a product that is more reliable and longer lasting, and offering the most value for the money (a combination of good quality, good service, and acceptable price)—to mention some of the most common competitive-edge possibilities. But whichever positioning strategy is pursued, the essential outcome to achieve competitive advantage is that a viable number of customers end up buying the firm's product because of the superior value they perceive it has. Superior value is nearly always created in one of two ways: either by offering buyers a *standard* product at a lower price or by using some differentiating technique to provide a *better* product that buyers think is worth paying a higher price for.

This chapter spotlights how a competitive advantage can be achieved or defended.[1] We begin with a discussion of the basic types of competitive strategies and then train attention on what it takes for the various competitive strategies, complemented with assorted offensive and defensive maneuvers, to produce a position of advantage in the marketplace.

THE THREE GENERIC TYPES OF COMPETITIVE STRATEGY

Competitive strategy is composed of all the specific moves and approaches a firm has taken and is taking to compete successfully in a given industry. In plainer terms, a firm's competitive strategy concerns how management is trying to knock the socks off rival companies and otherwise cope with the five competitive forces. It can be mostly offensive or mostly defensive, shifting from one to the other as seems appropriate.

Of course, companies the world over have imaginatively explored virtually every approach conceivable to competing successfully and winning an edge in the marketplace. And because company managements custom tailor strategy to fit the specifics of their own company's situation and market environment, thus producing a few unique wrinkles in each company's strategy, there are countless competitive-strategy variations. In this sense, there are as many competitive strategies as there are companies trying to compete. However, when one cuts beneath all the company-specific details and nuances to look at the basic character of the overall competitive approach that companies employ, the field of difference narrows considerably and three *generic* competitive-strategy approaches stand out:

1. Striving to be the overall low-cost producer in the industry.
2. Seeking to differentiate one's product offering in one way or another from rivals' products.
3. Focusing on a narrow portion of the market, rather than going out after the whole market.[2]

Table 5–1, found on page 124, profiles the distinctive features of the three generic strategies.

---

[1]Michael E. Porter of the Harvard Business School has done more than anyone else to expose the *hows* of achieving and defending competitive advantage. His 1980 book on *Competitive Strategy* quickly won status as a classic, totally reshaping the approach to analyzing business and competitive strategy; no discussion of the tools and techniques of industry and competitive analysis is adequate without relying heavily on Porter's work. His *Competitive Advantage*, published in 1985, is the definitive treatment of how to capture a competitive advantage. Because of the pathbreaking nature of Porter's work, this chapter of necessity draws heavily upon *Competitive Advantage* in an attempt to present the best, most up-to-date summary survey of how competitive advantages can be achieved and maintained. The material in this chapter can serve only as an introduction to the subject. Porter's *Competitive Advantage*, and the other references cited as sources for this chapter, offer more sweeping and intensive treatments.

[2]Michael E. Porter, *Competitive Strategy: Techniques for Analyzing Industries and Competitors* (New York: Free Press, 1980), chap. 2. The following discussion of these generic strategies relies on Porter's presentation, pp. 35–39 and 44–46.

TABLE 5–1
Distinctive Features of the Generic Competitive Strategies

Overall Low-Cost Leadership

- Production emphasis—"Nobody Does It Cheaper."
- Marketing emphasis—"Budget Prices/Good Value."
- Standardized products (only a few models and limited optional features).
- No-frills operating culture (lean-and-mean reputation).
- Stay out front in riding experience curve down (lower prices → added volume and market share → lower costs due to experience effects).
- High productivity per employee.
- Cost-cutting innovations.
- Can set the floor on market price (in best position to use price cutting as an offensive or defensive weapon).
- Accept low profit margins in return for high volume.

Differentiation

- Production emphasis—"Nobody Makes It Better."
- Marketing emphasis—"Ours Is Better than Theirs."
- Many frills (models, options, features, services).
- Frequent innovation.
- Premium pricing to cover added cost of differentiation.
- Intensive advertising and sales efforts.

Focus

- Production emphasis—"Made Especially for You."
- Marketing emphasis—"Ours Meets Your Needs Better."
- Specialization (buyer segments, geographic areas, end-use applications).
- Competitive advantage depends on:
  —being the low-cost leader *in the target segment*
     or
  —successful differentiation (doing something that is especially appealing to customers comprising the target segment).

Striving to Be the Low-Cost Producer

The impetus for striving to be the industry's low-cost producer can stem from sizable economies of scale, strong learning and experience curve effects, other cost-cutting/efficiency-enhancing opportunities, and a market comprised of many price-conscious buyers. Trying to be the industry leader in achieving an overall low-cost position typically entails being out in front of rivals in constructing the most efficient-sized plants, in implementing cost-reducing technological advances, in getting the sales and market share needed to capitalize on learning and experience curve effects, in maintaining a tight rein on overhead and other administrative types of fixed costs, and in containing costs in such areas as R&D, advertising, service, and distribution. Low cost *relative to competitors* is the theme of the firm's entire strategy—though low cost is not so zealously pursued that a firm's product offering loses its competitiveness as concerns those product attributes which buyers value highly (such as optional performance features, rapid delivery, spare parts availability, low maintenance, reliability, technical assistance, or whatever).

There are attractive advantages to being the low-cost producer in an industry:

- As concerns *rival competitors,* the low-cost company is in the best position to compete offensively on the basis of price, to defend against price war conditions, to use the appeal of a lower price as a weapon for grabbing sales (and market share) away from rivals and for attacking whatever success rivals have enjoyed with their competitive strategies, and to earn above-average profits (based on bigger profit margins or greater sales volume) in markets where price competition thrives.
- As concerns *buyers,* the low-cost company has partial profit margin protection from powerful customers, since the latter will rarely be able to bargain price down past the survival level of the next most cost-efficient seller.
- As concerns *suppliers,* the low-cost producer can, in some cases, be more insulated than competitors from powerful suppliers if its greater efficiency allows more pricing room to cope with upward pressure on the prices it must pay for important inputs.
- As concerns *potential entrants,* the low-cost producer is in a favorable competitive position because having the lowest costs not only acts as a barrier for a new entrant to hurdle but it also provides the leeway to use price cutting to defend against market inroads made by a new competitor.
- As concerns *substitutes,* a low-cost producer is, compared to its rivals, in a favorable position to use price cuts to defend against competition from attractively priced substitutes.

Consequently, a low-cost position provides a measure of protection against all five types of competitive forces. Whenever price competition is a major market force, less-efficient rivals get squeezed the most. Being the low-cost producer allows a firm to use its cost advantage to earn higher profit margins or to charge a lower price or both. Firms in a low-cost position relative to rivals have a significant edge in appealing to those buyers who are inclined to base their purchase decision on low price; plainly, *a low-cost producer has the ability to exert a heavy hand in determining the industry's price floor.*

A strategy of trying to be the low-cost producer is particularly powerful when:

1. Demand is so price-elastic that small price cuts produce much bigger percentage increases in customers' purchases.
2. All firms in the industry produce essentially standardized, commodity-type products, causing the marketplace to be dominated by price competition and making the name of the game for sellers one of being cost efficient and otherwise getting in a position to be an overall low-cost supplier to their customers.
3. There are not many ways to achieve product differentiation that have much value to buyers.
4. Most buyers utilize the product in the same ways and, thus, have common user requirements.
5. And buyers incur few if any switching costs in changing from one seller to another and, thus, are strongly inclined to shop for the best price.

However, trying to be the low-cost leader is not without risk and disadvantage. Technological changes can result in cost or process breakthroughs that nullify past investments and efficiency gains. Rival firms may find it comparatively easy and inexpensive to imitate the leader's low-cost methods, thereby making any advantage short-lived. A tunnel vision approach to cost reduction can result in a firm overlooking such things as a growing preference of buyers for added quality or service features, subtle shifts in buyers' uses of the product, and declining buyer sensitivity to price—thus, getting left behind if buyer interest swings more to quality, performance, service, and other differentiating features. Finally, heavy investments in cost minimization can lock a firm into both its present technology and present strategy, leaving it vulnerable to new state-of-the-art technologies and to growing customer interest in something other than a cheaper price. In short, being the low-cost leader imposes a significant burden in terms of staying on top of cost-saving technological improvements, scrapping existing equipment (even if it is not worn out) anytime something more efficient comes along, and risking technological and strategic inflexibility if buyers begin to be attracted by rivals' introduction of new product attributes. Moreover, strategic success in trying to be the low-cost producer usually requires a firm to be *the* overall cost leader, not just one of the several firms vying for this position.[3] When there is more than one aspiring low-cost producer, rivalry among them is typically fierce and, unless one firm can get a clear enough cost lead to "persuade" the others to abandon zealous pursuit of low-cost leadership, profitability suffers.

Examples of firms that are well known for their low-cost leadership strategies are Lincoln Electric in arc welding equipment, Briggs and Stratton in small-horsepower gasoline engines, BIC in ballpoint pens, Black & Decker in tools, Design and Manufacturing in dishwashers (marketed under the Sears Kenmore brand), Beaird-Poulan in chain saws, Ford in heavy-duty trucks, General Electric in major home appliances, R. J. Reynolds in cigarettes, and Southwest Airlines in commercial airline travel.

Differentiation Strategies

The approaches to differentiating one's product from rival firms take many forms: a different taste (Dr Pepper and Listerine), special features (Jenn-Air's indoor cooking tops with a vented built-in grill for barbecuing), superior service (IBM in computers and Federal Express in overnight package delivery), spare parts availability (Caterpillar guarantees 48-hour spare parts delivery to any customer anywhere in the world or else the part is furnished free), overall value to the customer (Sears and McDonald's), engineering design and performance (Mercedes in automobiles), unusual quality and distinctiveness (Rolex in watches and Chivas Regal in scotch), product reliability (Johnson & Johnson in baby products), quality manufacture (Karastan in carpets and Curtis Mathes in TV sets), technological leadership (Hyster in lift trucks and 3M Corporation in bonding and coating products), convenient payment (American Express), a full range of services (Merrill

---

[3]Michael E. Porter, *Competitive Advantage* (New York: Free Press, 1985), p. 13.

Lynch), a complete line of products (General Motors in automobiles and Campbell in soups), and top-of-the-line image and reputation (Brooks Brothers and Ralph Lauren in menswear, Kitchen Aid in dishwashers, and Cross in writing instruments).

Differentiation provides some buffer against the strategies of rivals because buyers establish a loyalty for the brand or model they like best and often are willing to pay a little (perhaps a lot!) more for it. In addition, successful differentiation (1) erects entry barriers in the form of customer loyalty and uniqueness that newcomers can find hard to hurdle; (2) mitigates the bargaining power of large buyers, since the products of alternative sellers are less attractive to them; and (3) puts a firm in a better position to fend off threats from substitutes, based on the attachments customers have for its brand version. To the extent that differentiation allows a seller to charge a higher price and bolster profit margins, then a seller is in a stronger economic position to withstand the efforts of powerful suppliers to jack up their prices. Thus, as with cost leadership, successful differentiation creates lines of defense for dealing with the five competitive forces.

The types of differentiation strategies that are most appealing are those least subject to quick or inexpensive imitation. Here is where having a distinctive competence comes into play. When a firm has skills and competences that competitors cannot match easily, it can use its ability as a basis for successful differentiation. Those areas where efforts to differentiate are likely to produce an attractive, longer-lasting competitive edge are:

- Differentiation based on *technical superiority*.
- Differentiation based on *quality*.
- Differentiation based on *giving customers more support services*.
- Differentiation based on the appeal of *more value for the money*.

As a rule, differentiation strategies work best in situations where (1) there are many ways to differentiate the product or service and these differences are perceived by some buyers to have value, (2) buyer needs and uses of the item are diverse, and (3) not many rival firms are following a differentiation strategy. Often, the most-attractive avenue for product differentiation is the one least traveled by rival firms—as the saying goes, "never follow the crowd."

Employing a differentiation strategy has its risks, however:

- The extra cost of adding enough product attributes to achieve differentiation can result in a selling price so much higher that buyers opt for lower-priced brands. Buyers are usually willing to pay only so much extra for differentiation; when this price premium is exceeded, low-cost/low-price firms gain an edge over firms pursuing high-cost differentiation. In such circumstances, despite the unique features that the products of the high-priced firms may have, a lower-cost/lower-price strategy can defeat an all-the-frills differentiation strategy.
- Over time, more and more buyers may decide that they do not need or want extra features, concluding that a less-expensive standard model serves their purpose just as well. As market emphasis shifts away from differ-

entiation toward that of a commodity product situation, the name of the game for competitive success becomes low-cost, efficient production of a more or less standardized product offering.

- Rival firms may imitate the product attributes of the leaders to such an extent that buyers begin to see very little, if any, meaningful differentiation from seller to seller. The differentiation attempts of rivals, thus, cancel each other and buyers shop mostly on the basis of price.

In addition to these pitfalls, experience indicates that it is hard to excel in more than one approach to differentiation simultaneously. Attempting to differentiate in many ways at once can deteriorate into trying to be too many things to too many people, thereby blurring the firm's image with buyers. In formulating a differentiation strategy, it is usually wise to stress one key value and to develop a distinctive competence in delivering it. It can also be a good tactic to select a basis for differentiation that *(a)* makes it easy for first-time buyers to try the product and *(b)* makes it hard for regular users to abandon the product (because the costs of switching to other brands or substitutes are high).

Focus and Specialization Strategies

A focus or specialization strategy aims at building a competitive edge and carving out a market position by catering to the special needs of a particular group of customers or by concentrating on a limited geographic market or by concentrating on certain uses for the product. *The distinguishing feature of a focus strategy is that the firm specializes in serving only a portion of the total market.* The underlying premise is that a firm can serve its narrow target market more effectively or more efficiently than rivals that position themselves broadly.

The competitive advantage of a focus strategy is earned either by differentiation from better meeting the needs of the target market segment, by achieving lower costs in serving the segment, or both. A focuser can gain a cost advantage because more than one cost curve can prevail in an industry. The cost curve for a specialist firm concentrating on custom orders and short production runs can differ substantially from the cost curve for a firm pursuing a high-volume, low-cost strategy, as shown in Figure 5–1. In such cases, small firms are positioned to be cost-effective focusers in the small-volume, custom-order buyer segments, leaving the mass market to large-volume producers.

Because of its specialized approach and unmatched skills in serving a limited market target, a focused firm gains a basis for defending against the five competitive forces. Rivals do not have the same ability to serve the focused firm's target clientele. Entry into the focused firm's market niche is made harder by the competitive edge generated by the focused firm's distinctive competence. The focused firm's distinctive competence also acts as a hurdle that substitutes must overcome. The bargaining leverage of powerful customers is blunted somewhat by their own unwillingness to shift their business to firms with lesser capabilities to serve their needs.

A competitive strategy based on focus or specialization has merit (1) when there are distinctly different groups of buyers who either have different needs or else

FIGURE 5–1

When a Focus Strategy Can Allow a Small Firm to Be Cost Competitive with a Large, Mass-Production Rival

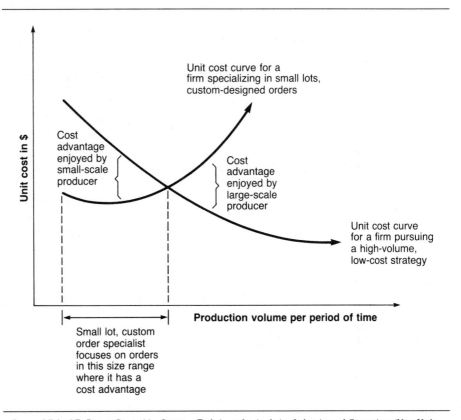

Source: Michael E. Porter, *Competitive Strategy: Techniques for Analyzing Industries and Competitors* (New York: Free Press, 1980), p. 245.

utilize the product in different ways; (2) when no other rival is attempting to *specialize* in the same target segment; (3) when a firm's resources do not permit it to go after a wide segment of the total market; and (4) when industry segments differ so widely in size, growth rate, profitability, and intensity of the five competitive forces that some segments are much more attractive than others.

Examples of firms employing a focus strategy include Tandem Computers (a specialist in "nonstop" computers for customers who need a "fail-safe" system that can support thousands of online terminals and preserve data integrity and reliability); Rolls-Royce (in super-luxury automobiles); Thermador (a maker of top-of-the-line refrigerators, freezers, trash compactors, and cooking appliances); Fort Howard Paper (specializing in paper products for industrial and commercial enterprises only); the numerous commuter airlines (which specialize in low-traffic, short-haul flights linking major airports with smaller population centers 50 to 250 miles away); and Ficks and Reed, a maker of premium-quality rattan furniture.

The risks of a focus strategy include (1) the possibility that broad-range competitors will find effective ways to match the focused firm in serving the narrow target market; (2) shifts in buyer preferences and needs that make the differences in product attributes desired by the target segment and the market as a whole enough narrower to allow broad-range rivals a strong competitive footing in the target markets of the focused firms; and (3) the chance that competitors will find subsegments within the target segment and outfocus the focuser.

BUILDING COMPETITIVE ADVANTAGE VIA LOW-COST LEADERSHIP

A cost advantage is achieved when a firm's cumulative costs across its overall production-cost chain are lower than competitors' cumulative costs.[4] How valuable a cost advantage is from a competitive-strategy perspective depends on its sustainability. Sustainability, in turn, hinges upon whether a firm's sources of cost advantage are difficult to copy or to match in some other way. A cost advantage generates superior profitability when the firm's product offering is deemed by buyers to be comparable enough to the offerings of competitors that the cost advantage is not eaten up in whole or in part by the need to underprice competitors to win sales. Two avenues can be used to pursue a cost advantage:[5]

- Do a better job than rivals of controlling the factors that give rise to costs.
- Revamp the makeup of the production-cost chain by doing things differently and saving enough in the process that customers can be supplied more cheaply.

Let's look at each of the two cost-saving approaches.

Controlling the Cost Drivers

A firm's cost position is the result of the behavior of costs in each one of the activities comprising its total activity-cost chain. There are nine *major types of cost drivers* which can come into play in determining costs in each activity segment of the chain:[6]

1. *Economies or diseconomies of scale.* Economies and diseconomies of scale can be found or created in virtually every segment of the activity-cost chain. For example, manufacturing economies can sometimes be achieved by simplifying the product line and scheduling longer production runs for fewer models. A geographically organized sales force can realize economies as regional sales volume grows because a salesperson can write larger orders at each sales call and/or because of reduced travel time between calls; on the other hand, a sales force organized by product line can encounter travel-related diseconomies if salespersons have to spend disproportionately more travel time calling on dis-

---

[4] The concept of activity-cost chains was presented in Chapter 4. Since we will have cause to draw upon the activity-cost chain idea repeatedly in the remainder of this chapter, you may wish to skim over the section on "Strategic Cost Analysis" in Chapter 4, paying particular attention to Figure 4–2.

[5] Michael E. Porter, *Competitive Advantage* (New York: Free Press, 1985), p. 97.

[6] This listing and explanation is condensed from Porter, *Competitive Advantage*, pp. 70–107.

tantly spaced customers. In global industries, modifying products by country instead of selling a standard product worldwide tends to boost unit costs, because of lost time in model changeover, shorter production runs, and inability to reach the most economic scale of production for each model. Boosting local or regional market share can lower sales and marketing costs per unit, whereas opting for a bigger national market share by entering new regions can create scale diseconomies unless and until the market penetration in the newly entered regions reaches efficient proportions.

2. *Learning and experience curve effects*. Experience-based cost savings can come from improved layout, gains in labor efficiency, debugging of technology, product design modifications that enhance manufacturing efficiency, redesign of machinery and equipment to gain increased operating speed, getting samples of a rival's products and having design engineers study how they are made, and tips from suppliers, consultants, and ex-employees of rival firms. Learning tends to vary with the amount of management attention devoted to capturing the benefits of experience of both the firm and others. Learning benefits can be kept proprietary by building or modifying production equipment in-house, retaining key employees, limiting the dissemination of information through employee publications, and enforcing strict nondisclosure provisions in employment contracts.

3. *The percentage of capacity utilization*. High fixed costs as a percentage of total costs create a stiff unit-cost penalty for underutilization of existing capacity. Increased capacity utilization spreads indirect and overhead costs over a larger unit volume and enhances the efficiency of fixed assets. The more capital-intensive the business, the more important this cost driver becomes. Finding ways to minimize the ups and downs in seasonal capacity utilization can be an important source of cost advantage.[7]

4. *Linkages with other activities in the chain*. When the cost of one activity is affected by how other activities are performed, there is opportunity to lower the costs of the linked activities via superior coordination and/or joint optimization. Linkages with suppliers tend to center on suppliers' product-design characteristics, quality-assurance procedures, delivery and service policies, and the manner by which the supplier's product is furnished (for example, delivery of nails in prepackaged 1-lb., 5-lb., and 10-lb. assortments instead of 100-lb. bulk cartons can reduce a hardware dealer's labor costs in filling individual customer orders). The easiest supplier linkages to exploit are those where both a supplier's and a firm's costs fall because of coordination and/or joint optimization. Linkages with forward channels tend to center on location of warehouses, materials handling, outbound shipping, and packaging.

5. *Sharing opportunities with other business units within the enterprise*. When an activity can be shared with a sister unit, there can be significant cost savings.

---

[7]A firm can improve its capacity utilization by *(a)* serving a mix of accounts having peak volumes spread throughout the year, *(b)* finding off-season uses for its products, *(c)* serving private-label customers that can intermittently use the excess capacity, *(d)* selecting buyers with stable demands or demands that are counter to the normal peak/valley cycle, *(e)* letting competitors serve the buyer segments whose demands fluctuate the most, and *(f)* sharing capacity with sister units having a different pattern of needs.

Cost sharing is potentially a way to achieve scale economies, ride the learning curve down at a faster clip, and/or achieve fuller capacity utilization. Sometimes the know-how gained in one division can be used to help lower costs in another; sharing know-how is significant when the activities are similar and know-how can be readily transferred from one unit to another.

6. *The extent of vertical integration.* Partially or fully integrating into the activities of either suppliers or forward channel allies can allow an enterprise to detour suppliers or buyers with considerable bargaining power; vertical integration can also result in cost savings when it is feasible to coordinate or closely mesh adjacent activities in the overall cost chain.

7. *Timing considerations associated with first-mover advantages and disadvantages.* The first major brand in the market may achieve lower costs of establishing and maintaining a brand name. Late-movers can, in a fast-paced technology development situation, benefit from purchasing the latest equipment or avoiding the high product/market development costs of early-moving pioneers.

8. *Strategic choices and operating decisions.* Managers at various levels can impact a firm's costs via a variety of decisions they make:

   - Increasing/decreasing the number of products offered.
   - Adding/cutting the services provided to buyers.
   - Incorporating more/less performance and quality features into the product.
   - Paying higher/lower wages and fringes to employees relative to rivals and firms in other industries.
   - Increasing/decreasing the number of different forward channels utilized in distributing the firm's product.
   - Raising/lowering the levels of R&D support relative to rivals.
   - Putting more/less emphasis on achieving higher levels of productivity and efficiency, as compared to rivals.
   - Raising/lowering the specifications set for purchased materials.

9. *Locational variables.* Locations differ in their prevailing wage levels, tax rates, energy costs, inbound and outbound shipping and freight costs, and so on. Opportunities may exist for reducing costs by relocating plants, field offices, warehousing, and headquarters operations. Moreover, the location of sister facilities relative to each other affects the cost of intrafirm shipping inventory, outbound freight on goods shipped to customers, and coordination.

A firm intent on being the low-cost producer has to scrutinize each cost-creating activity and identify the drivers of cost for that activity. Then it needs to use its knowledge about the cost drivers to reduce costs for each and every activity where cost-saving potential is believed to exist. It is important to recognize that the task of pushing costs down further and further (and not incurring some costs at all) is not easy or simple; rather, it is a task that has to be managed with both ingenuity and single-minded toughness.

Revamping the Makeup of the Activity-Cost Chain

Dramatic cost advantages can emerge from finding innovative ways to restructure activities, to cut out frills, and to provide the basics in more economical fashion.[8] The primary ways to achieve an advantage via revamping the makeup of the activity-cost chain include:

- Stripping away all the extras and offering only a basic, no-frills product or service.
- Using a different production process.
- Finding ways to use cheaper raw materials.
- Using new kinds of advertising media and promotional approaches relative to the industry norm.
- Selling directly through one's own sales force instead of indirectly through dealers and distributors.
- Relocating facilities closer to suppliers or customers, or both.
- Achieving a more economical degree of forward or backward vertical integration relative to competitors.
- Going against the "something for everyone" approach of others and focusing on a limited product/service to meet a special, but important, need of the target buyer segment.

Illustration Capsule 12 describes how two companies won strong competitive positions via restructuring the traditional activity-cost chain.

Cost-Cutting Strategies

The two cost-saving approaches of controlling the cost drivers and revamping the activity-cost chain are not mutually exclusive. Low-cost producers usually achieve their cost advantages from any and all avenues they can find. More often than not, low-cost producers have a strong cost-conscious operating culture undergirded by symbolic traditions of spartan facilities, frugal screening of all budget requests, and limited perks and frills for employees at all levels.

Using a focus strategy to achieve a cost breakthrough is a fairly common technique. Southwest Airlines has focused on the price-sensitive segment of the commercial air travel market. Budget-priced motel chains like Days Inn, Motel 6, and LaQuinta have all lowered their investment and operating cost per room by going to a no-frills approach and catering to price-conscious travelers. The discount stock brokerage houses have lowered costs by focusing on customers who were interested mainly in buying and selling transactions and were willing to forego all of the investment research, investment advice, and financial services offered by full-service firms like Merrill Lynch. Pursuing a cost advantage via focusing works well when a firm can find ways to lower costs significantly by reducing its customer base to a well-defined buyer segment.

Pitfalls in Pursuing a Cost Advantage

Gaining a sustainable cost advantage is no easy chore and there are a number of common pitfalls:[9]

---

[8]This section is adapted from the presentation by Porter, *Competitive Advantage*, pp. 107–11.
[9]Porter, *Competitive Advantage*, pp. 115–18.

ILLUSTRATION CAPSULE 12

Winning a Cost Advantage: Iowa Beef Packers and Federal Express

Iowa Beef Packers and Federal Express have been able to win strong competitive positions by restructuring the traditional activity-cost chains in their industries. In beef packing, the traditional-cost chain involved raising cattle on scattered farms and ranches, shipping them live to labor-intensive, unionized slaughtering plants, and then transporting whole sides of beef to grocery retailers whose butcher departments cut them into smaller pieces and packaged them for sale to grocery shoppers.

Iowa Beef Packers revamped the traditional chain with a radically different strategy—large automated plants employing nonunion labor were built near economically transportable supplies of cattle and the meat was partially butchered at the processing plant into smaller high-yield cuts (sometimes sealed in plastic casing ready for purchase), boxed, and shipped to retailers. IBP's inbound cattle transportation expenses, traditionally a major-cost item, were cut significantly by avoiding the weight losses that occurred when live animals were shipped long distances; major outbound shipping-cost savings were achieved by not having to ship whole sides of beef with their high waste factor. Iowa Beef's strategy was so successful that it was, in 1985, the largest U.S. meatpacker, surpassing the former industry leaders, Swift, Wilson, and Armour.

Federal Express innovatively redefined the activity-cost chain for rapid delivery of small parcels. Traditional firms like Emery and Airborne Express operated by collecting freight packages of varying sizes, shipping them to their destination points via air freight and commercial airlines, and then delivering them to the addressee. Federal Express opted to focus only on the market for overnight delivery of small packages and documents. These were collected at local drop points during the late afternoon hours, flown on company-owned planes during early evening hours to a central hub in Memphis where from 11 P.M. to 3 A.M. each night, all parcels were sorted, then reloaded on company planes, and flown during the early morning hours to their destination points, where they were delivered the next morning by company personnel using company trucks. The cost structure so achieved by Federal Express was low enough to permit it to guarantee overnight delivery of a small parcel anywhere in the United States for a price as low as $11. In 1986, Federal Express had a 58 percent market share of the air-express package-delivery market versus a 15 percent share for UPS, 11 percent for Airborne Express, and 10 percent for Emery/Purolator.

SOURCE: Based on information in Michael E. Porter, *Competitive Advantage* (New York: Free Press, 1985), p. 109.

- Focusing too heavily or even exclusively on manufacturing costs (in many businesses, a very significant portion of the activity-cost chain consists of sales and marketing, customer services, the development of new products and production process improvements, and internal staff support).
- Ignoring the payoff of first-rate, diligent efforts to reduce the cost of pur-

chased materials and equipment (many senior executives view purchasing as a secondary staff function).

- Overlooking activities that represent a small fraction of total costs.
- Not understanding what factors really drive costs per unit (for example, large regional market share may be more important to per-unit cost than is having a large national share arising from scattered sales across many regions).
- Striving exclusively for incremental-cost improvements in the existing activity-cost chain and not broadening the search to include ways to revamp the chain.
- Unwitting pursuit of conflicting functional strategies, as when a firm tries to gain market share to reap the benefits of scale economies and long production runs while at the same time dissipating the potential benefits of larger volume by adding more models and optional features.
- Pursuing cost reductions so zealously that differentiation of the firm's product is undermined by cutting out performance features, overstandardizing models, and eliminating helpful customer services.

BUILDING COMPETITIVE ADVANTAGE VIA DIFFERENTIATION

Successful differentiation requires being unique at something buyers consider valuable.[10] When differentiation offers value to the customer, it yields competitive advantage. Differentiation is unsuccessful when the forms of uniqueness pursued by a firm are not valued highly by enough buyers to cause them to prefer the firm's product to that of rivals. Successful differentiation allows a firm to:

- Command a premium price, and/or
- Sell more units of its product (because buyers are attracted to the differentiating features), and/or
- Realize greater degrees of buyer loyalty.

Differentiation can enhance profitability whenever the price premium achieved exceeds any added costs associated with achieving differentiation. Differentiation strategies may be aimed at broad customer groups or narrowly focused on a limited-buyer segment having particular needs.

Ways to Differentiate

Successful differentiation strategies can grow out of activities performed anywhere in the overall activity-cost chain; they do not arise solely from marketing and advertising departments. The places in the chain where differentiation can be achieved include:

1. *The procurement of raw materials* that affect the performance or quality of the

---

[10]Porter, *Competitive Advantage*, pp. 119–20. The content of this section is based on chapter 4 of *Competitive Advantage*. For an alternative treatment, see David A. Aaker, *Developing Business Strategies* (New York: John Wiley & Sons, 1984), pp. 251–57.

end product. (McDonald's is more selective and particular than its competitors in selecting the potatoes it uses in its french fries.)

2. *Product-oriented R&D efforts* that lead to improved designs, performance features, expanded end-uses and applications, product variety, shorter lead times in developing new models, and being the first to come out with new products.

3. *Production process-oriented R&D efforts* that lead to improved quality, reliability, and product appearance.

4. *The manufacturing process,* insofar as it emphasizes zero-defects, carefully engineered performance designs, long-term durability, improved economy to end-users, maintenance-free use, flexible end-use application, and consistent product quality.

5. *The outbound logistics system,* to the extent that it improves delivery time and accurate order filling.

6. *Marketing, sales, and customer service activities* that result in helpful technical assistance to buyers, faster maintenance and repair services, more and better product information provided to customers, more and better training materials for end-users, better credit terms, better warranty coverages, quicker order processing, more frequent sales calls, and greater customer convenience.

Differentiation, thus, goes deeper than just the catchall aspects of quality and service. Quality is primarily a function of the product's physical properties, whereas differentiation possibilities that create value to buyers can be found throughout the whole activity-cost chain. A full understanding of the sources of differentiation and the activities that drive uniqueness is a prerequisite to developing new ways to achieve differentiation and to diagnosing how sustainable any advantage gained by uniqueness might be.[11]

Creating a Differentiation-Based Advantage

Anything a firm can do to lower the buyer's total costs of using a product, or to raise the performance the buyer gets, represents a potential basis for differentiation.[12] To make it cheaper for a buyer to use a firm's brand, the firm can incorporate features that result in the buyer enjoying:

- Reduced waste and scrap in the use of raw materials.
- Lower labor costs (fewer hours, less training, lower skill requirements).
- Less down-time or idle-time (because of short lead-times in supplying spare parts).
- Faster processing times.
- Lower delivery, installation, or financing cost.
- Reduced inventory costs (because of reliable delivery capability from suppliers).
- Less maintenance and/or ease of maintenance.

---

[11]Porter, *Competitive Advantage,* p. 124.
[12]Porter, *Competitive Advantage,* pp. 135–38.

- Reduced need for other inputs (energy, safety equipment, security personnel, inspection personnel).
- Higher trade-in value for used models.
- Compatibility to interface with other ancillary equipment.
- Multipurpose flexibility to handle a variety of needs and potential applications (reduces buyer's needs for other equipment).
- Free advice and technical assistance on end-use applications (lowers the need for technical personnel, enhances efficiency of use).
- Less risk in the purchase decision should the product unexpectedly fail later.

Differentiation approaches that can be used to enhance the performance and value which the buyer receives can include such things as providing:

- Greater convenience and ease of use.
- More features that meet the full range of a buyer's requirements, compared to competitors' products.
- Capacity to add on or to change later.
- Optional extras to meet occasional needs.
- Flexible applications that give the buyer more options to tailor his own product to the needs of his customers.
- Ability to fill noneconomic needs, such as status, image, prestige, appearance, comfort.
- Capability for meeting the customer's future growth and expansion requirements.

Real Value, Perceived Value, and Signals of Value

Buyers will seldom pay for value they do not perceive, no matter how real the unique extras may be.[13] Thus, the price premium that a differentiation strategy commands is a reflection of *the value actually delivered* to the buyer and *the value perceived* by the buyer (even if not actually delivered). The difference between actual value and perceived value often emerges because buyers have a difficult time assessing in advance what their experience with the product will actually be. Sometimes, buyers cannot completely or accurately gauge value even *after* the product has been used; this is especially true in trying to compare the outcome with what might have been experienced with rival brands.

When buyers have incomplete knowledge about value, there is competitive opportunity for a seller to adopt a new differentiating feature, educate buyers to value it, and gain the first-mover advantage of reputation for being a leader. In addition, incomplete knowledge on the part of buyers often prompts buyers to

---

[13]This discussion draws from Porter, *Competitive Advantage*, pp. 138–42. Porter's insights here are particularly important to formulating differentiating strategies, because they highlight the relevance of "intangibles" and "signals."

judge and to infer what the real value may be on the basis of such *signals* as seller's word-of-mouth reputation, how attractively the product is packaged, how extensively the brand is advertised and, thus, how "well-known" it is, the content of the ads and the image they project, the manner in which information is presented in brochures and sales presentations, the attractiveness and aura of quality associated with the seller's facilities, the list of customers a seller has, the market share the firm has, the time the firm has been in business, the price being charged (where price connotes "quality"), and the professionalism, appearance, and personality of the seller's employees. These signals of value may be as important as actual value (1) when the nature of differentiation is subjective or hard to quantify, (2) when buyers are making their first-time purchases, (3) when repurchase is infrequent, and (4) when buyers are unsophisticated. A seller whose differentiation strategy delivers only modest extra value, but who signals the existence of extra value very effectively, may be able to command a higher price than a firm that actually delivers higher value but signals it poorly.

Keeping the Cost of Differentiation in Line

Attempts to achieve differentiation usually raise costs. The trick to profitable differentiation is either to raise unit costs by less than the price premium that the differentiation approach commands (this widens the profit margin per unit sold) or else to more than offset the cost increase with enough added volume to cause total profits to be greater (larger volume can make up for smaller margins, provided differentiation adds enough extra sales). In pursuing differentiation, a firm must be careful not to get its overall unit costs so far out of line with competitors that the resulting price premium it has to charge causes the brand to be priced out of the range buyers are willing to pay. From a cost perspective, the most attractive differentiating activities are those where a firm can enjoy either a cost advantage over competitors in achieving differentiation or a price premium that more than offsets the added costs of achieving uniqueness. There may also be good reason to pursue all sources of differentiation that are not costly.

The Risks of Pursuing a Differentiation-Based Competitive Advantage

There are, of course, no guarantees that differentiation will produce a meaningful competitive advantage. If buyers see little value in uniqueness and a standard item suffices to meet customer needs, then a low-cost strategy can easily defeat a differentiation strategy. In addition, differentiation can be defeated when competitors can quickly copy most any kind of differentiating attempt—rapid imitation, of course, means that real differentiation is never actually achieved, since competing brands keep changing in like ways despite the continued efforts of sellers to create uniqueness. Thus, to be successful at differentiation, a firm must search for durable sources of uniqueness that are protected by barriers to quick or cheap imitation. Aside from these considerations, other common pitfalls to pursuing differentiation include:[14]

---

[14]Porter, *Competitive Advantage*, pp. 160–62.

- Trying to differentiate on the basis of something that does not lower buyer cost or enhance the buyer's well-being, as perceived by the buyer.
- Overdifferentiating, so price is too high relative to competitors or that product quality or service levels go well past the needs of buyers.
- Trying to charge too high a price premium (the bigger the premium, the more buyers that can be lured away by lower-priced competitors).
- Ignoring the need to signal value and depending only on the "real" bases of differentiation.
- Not knowing the cost of differentiation and plodding ahead on the blind assumption that differentiation makes good economic and competitive sense.
- Not understanding or identifying what the buyer will consider as value.

BUILDING COMPETITIVE ADVANTAGE VIA FOCUSING

Buyer segments within an industry are far from being homogeneous.[15] The strengths of the five competitive forces vary from segment to segment, and different segments can have significantly different activity-cost chains. As a consequence, segments differ in their competitive attractiveness and in what it takes to achieve competitive advantage in each segment. It is these differences that give rise to the appeal of a focus strategy. The two crucial issues concerning adoption of a focus strategy revolve around (1) choosing which industry segments to compete in and (2) how to build competitive advantage in the target segments.

Deciding which segments to focus on hinges upon attractiveness of the various segments. Segment attractiveness is typically a function of segment size and growth rate, the intensity of the five competitive forces in the segment, segment profitability, the strategic importance of the segment to other major competitors, and the match between a firm's capabilities and the segment's needs. These are self-explanatory, except for the differences between analyzing the five forces at the segment level, compared to the industry level.[16] In five forces analysis at the segment level, potential entrants include firms serving other segments, as well as firms not presently in the industry. Substitutes for the product varieties already included in the segment can be product varieties in the rest of the industry, as well as products produced in other industries. Rivalry in the segment involves both the firms focusing exclusively on the segment and the firms that serve this and other segments. Buyer and supplier power, while mostly segment-specific, can be influenced by buyer purchases in other segments and supplier sales to other segments. As a rule, then, five forces analysis of a segment tends to be heavily influenced by conditions in other segments.

---

[15]This section is based on Porter, *Competitive Advantage*, chap. 7. For a different but related approach to focusing and segmentation, see Kenichi Ohmae, *The Mind of the Strategist* (New York: Penguin Books, 1983), chap. 9; also, Aaker, *Developing Business Strategies*, pp. 261–64.

[16]Porter, *Competitive Advantage*, pp. 256–57.

Choosing Whether to Focus on One or More Segments

The most attractive segments for focusing have one or more of the following characteristics:

- The segment is of sufficient size and purchasing power to be profitable.
- The segment has good growth potential.
- The segment is not crucial to the success of major competitors.
- The focusing firm has the skills and resources to serve the segment effectively.
- The focuser can defend itself against challengers via the customer goodwill it has built up and its superior ability to serve buyers in the segment.

However, segments are often related in ways that make it desirable to compete in two or three segments, rather than just one.[17] The thing to look for here is an opportunity to share activities in the overall activity-cost chain across segments. Multisegment focusing becomes a strong consideration when (1) the same sales force can effectively sell to different buyer groups, (2) the same manufacturing plants can produce enough product varieties to supply two or more segments, (3) R&D can be done simultaneously for several product groups within the industry family, or (4) outbound shipping and distribution activities for two or more buyer groups can be closely coordinated, all with resultant cost savings in serving multiple segments. In addition, there are times when sharing produces scale economies, more rapid learning, improved capacity utilization, increased differentiation, or lower differentiation costs. However, the cost-saving benefits associated with segment interrelationships can be offset when:

- The costs of coordinating shared activities are high (because of greater operating complexity).
- The activity-cost chain designed to serve one segment is not optimally suitable for serving another segment, thereby compromising a firm's ability to serve both segments well.
- Sharing activities across segments limits the flexibility of modifying strategies in the target segments.

The net competitive advantage of focusing on one versus several target segments is a function of the balance between the benefits and costs of sharing activities. In general, the stronger the interrelationships among several segments, the more attractive is a multisegment focus strategy.

The Focuser's Advantage: Differentiation or Low Cost?

A focuser, to achieve competitive advantage, has to succeed at low-cost leadership or at differentiation *in its chosen segment or segments*. If a focuser opts to pursue low-cost leadership, then the same kinds of cost-reducing approaches as explained above for industrywide cost leadership have to be used in managing the

---

[17]Philip Kotler, *Marketing Management: Analysis, Planning and Control*, 5th ed. (Englewood Cliffs, N.J.: Prentice-Hall, 1984), p. 411.

activity-cost chain for the segment. If a focusing firm opts for differentiation, then it must look at buyer needs and develop ways to lower these costs or enhance the performance they get from the product; the specific kinds of differentiating approaches are the same for focusers as for broad competitors. What sets the creation of competitive advantage by focusing apart is that focus strategies are grounded in differences among segments. A focuser excells in serving the target segment. However, what can give the focuser a special boost in winning a segment-based competitive advantage is the fact that differences across segments can impose significant costs of coordination, compromise, and inflexibility on broadly targeted competitors in trying to meet the specific needs of buyers in the focuser's target segments. This is the condition that makes focusing really attractive. When the differences among the segments are slight, a focuser has little defense against more broadly targeted competitors, because the latter can serve the needs of the buyer segment about as well as the focuser can.

Protecting a Focus-Based Competitive Advantage

For a focus strategy to be successful over time, three conditions must be present:[18]

1. A focuser must be able to defend its position against inroads from more broadly targeted competitors. This is easier when segment differences are big and harder when they are small.
2. A focuser needs to erect barriers to imitation from other focusers. Another competitor, either new to the industry or one dissatisfied with its current strategy, may try to replicate the focus strategy. The more attractive the segment and the more successful a focuser's strategy, the greater the threat of imitation (unless the focuser has built a good defense against fast followership).
3. A focuser must not be threatened by conditions that will cause the segment to dissolve into the broader market or to shrink to an unattractive size. Competitors serving broader parts of the industry may well use product innovation, advertising, promotional efforts, and other marketing tactics to induce buyers to leave the focuser's segment and come into theirs.

Absent these three conditions, it is an uphill struggle to make a success of focusing. Thus, it is a mistake to think of focusing per se as generating competitive advantage.[19] For focusing to work, the target segment must (1) involve buyers with materially different needs or (2) entail the use of an activity-cost chain that differs from the chain needed to serve other segments. Otherwise it is not likely that the segment can be successfully defended against challengers attracted by the segment's size and profitability.

USING OFFENSIVE STRATEGIES TO SECURE COMPETITIVE ADVANTAGE

To the extent that a firm can capture and maintain the initiative, competitors are forced to respond to the initiator's moves defensively and to do so under

---

[18]Porter, *Competitive Advantage,* pp. 267–69.
[19]These and other pitfalls were identified by Porter; see *Competitive Advantage,* pp. 270–72.

conditions not of their own choosing.[20] The strategic management challenge in capturing and retaining an offensive initiative involves:[21]

- Anticipating what the bases of industry leadership will be for the next round of strategic moves.
- Planning a *series* of moves aimed at throwing competitors off balance, keeping them on the defensive, and giving them little time to launch initiatives of their own.
- Gaining a shrewd understanding of offensive strategy tactics and what organizational capabilities are needed to carry them out.

As it turns out, military warfare principles are particularly instructive in designing offensive attacks on competitors' market positions. Three military maxims speak to how to attack an enemy:

Principle of Mass. Superior combat power must be concentrated at the critical time and place for a decisive purpose.

Principle of the Offensive. The commander who exercises the initiative, capitalizes on emergent opportunities, and exploits enemy weakness is in the best position to dominate the enemy and to maintain control of the campaign.

Principle of Surprise. Surprise results from striking an enemy at a time, place, and in a manner for which he is not prepared.

And four additional offensive guidelines have been proposed by business strategists:[22]

- A challenger firm should concentrate its strength against competitors' relative weaknesses.
- A major attack should never be launched against a competent, well-entrenched competitor without first neutralizing the competitor's ability to counterattack effectively.
- Any strategy of value requires that a firm follow a different course from its competitors *or* initiate action which will not be effective for an imitator *or* follow a course which will have quite different, and more favorable, consequences for it than for rivals.
- Capturing and retaining the initiative requires capitalizing on opportunities to preempt competitors and gain a prime market position—preemption occurs when one firm moves first (to tie up the best suppliers, to build new capacity, and so on), creating a condition where others find it extremely difficult to follow because of the "first occupancy" benefits gained by the aggressor.

---

[20]Ian C. MacMillan, "How Business Strategists Can Use Guerilla Warfare Tactics," *Journal of Business Strategy* 1, no. 2 (Fall 1980), p. 65.

[21]Ian C. MacMillan, "Seizing Competitive Initiative," *Journal of Business Strategy* 2, no. 4 (Spring 1982), pp. 45–49.

[22]Bruce D. Henderson, "On Corporate Strategy," reprinted in R.B. Lamb, *Competitive Strategic Management* (Englewood Cliffs, N.J.: Prentice-Hall, 1984, pp. 9, 10, and 14; and Ian C. MacMillan, "Preemptive Strategies," *Journal of Business Strategy* 4, no. 2 (Fall 1983), p. 16.

These military principles and experience-based business strategy admonitions have led to the identification of six offensive strategies.[23]

Frontal Attacks on Competitors' Strengths

An offensive-minded firm is said to employ a frontal attack when it moves against an opponent head-on, pitting its own strengths against those of rivals. The outcome depends on who has the greater competitive strength and commitment. For a pure frontal attack to succeed, the initiator needs a strength advantage over the intended victim(s). The military "principle of force" holds that whoever has the greatest resources will win out, except if the defender has greater firing efficiency or a terrain advantage. Military wisdom maintains that, for an aggressor's frontal attack to succeed against a well-entrenched opponent, the attacker needs at least a 3:1 advantage in combat firepower. When aggressor companies have fewer resources and weaker competitive strengths than entrenched defender firms, a frontal attack makes no sense and is generally doomed from the start.

All-out attacks upon a competitor's strengths can involve initiatives on any of several fronts—price-cutting, boosts in advertising and promotion, improved quality and performance, added customer services, the construction of major new plant capacity in a rival's "backyard," and much bigger R&D outlays. Head-on attacks can entail the use of one or more offensive initiatives. One of the most usual ploys is for the aggressor to attack with an equally good product offering and a lower price.[24] This can produce market share gains if the targeted rival has strong reasons for not resorting to matching price cuts of its own and if the challenger convinces buyers that its product is really just as good. However, whether such a strategy produces improved profits depends on the challenger's price-cost-volume relationships—will the price cuts result in lower margins and, if so, will the gains in volume offset the bottom-line impact of thinner margins per unit sold?

Another type of price-aggressive attack is based on first achieving overall low-cost leadership and then attacking competitors with a lower price.[25] Cost-related price-cutting is perhaps the strongest basis for launching and sustaining a price-aggressive frontal attack. Without a cost advantage, price cutting works only if the aggressor has more financial resources and can outlast its rivals in a war of attrition.

Attacks on Competitors' Weaknesses

This offensive approach draws upon the military principle of mass and involves concentrating one's competitive strengths and resources against the weaknesses of

---

[23]Philip Kotler and Ravi Singh, "Marketing Warfare in the 1980s," *Journal of Business Strategy* 1, no. 3 (Winter 1981), pp. 30–41; Kotler, *Marketing Management,* pp. 401–06; and MacMillan, "Preemptive Strategies," pp. 16–26.

[24]Kotler, *Marketing Management,* p. 402.

[25]Kotler, *Marketing Management,* p. 403.

rivals. The common weaknesses and openings that challengers are inclined to attack are:

- Geographic regions where the rival has low market share or is exerting less competitive effort, or both.
- Buyer segments which the rival is neglecting or is less equipped to serve, or both.
- Situations where rivals have neglected improving quality and product performance, thus creating opportunities to switch quality and performance-conscious buyers over to the challenger's better-quality offering.
- Instances where rivals have done a poor job of providing adequate customer service, making it relatively easy for a service-oriented challenger to win away the defenders' disenchanted customers.
- Where the defenders have under-advertised and otherwise failed to market the product to its fullest potential, thereby allowing a challenger with strong marketing skills to move in and win substantial sales and market share.
- Where the market leaders have gaps in their product line and opportunities exist to develop these gaps into strong, new market segments.
- Where the market leaders have failed to spot certain buyer needs, and an opportunity exists for an aggressor to jump in and serve them.

As a general rule, attacks on competitors' weaknesses have a better chance of succeeding than do frontal attacks on strengths. They may or may not involve the element of surprise.[26]

Simultaneous Attack on Many Fronts

There are times when aggressors launch a grand competitive offensive involving several major initiatives in an effort to throw a rival off balance, divert its attention in many directions, and force it into channeling resources to protect its front, sides, and rear simultaneously. Hunt's tried such an offensive several years ago in an attempt to wrest market share away from Heinz in the ketchup market. Simultaneously, Hunt's introduced two new ketchup flavors (pizza and hickory) to disrupt consumers' taste preferences, to try to create new-product segments, and to capture more retail shelf space in groceries. It lowered its price to 70 percent of Heinz's price; it offered sizable trade allowances to retailers; and it raised its advertising budget to over twice the level of Heinz's.[27] The offensive failed because not enough Heinz users tried the Hunt's brands and many of those who switched over to Hunt's soon switched back to Heinz. Grand offensives have their best chance of success when a challenger, because of superior resources, can overpower its rivals by outspending them across the board for a long enough time to buy its way into a position of market leadership and competitive advantage.

---

[26]For a discussion of the use of surprise to gain an offensive competitive edge, see William E. Rothschild, "Surprise and the Competitive Advantage," *Journal of Business Strategy* 4, no. 3 (Winter 1984), pp. 10–18.

[27]As cited in Kotler, *Marketing Management*, p. 404.

End-Run Offensives

End-run offensives avoid direct assault on entrenched positions and aim, instead, at being the first to occupy new ground. End-runs involve such moves as being the first to expand into new geographic markets, trying to create new segments via the introduction of products with different attributes and performance features, and leapfrogging into new technologies to supplant existing products and production processes. Technological leapfrogging is used often in high-tech industries; here, challengers concentrate on developing the next-generation technology and, when satisfied about its superiority, bring out a new wave of products that shift the competitive focus to its own new technological arena where a new trail is being blazed.

When end-run offensives can be made to appear as if they pose no *direct* or immediate threat to any particular rival, then they may not elicit any immediate competitive response. Aggressors who succeed in avoiding or delaying competitive retaliation may gain a significant first-mover advantage with a well-designed end-run, parlaying its newly won market success into a sustainable competitive advantage.

Guerrilla Offensives

Guerrilla offensives are particularly well suited to small challengers who have neither the resources nor the market visibility to mount a broad-based attack on the industry leaders. A guerrilla offensive uses the strategy of attacking in those locations and at those times in which the underdog can compete under conditions that suit it, rather than its bigger competitors. There are several options for designing a guerrilla offensive:[28]

1. Focus the offensive on a narrow, well-defined segment that is weakly defended by competitors.
2. Attack those fronts where rivals are overextended and have spread their resources most thinly (possibilities include serving less-populated geographic areas, enhancing delivery schedules at times when competitors' deliveries are running behind, adding to quality when rivals have quality-control problems, and boosting the technical services when buyers are confused by competitors' proliferation of models and optional features).
3. Make small, scattered, at-random raids on the leaders, with such harassing tactics as selective lowballing on price, intense bursts of promotional activity, and legal actions charging antitrust violations, patent infringement, and unfair advertising.

Preemptive Strategies

Preemptive strategies involve moving first to secure an advantageous position that rivals are foreclosed or discouraged from duplicating. There

---

[28]For more details, see MacMillan, "How Business Strategists Can Use Guerrilla Warfare Tactics," pp. 63–65 and Kathryn R. Harrigan, *Strategic Flexibility* (Lexington, Mass.: Lexington Books, 1985), pp. 30–45.

are several ways to win a prime strategic position with preemptive moves:[29]

- Expanding production capacity well ahead of market demand in hopes of discouraging rivals from following with expansions of their own—when rivals are bluffed out of adding capacity by a fear of creating long-term excess supply conditions and having to struggle with the bad profit economics of underutilized plants, the preemptor stands to win a bigger market share as market demand grows and its own plant capacity becomes filled.
- Tying up the best (or the most) raw material sources and the most reliable, high-quality suppliers via long-term contracts or backward vertical integration—this move can effectively relegate rivals to struggling for second-best supply positions.
- Securing the best geographic locations—big first-mover advantages are often locked in by quickly moving to obtain the most favorable sites along a heavily traveled thoroughfare, at a new interchange or intersection, in a new shopping mall, in a natural beauty spot, close to cheap transportation or raw material supplies or market outlets, and so on.
- Obtaining the business of prestigious customers.
- Establishing a psychological image and position in the minds of consumers that is unique and hard to copy and that establishes a compelling appeal and rallying cry—examples include Avis's well-known "We try harder" theme; Frito-Lay's guarantee to retailers of "99.5 percent service;" Holiday Inn's assurance of "no surprises," and Prudential's "piece of the Rock" image of safety and permanence.
- Securing exclusive or dominant access to the best distributors in an area.

Preemption has been used successfully on a number of occasions. General Mills' Red Lobster restaurant chain was notably successful in securing access to excellent seafood suppliers and in getting prime locations for its restaurant sites. DeBeers became the dominant world distributor of diamonds by tying up the production of nearly all of the important diamond mines. Du Pont's aggressive capacity expansions in titanium dioxide, while not blocking all competitors from expanding, did discourage enough competitors to give it a leadership position in the titanium dioxide industry. Coca-Cola has won a strong position in the fountain segment of the soft-drink industry by winning the business of McDonald's. Price Waterhouse's image as the most prestigious public accounting firm has always been linked to its list of blue-chip corporate clients.

To be successful, it is not necessary that a preemptive move totally blockade rivals from following or copying. It is enough to create a competitive advantage if preemption results in occupying a prime position. A *prime position* is one that is easier to defend and that makes a material difference in how the game of competition unfolds in the industry.

---

[29]The use of preemptive moves is treated comprehensively in MacMillan, "Preemptive Strategies," pp. 16–26. What follows in this section is based on MacMillan's article.

Choosing Whom to Attack

Aggressor firms need to analyze which of their rivals to attack as well as how to attack them. There are basically three types of firms at which an offensive can be aimed:[30]

1. *Attack the market leader(s).* This entails high risk but can carry a potentially big payoff. It makes the best sense when the leader in terms of size and market share is not a true leader in terms of serving the market well. The signs of leader vulnerability include unhappy buyers, low profitability, strong emotional commitment to a technology it has pioneered, a history of regulatory problems, and being "stuck in the middle"—lacking real strength based on low-cost leadership or differentiation. Attacks on leaders can also succeed when the challenger is able to revamp its activity-cost chain or to otherwise so innovate in the ways activities are performed that it gains a lockhold on a fresh cost-based or differentiation-based competitive advantage.[31] Attacks on leaders need not have the objective of making the aggressor the new leader, however; a challenger may win by simply wresting enough sales away from the leader to make the aggressor a far stronger runner-up.
2. *Attack runner-up firms.* Launching offensives against weaker runner-up firms whose positions are vulnerable often has strong appeal and carries relatively low risk. In such cases, frontal attacks may well work, even if the challenger has smaller resources to work with, because the targeted rival's vulnerabilities are so readily exploitable.
3. *Attack small local and regional firms that are not doing the job and whose customers are dissatisfied.*

As was argued earlier in this chapter, the most successful strategies tend to be grounded in competitive advantage. This goes for offensive strategies, too. The offensive options for getting a competitive advantage can be linked to low-cost leadership, differentiation, or focusing. The primary competitive offensive weapons include:[32]

- Coming up with a lower-cost product design.
- Developing product features that deliver superior performance to buyers or that lower buyers' user costs.
- Employing more efficient inbound and/or outbound logistical systems.
- Giving more responsive after-sale support to buyers.
- Escalating the marketing effort in an undermarketed industry.
- Utilizing a more technically proficient sales force.
- Making changes in production operations that lower costs or enhance differentiation.
- Pioneering a new distribution channel.
- Bypassing existing channels and selling direct to the end-user.

---

[30]Kotler, *Marketing Management,* p. 400.
[31]Porter, *Competitive Advantage,* p. 518.
[32]Porter, *Competitive Advantage,* pp. 520–22.

USING DEFENSIVE STRATEGIES TO PROTECT COMPETITIVE ADVANTAGE

In a competitive market, all firms are subject to attacks from rivals. Offensive attacks can come both from new entrants into the industry and from established firms seeking to improve their market positions. The purpose of defensive strategy is to lower the risk of being attacked, to lessen the intensity of any attack that occurs, and to influence challengers to opt for less threatening offensive strategies.[33] While defensive strategy usually doesn't enhance a firm's competitive advantage, it should definitely be capable of strengthening a firm's competitive position and, thus, sustaining whatever competitive advantage the firm has.

There are several basic defensive postures a firm can assume:[34]

- *Position defense*. This plays off the theme of fortification and is the defensive equivalent of the frontal assault. Resources are channeled into improving existing products, the existing organization, and the firm's traditional ways of doing business. Its appeal hinges upon a belief that the firm's future lies in "strengthening our existing position." However, the pitfall of position defense is that it can blind users to new driving forces and the signals of market and environmental change; as a consequence, it fosters a lethargy to adapt to changing conditions.

- *Mobile defense*. This defensive approach presents attackers with more of a moving target. The firm makes a conscious effort to monitor the market and competitive environment and to adjust to changing conditions promptly, thus avoiding out-of-date vulnerability. Product lines may be broadened, production facilities kept modern, and diversification into closely related areas pursued.

- *Preemptive defense*. This posture plays off the theme that prevention is better than cure and is an "offensive defense." Preemptive moves are made any time there are big first-mover advantages to be gained and, especially, when moving first tends to block rivals from undertaking like action (because there is much less to be gained from being an imitative second or because imitation is effectively foreclosed).

- *Diversion and dissuasion defenses*. Here the aim is to lessen the chances of attack and divert rivals' attention to other firms. Classic diversion and dissuasion approaches include appearing to be unworthy of attention, appearing to be unbeatable, being secretive and avoiding attention, appearing to be irrational, and trying to channel competitor's attention away from high potential areas.

The Kinds of Defensive Tactics

There are substantial numbers of defensive moves to choose from in protecting one's competitive position. One category of defensive tactics involves trying to

---

[33]Porter, *Competitive Advantage*, p. 482.

[34]Kotler and Singh, "Marketing Warfare in the 1980s," pp. 36–40; and Henderson, "On Corporate Strategy," pp. 10–11.

block the avenues that challengers can take in mounting an offensive; the options here include:[35]

- Broadening the product line to close vacant niches and gaps to would-be challengers.
- Introducing models or brands that match the characteristics that challengers' models already have or might have.
- Keeping prices low on those models that most closely match competitors' offerings.
- Signing exclusive agreements with dealers and distributors to keep competitors from using the same ones.
- Granting dealers and distributors sizable volume discounts to discourage them from experimenting with other suppliers.
- Offering free or low-cost training to buyers' personnel in the use of the firm's product.
- Making it harder for competitors to get buyers to try their brands by (1) giving special price discounts to buyers who are considering trial use of rival brands, (2) resorting to high levels of couponing and sample giveaways to buyers most prone to experiment, and (3) leaking information about impending new products or price changes that cause buyers to postpone switching decisions.
- Raising the amount of financing provided to dealers and to buyers.
- Reducing delivery times for spare parts.
- Increasing warranty coverages.
- Patenting the feasible alternative technologies.
- Maintaining a participation in alternative technologies.
- Protecting proprietary know-how in products, production technologies, and other parts of the activity-cost chain.
- Signing exclusive contracts with the best suppliers to block access of aggressive rivals.
- Purchasing natural resource reserves well in excess of present needs so as to preempt them from competitors.
- Avoiding suppliers that also serve competitors.
- Challenging rivals' products or practices in regulatory proceedings.

A second category of defensive tactics consists of ways to signal challengers that there is a real threat of strong retaliation if the challenger attacks. Such tactics are intended to dissuade challengers from attacking at all (by raising their expectations that the resulting battle will be bloody and more costly to the challenger than it is worth) or, at the least, to blunt and divert the attack to arenas that are less threatening to the defender. A number of defen-

---

[35]Porter, *Competitive Advantage*, pp. 489–94.

sive moves can be used to signal challengers of a defender's intent to the retaliate:[36]

- Publicly announcing management's commitment to maintain the firm's
  present market share.
- Publicly announcing plans to construct adequate production capacity to
  meet forecasted demand growth, and sometimes building just ahead of
  demand.
- Leaking advance information about a new product generation, a breakthrough in production technology, or the planned introduction of important
  new brands or models, thereby raising the risk perceived by challengers
  that such a move will actually be forthcoming and, hopefully, inducing
  them to delay moves of their own until they see if the signals are credible.
- Publicly commiting the firm to a policy of matching the prices or other
  terms offered by competitors (that is, touting and then following through
  on a "we will not be undersold" theme).
- Maintaining a war chest of cash reserves or other quickly tappable source
  of liquidity.
- Making an occasional strong counterresponse to the moves of weak competitors to enhance the firm's image as a tough defender.

A third category of defensive maneuvers involves trying to lower the inducement
for challengers to launch an offensive. Typically, profit is the inducement for
attack—in particular, the defender's current profits and the challenger's assumption
about future industry conditions and profitability. A defender can deflect attacks,
especially from new entrants, by not being too greedy and by deliberately forgoing
some short-run profits. When a firm's or an industry's profitability is very high,
challengers are more willing to try to hurdle high defensive barriers and to combat
strong retaliation.

Benefit-Cost Trade-offs.   The benefits of a successful defense can be hard to
measure because, when a defense works best, then nothing happens in the way
of serious challenges. On the other hand, a number of defensive options involve
substantial costs to a firm. Defensive tactics become more attractive when they
meet some or all of the following conditions:[37]

1. When the firm's position with buyers is strengthened—through enhanced differentiation or increased sales (as can occur from the defensive value of an
   advertising boost that raises the costs to challengers of attacking the firm's
   position) or through increased buyer loyalty (as can occur from better credit
   or financing terms and from stronger warranties).
2. When the cost of the defensive tactic imposes an even greater cost on a
   challenger.

---

[36]Porter, *Competitive Advantage*, pp. 495–97. The listing here is selective; Porter offers a greater number
of options.
[37]Porter, *Competitive Advantage*, pp. 500–02.

3. When the defensive tactic has a lasting effect in raising barriers or in creating a credible long-term threat of retaliation.
4. When there is strong likelihood that the defensive tactic will be noticed and well understood by potential challengers.
5. When the tactic will be taken seriously by challengers (because the defender has the resources to carry out its retaliatory threats and a resolve to do so).

Illustration Capsule 13 relates a fascinating example of the offensive and defensive maneuvers IBM once employed in mainframe computers.

FIRST-MOVER ADVANTAGES AND DISADVANTAGES

When to make a strategic move is often as crucial as *what* move to make. Timing is especially important when *first-mover advantages* or *disadvantages* exist.[38] Being the first competitor to initiate a fresh strategy can have a high payoff when (1) pioneering adds greatly to a firm's image and reputation with buyers; (2) early commitments to supplies of raw materials, new technologies, distribution channels, and so on can produce an absolute cost advantage over rivals; (3) customer loyalty is so high that long-term benefits accrue to the firm that first convinces the customer to use its product; and (4) moving first can be a preemptive strike, making imitation extra hard or unlikely. The stronger any first-mover advantages are, the more attractive the offensive move becomes.

However, being late or following a wait and see approach is wise if first-mover disadvantages exist. Pioneering is risky when (1) the costs of opening up a new market are great but customer loyalty is weak, (2) technological change is so rapid that early investments can be rendered obsolete (thus, allowing following firms to have the advantage of the newest products and processes), and (3) the industry is developing so rapidly that skills and know-how built up during the early competitive phase are easily bypassed and overcome by late-movers. "Good" timing, therefore, is an important ingredient in deciding whether to be aggressive or cautious in pursuing a particular move.

ANALYTICAL CHECKLIST

The challenge of competitive strategy—whether it be a low-cost, a differentiation, or a focus strategy, is to create a competitive advantage for the firm. Competitive advantage comes from so positioning a firm in the marketplace that it has an edge in coping with competitive forces and in attracting buyers.

A strategy of trying to be the low-cost producer works well in situations where:

- Demand is price-elastic (buyers are very price-sensitive).
- The industry's product is pretty much the same from seller to seller.
- The marketplace is dominated by the force of price competition (buyers are prone to shop around on price).

---

[38]Michael E. Porter, *Comparative Strategy* (New York: Free Press, 1980), pp. 232–33.

ILLUSTRATION CAPSULE 13

Competitive Strategy at IBM: The System/360 Product Line

IBM's System/360 computer models included a wide range of central processing unit (CPU) sizes, together with numerous options for tying in input-output equipment (printers, readers) and memory storage. IBM priced its memory and input-output equipment separately from its central processing computer units to allow customers maximum flexibility in choosing the best equipment combinations. The design characteristics of the System/360 models, however, allowed rival computer manufacturers to produce almost identical copies of the IBM input-output units and memories; they could then sell these at lower prices directly to users having IBM central processing units. Generally, IBM's central-processing units were protected from the competition of rival computer firms, because IBM customers were very reluctant to discard their investment in specialized programming and because of the difficulty in manufacturing a CPU having programming logic compatible with IBM processors. There was no such compatibility problem with input-output equipment or with memory units. Potter Instrument Company in 1967 initiated competition with IBM by introducing a replacement for IBM tape drives; a short time later, other peripheral equipment manufacturers came out with replacements for IBM disc drives and then for main memory units.

Because sales of input-output equipment and memory units accounted for over half of IBM's computer revenue, IBM was concerned in early 1970 about the threat posed by the competitive products of the peripheral equipment manufacturers and the great success they were having in getting IBM users to switch to lower-priced non-IBM equipment. At the time, IBM was preparing to introduce its new System/370 line, and, while the company felt it could safely ignore the threat to the System/360 memories, it wanted to avoid losing the new System/370 memories to rival firms. IBM assembled a task force to assess how well rival firms would fare in selling IBM-compatible memory units against IBM at various IBM prices; the study was done for a hypothetical new company and also for an established company having the capacity to produce IBM-compatible memory units. Insofar as the hypothetical new company was concerned, the analysis showed that IBM's primary protection from competition was the time required for a new company to become established in the marketplace. The IBM task force estimated that if IBM established a lease price of $16,000 to $18,000 per month per megabyte of memory (with initial shipments to begin in 1972), then a new company could not break even competing with IBM until around 1974; and, further, if the IBM lease price was $12,000 and above, the task force projected good profitability for a new company beyond 1976 but at prices of $10,000 and below no break-even point was envisioned until the far future.

For an established company, the task force projected that a firm could enter memory competition and reach the break-even point by 1973 at an IBM lease price of $18,000 per month per megabyte; and, by 1975, with a price of $10,000 to $12,000, with high profitability in later years for all lease rentals of $12,000 and above. The task force concluded that if IBM went ahead with its planned $12,000-per-megabyte monthly fee that a new company could be only marginally profitable but that an established peripheral equipment company would be very likely to enter

ILLUSTRATION CAPSULE 13 *(continued)*

the field, because they could make a 20 percent return on investment for a $10 million investment and would enjoy a healthy 23 percent profit margin.

However, additional studies indicated that of the $61 million-per-month rental value which IBM expected to have from its memory units by 1976, 26 percent would be protected through minimum-memory sizes tied directly to the CPU, 36 percent through customers who would resist mixing IBM equipment with that of other manufacturers, and 15 percent because of locations in outlying geographical areas where the smaller firms were not expected to compete. This left only 23 percent of IBM's memory business as a possible competitive target, regardless of the exact price set by IBM. Thus, based on the expected customer resistance to using non-IBM equipment and upon the estimated lag time between IBM's introduction to System/370 memory units and the availability of competitive memory units, IBM decided to go ahead with its planned price of $12,000 per month per megabyte for memory units on its 155 and 165 System/370 models. The 370/155 and 165 memory units utilized magnetic cores—the standard computer memory technology. But when IBM came out with its next System/370 model, the 145, a new all-semiconductor memory was used; this semiconductor memory was much faster than magnetic cores and, because it was a new technology, it was not considered subject to immediate competitive attack. As a result, IBM priced its new semiconductor memory units 60 percent higher than its magnetic core memory units. Within less than a year, though, IBM became concerned about the ability of rival firms to introduce not only magnetic core replacements for the earlier System/370 models but also replacement equipment for the new semiconductor unit.

Meanwhile, IBM studies indicated lower prices for central processing units prompted users to install the largest possible system and, thus, generate the maximum demand for memory and input-output equipment (subject to replacement by competitors), while higher prices on central processing units increased CPU profits but reduced the demand and profit earned on peripheral equipment sales and leases. IBM's solution to this profit trade-off was to package a large amount of memory with a central processing unit and charge a lower CPU price. This had the advantage of raising overall profits, while protecting at least the packaged portion of memory from competition.

Even so, within a few months, IBM saw that its previous forecast had underestimated the ability of rival firms to keep pace, and still another task force was set up to study alternatives for reducing the competitive threat. Basically, the plans the task force considered were various combinations of minimum memories, lower memory unit prices, and increased CPU prices. The task force also looked at reducing the number of memory options obtainable with a central processing unit and then refusing to sell CPUs without at least the minimum memory. Nonetheless, the final decision was to raise the central processing unit prices by a maximum of 8 percent, cut the purchase price of memory units on 155 and 165 models, and make no change in the rental price of memory units.

This action shortly proved to be ineffective, and IBM came up with a strategy of introducing upgraded 155 and 165 models as new machines having higher CPU

ILLUSTRATION CAPSULE 13 *(concluded)*

prices and lower memory prices. In August 1972, IBM announced new versions of its 155 and 165 models, to be known as the 158 and 168 models (a revision known inside IBM as the SMASH program). The basic CPU price was raised 36 percent on the 165 model and 54 percent on the model 155. The memory price was cut 57 percent, and a larger minimum memory size was tied to the basic central processing unit on both models, neither of which could be acquired without the memory units. The effect of the changes was to make the total price of the 158 and 168 models higher in small configurations and lower in large configurations than the original 155 and 165 models. The semiconductor memory was not made available to users of the original 155 and 165 models, thereby prohibiting users from buying the cheaper central process unit and putting on the cheaper memory as well. The SMASH program effectively foreclosed rival firms from the memory market for several months.

In trying to unravel IBM's actions, it is important to understand that there are high barriers to entry in the full-line computer systems market but low barriers to entry in the peripheral equipment market. The barriers that do exist in the peripheral equipment market are related primarily to brand loyalty to IBM (including a fear of problems of mixing the equipment of different manufacturers) and the difficulty of producing IBM-compatible products which will match IBM interface specifications. The latter problem causes a lag between the time IBM introduces a product and the time it can be copied. This time lag reduces the rental life of the product of rival firms and gives IBM some time after a new product introduction without competition. Additional barriers to entry in the peripheral market include raising enough working capital to finance a rental business and some small manufacturing economies of scale. However, the disadvantages of small size are not so large as to preclude a satisfactory profit by undercutting IBM's existing price—unless and until IBM also cuts prices.

A second aspect of the computer equipment market is the disruption caused by equipment installation and removal, even if compatibility is not a problem. Normally, lower-priced equipment is introduced as a "new" product having essentially identical performance specifications as existing products. The customer can get the price cut only by physically removing the old model and installing the new one. The freight charges and disruption involved, as well as lack of information or lethargy on the part of some computer users, allowed IBM to come out with a competitive low-priced product while still receiving the higher rent from many users for some time after the price cut.

The third feature which IBM used to good advantage related to the time lag between IBM's introduction of a new product and a rival's introduction of its equivalent. As part of its introductory scheme, IBM induced users to agree to a fixed-term lease period, with heavy penalties for early termination. This effectively locked out competitors until users completed their lease agreements.

- There are not many ways to achieve product differentiation that have much value to buyers.
- Most buyers use the product in about the same ways and, thus, have common user requirements.
- Buyers' costs in switching from one seller or brand to another are low (or even zero).

To achieve a low-cost advantage, a company must become more skilled than rivals in controlling cost drivers or it must find innovative cost-saving ways to revamp the activity-cost chain, or do both.

Differentiation strategies can produce a competitive edge based on technical superiority, quality, service, or more value for the money. Differentiation strategies work *best* when:

- There are many ways to differentiate the product/service that buyers think have value.
- Buyer needs or uses of the product/service are diverse.
- Not many rival firms are following a differentiation strategy.

Successful differentiation must usually be keyed to lowering the buyer's cost of using the item or else raising the performance and value the buyer gets in using the product.

The competitive advantage of focusing is earned either by differentiation from better meeting the needs of the target market segments or by achieving lower costs in serving the segment. Focusing works best when:

- Buyer needs or uses of the item are diverse.
- No other rival is attempting to *specialize* in the same target segment.
- A firm lacks the capability to go after a wider part of the total market.
- Buyer segments differ widely in size, growth rate, profitability, and intensity in the five competitive forces, making some segments more attractive than others.

A variety of offensive strategic moves are available for securing a competitive advantage. Strategic offensives can be aimed either at competitors' strengths or at their weaknesses; they can involve one or many points of attack; they can be designed as guerrilla actions, as head-on assaults, or as end-runs to outflank a rival; and the target of the offensive can be a market leader, a runner-up firm, or the smallest and weakest firms in the industry.

The strategic approaches to defending a company's position can entail (1) fortifying the company's present position, (2) presenting competitors with a moving target, (3) using an offensive-type defense that preempts rivals from making aggressive moves, and (4) diverting and dissuading rivals from even trying to attack.

SUGGESTED READINGS

Cohen, William A. "War in the Marketplace." *Business Horizons* 29, no. 2 (March–April 1986), pp. 10–20.

Coyne, Kevin P. "Sustainable Competitive Advantage—What It Is, What It Isn't." *Business Horizons* 29, no. 1 (January–February 1986), pp. 54–61.

Harrigan, Kathryn. "Guerilla Strategies for Underdog Competitors." *Planning Review* 14, no. 6 (November 1986), pp. 4–11.

Henderson, Bruce D. "On Corporate Strategy." Reprinted in R. B. Lamb, ed., *Competitive Strategic Management*. Englewood Cliffs, N.J.: Prentice-Hall, 1984, pp. 1–34.

Hout, Thomas; Michael E. Porter; and Eileen Rudden. "How Global Companies Win Out." *Harvard Business Review* 60, no. 5 (September–October 1982), pp. 98–108.

Kotler, Philip, and Ravi Singh. "Marketing Warfare in the 1980s." *Journal of Business Strategy* 1, no. 3 (Winter 1981), pp. 30–41.

MacMillan, Ian C. "Seizing Competitive Initiative." *Journal of Business Strategy* 2, no. 4 (Spring 1982), pp. 43–57.

————. "How Business Strategies Can Use Guerilla Warfare Tactics." *Journal of Business Strategy* 1, no. 2 (Fall 1980), pp. 63–65.

————. "Preemptive Strategies." *Journal of Business Strategy* 4, no. 2 (Fall 1983), pp. 16–26.

Ohmae, Kenichi. *The Mind of the Strategist*. (New York: Penguin Books, 1983), chaps. 4 and 5.

Porter, Michael E. *Competitive Advantage*. New York: Free Press, 1985, chaps. 3, 4, 5, 7, 14, and 15.

Rothschild, William E. "Surprise and the Competitive Advantage." *Journal of Business Strategy* 4, no. 3 (Winter 1984), pp. 10–18.

Thompson, Arthur A. "Strategies for Staying Cost Competitive." *Harvard Business Review* 62, no. 1 (January–February 1984), pp. 110–17.

6

Matching Strategy to the Situation

Strategy isn't something you can nail together in slap-dash fashion by sitting around a conference table.

Terry Haller

The essence of formulating competitive strategy is relating a company to its environment . . . the best strategy for a given firm is ultimately a unique construction reflecting its particular circumstances.

Michael E. Porter

Which of the many available strategy alternatives best suits a particular business is conditioned partly by the industry environment in which it competes and partly by its situation in that environment. To demonstrate the kinds of considerations that go into matching strategy to the situation, this chapter surveys nine classic types of generic industry environments and company situations:

1. Competing in a young, emerging industry.
2. Competing during the transition to industry maturity.
3. Competing in mature or declining industries.
4. Competing in fragmented industries.
5. Competing in global markets.
6. Strategies for industry leaders.
7. Strategies for runner-up firms.
8. Strategies for weaker firms.
9. Turnaround strategies for distressed businesses and crisis situations.

STRATEGIES FOR COMPETING IN YOUNG, EMERGING INDUSTRIES

Two crucial strategic issues confront firms trying to participate in a young, emerging industry with high-growth potential: (1) how to acquire the resources needed to support a *grow-and-build strategy* aimed at growing faster than the market as a whole and achieving/maintaining a position among the industry leaders and (2) what market segments and competitive advantage to go after in preparation for the time when growth slows and the weakest firms fall prey to competitive shakeout and industry consolidation.[1] Ironclad prescriptions cannot be given for just how these two issues should be resolved, since emerging industries are not all alike. The form of the grow-and-build strategy has to be geared to match the firm's situation and the character of the emerging industry itself—it can emphasize differentiation or low cost. The market environments of emerging industries have several strategy-shaping features:[2]

- There are no proven key success factors; the issue of how the industry will evolve and what it will take to compete successfully is open ended.
- Much of the technological know-how tends to be proprietary, having been developed in-house by pioneering firms.
- There is uncertainty over which production technology will prove to be the most efficient and which product attributes will be preferred by buyers—the result is erratic product quality, industrywide absence of product and technological standardization, and a situation where each firm is, at least until a broader consensus develops, committed to pioneering its own approach to technology, product design, marketing, and distribution.
- Firms lack solid information about competitors, buyer needs and preferences, when demand will take off, how fast the market will grow, and how big the market will get; industry participants are forced to grope for the right strategy and the right timing.
- Experience curve effects permit significant cost reductions as volume builds.
- Low entry barriers exist (even for newly formed companies) unless initial investment costs in new technology create a high financial barrier.
- Since all buyers will be first-time users, the marketing task is one of inducing initial purchase and eliminating customer confusion over the multiplicity of product attributes, technologies, and claims of rival firms. Many potential buyers may perceive that second- or third-generation technologies will make current products obsolete; hence, they may delay purchase until the product matures and a consensus emerges regarding design and technology.
- Difficulties in securing ample supplies of raw materials and components may be encountered (until suppliers gear up to meet the industry's needs).
- Because of the above conditions, firms in an emerging industry need enough financial strength to get over the hump of industry start-up problems and to begin to realize the cash flow benefits of strong sales growth and a declining experience curve. Still, raising the capital to finance rapid growth can be a strain.

---

[1]Charles W. Hofer and Dan Schendel, *Strategy Formulation: Analytical Concepts* (St. Paul, Minn.: West Publishing, 1978), pp. 164–65.

[2]Michael E. Porter, *Competitive Strategy* (New York: Free Press, 1980), pp. 216–23.

Dealing with these conditions is a challenging business strategy problem. The experiences of firms in emerging industries have produced the following growth-stage strategy guidelines.[3]

1. Manage the business in an entrepreneurial mode with the aim of positioning the firm for future growth. In an emerging industry there are no established rules of the game, and a wide variety of strategic approaches are often tried by industry participants. Because firms enjoy wide strategic freedom, a pioneering firm that makes a good strategic choice can shape the rules, gain first-mover advantages, and achieve leadership recognition.
2. Work hard at improving product quality and developing attractive performance features.
3. Try to capture any advantages associated with adding more models, better styling, early commitments to technologies and raw materials suppliers, experience curve effects, and pioneering new distribution channels.
4. Search out new customer groups, new geographical areas to enter, and new user applications. Make it easier and cheaper for first-time buyers to try the industry's new product.
5. Gradually shift the advertising focus from building product awareness to increasing frequency of use and to creating brand loyalty.
6. Move quickly when technological uncertainty clears and a dominant technology emerges; try to pioneer the "dominant design" approach (but be cautious when technology is moving so rapidly that early investments are likely to be rendered obsolete).
7. Use price cuts to attract the next layer of price-sensitive buyers into the market.
8. Expect large, established firms looking for growth opportunities to enter the industry, attracted by the more certain prospects the industry is offering. Try to prepare for the entry of powerful competitors by forecasting *(a)* who the probable entrants will be (based on present and future entry barriers) and *(b)* the types of strategies they are likely to employ.

However, the value of winning the early race for growth and market share leadership has to be balanced against the longer-range need to build a durable competitive edge and a defendable market position.[4] Powerful firms may enter, attracted by the growth potential. And sooner or later, the battle for market share will trigger a competitive shakeout and the industry will consolidate to a smaller number of competitors. A young, single-business enterprise in a fast-developing industry can help its cause by selecting knowledgeable members to its board of directors, bringing to entrepreneurially-oriented managers with experience in guiding young businesses through the developmental and takeoff stages, or gaining added expertise and a stronger resource base via merger with other firms in the industry.

---

[3]Philip Kotler, *Marketing Management,* 5th ed. (Englewood Cliffs, N.J.: Prentice Hall, 1984), p. 366; and Porter, *Competitive Strategy,* chap. 10.
[4]Hofer and Schendel, *Strategy Formulation,* pp. 164–65.

STRATEGIES FOR COMPETING DURING THE TRANSITION TO INDUSTRY MATURITY

Rapid industry growth cannot go on forever. The transition to a slower-growth, maturing industry environment does not, of course, occur after any fixed period and it can be forestalled by innovations or other driving forces that renew rapid growth. Nonetheless, when growth slows, the transition usually produces fundamental changes in the industry's competitive environment:[5]

1. *Slowing growth in buyer demand generates more head-to-head competition for market share.* Since firms are unable to maintain their historical rates of growth by merely holding the same market share, rivalry turns toward trying to take customers away from other firms. Outbreaks of price-cutting, increased advertising, and other aggressive tactics are common.

2. *Buyers become more sophisticated, often driving a harder bargain on repeat purchases.* Since the product is no longer new but an established item with which buyers are familiar, the attention of buyers is on which of several brands to buy the next time.

3. *Competition often produces a greater emphasis on cost and service.* As sellers all begin to offer the product attributes that buyers prefer, buyer choice among competing brands hinges more and more on which seller offers the best combination of price and service.

4. *Firms have a "topping out" problem in adding production capacity.* Slower rates of industry growth mean slower rates of capacity additions—or else industry over capacity results. Each firm has to monitor rivals' capacity additions carefully and to so time its own capacity additions that excess capacity is minimized. Rapid industry growth no longer quickly covers up the mistake of adding too much capacity too soon.

5. *Product innovation and new end-use applications are harder to come by.* Whereas R&D usually produces a stream of new-product attributes and applications during the takeoff and rapid-growth stages, the ability to continue to generate marketable innovations tend to drop off. Firms run out of big new ideas and ways to stimulate product excitement.

6. *International competition increases.* Technological maturity, product standardization, and increased emphasis on low-cost production often generate a more globally competitive industry. Growth-minded domestic firms seek new foreign markets and, also, become interested in locating plant facilities in countries where production costs are lower; domestic and foreign firms are drawn into head-to-head competition, creating political issues over trade barriers and protectionism. Industry leadership passes to those companies intent on winning the biggest global market shares with strategies designed to build strong competitive positions in most of the major geographic markets of the world.

7. *Industry profitability falls, sometimes temporarily and sometimes permanently.* Slower growth, increased competition, more sophisticated buyers, and the erosion of competitive advantages frequently shrink industry profits. The profits

---

[5]Porter, *Competitive Strategy*, pp. 238–40.

of weaker, less-efficient firms are usually more adversely affected than are those of strong competitors.

8. *The resulting competitive shakeout induces a number of mergers and acquisitions among former competitors, drives some firms out of the industry, and, in general, produces industry consolidation.* Whereas even inefficient firms and firms with weak competitive strategies can survive in a rapid-growth industry, the stiffer competition accompanying industry maturity generally exposes competitive weakness and opens the door for a survival-of-the-fittest contest to unfold.

These characteristics usually force firms to reexamine their business strategies. A refashioned competitive approach can sometimes be a matter of survival. There are several strategic moves that are well-suited for maturing industries.[6]

Pruning the Product Line. Although numerous models, sizes, and product options may have been competitively useful in a rapidly growing market, product-line proliferation can be costly in a mature environment characterized by price competition and battles for market share. Squeezed profit margins prompt cost studies that become the basis for pruning unprofitable items from the line and for concentrating on items where margins are highest or where the firm has a comparative advantage, or both. Average costing for groups of products and arbitrary allocations of overhead become inadequate for evaluating the product line and deciding what new items to add. Unwittingly subsidizing the losses on one item with above-average profits on another hides items whose demand does not support their true costs and invites price-cutting or new product introductions by rivals against items that may be priced high. In general, a much enhanced "profit consciousness" is needed to be successful in intensely competitive markets.

More Emphasis on Process Innovation. The intensifying of price competition that accompanies market maturity puts greater relative importance on process-oriented technological innovation. Innovations that permit lower-cost distribution have high competitive value in markets where buyers are increasingly price-conscious. Japanese firms have been quite successful emphasizing technological process strategies aimed at becoming the low-cost producer of a quality product.

A Stronger Focus on Cost Reduction. Stiffening price competition gives firms the incentive to reduce unit costs. The efforts can cover a broad front: pushing suppliers for better prices, switching to lower-priced components, adopting more economical product designs, emphasizing manufacturing and distribution efficiency, retrenching sales efforts (to concentrate on the best types of buyers), and trimming administrative overhead.

Increasing Sales to Present Customers. In a mature market, growing by taking customers away from rivals may not hold as much appeal as may a strategy of expanding sales to existing customers. Increasing the purchases of existing customers can take the form of broadening the lines offered to include complementary products and ancillary services, finding more ways for customers to use

---

[6]The following discussion draws from Porter, *Competitive Strategy*, pp. 241–46.

the product, performing more functions for the buyers (assembling components prior to shipment), and so on.

Purchasing Weaker Rivals at Bargain Prices.   Sometimes the facilities and assets of distressed rivals can be acquired cheaply. Such acquisitions can improve margins and help create a low-cost position if these facilities are not inefficient or likely to be rendered obsolete by technological change. Heileman Brewing Company rose from relative obscurity to become the fourth largest beer company by acquiring small regional brewers and used equipment at bargain prices.

Expanding Internationally.   As its domestic market matures, a firm may seek to enter foreign markets where attractive growth potential still exists and where competitive pressures are not so strong. Foreign expansion can also be attractive if manufacturing facilities that have become obsolete domestically are still suitable for competing in less-developed foreign markets (a condition that lowers entry costs); such can occur when (1) foreign buyers have less-sophisticated needs and have simpler, old-fashioned end-use applications; (2) foreign competitors are smaller, less formidable, and do not employ the latest production technology; (3) continuing to squeeze production out of fully depreciated plants and equipment offers the prospects of bigger profit margins; and (4) a domestic firm's skills and reputation are readily transferable to foreign markets.

Strategic Pitfalls

Perhaps the biggest pitfall during the transition to industry maturity is not making a clear strategic choice and, instead, steering a middle course between low cost, differentiation, and focus. Such strategies leave the firm stuck in the middle, without a solid competitive advantage and an "average" image with buyers. Other pitfalls include sacrificing long-term position for short-term profit, waiting too long to respond to price-cutting, not getting rid of excess capacity as growth slows, and overinvesting in efforts to boost sales growth.

STRATEGIES FOR FIRMS IN MATURE OR DECLINING INDUSTRIES

Many firms operate in industries where demand is growing slower than the economywide average or is even declining. Although harvesting, selling out, and closing down are candidate strategies for weaker competitors with dim survival prospects, strong competitors may well find it possible to work within a stagnant market environment and achieve good performance.[7] Stagnant demand by itself is not enough to make an industry unattractive. Selling out may or may not be practical, and closing down operations is always a last resort.

Businesses competing in slow-growth/declining industries have to accept the difficult realities of continuing stagnancy, and they must resign themselves to performance goals consistent with the market opportunities that are available. Cash flow and return on investment criteria are more appropriate than growth-oriented performance measures, but sales and market share growth are by no means ruled

---

[7]R.G. Hamermesh and S.B. Silk, "How to Compete in Stagnant Industries," *Harvard Business Review* 57, no. 5 (September–October 1979), p. 161.

out. Strong competitors may well be able to take sales away from rivals, and either the acquisition of or exit of weaker firms creates opportunities for the market shares of the remaining companies to rise.

In general, three themes characterize the strategies of firms that have succeeded in stagnant industries:[8]

1. *Pursue a focus strategy by identifying, creating, and exploiting the growth segments within the industry.* Slow-growth or declining markets, like other markets, are composed of numerous segments and subsegments. Frequently, one or more of these segments is growing rapidly, despite a lack of growth in the industry as a whole. An astute competitor who is first to concentrate on the most attractive segments can escape stagnating sales and profits and possibly achieve competitive advantage in serving the target segments.

2. *Emphasize quality improvement and product innovation.* Either enhanced quality or innovation can rejuvenate demand by creating important new growth segments or by attracting buyers to trade up. Successful product innovation opens up an avenue for competing besides that of meeting or beating the prices of rival sellers. Differentiation based on successful innovation has the additional advantage of being difficult and expensive for rival firms to imitate.

3. *Work diligently and persistently to improve production and distribution efficiency.* When increases in sales cannot be counted on to generate increases in earnings, an alternative is to improve profit margins and return on investment by reducing operating costs. The paths for achieving a lower-cost position include (1) improving the manufacturing process via automation and increased specialization, (2) consolidating underutilized production facilities, (3) adding more distribution channels to ensure the unit volume needed for low-cost production, and (4) closing down low-volume, high-cost distribution outlets.

Plainly enough, these three strategic themes are not mutually exclusive.[9] Attempts to introduce new innovative versions of a product can *create* a fast-growing market segment. Similarly, concentrating on operating efficiencies paves the way to initiate price reductions that create price-conscious growth segments. Note, also, that all three themes are variations of the three generic competitive strategies— what is creative is how they have been applied to fit opportunities and conditions in an otherwise unattractive industry environment.

The most attractive declining industries are those where the decline is reasonably slow and smooth and where some profitable niches remain. The pitfalls of choosing to continue to compete in a stagnating market are (1) getting trapped in a profitless war of attrition, (2) trying to harvest from a weak initial position, and (3) over-optimism about the industry's future.

STRATEGIES FOR COMPETING IN FRAGMENTED INDUSTRIES

Many firms compete in an industry made of numerous small and medium-sized companies, many of which are privately held and none of which has a king-sized

---

[8]Ibid., p. 162.
[9]Ibid., p. 165.

share of total industry sales.[10] The key competitive feature of a fragmented industry is the absence of highly visible, well-known market leaders with the power to dominate the industry and set the tone of competition. Examples of fragmented industries include book publishing, landscaping and plant nurseries, kitchen cabinets, oil tanker shipping, auto repair, the restaurant business, public accounting, women's dresses, poultry processing, metal foundries, meat packing, paperboard boxes, log homes, hotels and motels, and furniture.

An industry can be populated with a host of a fairly small competitors for many reasons, some historical and some economic:

- Low entry barriers.
- An absence of scale economies.
- Such diverse market needs from geographic area to geographic area that the demand for any particular product version is small, and adequate volume is not present to support producing, distributing, or marketing on a scale that yields advantages to a large firm.
- The need of buyers for relatively small quantities of customized products (as in the business forms industry, in advertising, and in interior design).
- High degrees of product differentiation based on image.
- High transportation costs (which limit the radius a plant can economically service—as in concrete blocks, mobile homes, milk, and gravel).
- Local regulatory requirements that make each geographic area somewhat unique.
- Newness of the industry, such that no firms have yet developed the skills and resources to command a significant market share.

Some fragmented industries consolidate naturally as they mature—the stiffer competition that comes with a slow-growth industry environment produces a shake-out of weak, inefficient firms and a greater concentration of fairly large, visible sellers. Other fragmented industries remain atomistically competitive, because it is inherent to the nature of their business. And still others remain stuck in a fragmented state, because existing firms lack the resources or ingenuity to employ a strategy that might promote industry consolidation.

Firms in fragmented industries usually are in a weak bargaining position with buyers and its suppliers. Entry is usually easy. Competition from substitutes may or may not be a major factor. In such an environment, about the best a firm can hope for is to create a loyal customer base and to garner a big enough sales volume to be successful. Competitive strategies based on low cost, on some kind of differentiation theme, or on focus approaches are all viable except when the industry's product is highly standardized; then competitors are relegated to a strategy based on low cost or on focused specialization. Specific competitive strategy options include:

- *Constructing and operating "formula" facilities.* This is an attractive ap-

---

[10]This section is summarized from Porter, *Competitive Strategy,* chap. 9.

proach to achieving low cost when the firm must operate facilities at multiple locations. It involves designing a standard facility, constructing it in an optimum location at minimum cost, and then polishing to a science how to operate it in super-efficient manner. McDonald's and 7-Eleven have pursued this strategy to perfection, earning excellent profits in their respective industries.

- *A bare-bones/no-frills strategy.* When price competition is intense and profit margins are constantly under pressure, a lean operation based on low overhead, use of high-productivity/low-cost labor, tight budget control, and rigid adherence to a no-frills expenditure policy can place a firm in the best position to play the price-cutting game and still earn profits above the industry average.

- *Increasing customer value through integration.* Backward or forward integration may contain opportunities to lower costs or enhance the value given to customers (like cutting to size or by doing assembly of components before shipment to customers or by providing technical advice to customers).

- *Specializing by product type.* When a fragmented industry is engaged in producing a broad product line with many models and styles, a focus strategy based on specialization in a particular area of the whole line can be very effective. In furniture, there are firms that specialize in only one furniture type, such as brass beds, rattan and wicker, lawn, and Early American. In auto repair, there are specialist firms for transmission repair, for body work, and for mufflers, brakes, and shocks.

- *Specializing by customer type.* A firm can try to cope with the intense competition of a fragmented industry by catering to customers with the least bargaining leverage (because they are small in size or because they purchase small annual volumes), by specializing in serving customers who are the least price-sensitive, by going after those buyers who are interested in additional services or product attributes or other extras, by serving customers who place custom orders, or by targeting buyers who have special needs or tastes.

- *Focusing on a limited geographic area.* Even though a firm in a fragmented industry is blocked from winning a big industrywide market share, it may still be able to realize significant internal operating economies by blanketing a local/regional geographic area. Concentrating facilities and marketing activities on a limited territory can produce greater sales force efficiency, speed delivery and customer services, and permit saturation advertising, while avoiding the diseconomies of trying to duplicate the strategy on a national scale. Convenience food stores, dry cleaning establishments, savings and loan associations, and department store retailers have been successful in operating multiple locations within a limited geographic area.

In fragmented industries, firms have a wide degree of strategic freedom—many different strategic approaches can exist side by side.

STRATEGIES FOR COMPETING IN GLOBAL INDUSTRIES

A global industry is one where the marketplace is worldwide and major firms are driven to employ some type of worldwide competitive strategy or else face strategic disadvantages.[11] Goodyear's strategic position in competing for tire sales in Europe, for example, is bolstered significantly by the tire-making and tire-marketing skills developed in the company's U.S. operations and by the company's worldwide network of tire-manufacturing plants. Global competition exists in computers, automobiles, television receivers, motorcycles, sewing machines, tires, heavy construction, aircraft, telecommunications equipment, and clothing.

To craft a strategy in a globally competitive industry, it is necessary to examine the industry and the competitive situation from a worldwide perspective, as opposed to considering only the conditions in one country. Competing internationally brings into play an *additional* set of situational considerations:

- The problems of sharply fluctuating exchange rates.
- Sharp variations in manufacturing costs from country to country, owing to differences in wage rates, worker productivity, rates of price inflation, energy costs, tax rates, raw material costs, and so on.
- Differences in buyer habits and buyer needs from country to country.
- Differences among foreign governments on tariffs, import quotas and restrictions, and assorted trade rules and regulations.
- Differences in competitors, competitive forces, and market conditions from country to country.

While a company in a global industry does not always have to compete internationally to be successful, it does need to know the advantages that global competitors have, the strategic positions and approaches that the major global companies have, and the moves they have made and are likely to make; otherwise, it is problematic whether it can fashion a workable strategy of its own. The strategic advantages which accrue to companies with global strategies and competitive positions vary a great deal from industry to industry; but given the movement to globalization that has occurred during the 1980s, strategy managers must consider global competition a possibility even where it is not already a reality.[12] The problem of matching company strategy to the situation in a global industry is framed by two questions:

1. Can a strategic advantage be gained from competing on a global basis?
2. How threatened will the company be by international competitors?

The Pros and Cons of a Globally Competitive Approach

There are primary advantages that can accrue to companies competing globally.[13] One is the existence of *comparative advantage*. Whenever a country or countries

---

[11]This section is adapted from Porter, *Competitive Strategy,* chap. 13.
[12]Porter, *Competitive Strategy,* p. 276.
[13]Porter, *Competitive Strategy,* pp. 278–81.

have significant manufacturing advantages (in terms of lower input costs or better-quality inputs, or both), these countries will become the principal production sites and exports will flow to other parts of the world. Companies with facilities in these locations will have a competitive advantage over those that do not. A second advantage of competing globally arises from scale economies and learning curves that extend beyond what can be gotten by competing only in one or two individual national markets. Global scale economies can derive from centralizing production in one or several giant-scale plants (where the output is greater than the size of national markets and the excess is exported to markets in other countries), from opportunities to achieve cost-savings in purchasing essential raw materials, from opportunities to achieve cost-savings in shipping or distribution, from opportunities to achieve cost-savings in the marketing area, and from opportunities to transfer technological skills and business expertise to another geographic area at little or no incremental cost. The third advantage has to do with the fact that competing worldwide can give a company an edge in reputation, in credibility, and in serving the needs of international customers.

On the other hand, there are forces that raise barriers to the emergence of globally competitive markets: (1) prohibitively high international transportation and distribution costs; (2) important country-to-country differences in the buying habits of customers, the product attributes they prefer, and the needs they have; (3) high barriers to gaining access to distribution channels in different countries; (4) lack of a worldwide demand for the product; (5) differing technologies among country markets stemming from different rates of technological change; (6) government-imposed trade barriers (to protect domestic industry from foreign competition); and (7) a need for intensive services on a locality-by-locality basis to support customer-use of the product. The advantages of competing globally *may* or *may not* outweigh the foregoing impediments. But even when they do, a company is not necessarily driven into competing more broadly with a global strategy. The impediments can still create viable market niches for national companies that do not sell in foreign countries.

Strategic Alternatives for Global Situations

There are six generic approaches to competing on a global scale:

1. *Licensing foreign firms to produce and distribute one's products* (in which case, revenues from international sales will equal only the royalty income from sales made by licensees).
2. *Maintaining a national (one-country) production base and exporting goods to foreign markets,* utilizing either company-owned or foreign-controlled forward distribution channels.
3. *Full-scale global competition*—where strategy is directed at competing worldwide with a broad product line, plant locations in many countries, and sales capabilities in most or all major national markets.
4. *A global focus strategy*—where competitive energies are aimed at serving the same identifiable market segment in each of many target countries.
5. *A national focus strategy*—where a firm tries to outcompete global firms by

doing a better job of serving the particular needs of buyers in a particular national market; this approach is best suited for situations where buyer needs in a given country are sufficiently different from those in other countries as to create unique impediments for global firms to hurdle.

6. *A protected niche strategy*—where a firm concentrates on serving limited market segments within a national market that are costly for firms with global or national approaches to access; protected niche situations emerge when some customers insist on special-order or highly customized products and when local government bodies enact codes or statutes requiring that certain products have unusually strict manufacturing specifications and performance attributes to qualify for use in their jurisdictions.

STRATEGIES FOR INDUSTRY LEADERS

The competitive positions of industry leaders normally range from stronger than average to powerful. Leaders typically enjoy a well-known reputation, and strongly entrenched leaders have proven strategies (keyed either to low-cost leadership or to differentiation). Some of the best-known leaders are Anheuser-Busch (beer), IBM (computers), McDonald's (fast food), Gillette (razor blades), Campbell Soup (canned soups), Gerber (baby food), Xerox (copying machines), AT&T (long-distance telephone service), and Levi Strauss (jeanswear).

The main strategic issue for a leader revolves around how best to sustain what has been achieved and how to become or remain *the* leader as opposed to *a* leader. However, the pursuit of industry leadership and large market share per se is seldom competitively important; what matters more is the competitive advantage that the leader can secure. At least three contrasting strategic postures are open to industry leaders and dominant firms:[14]

1. *Seize-the-offensive strategy.* This strategy rests upon the principle that the best defense is a good offense. Offensive-minded leaders try to be "first-movers," the aim being to translate "being first" into a sustainable competitive advantage as well as into solidifying their reputation as *the* leader. The key to staying on the offensive is relentless pursuit of innovation and launching initiatives that keep rivals guessing, off-balance, and scrambling to respond. The innovation objective is to be *the source* of new products, better performance features, quality enhancements, improved customer services, ways to cut production costs, and whatever else it takes to stay in the lead and sustain a competitive edge. The array of offensive options also includes initiatives to expand overall industry demand—discovering new uses for the product, attracting new users of the product, and promoting more frequent usage of the product. In addition, a clever offensive leader stays alert for ways to make it easier and less costly for potential customers to switch their purchases over from runner-up firms. Unless a leader's market share is already so dominant that it presents a threat

---

[14]Kotler, *Marketing Management*, chap. 23; Michael E. Porter, *Competitive Advantage* (New York: Free Press, 1985), chap. 14; and Ian C. MacMillan, "Seizing Competitive Initiative," *Journal of Business Strategy* 2, no. 4 (Spring 1982), pp. 43–57.

of antitrust action (a market share under 60 percent is usually safe), then a stay-on-the-offensive posture almost surely involves trying to grow *faster* than the industry as a whole and to wrest market share points away from rivals— unless a leader's growth equals or outpaces the industry average, then it is, of course, losing ground to competitors.

2. *Hold and maintain strategy.* The essence of hold and maintain is a good defense—one which makes it harder for new firms to enter and for challengers to gain ground, one which lowers the probability of attack, lessens the intensity of attack, or diverts attack to less-threatening arenas. The goal of a strong defense is to make the leader's competitive advantage more sustainable by erecting fortifications that protect its present market position. Specific defensive actions can include:

   - Attempting to raise entry barriers via increased spending for advertising, customer service, and production capacity.
   - Introducing more of the company's own brands to match the product attributes that challenger brands have or could employ.
   - Figuring out ways to increase the costs of customers switching to rival products.
   - Broadening the product line to close off possible vacant niches for competitors to slip into.
   - Keeping prices reasonable and quality attractive.
   - Preserving or even raising the level of customer service.
   - Investing enough to remain cost-competitive, to stay technologically progressive, and to maintain the firm's existing share of new market growth, thus staving off any market share slippage and decline.
   - Patenting the feasible alternative technologies (as Xerox did early in the development of the copier industry).
   - Signing exclusive contracts with the best suppliers.

The primary appeals of "hold and maintain" are to lessen the chances of antitrust charges (if the leader's market share approaches monopoly proportions) and to "milk" the firm's present position for profits and cash flow (if the industry's prospects for growth are low or if further gains in market share are not profitable enough to go after). Hold and maintain always entails trying to grow as fast as the market as a whole (to preserve market share) and reinvesting enough capital in the business to protect the leader's ability to compete.

3. *Competitive harassment strategy.* With this strategy the leader sends a clear message to rivals that any moves to cut into the leader's business will be bloody and will provoke heavy-handed retaliation. The strategic themes include being quick to meet all competitive price cuts (with even larger cuts if necessary), being ready to counter with large-scale promotional campaigns if lesser-sized firms boost their advertising budgets in an attempt to increase market share of their own, offering better deals to the major customers of next-in-line or maverick firms, and using hardball measures to signal aggressive-minded small

firms regarding who should lead and who should follow (possible signalling options include pressuring distributors not to carry rivals' products, having salespersons bad-mouth the products of aggressive small firms, or trying to hire away the better executives of firms that get out of line). The objective of a harassment/confrontation type of competitive strategy is to enforce an unwritten but well-understood tradition among lesser-sized firms of their playing follow the leader. Assuming the role of industry policeman gives the leader added strategic flexibility, as well as raising the ante for would-be challengers to take the offensive.

STRATEGIES FOR RUNNER-UP FIRMS

Runner-up firms occupy weaker market positions than do the industry leader(s). Some runner-up firms are market challengers, in that they are willing to fight one another and the leader(s) for a bigger market share and a stronger market position. Other runner-up firms play the role of followers, with no overt desire to rock the boat and a willingness to coast along in their current position. If a firm is content to be a follower, perhaps because profits are still adequate, then it has no urgent strategic issue to confront beyond that of "What kinds of strategic changes do the leaders seem to have in mind and what do we need to do to follow along?"

For a challenger firm to improve its market standing, it will need a strategy aimed at building a competitive advantage of its own. Rarely can a runner-up firm improve its competitive position just by trying harder or by imitating what leading firms in the industry are doing; indeed, a cardinal rule in offensive strategy is to avoid attacking a leader head-on with an imitative strategy, regardless of the resources and staying power an underdog may have.[15] Moreover, if an underdog has a 5 percent market share and needs a 20 percent share to earn attractive returns, then it needs a more creative approach to competing than just "try harder."

In cases where large size yields significantly lower unit costs and gives large-share firms an important cost advantage, small-share firms have only two viable strategic options: move to increase their market share or withdraw from the business (gradually or quickly). The most-used competitive strategies to building market share are based on (1) becoming a lower-cost producer and then using the attractiveness of a lower price to win increased customer favor from weak, higher-cost rivals and (2) differentiation strategies based on quality or technological superiority or better customer service or innovation. Achieving overall low-cost leadership is usually open to an underdog only when one of the market leaders is not already solidly positioned as the industry's low-cost producer. But a small-share firm may still be able to reduce its cost disadvantage by merging with or acquiring lesser-sized firms; the combined market shares may provide the needed access to size-related economies. Other options include ramping its activity-cost chain in a manner that produces the needed cost-savings and finding ways to better control the cost drivers.

In situations where scale economies or experience curve effects are small and

---

[15]Porter, *Competitive Advantage*, p. 514.

a large market share produces no cost advantage of competitive consequences, then runner-up companies have more strategic flexibility and can consider any of the following six approaches:[16]

1. *Vacant niche strategy.* The principle underlying this competitive positioning approach is to concentrate on those customer or end-use applications that major firms have bypassed or neglected. An ideal vacant niche is of sufficient size and scope to be profitable, has some growth potential, and is well suited to a firm's own capabilities and skills, as well as being outside the realm of interest of leading firms. Two examples of successful use of a vacant niche type of focus strategy are the regional commuter airlines, which serve small and medium-sized population centers having too few passengers to attract the interest of the major airlines, and the small "no-name" tire manufacturers (like Armstrong Tire and Cooper Tire) that have managed to find enough holes in the market to survive alongside Goodyear, Michelin, Bridgestone, Uniroyal-Goodrich, and Firestone.

2. *Specialist strategy.* A specialist firm trains its competitive efforts on a few carefully chosen product/customer-use segments and does not try to compete for all types of customers with a full product line appealing to all different needs and functions. Stress is placed only on those differentiating variables where the company has or can develop special expertise and where such expertise will be highly valued by customers. Smaller companies that have successfully used a specialist type of focus strategy include Formby's (which specializes in making stains and finishes for wood furniture, especially refinishing); Liquid Paper Company (which made a reputation for itself producing correction fluid for use by typists); Canada Dry (known for its ginger ale, tonic water, and carbonated soda water); and American Tobacco (which specializes in chewing tobacco and snuff).

3. *"Ours-is-better-than-theirs" strategy.* The approach here is to use a combination focus-differentiation strategy keyed to product quality. Sales and marketing efforts are focused on quality-conscious and performance-oriented buyers. Fine craftsmanship, prestige quality, frequent product innovations, and working closely with customers to develop a better product usually undergird this "superior product" type of approach. Some examples: Beefeater and Tanqueray in gin, Tiffany in diamonds and jewelry, Chicago Cutlery in premium-quality kitchen knives, Baccarat in fine crystal, Mazola in cooking oil and margarine, Bally in shoes, Pennzoil in motor oil, and Neiman-Marcus's approach to department store retailing.

4. *Contented-follower strategy.* Follower firms deliberately refrain from initiating trend-setting strategic moves and from aggressive attempts to steal customers away from the leaders. Followers prefer approaches that will not provoke competitive retaliation, often opting for focus and differentiation strategies that keep them out of the leaders' paths. They react and respond, rather than initiate

---

[16]For more details, see Kotler, *Marketing Management,* pp. 397–412; R.G. Hamermesh, M.J. Anderson, Jr., and J.E. Harris, "Strategies for Low Market Share Businesses," *Harvard Business Review* 56, no. 3 (May–June 1978), pp. 95–102; and Porter, *Competitive Advantage,* chap. 15.

and attack. They prefer defense to offense. And they rarely get out of line with the leaders on price. Burroughs (in computers) and Union Camp (in paper products) have been successful market followers by consciously concentrating on selected product uses and applications for specific customer groups, effectively focused R&D, profit emphasis (rather than market share emphasis), and cautious, but efficient, management.

5. *Guppy strategy.* A "swallow up the small fish" approach has appeal when a financially strong underdog is able to grow at the expense of still-weaker rivals either by directly taking sales away from them or by acquiring them outright to form an enterprise that has more competitive strength. Such beer manufacturers as Heileman, Stroh, and Pabst owe their market share growth in the early 1980s to having acquired smaller brewers. Likewise, a number of public accounting firms have achieved rapid growth and broader geographic coverage by acquiring or merging with smaller CPA firms.

6. *Distinctive image strategy.* Some runner-up companies build their strategies around ways to make themselves stand out from competitors. A variety of strategic approaches have been used: creating a reputation for charging the lowest prices, providing prestige quality at a good price, going all out to give superior customer service, designing unique product attributes, being a leader in new-product introduction, or coming up with unusually creative advertising. Examples include Dr Pepper's strategy of calling attention to its distinctive taste, 7UP's campaign to promote caffeine-free soft drinks, Apple Computer's approach to making it easier and more interesting for people to use a personal computer, and Hyatt's use of architecture and luxurious hotel accommodations to appeal to upscale travelers and conventions.

Table 6–1 highlights risks and pitfalls associated with various market challenger strategies.

Without a doubt, in industries where big size is definitely a key success factor, firms with low market shares have some obstacles to overcome: (1) less access to economies of scale in manufacturing, distribution, or sales promotion; (2) difficulty in gaining customer recognition; (3) an inability to afford mass-media advertising on a grand scale; and (4) difficulty in funding capital requirements.[17] But *it is erroneous to view runner-up firms as necessarily being less profitable or being unable to hold their own against the biggest firms.* Many lesser-sized firms earn healthy profits and enjoy good reputations with customers. Often, the handicaps of smaller size can be surmounted and a profitable competitive position established by: (1) focusing on carefully chosen market segments, where particular strengths can be developed, and not attacking dominant firms head-on with price cuts and increased promotional expenditure; (2) developing a distinctive competence in new-product development or technical capabilities, but only for the target market segments; and (3) using innovative/"dare to be different"/"beat the odds" entrepreneurial approaches to outmanage stodgy, slow-to-change market leaders. Runner-up companies have a golden opportunity to make major market share gains if they make a leapfrogging technological breakthrough, if the leaders stumble or become

---

[17]Hamermesh, Anderson, and Harris, "Strategies for Low Market Share Businesses," p. 102.

TABLE 6–1
Risks and Pitfalls of Market Challenger Strategies

Higher-Risk Strategy Alternatives	*Lower-Risk Strategy Alternatives*
• Price-cutting (without having a cost advantage).	• Improving the levels of customer service.
• Cheapening the quality (to save on cost and fund price cuts).	• Opening new channels of distribution.
• Product innovation (R&D can be expensive and many new-product ideas fail in the marketplace).	• Looking for ways to reduce costs.
• Going after the high end of the market (without having the reputation to attract buyers who want name-brand prestige goods).	

Pitfalls

- Adding lots of models and optional features (product-line proliferation is costly and often leads to lower profit margins).
- Spending heavily on promotional and advertising (may provoke a promotional war; the sales gains may not offset the added costs).
- Imitating what the leaders do (me-too strategies seldom close the gap on the leaders).
- Depending on cosmetic product improvements to serve as a substitute for real innovation and extra customer value.

complacent, or if they have patience to nibble away at the leaders and build up their customer base over a long time.

STRATEGIES FOR WEAK BUSINESSES

A firm in an also-ran or declining competitive position has four basic strategic options. If the financial wherewithal is available, it can launch a modest *grow-and-build* strategy keyed either to low-cost production or to new differentiation themes, pouring enough money and talent into the effort to become a respectable market contender within five years or so. It can adopt a *hold-and-maintain* mode, continuing the present strategy and scrounging up enough resources to keep sales, market share, profitability, and competitive position at survival levels. It can opt for an *abandonment* strategy and get out of the business, either by selling out to another firm or by closing down operations if a buyer cannot be found. Or, it can employ a *harvest strategy,* whereby reinvestment in the business is held to a bare-bones minimum and the overriding management objective is to generate the largest feasible short-term cash flow; the long-term objective of harvesting is orderly market exit. The gist of the first three options is self-explanatory. The fourth deserves more explanation.

A *harvest strategy* steers a middle course between maintenance and abandonment. Harvesting entails resource commitments in between what is required to maintain the company's market position and a decision to get out as soon as possible. Harvesting is a phasing down or endgame approach, in which strategy is aimed at an orderly market pullback and surrendering of market share but, in the process, reaping a harvest of cash to deploy to other business endeavors.

The actions to harvest are fairly standard. The operating budget is reduced to a bare-bones level; stringent cost control is pursued. Capital investment in new equipment is given little, if any, financial priority—depending on the current condition of fixed assets and on whether the harvest is to be fast or slow. Price may be raised, promotional expenses cut, quality reduced in not so visible ways, nonessential customer services curtailed, equipment maintenance decreased, and the like. The harvest objective is to *maximize short-term cash flow*, withdraw the funds from the business, and shift them into activities where the returns are more promising. It is understood that sales will shrink; but if costs can be cut in proportion, then profits will erode slowly, rather than rapidly.

Professor Kotler has suggested seven indicators of when a business should be harvested:[18]

1. When the business is in a saturated or declining market, and the industry's long-term prospects are unattractive.
2. When the business has gained only a small market share, and building it up would be too costly or not profitable enough; or when it has a respectable market share that is becoming increasingly costly to maintain or defend.
3. When profit prospects are subpar, because of the firm's competitive weakness or because poor long-term market conditions are forecast.
4. When reduced levels of competitive effort will not immediately trigger sharp declines in sales and market position.
5. When the enterprise can redeploy the freed-up resources in higher-opportunity areas.
6. When the business is *not* a major component of a diversified corporation's portfolio of existing business interests.
7. When the business does not contribute other desired features (sales stability, prestige, a well-rounded product line) to a company's overall business portfolio.

The more of these seven conditions that are present, the more ideal the business is for harvesting.

Harvesting strategies make the most sense in diversified companies having business units that are in the declining stages of the life cycle or that are "dogs." In such situations, the cash flows from harvesting unattractive business units can be reallocated to business units with greater profit potential and better long-term industry attractiveness.

TURNAROUND STRATEGIES FOR DISTRESSED BUSINESSES

Turnaround strategies come into play when a business worth rescuing has fallen into disrepair and perhaps into a crisis situation. The objective is to arrest and

---

[18]Philip Kotler, "Harvesting Strategies for Weak Products," *Business Horizons* 21, no. 5 (August 1978), pp. 17–18.

reverse the sources of competitive and financial weakness as quickly as possible. The first task of rescue is diagnosis: What lies at the root of poor performance? Is it bad competitive strategy? Or poor implementation and execution of an otherwise workable strategy? Or are the causes of distress beyond management control? Can the business be saved? Discerning what is wrong and how serious the firm's strategic problems are is a prerequisite to formulating a turnaround strategy.

Some of the most common causes of business trouble are ignoring the profit-depressing effects of an overly aggressive effort to buy market share with deep price cuts; being burdened with heavy fixed costs because of an inability to utilize plant capacity; betting on R&D efforts to boost competitive position and profitability and failing to come up with effective innovations; betting on technological long shots; being too optimistic about the ability to penetrate new markets; making frequent changes in strategy (because the previous strategy didn't work out); and being overpowered by the competitive advantages enjoyed by more successful rivals. There are five generic approaches to achieving a business turnaround:[19]

- Revamping the existing strategy.
- Revenue-increasing strategies.
- Cost-reduction strategies.
- Asset reduction/retrenchment strategies.
- A combination of these.

When the cause of weak performance is diagnosed as "bad" strategy, the task of strategy overhaul can proceed along any of several paths: (1) shifting to a new competitive approach and, thus, trying to rebuild the firm's market position, (2) overhauling internal operations and functional-area strategies to produce better support of the same basic overall business strategy, (3) merging with another firm in the industry and forging a new strategy keyed to the newly merged firm's strengths, and (4) retrenching into a reduced core of products and customers more closely matched to the firm's strengths. Which of these paths proves most appealing depends on conditions prevailing in the industry, on the firm's particular strengths and weaknesses vis-à-vis rival firms, and on the severity of the crisis. Consequently, situation analysis of the industry, major competitors, the firm's own competitive position, and its skills and resources are prerequisites to action. As a rule, successful rescue of an ailing business needs to be predicted on a firm's strengths and its very best opportunities.

Revenue-increasing turnaround efforts aim at generating increases in sales volume. There are a number of revenue-building options: price cuts, increased promotion, a bigger sales force, added customer services, and quickly achieved product improvements. If demand happens to be price-inelastic, revenues can be boosted by instituting a price increase instead of a price cut. Attempts to increase sales revenues are necessary (1) when there is little or no room in the operating budget

---

[19]For excellent discussions of the ins and outs of rescuing distressed firms, see Charles W. Hofer, "Turnaround Strategies," *Journal of Business Strategy* 1, no. 1 (Summer 1980), pp. 19–31; Donald F. Heany, "Businesses in Profit Trouble," *Journal of Business Strategy* 5, no. 4 (Spring 1985), pp. 4–13; and Eugene F. Finkin, "Company Turnaround," *Journal of Business Strategy* 5, no. 4 (Spring 1985), pp. 14–25.

to cut back on expenses and still break even and (2) when the key to restoring profitability is increased utilization of existing capacity.

Cost-reducing turnaround strategies work best when an ailing firm's cost structure is flexible enough to permit radical surgery, when operating inefficiencies are identifiable and readily correctable, and when the firm is relatively close to its break-even point. Accompanying a general belt-tightening can be an increased emphasis on budgeting and cost control, elimination of jobs and hirings, modernization of existing plant and equipment to gain greater productivity, or postponement of capital expenditures.

Asset reduction/retrenchment strategies become essential to rescue when cash flow is a critical consideration and when the most practical way to generate cash is (1) through sale of some of the firm's assets (plant and equipment, land, patents, inventories, or profitable subsidiaries) and (2) through retrenchment (pruning of marginal products from the product line, closing or sale of older plants, a reduced work force, withdrawal from outlying markets, cutbacks in customer service, and the like). Sometimes, though, selling off some of a firm's assets is not so much for the purpose of unloading money-losing operations as it is for the purpose of raising funds to plow back into a strengthening of the remaining activities.

Combination turnaround strategies are usually essential in grim situations where fast action on a broad front is required. Likewise, combination actions frequently come into play when the rescue effort entails bringing in new managers and giving them a relatively free hand to make whatever changes they see fit in restoring the business to a good condition. The tougher the problems, the more likely that the solutions will involve a multipronged approach, rather than just one category of turnaround actions.

Turnaround efforts tend to be high-risk undertakings and often fail. A recent study of 64 companies found no successful turnarounds among the most troubled companies in eight basic industries.[20] Many waited too late to begin a turnaround, and others found themselves short of both cash and entrepreneurial talent to compete in a mature industry characterized by a fierce battle for market share; better-positioned rivals simply proved too strong to defeat in head-to-head combat for the market share needed to survive. This study found that, as market maturity approaches and competitive hostility intensifies, a firm's range of strategic options narrows. For a crisis-ridden firm to be successful in a turnaround effort, its management has to be alert to the signs of an impending competitive shakeout and launch an early effort to reposition the firm and rebuild its competitive status.

As a conclusion to our review of generic business strategies, read Illustration Capsule 14 describing 10 of the most common business strategy mistakes.

ANALYTICAL CHECKLIST

Identifying the different strategic options is fairly routine; the hard part is deciding which strategy option best fits the firm's overall situation and, most particularly, its industry environment and competitive position. Table 6–2 provides

---

[20]William K. Hall, "Survival Strategies in a Hostile Environment," *Harvard Business Review* 58, no. 5 (September–October 1980), pp. 75–85.

ILLUSTRATION CAPSULE 14

10 Common Strategic Mistakes

Experience has shown that some strategic actions fail more often than they succeed. Ten examples of strategic moves that usually produce poor results are presented below:

1. Imitating the moves of leading or successful competitors when the market has no more room for copy-cat products and look-alike competitors.
2. Spending more money on marketing and sales promotion to try to get around problems with product quality and product performance.
3. Establishing many weak market positions instead of a few strong ones.
4. Trying to achieve greater productivity and lower unit costs by making heavy investments in new facilities and equipment (the risk here is that an unforeseen downturn in industry demand will give rise to excess capacity and put the firm in a bind to meet high fixed-overhead costs and debt-repayment obligations).
5. Allocating R&D efforts to weak products instead of to strong products.
6. Attacking the market leaders head-on without having either a good competitive advantage or adequate financial strength.
7. Making such aggressive attempts to take market share that rivals are provoked into strong retaliation and a costly "arms-race" struggle ensues (such battles seldom produce a substantial change in market shares; the usual outcome is higher costs and profitless sales growth).
8. Harvesting a weak business in a declining industry (such a strategy can *sometimes* turn a weak business into a distressed business very, very quickly).
9. Trying to repeat the same strategy in a new business (what worked elsewhere may not work again, even in similar industry environments, because of subtle differences in industry key success factors and competitive forces).
10. Giving higher priority to cost reduction than to opportunities for building a stronger position in selected market segments.

These mistakes usually are born out of acts of desperation, poor analysis of industry and competitive conditions, and misjudgments of one sort or another.

a summary checklist of the optional strategies and generic situations. The first analytical step in matching strategy to the situation is to diagnose the industry environment and the firm's competitive standing in the industry. Answers to the following questions need to be developed:

1. In what basic type of industry environment does the company operate (emerging, growth, transition to maturity, mature, fragmented, global)? What strategic options and strategic postures are usually best suited for this generic type of environment?
2. What position does the firm have in the industry (strong versus weak versus crisis-ridden; leader versus runner-up versus also-ran)? How does the firm's

TABLE 6–2
Matching Strategy to the Situation: A Checklist of Optional Strategies and Generic Situations

Market Share and Investment Options	Generic Competitive Strategy Options	Generic Industry Environments	Generic Company Positions/Situations
• Grow and build: —capture a bigger market share by growing faster than industry as a whole; —employ offensive strategies. • Hold and maintain: —protect market share; grow at least as fast as whole industry; —invest enough resources to maintain competitive strength and market position; —employ defensive strategies. • Withdraw and abandon: —give up market share gradually; —harvest; prepare for orderly market withdrawal; —maximize short-term cash flow; —minimize reinvestment of capital in the business. • Liquidate: —sell out; —close down.	• Overall low-cost leadership. • Differentiation. • Focus: —based on low cost; —based on differentiation.	• Young, emerging industry. • Rapid growth. • Heading into maturity/competitive shake-out and industry consolidation. • Mature/slow growth. • Aging/declining. • Fragmented. • Globally competitive.	• Dominant leader. • Leader. • Strong runner-up/aggressive challenger. • Weak runner-up. • Weak/in trouble/distressed. • Aggressive newcomer. • Candidate for exit/failing. • No-name/also-ran.

standing influence its strategic options, given the stage of the industry's development—in particular, which options have to be ruled out?

Given the answers to these questions, step 2 is to choose which of the three generic competitive approaches to build the firm's strategy around:

- Strive to be the low-cost producer and become the overall cost leader.
- Pursue some sort of differentiation theme (which one?).
- Specialize or focus on selected market segments (as opposed to trying to compete across the board).

To this must be added the firm's market share and investment options (column 1 of Table 6–2).

Step 3 is to custom-tailor the chosen generic approaches (columns 1 and 2 of

Table 6–2) to fit *both* the industry environment and the firm's standing vis-à-vis competitors. Here, it is important to be sure that (1) the customized aspects of the proposed strategy are well matched to the firm's skills and capabilities and (2) the strategy addresses all of the strategic issues confronting the firm.

Weighing the Different Alternatives

The strategist's task is to judge "how all the factors add up" and "which strategy and competitive approach make the most sense, all things considered." In singling out stronger candidate strategies from the weaker ones and weighing the pros and cons of the most attractive strategic options, the answers to the following questions often indicate the way to go:

- What kind of competitive edge can the company realistically hope to have and what strategic moves/approaches will it take to secure this edge?
- Are the skills and resources available to be successful in pursuing these moves and approaches—if not, can they be gotten?
- Once built, how can the competitive advantage be protected? What defensive strategies need to be employed? Will rivals counterattack? What will it take to blunt their efforts?
- Are any rivals particularly vulnerable? Should the firm mount an offensive to capitalize on these vulnerabilities? What offensive moves need to be employed?
- What additional strategic moves are needed to deal with driving forces in the industry, specific threats and weaknesses, and any other issues/problems unique to the firm?

As the choice of strategic initiatives is developed, there are some specific pitfalls to watch out for:

- Underestimating the reactions of rival firms.
- Designing an overly ambitious strategic plan—one that calls for a lot of different strategic moves or one that overtaxes the company's resources and capabilities, or both.
- Selecting a strategy that represents a radical departure from or abandonment of the cornerstones of the company's prior success—this is not to say that a radical strategy change should automatically be rejected, but it is to say that it should be undertaken only after careful analysis.
- Choosing a strategy that is capable of succeeding only under the best of circumstances.
- Choosing a strategy that goes against the grain of the organization's culture or that conflicts with the values and philosophies of the most senior executives.
- Forming a strategy that leaves the firm stuck in the middle, with no clearly defined strategic theme and no basis on which to distinguish itself from rivals—that is, it is regarded as average.

SUGGESTED READINGS

Bolt, James F. "Global Competitors: Some Criteria for Success." *Business Horizons* 31, no. 1 (January–February 1988), pp. 34–41.

Carroll, Glenn R. "The Specialist Strategy." In *Strategic and Organization: A West Coast Perspective,* ed. Glenn Carroll and David Vogel. Boston: Pitman Publishing, 1984, pp. 117–28.

Feldman, Lawrence P., and Albert L. Page. "Harvesting: The Misunderstood Market Exit Strategy." *Journal of Business Strategy* 5, no. 4 (Spring 1985), pp. 79–85.

Finkin, Eugene F. "Company Turnaround." *Journal of Business Strategy* 5, no. 4 (Spring 1985), pp. 14–25.

Hall, William K. "Survival Strategies in a Hostile Environment." *Harvard Business Review* 58, no. 5 (September–October 1980), pp. 75–85.

Hamermesh, R.G., and S.B. Silk. "How to Compete in Stagnant Industries." *Harvard Business Review* 57, no. 5 (September–October 1979), pp. 161–68.

Harrigan, Kathryn R. *Strategic Flexibility.* Lexington, Mass.: Lexington Books, 1985, chaps. 6 and 8.

Heany, Donald F. "Businesses in Profit Trouble." *Journal of Business Strategy* 5, no. 4 (Spring 1985), pp. 4–13.

Hofer, Charles W. "Turnaround Strategies." *Journal of Business Strategy* 1, no. 1 (Summer 1980), pp. 19–31.

Hout, Thomas; Michael E. Porter; and Eileen Rudden. "How Global Companies Win Out." *Harvard Business Review* 60, no. 5 (September–October 1982), pp. 98–108.

Kotler, Philip. *Marketing Management: Analysis, Planning, Control.* 5th ed. Englewood Cliffs, N.J.: Prentice-Hall, 1984, chap. 11.

Mayer, Robert J. "Winning Strategies for Manufacturers in Mature Industries." *Journal of Business Strategy* 8, no. 2 (Fall 1987), pp. 23–31.

Ohmae, Kenichi. *The Mind of the Strategist.* New York: Penguin Books, 1983, chaps. 8, 9, and 11.

Porter, Michael E. *Competitive Strategy: Techniques for Analyzing Industries and Competitors.* New York: Free Press, 1980, chaps. 9–13.

Thompson, Arthur A. "Strategies for Staying Cost Competitive." *Harvard Business Review* 62, no. 1 (January–February 1984), pp. 110–17.

Reading 3

SUSTAINABLE COMPETITIVE ADVANTAGE—WHAT IT IS, WHAT IT ISN'T*

Kevin P. Coyne

I shall not today attempt to define the kinds of material to be embraced within that shorthand description; and perhaps I could never succeed in intelligibly doing so. But I know it when I see it.

Supreme Court Justice Potter Stewart (Jacobellis v. State of Ohio)

Although it was pornography, not sustainable competitive advantage, the late Justice Stewart doubted his ability to define, his remark neatly characterizes the current state of thinking about the latter subject as well. Explicitly or implicitly, sustainable competitive advantage (SCA) has long occupied a central place in strategic thinking. Witness the widely accepted definition of competitive strategy as "an integrated set of actions that produce a sustainable advantage over competitors."[1] But exactly what constitutes sustainable competitive advantage is a question rarely asked. Most corporate strategists are content to apply Justice Stewart's test; they know an SCA when they see it—or so they assume.

But perhaps an SCA is not always so easy to identify. In developing its liquid hand soap, Minnetonka, Inc., focused its efforts on building an advantage that was easily copied later. In the wristwatch market, Texas Instruments attempted to exploit an advantage over its competitors that turned out to be unimportant to target consumers. RCA built barriers to competition in the vacuum tube market in the 1950s only to find these barriers irrelevant

when transistors and semiconductors were born. CB radio producers built capacity to fill a demand that later evaporated. In each case, the companies failed to see in advance that, for one reason or another, they lacked a sustainable competitive advantage.

Perhaps it is because the meaning of sustainable competitive advantage is superficially self-evident that virtually no effort has been made to define it explicitly. After all, it can be argued that the dictionary's definitions of the three words bring forth the heart of the concept. But every strategist needs to discover whether an SCA is actually or potentially present, and, if so, what its implications are for competitive and business strategy.

Therefore, this article will describe a number of established strategic concepts and build on them to develop a clear and explicit concept of SCA.

Specifically, we will examine:

1. The conditions for SCA. When does a producer have a competitive advantage? How can the strategist test whether such an advantage is sustainable?
2. Some implications of SCA for strategy. Does having SCA guarantee success? Can a producer succeed without an SCA? Should a producer always pursue an SCA?

Conditions for SCA

Any producer who sells his goods or services at a profit undeniably enjoys a competitive advantage with those customers who choose to buy from him instead of his competitors, though these competitors may be superior in size, strength, product quality, or distribution power. Some advantages, however,

Business Horizons: Copyright, 1986, by the Foundation for the School of Business at Indiana University. Reprinted by permission.

[1]*Competitive strategy,* as the term is used in this article, is exclusively concerned with defeating comptitiors and achieving dominance in a proditct/market segment. It is thus—in concept, and usually in practice—a subset of business strategy, which addresses the broader goal of macimizing the walth of shareholders.

are obviously worth more than others. A competitive advantage is meaningful in strategy only when three distinct conditions are met:

1. Customers perceive a consistent difference in important attributes between the producer's product or service and those of his competitors.
2. That difference is the direct consequence of a capability gap between the producer and his competitors.
3. Both the difference in important attributes and the capability gap can be expected to endure over time.

In earlier strategy work, these conditions have been jointly embedded in the concepts of "key factors for success" (KFS), "degrees of freedom," and "lower costs or higher value to the customer." In the interest of clarity, however, they deserve separate consideration.

Differentiation in Important Attributes

Obviously, competitive advantage results from differentiation among competitors—but not just any differentiation. For a producer to enjoy a competitive advantage in a product/market segment, the difference or differences between him and his competitors must be felt in the marketplace: that is, they must be reflected in some *product/delivery attribute* that is a *key buying criterion* for the market. And the product must be differentiated enough to win the loyalty of a significant set of buyers; it must have a *footprint in the market*.

Product/Delivery Attribute

Customers rarely base their choice of a product or service on internal characteristics of the producer that are not reflected in a perceived product or delivery difference. Indeed, they usually neither know nor care about those characteristics. Almost invariably, the most important contact between the customer and the producer is the marketplace—the "strategic triangle" where the producer meets his customers and competitors. It is here that the competitive contest for the scarce resource, the sales dollar, is directly engaged.

Just as differences among animal species that are

unrelated to scarce resources do not contribute to the survival of the fittest, so producer differences that do not affect the market do not influence the competitive process. Differences among competitors in plant locations, raw material choices, labor policies, and the like matter only when and if those differences translate into product/delivery attributes that influence the customers' choice of where to spend their sales dollars.

"Product/delivery attributes" include not only such familiar elements as price, quality, aesthetics, and functionality, but also broader attributes, such as availability, consumer awareness, visibility, and after-sales service. Anything that affects customers' perceptions of the product or service, its usefulness to them, and their access to it is a product/delivery attribute. Anything that does not affect these perceptions is not.

Having lower costs, for example, may well result in significantly higher margins. But this *business* advantage will become a *competitive* advantage only if and when the producer directly or indirectly recycles the additional profits into product/delivery attributes, such as price, product quality, advertising, or additional capacity that increases availability. Only then is the producer's competitive position enhanced. Two examples illustrate this point.

- For years, the "excess" profits of a major packaged good company—the low-cost producer in its industry—have been siphoned off by its corporate parent for reinvestment in other subsidiaries. The packaged good subsidiary has, therefore, been no more able to take initiatives or respond to competitive threats than if it did not produce those excess profits. Thus, business advantage may exist, but competitive advantage is lacking. If risk-adjusted returns available from investments in other business exceed those of additional investment in the packaged good subsidiary, the corporate parent may be making the best business decisions. However, the packaged goods subsidiary has gained no competitive advantage from its superior position.

- The corporate parent of a newly acquired, relatively high-cost producer in an industrial products market has decided to aggressively expand its subsidiary. This expansion is potentially at the expense of the current market leader, an independent company occupying the low-cost position in the industry. The resources that the new parent is willing to invest are far larger than the incremental profits generated by the market leader's lower costs. Because the new subsidiary can invest more than the market leader in product design, product quality, distribution, and so forth, it is the subsidiary that has, or soon will have, the competitive advantage.

In short, it is the application, not just the generation, of greater resources that is required for *competitive* advantage.

Key Buying Criterion

Every product has numerous attributes that competitors can use to differentiate themselves to gain some degree of advantage. To be strategically significant, however, an advantage must be based on positive differentiation of an attribute that is a *key buying criterion* for a particular market segment and is not offset by a negative differentiation in any other key buying criterion. In the end, competitive advantage is the result of all net differences in important product/delivery attributes, not just one factor, such as price or quality. Differences in other, less important attributes may be helpful at the margin, but they are not strategically significant.

Key buying criteria vary, of course, by industry and even by market segment. In fact, because market segments differ in their choice of key buying criteria, a particular product may have a competitive advantage in some segments while being at a disadvantage in others. Price aside, the elaborate technical features that professional photographers prize in Hasselblad cameras would baffle and discourage most of the casual users who make up the mass market.

In any one product/market segment, however, only a very few criteria are likely to be important enough to serve as the basis for a meaningful competitive advantage. These criteria are likely to be basic—that is, central to the concept of the product or service itself, as opposed to "add-ons" or "features." For example, in the tubular steel industry, there are just two key product/delivery attributes: a single measure of quality (third-party testing reject rate), and local availability on the day required by the customer's drilling schedule.

Texas Instruments (TI) apparently did not fully understand the importance of differentiation along key buying criteria when it entered the wristwatch market. Its strategy was to build upon its ability to drive down costs—and therefore, prices (the product attribute)—beyond the point where competitors could respond. But this competitive strategy, which had worked in electronic components, failed in wristwatches because price, past a certain point, was no longer a key buying criterion: customers cared more about aesthetics. TI had surpassed all of its competitors in an attribute that did not matter in the marketplace.

Footprint in the Market

To contribute to an SCA, the differences in product/delivery attributes must command the attention and loyalty of a substantial customer base: in other words, they must produce a "footprint in the market" of significant breadth and depth.

Breadth. How many customers are attracted to the product above all others by the difference in product attributes? What volume do these customers purchase?

Depth. How strong a preference has this difference generated? Would minor changes in the balance of attributes cause the customers to switch?

Breadth and depth are usually associated in marketing circles with the concept of "branding." Branding can indeed be a source of competitive advantage, as shown by Perrier's spectacular advantage in a commodity as prosaic as bottled mineral water.

But the importance of breadth and depth are not limited to branding strategies. Even a producer who is pursuing a low-price strategy must ensure that his lower price will cause customers to choose his product and that changes in nonprice attributes by competitors would be unlikely to lure them away.

Durable Differentiation

Positive differentiation in key product/delivery attributes is essential to competitive advantage. However, a differentiation that can be readily erased does not by itself confer a meaningful advantage. Competitive advantages described in such terms as *faster delivery* or *superior product quality* are illusory if competitors can erase the differentiation at will.

For example, Minnetonka, Inc., created a new market niche with "Softsoap." As a result, its stock price more than doubled. Before long, however, 50 different brands of liquid soap, some selling for a fifth of Softsoap's price, appeared on the market. As a result, Minnetonka saw its earnings fall to zero and its stock price decline by 75 percent.

An advantage is durable only if competitors cannot readily imitate the producer's superior product/delivery attributes. In other words, a gap in the *capability* underlying the differentiation must separate the producer from his competitors; otherwise no meaningful competitive advantage exists. (Conversely, of course, no meaningful advantage can arise from a capability gap that does not produce an important difference in product/delivery attributes.)

Understanding the capability gap, then, is basic to determining whether a competitive advantage actually exists. For example, such an attribute as faster delivery does not constitute a real competitive advantage unless it is based on a capability gap, such as may exist if the company has a much bigger truck fleet than its competitors can afford to maintain. Higher product quality does not in itself constitute a competitive advantage. But unique access to intrinsically superior raw materials that enable the producer to deliver a better-quality product may well do so.

A capability gap exists when the function responsible for the differentiated product/delivery attribute is one that only the producer in question can perform, or one that competitors (given their particular limitations) could do only with maximum effort. So defined, capability gaps fall into four categories.

1. *Business system gaps* result from the ability to perform individual functions more effectively than competitors and from the inability of competitors to easily follow suit. For example, differences in labor union work rules can constitute a capability gap resulting in superior production capability. Superior engineering or technical skills may create a capability gap leading to greater precision or reliability in the finished product.

2. *Position gaps* result from prior decisions, actions, and circumstances. Reputation, consumer awareness and trust, and order backlogs, which can represent important capability gaps, are often the legacy of an earlier management generation. Thus, current competitive advantage may be the consequence of a past facilities location decision. BHP, the large Australian steel maker, enjoys important production efficiencies because it is the only producer to have located its smelter adjacent to its iron ore source, eliminating expensive iron ore transportation costs.

3. *Regulatory/legal gaps* result from government's limiting the competitors who can perform certain activities, or the degree to which they can perform those activities. Patents, operating licenses, import quotas, and consumer safety laws can all open important capability gaps among competitors. For example, Ciba-Giegy's patent on a low-cost herbicide allowed it to dominate certain segments of the agricultural chemical market for years.

4. *Organization or managerial quality gaps* result from an organization's ability consistently to innovate and adapt more quickly and effectively than its competitors. For example, in industries like computers or financial services, where the competitive environment is shifting rapidly, this flexibility may be the single most important capability gap. In other industries, the key capability gap may be an ability to out-innovate competitors, keeping them always on the defensive.

Note that only the first category, business system gaps, covers actions that are currently under the control of the producer. Frustrating as it may be to the strategist, competitive advantage or disadvantage is often the result of factors he or she is in no position to alter in the short term.

The broad concept of a capability gap becomes useful only when we succeed in closely specifying a producer's *actual* capability gap over competitors in a *particular* situation. Analysts can detect the existence of a capability gap by examining broad functions in the business system, but they must then go further and determine the root cause of superior performance in that function.

Individual capability gaps between competitors are very specific. There must be a precise reason why one producer can outperform another, or there is no competitive advantage. The capability gap consists of specific, often physical, differences. It is likely to be prosaic and measurable, not intangible. Abstract terms, such as *higher labor productivity* or *technological leadership,* often serve as useful shorthand, but they are too general for precise analysis. Moreover, they implicitly equate capability gaps with marginal performance superiority, rather than with discrete differences—such as specific work rule differences or technical resources capacity—that are not easily imitated.

For example, if marginal performance superiority constituted competitive advantage, one would expect "focus" competitors—those who have no capability advantage but excel in serving a particular niche through sheer concentration of effort—to win out over more general competitors who decide to invade that niche. But as American Motors learned when Detroit's "Big Three" began producing small cars, and as some regional banks are learning as money center banks enter their markets, "trying harder" is no substitute for the possession of unique capabilities.

Only by understanding specific differences in capability can the strategist accurately determine and measure the actions that competitors must take to eliminate the gap and the obstacles and costs to them of doing so.

Lasting Advantage (Sustainability)

If a meaningful advantage is a function of a positive difference in important attributes based on an underlying capability gap, then the sustainability of the competitive advantage is simply a function of the durability of both the attributes and the gap.

There is not much value in an advantage in product/delivery attributes that do not retain their importance over time. Manufacturers of CB radios, video games, and designer jeans saw their revenues decline and their financial losses mount not because their competitors did anything to erode their capa-

bility advantages but because most of their customers simply no longer valued those products enough to pay the price. In each case, industry participants believed that they had benefited from a permanent shift in consumer preferences and began to invest accordingly. In each case they were wrong.

Whether consumers will continue to demand a product over time, and how they can be influenced to prefer certain product attributes over time, are essentially marketing issues, subject to normal marketing analytical techniques. How basic is the customer need that the product meets? How central to its function or availability is the attribute in each question? These may be the key questions to ask in this connection.

The sustainability of competitive advantage is also a function of the durability of the capability gap that created the attractive attribute. In fact, the most important condition to sustainability is that existing and potential competitors either cannot or will not take the actions required to close the gap. If competitors can and will fill the gap, the advantage is by definition not sustainable.

Obviously, a capability gap that competitors are unable to close is preferable to one that relies on some restraint. Unfortunately, a producer cannot choose whether a particular capability gap meets the former or the latter condition.

Consider the two cases more closely.

- *Case I: Competitors cannot fill the gap.* This situation occurs when the capability itself is protected by specific entry and mobility barriers, such as an important product patent or unique access to a key raw material (for example, DeBeer's Consolidated Mines). In a Case 1 situation, sustainability is assured at least until the barrier is eroded or eliminated (converting the situation to Case 2). Barriers can erode or be eliminated over time, unless they are inherent in the nature of the business.[2]

A more significant danger to Case 1 advantages,

---

[2]For example, if the business is a "natural monopoly." A natural monopoly exists where either (1) economies of scale cause marginal costs to decline past the point where production volume equals market demand (that is, where the most efficient economic system is to have only one producer); or (2) the social costs of installing duplicate production/distribution systems outweigh the benefits, a situation usually leading to the establishment of a legal monopoly by government fiat.

however, probably lies not in the gradual erosion of barriers but in the possibility that competitors may leapfrog the barriers by a new game strategy.

For example, the introduction of the transistor in 1955 did nothing to erode the barriers that RCA had created in vacuum tubes; it simply made RCA's leadership irrelevant. Therefore, although sustainability can be estimated by (1) considering all the changes (environmental forces or competitor actions) that could erode the barriers and (2) assessing the probabilities of their occurrence over a specified time horizon, there will, of course, always be uncertainty in the estimate.

• *Case 2: Competitors could close the capability gap but refrain from doing so.* This situation might occur for any one of four reasons.

1. *Inadequate potential.* A simple calculation may show competitors that the costs of closing the gap would exceed the benefits, even if the possessor of the advantage did not retaliate.

For example, the danger of cannibalizing existing products may preclude effective response: MCI, Sprint, and others were able to create the low-price segment of the U.S. long-distance telephone market largely because AT&T did not choose to respond directly for some time. Most likely it considered that the cost of cutting prices for 100 percent of its customers in order to retain the 1 to 2 percent in the low-price segment was simply too high, and that only when the segment grew to sufficient size would a response become worthwhile.

Other examples of situations where a payoff is not worth the required investment include investing in capacity to achieve "economies of scale" when the capacity required to achieve the required economy exceeds the likely additional demand in the industry; and labor work rules, where the additional compensation demanded by the union in return for such changes would more than offset the potential savings.

The inadequate-potential situation represents a sustainable advantage because the "end game" has already been reached: there are no rational strategic countermoves for competitors to take until conditions change.

2. *Corresponding disadvantage.* Competitors may believe that acting to close the capability gap will open gaps elsewhere (in this or other market segments) that will more than offset the value of closing this one.

For example, a "niche" competitor often relies on this factor to protect him against larger competitors, who (or so he hopes) will reckon that an effective attack on his niche advantage would divert resources (including management time) needed elsewhere, destroy the integrity of their own broader product lines (opening gaps in other segments), or create some other gap.

A "corresponding disadvantage" situation constitutes at least a temporarily sustainable advantage, because for the moment an "end game" has been reached. However, as the attractiveness of competitors' other markets changes, so does their estimate of whether a corresponding disadvantage is present in the niche (as American Motors learned to its cost). In addition, competitors will always be searching for ways to fill the capability gap without creating offsetting gaps. Only if the creation of offsetting gaps is an automatic and inevitable consequence of any such action will the producer's advantage be assured of sustainability in the long run.

3. *Fear of reprisal.* Even though it initially would appear worth doing so, competitors may refrain from filling the capability gap for fear of retaliatory action by the producer. The sustainability of the producer's existing advantage depends, in this case, on the competitors' continuing to exercise voluntary restraint, accepting in effect the producer's position in this market segment.

For example, Japanese steel makers voluntarily refrain from increasing their U.S. market share for fear that American producers can and will persuade the U.S. government to take harsh protectionist measures.

"Fear of reprisal" is probably among the most common strategic situations in business, but it must be considered unstable over time, as competitors' situations and managements shift.

4. *Management inertia.* Finally, there are cases where competitors would benefit from closing the capability gap but fail to do so, either because management has incorrectly assessed the situation or because it lacks the will, the ability, or the energy to take the required action.

For example, Honda's success in dominating the

British motorcycle industry is generally attributed to Norton Villiers Triumph's failure to respond to a clear competitive threat until too late.

Psychologists tell us that managers will implement real change only when their discomfort with the status quo exceeds the perceived personal cost of taking the indicated action. This may well explain why competitors often tolerate a performance gap that they could profitably act to close. But it is risky for a producer to rely for long on the weakness or inertia of competitors' management to protect a competitive advantage; by definition the end game has not been reached.

In all four cases, how long competitors will tolerate capability gaps they are capable of closing depends largely on the relationship between the value of the advantage created by the gap and the cost (to each competitor) of closing it. The worse the cost-to-benefit ratio, the longer the advantage is likely to be sustainable, because greater changes in the environment are required before value would exceed cost. Coupled with an informed view of the rate of environmental change in the industry, this ratio thus allows the analyst to estimate sustainability.

SCA and Strategy

The classic definition of competitive strategy as "an integrated set of actions designed to create a sustainable advantage over competitors" might suggest that possessing an SCA is synonymous with business success—that those producers who have an SCA are guaranteed winners, and that those competitors who lack one should simply exit the business to avoid financial disaster.

This apparently reasonable conclusion is, however, incorrect. Although an SCA is a powerful tool in creating a successful business strategy, it is not the only key ingredient. In fact:

1. Possessing an SCA does not guarantee financial success.
2. Producers can succeed even when competitors possess an SCA.
3. Pursuing an SCA can sometimes conflict with sound business strategy.

Losing with an SCA

Although an SCA will help a producer to achieve, over time, higher returns than his competitors, there are at least three circumstances where its possessor can fail financially:

1. *If the market sector is not viable.* In many cases (including most new-product introductions), the minimum achieveable cost of producing and selling a particular produce or service exceeds its value to the customer. In this situation, an SCA will not guarantee the survival of its possessor; it will tend merely to ensure that his competitors will fare even worse.

2. *If the producer has severe operational problems.* An SCA can allow management the luxury of focusing more fully on achieving operational excellence, but thousands of companies have failed for operational, rather than strategic, reasons.

3. *If competitors inflict tactical damage.* An SCA rarely puts a producer completely beyond the reach of competitor actions, such as price cuts and "buying" market share, which may be unrelated to the SCA itself. A producer will be particulary vulnerable to such competitive tactics if the SCA is not very important, either because the depth of the "footprint" described earlier is shallow or because the gap in capability is minor.

In these cases, producers must select their actions very carefully. Actions that can and will be imitated may result only in intensified competitive rivalry. And, where the producer's advantage is unimportant, he will have little cushion against the competitive repercussions. For example, recent airline pricing policies and "frequent flyer" programs have done nothing to contribute to the long-term profitability or competitive positions of their originators. Unimaginative direct cost-reduction efforts (cutting overhead or staffs, for example) may improve profitability in the short term. But if competitors can and will imitate these efforts, the only long-run effect may be to raise the general level of misery throughout the industry.

Competing against an SCA

By definition, not all producers can possess an SCA in a given product market segment. Other competitors face the prospects of competing (at least for some time) from a handicapped position. Under certain circumstances, however, it is still possible for some to succeed.

Rapidly growing markets constitute one such situation. As long as real market growth over a given period exceeds the additional capacity advantaged competitors can bring on line during that time (due to organizational constraints, risk aversion, and so forth), even weak competitors can thrive. For example, the booming market for microcomputer software over the past five years has enabled many weak competitors to grow rich. Only when market growth slows or the advantaged competitors increase the rate at which they can grow will true competition begin and the impact of an SCA make itself felt.

In markets where true competition for scarce sales dollars is taking place, the number of disadvantaged competitors who can succeed, the degree to which they can prosper, and the conditions under which they can prosper will vary, depending on the value of the advantage held by the "number one" competitor.

If the number one competitor has only a shallow or unimportant advantage, many disadvantaged competitors can prosper for long periods. As noted earlier, each competitor is unique. When all attributes are considered, each will have a competitive advantage in serving some customers. The disadvantaged competitors are more likely to receive lower returns than the number one producer, but they certainly may be viable.

If the number one competitor has an important advantage in a given product/market segment, some theorists assert that over the long run there will be only one viable competitor. Others may remain in the segment, but they will be plagued by losses and/or very inadequate returns. If there are six different ways to achieve a major advantage, this reasoning runs, then the market will split into six segments, each ruled by a different competitor, who uniquely excels in the attribute most valued by the customers in that segment.

Be that as it may, in practice other strong competitors may also profitably exist alongside Number One under two conditions:

1. *If the number one producer's advantage is limited by a finite capacity* that is significantly less than the size of the market; that is, he may expand further,

but will not retain his advantage on the incremental capacity. Obstacles to continued advantaged expansion are common: limited access to superior raw materials, finite capacity in low-cost plants, prohibitive transportation costs beyond certain distances. Antitrust laws also tend to act as barriers to expansion beyond a certain level by number one competitors.

2. *If the size of the individual competitors is small* relative to the size of the market. In this case, a number of strong competitors can expand for many years without directly competing with each other, by taking share from weak competitors rather than each other.

Weak competitors, of course, are likely to fare badly when competition is intense and the depth of the advantage enjoyed by others is great. Their choices are:

1. To leave the business.
2. To endure the situation until the advantage is eroded.
3. To seek to create a new advantage.

If a weak competitor chooses to pursue a new advantage, then he must ensure that it will be preemptive, or that competitors will not notice his move and will fail to respond until he has consolidated his position. Otherwise, his action is virtually certain to be copied and the intended advantage erased.

Pursuing the Wrong SCA

Although its attainment is the goal of *competitive* strategy, sustainable competitive advantage is not an end in itself but a means to an end. The corporation is not in business to beat its competitors, but to create wealth for its shareholders. Thus, actions that contribute to SCA but detract from creating shareholder wealth may be good strategy in the competitive sense but bad strategy for the corporation. Consider two examples:

• *Low-cost capacity additions in the absence of increased industry demand.* Adding low-cost capacity and recycling the additional profits into product/delivery attributes that attract enough customers to fill that capacity is usually a sound business strategy. However, as industry cost curve analysis has demonstrated, if the capacity addition is not accompanied by increases in industry demand, the effect may well be to displace the high-cost, but previously viable, marginal producer. When this happens, prices in the industry will fall to the level of the costs of the new marginal producer, costs which by definition are lower than the costs of the former marginal producer. Thus, the profit per unit sold of all participants will be reduced.

Depending on the cost structure of the industry, the declines in the profit per unit sold can be dramatic (for example, if all the remaining producers have similar costs). In this case, even the producer who added the new capacity will face declining profitability on his preexisting capacity; in extreme cases, his total profit on new and old capacity may fall below the profit he had previously earned on the old capacity alone. While gaining share and eliminating a competitor (good competitive strategy), he has invested *more* to profit *less* (bad business strategy).

• *Aggressive learning curve pricing strategies that sacrifice too much current profit.* Under these strategies, prices are reduced at least as fast as costs in order to buy market share and drive out competitors. The assumption is that the future payoff from market dominance will more than offset the costs of acquiring it. The value of new business, however, is likely to be very sensitive to the precise relationship between prices and costs. This is true particularly in the early stages of the learning curve, when the absolute levels of prices, costs, and margins are relatively high and the profit consequences are, therefore, greater for any given volume. Especially in high-tech industries, such as electronics, where the lifetime of technologies is short, the long-term value of the market share bought by overly aggressive learning curve strategies can be less than the profit eliminated in the early stages by pricing too close to costs.

The framework for SCA proposed in this article is far from complete. Its treatment of product/delivery attributes and capability gaps (notably organizational strength) is impressionistic rather than detailed. It leaves other aspects of the topic (for example, the sustainability of competitive advantage at the corporate level) unexplored.

But a major concern of the business-unit strategist is to determine whether the enterprise (or a competitor's) possesses or is in a position to capture an SCA, and, if so, to examine is strategic implications. The conditions for SCA and the implications of SCA for strategy that have been proposed provide an initial framework for these tasks.

PART III

Strategic Analysis in Diversified Companies

7

Corporate Strategies

. . . to acquire or not to acquire: that is the question.
Robert J. Terry

Doing too many things isn't always a good idea—no matter how much better you think you can do them than someone else.

Dan Ciampi

In this chapter and the next, the spotlight is focused on corporate-level strategy. The task of forming corporate strategy is broader than that of line-of-business strategy. Business strategy concerns the managerial game plan for competing in a single line of business (given the context of the industry's environment and competitive forces), whereas corporate strategy goes on beyond to address diversification—the present and future scope for the whole company and plans for getting peak performance from what may already be a number of different business divisions competing in distinctly different industries. Business strategy is developed principally by the managers of line-of-business units, whereas corporate strategy is nearly always formulated by senior corporate officers. Business strategy and corporate strategy are the same only when the managerial game plan is strictly to remain in one single business.

As explained in Chapter 2, corporate strategy concerns four specific areas:

1. How can the long-term performance of the corporation's diversified business portfolio be improved—what scope and mix of business units makes the most sense, which businesses should be divested, and what new businesses should be added?
2. What major moves can be initiated to strengthen the position of existing businesses?
3. To what extent should the strategies of the firm's individual business units be coordinated in an attempt to produce corporate-level competitive advantage?
4. How should the available corporate resources be allocated across all of the company's various activities to get maximum performance from the whole portfolio—which business units deserve what kind of resource and investment priority?

In this chapter we will survey the generic approaches to building and then managing a diversified company. In Chapter 7 we will examine the techniques for analyzing a multibusiness corporate portfolio and for creating competitive advantage using various diversification approaches.

How Complex Organizations Develop—General Patterns of Corporate Strategy Evolution

Within the corporate sector where enterprises are complex enough to consist of several distinct business units, companies seem to have developed by following a fairly standard strategic path. The majority of companies begin as small single-business enterprises serving a local or at most a regional market. During a company's early years, the product line tends to be limited, the capital base thin, and the company's competitive position tenuous to weak. Nearly always, the initial strategic theme is grow and build, with chief strategic thrusts aimed at increasing sales volume, improving market share, and cultivating customer loyalty. Much attention is devoted to building a stronger competitive position vis-à-vis rival firms. Price, quality, service, and promotion are fine-tuned to respond more precisely to a detailed market need. The product line is broadened to meet variations in customer wants and end-use applications.

Opportunities for geographical market expansion customarily are pursued next. Usually the sequence of geographic expansion proceeds from local to regional to national to international markets, though the degree of penetration may be uneven from area to area because of varying profit potentials. Geographic expansion may, of course, stop well short of global or even national proportions, because of intense competition, lack of resources, or the unattractiveness of further market coverage.

When the opportunities for geographic expansion start to peter out, the third generation of corporate strategy may be toward opportunities for vertical integration—either backward to sources of supply or forward to the ultimate consumer. For some companies, this is an attractive strategic move, owing to the strengths vertical integration adds to the firm's core business.

Once a firm has reached the practical limits of geographical market expansion for its original product line and has also come to terms with the possibilities of forward and backward integration, the strategic options are either to attempt a more intensive implementation of the current line-of-business strategy or to begin to focus on diversification opportunities and on expanding the kind of businesses the company is in. The strategy of building a diversified business portfolio raises the issue of what new businesses to get into. Obviously, there are many, many ways to answer "What kind and how much diversification?" An almost infinite number of diversified business portfolios can be created; the different businesses can be closely related and have a high degree of strategic fit or they can be mostly unrelated, with little strategic fit at all. And after a diversified portfolio has been put together, the time will come when management has to consider "What businesses do we need to get out of?"—planned abandonment, divestiture, or liquidation of those business units that no longer are attractive, all now become realistic options. Somewhere along the way and for any number of reasons, a company's portfolio of businesses may fall into disarray and start to perform poorly; then the task of corporate strategy becomes one of concocting a game plan to restructure and rebuild the portfolio to fit new conditions and new corporate priorities.

GENERIC CORPORATE STRATEGY APPROACHES

The foregoing sketch of the way companies evolve correctly suggests that there are many paths managers can take in building and managing a diversified group of businesses. Seven generic corporate strategy approaches stand out:

1. Concentration on a single business, with little or no diversification.
2. A strategy of partial or full vertical integration.
3. A strategy of related diversification.
4. A strategy of unrelated diversification.
5. Abandonment, divestiture, and liquidation strategies.
6. Corporate turnaround, retrenchment, and portfolio restructuring strategies.
7. Combination strategies (mixing approaches 2 through 6 in varying ways).

Let's explore each of these basic corporate strategy options in some detail.

The Single-Business Corporate Strategy

The number of firms that have become household words concentrating in one line of business is impressively long. The power of single-business concentration is testified to by the market prominence of such familiar companies as McDonald's, Holiday Inn, Coca-Cola, BIC Pen, Apple Computer, Timex, Campbell Soup, Anheuser-Busch, Xerox, Gerber, and Polaroid, all of which gained their reputations in a single business. In the nonprofit sector, single-activity emphasis has proved successful for the Red Cross, the Salvation Army, the Christian Children's Fund, the Girl Scouts, Phi Beta Kappa, and the American Civil Liberties Union.

Concentrating on a single line of business (whether it be totally or with a small dose of diversification) offers some impressive competitive strengths and advantages. To begin, single-business concentration breeds directional clarity and unity of purpose up and down the whole organization—there is no confusion about "who we are and what we do." A number of key strategic tasks become more manageable: The efforts of the *total* organization can be directed down the *same* business path, rather than becoming fragmented into the pursuit of several different business directions simultaneously; the job of setting precise performance objectives for each department, work unit, and employee is less complex; and all entrepreneurial eyes can be trained squarely on keeping the firm's business strategy and competitive approach responsive to the winds of industry change and fine-tuned to specific customer needs. There is less chance that senior management's attention and limited organizational resources will be stretched thinly over too many diverse activities. All of the firm's managers, and especially those at the top executive level, can maintain hands-on contact with the core business and be expected to have in-depth knowledge about operations (most senior officers will probably have come up through the ranks and possess firsthand experience in field operations—something that is hard to expect of corporate managers in broadly diversified enterprises).

The competitive strength and earning power often associated with single-business concentration cannot be lightly dismissed. There are important sources of competitive advantage that attach to the single-business corporate strategy approach; concentration offers opportunity for a firm to:

1. Build a distinctive competence by bringing the full force of organizational resources and managerial know-how behind becoming proficient at doing one thing very well and very efficiently.
2. Use its accumulated experience and distinctive expertise to pioneer fresh approaches in production technology and/or in meeting customer needs and/or in product innovation and/or in any other part of the overall activity/cost chain.
3. Translate its distinctive competence and ability to innovate into a reputation for leadership and excellence.

Many single-business enterprises have parlayed their efforts into a sustainable competitive advantage and a prominent leadership position in their industry.

Concentrating exclusively or mostly on a single line of business need not inhibit company growth, especially as long as the industry is growing rapidly enough that the firm has its hands full just trying to capitalize on all the expansion opportunities in its present business. Nor does concentrating have to be strategically boring. Just how firms can concentrate on a single business, achieve growth, and still keep their strategies fresh and effective is illustrated by the strategic approaches and actual examples below:

1. *Create and promote more uses for the product.* Arm & Hammer baking soda sales increased markedly after the product was promoted for freshening refrigerators, cat litter boxes, and swimming pools.
2. *Take a standard commodity item and make a differentiated product out of it.* Frank Perdue succeeded in convincing people that his brand of chickens tasted better; Sunkist has done the same with oranges and lemons.
3. *Use advertising and promotional efforts to stimulate demand.* International Playtex and Johnson & Johnson discovered that tampons were "underadvertised" and scored major sales gains with increased television advertising.
4. *Attract nonusers to buy the product.* Procter & Gamble reversed declining Ivory soap sales in 1971 after promoting it for adults, instead of just for babies.
5. *Turn an apparent disadvantage into an advantage.* J. M. Smucker put its funny-sounding name to good use with an advertising slogan: "With a name like Smucker's, it has to be good."
6. *Use price cuts to build volume, market share, and profitability.* Telephone companies increased the use and profitability of their long-distance call business by giving substantial rate discounts on night and weekend calls.
7. *Seek market outlets for complementary by-products.* Several lumber and wood products firms have made use of scrap materials and started marketing pine bark for landscaping purposes and cat litter and wood shavings for household pets.
8. *Develop a more compelling sales appeal.* Procter & Gamble's Pampers disposable diapers were only a modest success when touted as a convenience

item for mothers, but sales took off after ads were changed to say that Pampers kept babies dry and happy.

9. *Capitalize on social concerns.* Sales of Dannon Yogurt, salt-free and sugar-free products of all kinds, caffeine-free herbal teas, and low-calorie beers all rose sharply after ads and media publicity helped health-conscious consumers "discover" the products.

10. *Make the product available through additional types of distribution channels.* Hanes captured additional sales and market share when it began to sell L'eggs panty hose in supermarkets.

Still other concentration strategy options include (1) stimulating greater customer use via quantity discounts and faster rates of product innovation, (2) expanding into additional geographic markets, (3) improving quality, (4) offering more support services to customers, and (5) introducing a wider variety of models, sizes, and features to cater to specific buyer needs and preferences.

Concentrating on a single line of business does pose the risk of putting all of a firm's eggs in one industry basket. If the industry stagnates, declines, or otherwise becomes unattractive, then the single-business enterprise's future outlook dims, the company's growth rate becomes tougher to sustain, and superior profit performance is much harder to achieve. In fact, there are times when changing customer needs, technological innovation, or new substitute products can undermine or virtually wipe out a single-business firm; one has only to recall what plastic bottles and paper cartons did to the market for glass milk bottles, what handheld calculators did to the makers of slide rules, and what electric typewriters did to the manual typewriter business. It is for this reason that most single-business companies sooner or later turn their attention in the direction of diversification.

Vertical Integration Strategies

Vertical integration strategies *extend a firm's competitive scope within the same overall industry.* They involve expanding the firm's range of activities backward into sources of supply and/or forward toward end-users of the final product. Thus, if a manufacturer elects to build a new plant to make certain component parts, rather than purchase them from outside suppliers, it remains in essentially the same industry as before—all that has changed is that it has business units in two stages of production in the industry's total activity chain. Similarly, if a personal computer manufacturer elects to integrate forward by opening 100 retail stores to market its brands directly to users, it remains in the personal computer business even though its *competitive scope* within the industry extends further forward in the industry chain.

Plainly, the generic corporate approaches to vertical integration can involve integrating backward or integrating forward, or doing both. Corporate strategy can aim at becoming *fully integrated,* participating in all stages of the process of getting products in the hands of final-users, or the strategic objective may be limited to becoming *partially integrated* and building positions in just some stages of the industry's total production-distribution chain. A firm can accomplish vertical integration via its own internal startup entry into more stages in the industry's activity chain, or it can choose to acquire an enterprise already positioned in the stage into which it wishes to integrate.

The best reason for pursuing vertical integration is to strengthen a firm's market position and/or to secure a competitive advantage.[1] Integrating backward into the business of one's suppliers can convert a cost center into a profit producer—an attractive option when suppliers have sizable profit margins. Moreover, integrating backward spares a firm the uncertainty of being dependent on suppliers of crucial raw materials or support services, as well as lessening the firm's vulnerability to powerful suppliers intent on jacking up the prices of important component materials at every opportunity. Stockpiling, fixed-price contracts, or the use of substitute inputs may not be attractive ways for dealing with uncertain supply conditions or with economically powerful suppliers. When this is the case, backward integration can be an organization's most profitable and competitively secure option for accessing reliable supplies of essential materials and support services at favorable prices.

The strategic impetus for forward integration has much the same roots. Undependable sales and distribution channels can give rise to costly inventory pileups and frequent underutilization of capacity, thereby undermining the economies of steady, near-capacity production operation. When the loss of these economies proves substantial, it is often advantageous for a firm to set up its own wholesale-retail distribution network in order to gain dependable channels through which to push its products to end-users. Sometimes even a few percentage point increases in the average rate of capacity utilization can boost manufacturing margins enough to make forward integration economical. On other occasions, forward vertical integration into distribution and retailing is cheaper than going through independent distributors and dealers, thus providing a source of relative cost advantage.

For a raw materials producer, integrating forward into manufacturing may help achieve greater product differentiation and allow escape from the price-oriented competition of a commodity business. Often, in the early phases of the vertical product flow, intermediate goods are "commodities" in the sense that they have essentially identical technical specifications irrespective of producer (as in the case with crude oil, poultry, sheet steel, cement, and textile fibers). Competition in the markets for commodity or commodity-like products is usually fiercely price-competitive, with the shifting balance between supply and demand giving rise to volatile profits. However, the closer the production stage is to the ultimate consumer, the greater are the opportunities for a firm to break out of a commodity-like competitive environment and differentiate its end-product via design, service, quality features, packaging, promotion, and so on. Often, product differentiation causes the importance of price to shrink in comparison to other competitive variables and allows for improved profit margins.

For a manufacturer, integrating forward may take the form of building a chain

---

[1]See Kathryn R. Harrigan, "Matching Vertical Integration Strategies to Competitive Conditions," *Strategic Management Journal* 7, no. 6 (November–December 1986), pp. 535–56; for specific advantages and disadvantages of vertical integration, see Kathryn R. Harrigan, *Strategic Flexibility* (Lexington, Mass.: Lexington Books, 1985), p. 162.

of closely supervised dealer franchises or it may mean establishing company-owned and -operated retail outlets. Alternatively, it could entail simply staffing regional and district sales offices instead of selling through manufacturer's agents or independent distributors.

Whatever its specific format, forward integration is usually motivated by a desire to realize the profit potential of (1) a smoother and more economical production flow, (2) product differentiation, (3) having one's own capability for accessing end-user markets, and/or (4) a distribution cost advantage.

There are, however, some strategic disadvantages of vertical integration. The larger capital requirements that sometimes accompany a strategy of full vertical integration may place a heavy strain on an organization's financial resources. Second, integration introduces additional risks, since the effect is to extend the enterprise's scope of activity across the industry chain. Third, vertical integration can so increase a firm's vested interests in technology, production facilities, and ways of doing things that it becomes reluctant to abandon heavy fixed investments even though they are becoming obsolete; because of this inflexibility, fully integrated firms are more vulnerable to new technologies and new products than are partially integrated or nonintegrated firms.

Fourth, vertical integration can pose problems of balancing capacity at each stage in the activity chain. The most efficient scale of operation at each step in the activity chain can be at substantial variance. Exact self-sufficiency at each interface is the exception not the rule. Where internal capacity is deficient to supply the next stage, the difference will have to be bought externally. Where internal capacity is excessive, customers will need to be found for the surplus. And if by-products are generated, they will require arrangements for disposal.

All in all, therefore, a strategy of vertical integration can have both important strengths and weaknesses. Which direction the scales tip on vertical integration depends upon (1) how compatible it is with the organization's long-term strategic interests and performance objectives, (2) how much it strengthens an organization's position in the overall industry, and (3) the extent to which it creates competitive advantage. Unless these considerations yield solid benefits, vertical integration is not likely to be an attractive corporate strategy option.[2]

Related Diversification Strategies

There are two generic approaches to corporate diversification: *related* and *unrelated*. In related diversification a firm's several lines of business, although distinct, still possess some kind of "fit." The nature of the fit in related diversification can be based on any of several factors: shared technology, common labor skills and requirements, common distribution channels, common suppliers and raw material sources, similar operating methods, similar kinds of managerial know-how, marketing-distribution channel complementarity, or customer overlap—virtually any aspect where meaningful relatedness or sharing opportunities exist in the

---

[2]For an extensive, well-researched, and fresh look at the whole family of corporate approaches to vertical integration, see Kathryn R. Harrigan, "Formulating Vertical Integration Strategies," *Academy of Management Review* 9, no. 4 (October 1984), pp. 638–52.

respective activity-cost chains. In contrast, with unrelated diversification there is no common linkage or element of fit among a firm's several lines of business; in this sense, unrelated diversification is *pure* diversification.

Related diversification has considerable appeal as a portfolio-building strategy. It allows a firm to maintain a degree of unity in its business activities and gain any benefits of fit and cost sharing, while at the same time spreading the risks of enterprise over a broader base. But more important, perhaps, when a firm has been able to build a distinctive competence in its original business, related diversification offers a way to exploit what a company does best and to transfer a distinctive competence-based competitive advantage from one business to another. Diversifying in ways that extend a firm's expertise to related businesses is a principal way to build corporate-level competitive advantage in a diversified firm and, thereby, result in the diversifier earning a profit greater than the total that would be earned if each business operated as an independent company. Specific approaches to related diversification include:

- *Entering businesses where sales force, advertising, and distribution activities can be shared* (a bread bakery buying a maker of crackers and salty snack foods).

- *Exploiting closely related technologies* (a maker of agricultural seeds and fertilizers diversifying into chemicals for insect and plant-disease control).

- *Seeking to increase capacity utilization* (an aluminum window manufacturer with idle equipment and unused plant space deciding to add aluminum lawn furniture to its product lineup).

- *Increasing the utilization of existing natural resource and raw material holdings* (a paper products firm electing to harvest more of its timberland and building a new plant to produce plywood).

- *Acquiring a firm where the buyer has a distinctive ability to improve the operations of the seller* (a successful mass marketer of women's cosmetics buying a chain of retail stores specializing in women's jewelry and accessories).

- *Building upon the organization's brand name and reputation with consumers* (a tire manufacturer diversifying into automotive repair centers).

- *Acquiring new businesses that will uniquely help the firm's position in its existing businesses* (a canned fruit juice firm diversifying into canned vegetables and frozen pies to give it more clout with food brokers and an expanded distribution system).

Actual examples of related diversification abound. BIC Pen, which pioneered inexpensive throw-away ballpoint pens, used the distinctive low-cost production and mass-merchandising competences it built in writing instruments as the basis for diversifying into disposable cigarette lighters, disposable shaving razors, and pantyhose, all three of which were businesses that relied heavily upon low-cost production know-how and skilled consumer marketing for competitive success. Tandy Corporation practiced related diversification when its chain of Radio Shack outlets, which originally handled mostly radio and stereo equipment, added telephones, intercoms, calculators, clocks, electronic and scientific toys, microcomputers, and peripheral computer equipment; the Tandy strategy was to use the marketing access provided by its thousands of Radio Shack locations to become one of the world's leading retailers of electronic technology to individual consumers. Philip Morris, a leading cigarette manufacturer, employed a marketing-related diversification strategy when it purchased Miller Brewing, General Foods, and Kraft, thus transferring many of its cigarette marketing skills to the marketing of beer and foods. Lockheed pursued a customer needs-based diversification strategy in creating business units to supply the Department of Defense with missiles, rocket engines, aircraft, electronic equipment, ships, and contract R&D for weapons. Sears understood that the diverse nature of TV sets, auto repair centers, men's suits, draperies, refrigerators, paint, and homeowner's insurance posed no difficulty to its corporate strategy, because the same customer buys them, in very much the same way and with the same value expectations, thereby providing the essential link for its version of customer-based related diversification. Technology-based related diversification has proved successful in process industries (steel, aluminum, paper, and glass), where a single processing technique spawns a multitude of related products.

The Nature and Value of Strategic Fit. The thing that makes related diversification so attractive, in comparison with unrelated diversification, is the opportunity to capitalize upon strategic fit. *Strategic fit* exists when different businesses have sufficiently related activity-cost chains that there are sizable opportunities to reduce costs, to enhance differentiation, or to manage more effectively by coordinating those particular activities in the industry chains that are closely related.[3] *A diversified firm which exploits these activity-cost chain interrelationships and captures the benefits of strategic fit achieves a consolidated performance that is more than the sum of what the businesses can earn pursuing independent strategies.* The presence of strategic fit within a diversified firm's business portfolio, together with corporate management's skill in capturing the benefits of the interrelationships, makes related diversification capable of being a $2 + 2 = 5$ phenomenon.

There are three broad categories of strategic fit. *Market-related fits* arise when the activity-cost chains of different businesses so overlap that the products are used by the same customers and/or are sold via essentially the same marketing and sales methods in the same geographic market and/or are distributed through common dealers and retailers. A variety of opportunities for cost sharing and coordination spring from market-related strategic fit: use of a common sales force to call on customers, advertising the related products in the same ads and brochures, use of the same brand names, coordinated delivery and shipping, combined after-the-sale service and repair organizations, coordinated order processing and billing, use of common promotional tie-ins (cents-off couponing, free samples and trial offers, seasonal specials, and the like), and combined dealer networks. In general,

---

[3]Michael E. Porter, *Competitive Advantage* (New York: Free Press, 1985), pp. 318–19. Porter has added substantially to the concept of strategic fit. The remainder of this section incorporates Porter's contributions into the presentation; for more details see chapter 9 of *Competitive Advantage*, especially pp. 337–53. The various ways to share resources across business units have also been discussed in Kenichi Ohmae, *The Mind of the Strategist* (New York: Penguin Books, 1983), pp. 121–24; the discussion here incorporates his ideas, too.

market-related strategic fits enhance a firm's overall ability to economize on its marketing, selling, and distribution costs and/or to enhance the customer appeal of its product mix and lines of product offspring.

Operating fits arise from interrelationships in the procurement of purchased inputs, in production technology, in manufacture and assembly, and in such administrative support areas as hiring and training, finance (efficiency in raising investment capital and in utilizing working capital), government relations, accounting and information systems, security, and facility maintenance. Operating fits nearly always present cost-saving opportunities; some derive from the potential to tap into more scale economies and some derive from ways to boost operating efficiency through sharing of related activities. The bigger the proportion of cost that an activity represents, the more significant the shared-cost savings become and the bigger the competitive advantage that accrues to capturing the benefits of operating fit.

Management fit emerges when different business units present managers with comparable or similar types of entrepreneurial, technical, administrative, or operating problems, thereby allowing the accumulated managerial know-how associated with one line of business to spill over and be useful in managing another line of business. Transfers of managerial know-how can occur anywhere in the activity-cost chain. United Airlines transferred its reservation systems know-how in air travel to hotels when its corporate parent acquired Westin Hotels; Emerson Electric transferred its skills in being a low-cost producer to its newly acquired Beaird-Poulan chain saw business division. In Beaird-Poulan's case, the transfer of management know-how drove its new strategy, changed the way its chain saws were designed and manufactured, and paved the way for new pricing and distribution emphasis. Management fit can also be based on (1) use of the same type of generic business strategy and competitive approach, (2) similar configuration of the activity-cost chains (the chain for operating large numbers of convenience food stores is remarkably similar to the chain for operating a group of retail auto parts centers for repair-it-yourself car owners), and (3) the application of proprietary technology in related products or production processes.

Table 7–1 provides a selective summary of the generic types of sharing opportunities associated with strategic fit, the likely kinds of competitive advantages that can result from each sharing opportunity, and the hidden factors that can result in the promise of fit never being realized.

Unrelated Diversification Strategies

While in many companies managers have opted to pursue related diversification because of the considerable appeal of benefiting from strategic fit opportunities, the managements of some firms have been more attracted to unrelated diversification. A simple criterion of venturing into "any industry in which we think we can make a profit" captures the essence of the corporate strategy of the most broadly diversified firms. Textron, for example, built its business portfolio out of such diverse businesses as Bell helicopters, Gorham silver, Homelite chain saws, Sheaffer pens, Fafnir bearings, Speidel watchbands, Polaris snowmobiles, Sprague gas meters and fittings, Bostitch staplers, air cushion vehicles, iron castings, milling

TABLE 7–1

Specific Types of Strategic Fit, the Competitive Advantage Potentials, and the Impediments to Actually Realizing Strategic Fit Benefits

Types of Strategic Fit and Opportunities for Sharing	Potential Competitive Advantages	Impediments to Capturing Strategic Fit Benefits
Market-related strategic fits:		
Shared sales force activities or shared sales offices, or both	• Lower selling costs. • Better market coverage. • Stronger technical advice to buyers. • Enhanced buyer convenience (can single-source). • Improved access to buyers (have more products to sell).	• Buyers have different purchasing habits toward the products. • Separate sales forces are more effective in representing the products. • Some products get more attention than others. • Buyers prefer to multiple-source, rather than single-source, their purchases.
Shared after-the-sale service and repair work	• Lower servicing costs. • Better utilization of service personnel (less idle time). • Faster servicing of customer calls.	• Different equipment or different labor skills, or both, are needed to handle repairs. • Buyers may do some in-house repairs.
Shared brand name	• Stronger brand image and company reputation. • Increased buyer confidence in the brand.	• Hurts reputation if quality of one product is lower.
Shared advertising and promotional activities	• Lower costs. • Greater clout in purchasing ads.	• Appropriate forms of messages are different. • Appropriate timing of promotions is different.
Common distribution channels	• Lower distribution costs. • Enhanced bargaining power with distributors and retailers to gain shelf space, shelf positioning, stronger push and more dealer attention, and better profit margins.	• Dealers resist being dominated by a single supplier and turn to multiple sources and lines. • Heavy use of the shared channel erodes willingness of other channels to carry or push the firm's products.
Shared order processing	• Lower order-processing costs. • One-stop shopping for buyer enhances service and, thus, differentiation.	• Differences in ordering cycles disrupt order-processing economies.
Operating fits:		
Joint procurement of purchased inputs	• Lower input costs. • Improved input quality. • Improved service from suppliers.	• Input needs are different in terms of quality or other specifications. • Inputs are needed at different plant locations, and centralized purchasing is not responsive to separate needs of each plant.

TABLE 7–1 *(concluded)*

Types of Strategic Fit and Opportunities for Sharing	Potential Competitive Advantages	Impediments to Capturing Strategic Fit Benefits
Shared manufacturing and assembly facilities	• Lower manufacturing/assembly costs. • Better capacity utilization, because peak demand for one product correlates with valley demand for other. • Bigger scale of operation improves access to better technology and results in better quality.	• Higher changeover costs in shifting from one product to another. • High-cost special tooling or equipment is required to accommodate quality differences or design differences.
Shared inbound or outbound shipping and materials handling, or both	• Lower freight and handling costs. • Better delivery reliability. • More frequent deliveries, so inventory costs are reduced.	• Input sources or plant locations, or both, are in different geographic areas. • Needs for frequency and reliability of inbound/outbound delivery differ among the business units.
Shared product or process technologies or technology development, or all three	• Lower product and process design costs, because of shorter design times and transfers to knowledge from area to area. • More innovative ability, owing to scale of effort and attraction of better R&D personnel.	• Technologies are same, but the applications in different business units are different enough to prevent much sharing of real value.
Shared administrative support activities	• Lower administrative and operating overhead costs.	• Support activities are not a large proportion of cost, and sharing has little cost impact (and virtually no differentiation impact).
Management fits: Shared management know-how, operating skills, and proprietary information	• Efficient transfer of a distinctive competence—can create cost savings or enhance differentiation. • More effective management as concerns strategy formulation, strategy implementation, and understanding of key success factors.	• Actual transfer of know-how is costly and stretches the key skill personnel too thinly. • Increased risks that proprietary information will leak out.

Source: Compiled and adapted from Michael E. Porter, *Competitive Advantage* (New York: Free Press, 1985), pp. 337–51.

machines, rolling mills, industrial fasteners, insurance, and missile and spacecraft propulsion systems. International Telephone and Telegraph (ITT), another pioneer of unrelated diversification, has had in its portfolio at one time or another such broad-ranging businesses as telephone equipment, Sheraton hotels, Wonder Bread, Smithfield Hams, Bobbs-Merrill Publishing, Hartford Insurance, Aetna Finance, Avis Rent-a-Car, Jabsco Pump, Gotham Lighting, Speedwriting, Inc., Transportation Displays, Rayonier chemical cellulose, Bramwell Business School, South Bend Window Cleaning, and Scott lawn care products.

Unrelated diversification can offer several different advantages:

1. Business risk is scattered over a variety of industries, making the company less dependent on any one business.
2. Capital resources can be invested in whatever industries offer the best profit prospects; cash flows from businesses with lower profit prospects can be diverted to supporting business units with higher profit potential.
3. Company profitability is made somewhat more stable, because hard times in one industry may be offset by good times in another industry—that is, the ups and downs of various industries can even one another out.
4. To the extent that corporate managers are exceptionally astute at picking what industries to get into and what companies to acquire in these industries, then shareholder wealth can be enhanced.

While there are circumstances where unrelated diversification is attractive, such a strategy has three big drawbacks. The Achilles' heel of unrelated diversification is the big demand it places on corporate-level management. The greater the number of diverse businesses that corporate managers must oversee and the more diverse these are, the harder it is for them (1) to stay on top of what is really going on in the divisions, (2) have in-depth familiarity with the strategic issues facing each business unit, and (3) probe deeply into the strategic actions and plans of business-level managers. As one president of a diversified firm expressed it:

> We've got to make sure that our core businesses are properly managed for solid, long-term earnings. We can't just sit back and watch the numbers. We've got to know what the real issues are out there in the profit centers. Otherwise, we're not even in a position to check out our managers on big decisions. And considering the pressures they're under, that's pretty dangerous for all concerned.[4]

With broad diversification, one has to hope that corporate managers will (1) have the ability to select capable managers to head each of many entirely different businesses; (2) discern when the major strategic proposals of business-unit managers are "sound" versus when they represent "good snow jobs"; and (3) be shrewd in acquiring businesses of widely varying character. Because every business sooner or later gets into trouble, one test of the risk of diversifying into new unrelated areas is to ask, "If the new business got into trouble, would we know how to bail it out?" If the answer is no, the risk of trouble is high and the profit prospects

---

[4]Carter F. Bales, "Strategic Control: The President's Paradox," *Business Horizons* 20, 4 (August 1977), p. 17.

chancy.[5] As the former chairman of a Fortune 500 company put it, "Never acquire a business you don't know how to run."

Second, without some kind of strategic fit, consolidated performance of an unrelated multibusiness portfolio will tend to be no better than the sum of what the individual business units could achieve if each were independent firms, and it may be worse to the extent that centralized management policies hamstring the line of business units. Except, perhaps, for the added financial backing that a cash-rich corporate parent can provide, a strategy of unrelated diversification adds little to the competitive strength of the individual business units. The value added by corporate managers in a widely diversified firm is primarily, therefore, a function of how good they are at portfolio management—deciding what new businesses to add to the portfolio, which ones to get rid of, and how best to deploy the available financial resources in building a higher-performing portfolio.

Third, although in theory unrelated diversification might seem to offer the potential of greater sales-profit stability over the course of the business cycle, in practice the attempts at countercyclical diversification appear to have fallen short of the mark. The consolidated profits of broadly diversified firms have not been found to be any more stable or less subject to reversal in periods of recession and economic stress than have the profits of firms in general.[6]

Despite its drawbacks, unrelated diversification cannot be ruled out as a desirable corporate strategy alternative. It plainly makes sense for a firm to consider some kind of diversification when its existing business has been expanded to its practical limits and/or when it is severely threatened by outside forces (it may or may not make sense to diversify before this occurs, however). And occasions will arise when the opportunity of acquiring a particular unrelated business is simply too good to pass up. A reasonable answer to how much diversification is enough comes from compromising the answers to two questions: "What is the least diversification we need to generate attractive performance over the long term?" and "What is the most diversification we can manage given the complexity it adds?"[7] In all likelihood, the optimal amount of diversification lies in between these two extremes.

Strategies for Entering New Businesses

Entry into new businesses can take any of three forms: acquisition, internal start-up, and joint ventures. *Acquisition of an existing business* is probably the most popular approach to corporate diversification.[8] Acquiring an established or-

---

[5]Of course, management may be willing to assume the risk that trouble will not strike before it has had time to learn the business well enough to bail it out of most any difficulty. See Peter Drucker, *Management: Tasks, Responsibilities, Practices* (New York: Harper & Row, 1974), p. 709.

[6]Drucker, *Management*, p. 767. Research studies in the interval since 1974, when Drucker made his observation, uphold his conclusion—on the whole, broadly diversified firms do not outperform less-diversified firms over the course of the business cycle.

[7]Drucker, *Management*, pp. 692–93.

[8]In recent years, takeovers have become an increasingly used approach to acquisition. The term *takeover* refers to the attempt (often sprung as a surprise) of one firm to acquire ownership or control over another firm against the wishes of the latter's management (and perhaps some of its stockholders).

ganization has the advantage of much quicker entry into the target market while, at the same time, offering a way to hurdle such barriers to entry as patents, technological inexperience, gaining access to reliable sources of supplies, being of a size to match rival firms in terms of efficiency and unit costs, having to spend enough on introductory promotions to gain market visibility and brand recognition, and getting adequate distribution access. Internally developing the knowledge, resources, scale of operation, and market reputation necessary to become an effective competitor can take years and entails all the problems of start-up. Finding the right kind of company to acquire can sometimes present a challenge, though.[9] Conceivably, an acquisition-minded firm may face the dilemma of buying a successful company at a high price or a struggling company at a low price. If the buying firm has very little knowledge about the industry it is seeking to enter but has ample capital, then it may be better off acquiring a capable firm—irrespective of the higher price. On the other hand, it can be advantageous to acquire a struggling firm at a bargain price when the new parent sees promising ways for transforming the weak firm into a strong one and has the money, the know-how, and the patience to transform it into a much stronger competitor.

Achieving diversification through *internal development* involves creating a new business entity in the desired industry and, starting from scratch, establishing new production capacity, developing sources of supply, building channels of distribution, growing a customer base, and so on. Generally, internal entry is more attractive when (1) there is ample time to launch the business from the ground up, (2) incumbent firms are likely to be slow or ineffective in responding to new entry, (3) the entrant has lower entry costs than other potential entrants, (4) the entrant has a distinctive ability to compete effectively in the business, (5) the additional capacity will not adversely impact the supply/demand balance in the industry, and (6) the targeted industry is young, fragmented (populated with many relatively small firms), and has potential for rapid growth over the long run.[10]

Joint ventures are a useful way to gain access to a new business in at least three types of situations.[11] *First,* a joint venture is a good device for doing something that is uneconomical or risky for an organization to do alone. *Second,* joint ventures make sense when pooling the resources and competences of two or more independent organizations produces an organization with more of the skills needed to be a strong competitor. In such cases, each partner brings to the deal the special talents or resources which the other doesn't have and which are important enough that they can spell the difference between success and near success. *Third,* joint ventures with foreign partners are sometimes a good way to surmount import quotas, tariffs, nationalistic political interests, and cultural roadblocks. Economic, competitive, and political realities of nationalism often require a foreign company to team up with a domestic partner to gain access to the national market in which the domestic partner is located. The drawback to joint ventures is that they create

---

[9]Michael E. Porter, *Competitive Strategy: Techniques for Analyzing Industries and Competitors* (New York: Free Press, 1980), pp. 354–55.

[10]Porter, *Competitive Strategy,* pp. 344–45.

[11]Drucker, *Management,* pp. 720–24.

complicated questions about the division of efforts among the partners and who has effective control.[12]

Abandonment, Divestiture, and Liquidation Strategies

Even a shrewd corporate diversification strategy can result in the acquisition of business units that, down the road, just do not work out. Misfits or partial fits cannot be completely avoided because it is impossible to predict precisely how getting into a new line of business will actually work out. In addition, long-term industry attractiveness changes with the times and what once was a good diversification move into an attractive industry may later turn sour. Subpar performance by some business units is bound to occur, thereby raising questions of whether to continue. Other business units may simply not mesh as well with the rest of the firm as was originally thought.

Sometimes, a diversification move that seems sensible from the standpoint of common markets, technologies, or channels turns out to lack the compatibility of values essential to a *temperamental fit*.[13] Several pharmaceutical companies had just this experience. When they diversified into cosmetics and perfumes, they discovered their personnel had little respect for the "frivolous" nature of such products, compared to the far nobler task of developing miracle drugs to cure the ill. The absence of "temperamental unity" between the chemical and compounding expertise of the pharmaceutical companies and the fashion-marketing orientation of the cosmetics business was the undoing of what otherwise was diversification into a business with related technology and logical product fit.

When a particular line of business loses its appeal, the most attractive solution may be to abandon it. Normally, such businesses should be divested as fast as practical. To drag things out merely drains away valuable organization resources. The more business units in a firm's portfolio, the more it will need a systematic planned abandonment strategy for divesting itself of poor performers, dogs, and misfits. A useful guide for determining if and when to divest a particular line of business is to ask the question, "If we were not in this business today, would we want to get into it now?"[14] When the answer is no or probably not, then divestiture needs to become a priority consideration.

Divestiture can take either of two forms. In some cases, it works fine to divest a business by spinning it off as a financially and managerially independent company, with the parent company retaining partial ownership or not. In other cases, divestiture is best accomplished by selling the unit outright, in which case a buyer needs to be found. As a rule, divestiture should not be approached from the angle of "Who can we pawn this business off on and what is the most we can get for it?"[15] Instead, it is wiser to proceed by addressing "For what sort of organization would this business be a good fit and under what conditions would it be viewed

[12]Porter, *Competitive Strategy,* p. 340.
[13]Drucker, *Management,* p. 709.
[14]Drucker, *Management,* p. 94.
[15]Ibid., p. 719.

as a good deal?" In identifying organizations for whom the business is a good fit, one also finds the buyers who will pay the highest price.

Of all the strategic alternatives, liquidation is the most unpleasant and painful, especially for a single-business enterprise where it means terminating the organization's existence. For a multi-industry, multibusiness firm to liquidate one of its lines of business is less traumatic; the hardships of suffering through layoffs, plant closings, and so on, while not to be minimized, still leaves an ongoing organization, perhaps one that eventually will turn out to be healthier after its pruning than before. In hopeless situations, an early liquidation effort usually serves owner-stockholder interests better than an inevitable bankruptcy. Prolonging the pursuit of a lost cause simply exhausts an organization's resources and leaves less to liquidate; it can also mar reputations and ruin management careers. Unfortunately, of course, it is seldom simple for management to differentiate between when a cause is lost and when a turnaround is achievable. This is particularly true when emotions and pride get mixed with sound managerial judgment—as often they do.

Corporate Turnaround, Retrenchment, and Portfolio Restructuring Strategies

Corporate turnaround, retrenchment, and portfolio restructuring strategies come into play when senior management undertakes to restore an ailing corporate business portfolio to good health. The first task here is always diagnosis of the underlying reasons for poor corporate performance. Crafting turnaround strategies then follows. Poor performance can be caused by large losses in one or more business units that pull overall performance down, having a disproportionate number of businesses in unattractive industries, a bad economy which has adversely impacted many of the firm's business units, or having weak management at either the corporate or business levels.

How to attempt a *turnaround* necessarily depends on the roots of poor profitability and the urgency of any crisis. Depending on the causes, there are six action approaches that can be used singly or in combination to pull off a turnaround in a diversified enterprise: (1) concentrate on restoring profitability in the money-losing units, (2) implement harvest strategies in the poorly performing units and divert cash flows to opportunities in better-performing units, (3) institute across-the-board economies in all business units, (4) revamp the composition of the business portfolio by selling off weak businesses and replacing them with new acquisitions in more attractive industries, (5) replace key management personnel at the corporate or business levels, or both, and (6) launch sales and profit improvement programs in all business units.

Retrenchment differs from turnaround in that retrenchment is a pullback and leaning-up in the face of adverse conditions. The strategic posture of retrenchment is one of defensively "battening down the hatches and weathering out the storm," withdrawing from activities where return on investment is subpar. Conditions of general economic recession, sharp increases in interest rates, periods of economic uncertainty, a sudden downturn in market demand, harsh regulation, and internal financial crisis can all make retrenchment wise or necessary. Retrenchment strategies in diversified companies are usually triggered by unsuccessful forays into industries where diversification did not turn out as well as originally expected; curtailments then have to be instituted.

Retrenchment can be approached in either of two ways: (1) pursuing stringent across-the-board internal economies aimed at wringing out waste and improving efficiency and (2) singling out the weakest performing businesses in the corporate portfolio for divestiture or severe pruning back, thus *narrowing* the diversification base. In the first instance, a firm that finds itself in a defensive or overextended position elects to remain in most or all of its current businesses and tries to ride out the bad times with various internal economy measures. Ordinarily, this type of corporate retrenchment strategy is highlighted by directives to reduce operating expenses, boost productivity, and increase profit margins. It can involve curtailing the hiring of new personnel, trimming the size of corporate staff, postponing capital expenditure projects, stretching out the use of equipment and delaying replacement purchases to economize on cash requirements, retiring obsolete equipment, dropping marginally profitable products, closing older and less-efficient plants, reorganizing internal work flows, reducing inventories, and the like.

The second variation of corporate retrenchment singles out the weakly performing parts of the corporate business portfolio for major strategy revisions, internal overhaul, or divestiture. Performing radical surgery on those units that are least profitable is nearly always a by-product of poor overall corporate performance and/or persistently poor performance in the targeted business units. Some diversified firms have been forced into drastic surgery on one or more business units because of an inability to make them profitable after several frustrating years of trying, or because ongoing operating problems proved intractable, or because funds were lacking to support the investment needs of all the businesses in their corporate portfolios. More usually, however, diversified companies that have one or more business units that have not performed up to expectations or that do not "fit" will retrench by divesting the problem businesses, using the proceeds to reduce debt or to pursue opportunities in the remaining business units—the strategy is to withdraw to a narrower set of industry groups and become less broadly diversified than before.

Portfolio restructuring strategies involve radical surgery on the mix and percentage makeup of the types of businesses in the portfolio. Restructuring can be prompted by any of several conditions: (1) when a strategy review reveals that the long-term performance prospects for the corporation as a whole have become unattractive (because the portfolio contains too many slow-growth or declining or competitively weak business units), (2) when one or more of the firm's key business units fall prey to hard times, (3) when a new CEO takes over the reins and decides that it is time to redirect where the company is headed, (4) when "wave of the future" technologies or products emerge and make a series of foothold acquisitions an attractive way to get a position in a potentially big new industry, or (5) when a "unique opportunity" presents itself to make an acquisition so big that several existing business units have to be sold off to raise money to finance the new acquisition.

Portfolio restructuring frequently involves both divestitures and new acquisitions. The candidate business units for divestiture include not only those that may be competitively weak or are up-and-down performers or are in unattractive industries but also those that no longer fit (even though they may be profitable and in attractive industries). Indeed, many broadly diversified corporations, disenchanted with how some of their acquisitions have performed and beset with the thorny problems of making successes out of so many unrelated business units, have restructured their business portfolios. Business units found not to be compatible with newly established related-diversification criteria have been divested and the remaining units regrouped and aligned to capture more strategic-fit benefits. The trend to demerge and deconglomerate has been driven by a growing preference to gear diversification around creating strong competitive positions in a few, well-selected industries as opposed to scattering corporate investments across many industries.

Combination Strategies

The six corporate strategy alternatives discussed above are not mutually exclusive. They can be used in combination, either in whole or in part, and they can be chained together in whatever sequences may be appropriate for adjusting to changing internal and external circumstances. For instance, one well-known company over a two-year period added 25 new lines of business to its corporate portfolio (16 through acquisition and 9 through internal start-up), divested 4, and closed down the operations of 4 others. Moreover, there are endless variations of each of the six alternatives, allowing ample room for enterprises to create their own individualized corporate strategy.

Although each firm's corporate strategy tends to be idiosyncratic and otherwise tailor-made to its own particular situation, there are several distinctive types of enterprises that emerge. The most common business portfolios created by corporate strategies are:

- A single-business enterprise operating in only one stage of an industry's activity-cost chain.
- A partially integrated, single-business enterprise operating in *some* of the stages of an industry's activity-cost chain.
- A fully integrated, single-business enterprise operating in *all* stages of an industry's activity-cost chain.
- A dominant-business enterprise with sales concentrated in one major core business but with a modestly diversified portfolio of either related or unrelated businesses (amounting to one third or less of total corporatewide sales).
- A narrowly diversified enterprise having a *few* (3 to 10) *related* business units.
- A broadly diversified enterprise made up of *many* mostly *related* business units.
- A narrowly diversified enterprise whose business portfolio includes a *few* (3 to 10) business units in *unrelated* industries

- A broadly diversified enterprise having *many* business units in mostly *unrelated* industries.
- A multibusiness enterprise which has deliberately diversified into several different and unrelated areas but which has a portfolio of related businesses within each area—thus giving it *several unrelated groups of related businesses.*

Illustration Capsule 15 shows the business portfolios of eight prominent diversified companies.

ILLUSTRATION CAPSULE 15

Business Portfolios of Well-Known Diversified Companies

Listed below are the business portfolios of a selected number of diversified companies:

Philip Morris Companies
- Cigarettes (Marlboro, Virginia Slims, Benson & Hedges, and Merit)
- Miller Brewing Company
- General Foods (Maxwell House, Sanka, Oscar Mayer, Kool-Aid, Jell-O, Post cereals, Birds Eye frozen foods)
- Mission Viejo Realty
- Kraft (cheeses, Sealtest, Breyer's ice cream)

Anheuser-Busch Companies
- Beer (Budweiser, Michelob, Busch, Bud Light)
- Eagle Snacks
- Campbell Taggart (Colonial and Earth Grains breads, plus other bakery products)
- Busch Entertainment Corporation (Busch Gardens, Sesame Place, Dark Continent)
- St. Louis Cardinals (major league baseball)
- St. Louis Refrigerator Car Company
- Busch Properties (real estate development)

RJR Nabisco, Inc.
- Cigarettes (Winston, Salem, Camel, Vantage, Doral and others)
- Nabisco Brands (Oreos, Ritz crackers, vanilla wafers, Cream of Wheat)
- Planters LifeSavers Company (nuts, popcorn, Butterfingers, Baby Ruth, LifeSavers, Carefree chewing gum)
- Del Monte (canned fruits and vegetables)

General Electric
- Aircraft engines
- Plastics
- National Broadcasting System (NBC)
- Major appliances (refrigerators, ranges, TVs, and so on)
- Lighting
- RCA (aerospace and electronics)
- Power generation systems (turbines, nuclear plants, construction and engineering services)
- Transit systems and locomotives
- Electric motors
- Kidder, Peabody (investment banking)
- General Electric Credit Corporation

ILLUSTRATION CAPSULE 15 *(concluded)*

Union Pacific Corporation
- Railroad operations (Union Pacific Railroad Company)
- Oil and gas exploration
- Mining
- Microwave and fiber optic transportation information and control systems
- Hazardous waste management disposal
- Trucking (Overnite Transportation Company)
- Oil refining
- Real estate

United Technologies
- Pratt & Whitney aircraft engines
- Carrier heating and air-conditioning equipment
- Otis elevators
- Sikorsky helicopters
- Essex wire and cable products
- Norden defense systems
- Hamilton Standard controls
- Space transportation systems
- Automotive components

Time, Inc.
- Magazine publishing (*Time, Fortune, Sports Illustrated, People, Money, Southern Living, Progressive Farmer,* and 10 others)
- Book publishing (Time-Life; Scott, Foresman; Book-of-the-Month Club; Little, Brown)
- TV Programming (Home Box Office, Cinemax, HBO Video)
- Cable TV operations (3.7 million subscribers in 32 states)

PepsiCo
- Soft drinks (Pepsi, Slice, Mountain Dew)
- Kentucky Fried Chicken
- Frito-Lay
- Pizza Hut
- Taco Bell
- 7Up International (non-U.S. sales of 7Up only)

Can you determine from these listings which companies have pursued related diversification, unrelated diversification, or both?

Fitting Strategy to a Firm's Situation

Some corporate strategy alternatives offer a stronger fit with a corporation's situation than do others. As one way of analyzing situational fit, consider Figure 7–1, where the variable of competitive position is plotted against various rates of market growth to create four distinct strategic situations that might be occupied by a single-business or dominant-business firm.[16] Firms that fall into the rapid market growth/strong competitive position box have several logical corporate strategy options as indicated, the strongest of which in the near term may well be single-business concentration. Given the industry's high growth rate (and implicit long-term attractiveness), it makes sense for firms in this position to push hard to

---

[16]C. Roland Christensen, Norman A. Berg, and Malcolm S. Salter, *Policy Formulation and Administration,* 7th ed. (Homewood, Ill.: Richard D. Irwin, 1976), pp. 16–18.

FIGURE 7–1
Matching Corporate Strategy Alternatives to Fit an Undiversified Firm's Situation

	COMPETITIVE POSITION	
	Weak	*Strong*
Rapid (MARKET GROWTH RATE)	**Strategy Options** (in probable order of attractiveness): 1. Reformulation of single-business concentration strategy. 2. Merger with another firm in the same business (to strengthen competitive position). 3. Vertical integration (forward or backward if it strengthens competitive position). 4. Diversification. 5. Abandonment.	**Strategy Options** (in probable order of attractiveness): 1. Concentration on a single business. 2. Vertical integragion (if it strengthens the firm's competitive position). 3. Related diversification.
Slow	**Strategy Options** (in probable order of attractiveness): 1. Reformulate single-business concentration strategy. 2. Merger with a rival firm (to strengthen competitive position). 3. Vertical integration (if it strengthens competitive position). 4. Diversification. 5. Harvest/divest. 6. Liquidation.	**Strategy Options** (in probable order of attractiveness): 1. Related diversification. 2. Unrelated diversification. 3. Joint ventures into new areas. 4. Vertical integration (if it strengthens competitive position). 5. Single-business concentration.

maintain or increase their market shares, to develop further their distinctive competences, and to make whatever capital investments are necessary to continue in a strong industry position. At some juncture, a company in this box may find it desirable to consider vertical integration as strategy for undergirding its competitive strength. Later, when market growth starts to slow, prudence dictates looking into related diversification as a means of spreading business risks and capitalizing on the expertise the company has built up.

Firms falling into the rapid-growth/weak-position category should, first of all, consider what options they have for reformulating their present competitive strategy (given the high rate of market growth) and address the questions of (1) why their current approach to the market has resulted in a weak competitive position and (2) what it will take to become an effective competitor. With the market expanding rapidly, there should be ample opportunity for even a weak firm to improve its performance and to make headway in becoming a stronger competitor. If the firm is young and struggling to develop, then it usually has a better chance for survival in a growing market, where plenty of new business is up for grabs, than it does in a stable or declining industry. However, if a weakly positioned company in a rapid-growth market lacks the resources and skills to hold its own, then either merger with another company in the industry that has the missing pieces or else merger with an outsider having the cash and resources to support the company's development may be the best corporate strategy alternative. Vertical integration, either forward or backward or both, becomes a necessary consideration for weakly positioned firms whenever such a move can materially strengthen the firm's competitive position. A third option is diversification into related or unrelated areas (if adequate financing can be found). If all else fails, then abandonment—divestiture in the case of a multibusiness firm or liquidation in the case of a single-business firm—has to become an active corporate-strategy option. While getting out of the business may seem extreme, because of the high-growth potential, it is well to remember that a company that is unable to make a profit in a booming market probably does not have the ability to make a profit at all and has little prospect of survival—particularly if recession hits or if competition stiffens.

Companies with a weak competitive position in a relatively slow-growth market should look at (1) reformulating the present competitive strategy—to turn the firm's situation around and create a more attractive competitive position; (2) integrating forward or backward, provided good profit improvement and competitive positioning opportunities exist; (3) diversifying into related or unrelated areas; (4) merger with another firm; (5) employing a harvest-then-divest strategy; and (6) liquidating its position in the business—by either selling out to another firm or closing down operations.

Companies that are strongly positioned in a slow-growth industry almost certainly will want to consider the strategy of using the excess cash flow from their existing business to begin a program of diversification. A related-diversification approach keyed to the distinctive competence that gave the company its dominant position is an obvious option, but unrelated diversification is an option when none of the related business opportunities appear especially attractive. Joint ventures with other organizations into new fields of endeavor are another logical possibility, and vertical integration could be attractive if solid profit-improvement opportunities exist. Whichever, the firm will likely wish to put a damper on much new investment in its present facilities (unless important growth *segments* within the industry merit grow-and-build approaches) to free the maximum amount of cash to deploy in new endeavors.

Comparing firms on the basis of competitive position and market growth rate (or any other two variables) is useful for the insight it provides into the importance of situational fit and into why companies in the same industry may have good reason to pursue different corporate strategies. The nature of a firm's current business portfolio, how well the portfolio is performing, the firm's financial strength, capital investment requirements, ability to respond to emerging market opportunities, distinctive competences, and so on all combine to define its situation and what corporate strategy options it should realistically consider.

ANALYTICAL CHECKLIST

Figure 7–2 presents a summary schematic of the generic corporate-strategy alternatives. At the onset, the dominant corporate-strategy consideration is single-business concentration; vertical integration may or may not enter the picture,

FIGURE 7–2
Checklist of Major Corporate Strategy Alternatives

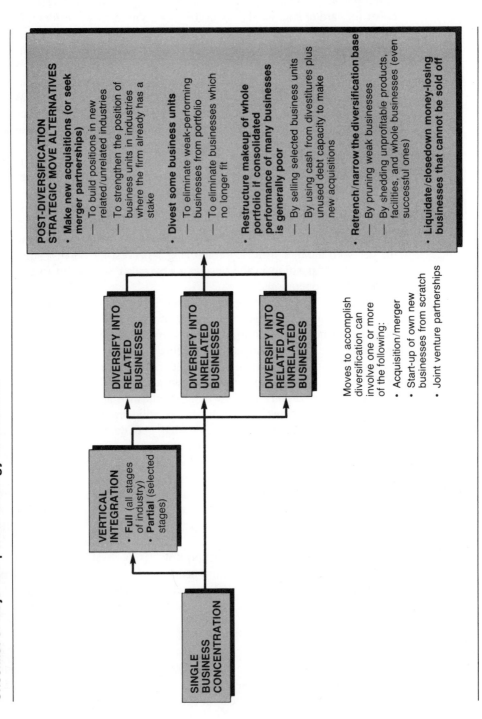

depending on the extent to which it strengthens a firm's competitive position or helps it secure a competitive advantage. When diversification becomes a serious strategic option, a choice must be made whether to pursue related diversification, unrelated diversification, or some mix of both. There are advantages and disadvantages to all three options. Once diversification has been accomplished, management's task is to figure out how to manage the existing business portfolio. The five primary post-diversification alternatives are (1) make new acquisitions, (2) divest those business units which are weak performers or which no longer fit, (3) restructure the makeup of the portfolio if overall performance is poor, (4) retrench to a narrower diversification base, and (5) close down/liquidate the assets of money-losing business units that cannot be sold off.

SUGGESTED READINGS

Ansoff, H. Igor. *Corporate Strategy*. New York: McGraw-Hill, 1965, chap. 7.

Bright, William M. "Alternative Strategies for Diversification," *Research Management* 12, no. 4 (July 1969), pp. 247–53.

Buzzell, Robert D. "Is Vertical Integration Profitable?" *Harvard Business Review* 61, no. 1 (January–February 1983), pp. 92–102.

Drucker, Peter. *Management: Tasks, Responsibilities, Practices*. New York: Harper & Row, 1974, chaps. 55, 56, 57, 58, 60, and 61.

Guth, William D. "Corporate Growth Strategies," *Journal of Business Strategy* 1, no. 2 (Fall 1980), pp. 56–62.

Hall, William K. "Survival Strategies in a Hostile Environment," *Harvard Business Review* 58, no. 5 (September–October 1980), pp. 75–85.

Harrigan, Kathryn R. "Matching Vertical Integration Strategies to Competitive Conditions," *Strategic Management Journal* 7, no. 6 (November–December 1986), pp. 535–56.

———. "Formulating Vertical Integration Strategies," *Academy of Management Review* 9, no. 4 (October 1984), pp. 638–52.

———. *Strategic Flexibility*. Lexington, Mass: Lexington Books, 1985, chap. 4 and Table A–8 (p. 162).

Hofer, Charles W. "Turnaround Strategies," *Journal of Business Strategy* 1, no. 1 (Summer 1980), pp. 19–31.

Kumpe, Ted, and Piet T. Bolwign, "Manufacturing: The New Case for Vertical Integration," *Harvard Business Review* 88, no. 2 (March–April 1988), pp. 75–82.

Lauenstein, Milton, and Wickham Skinner. "Formulating a Strategy of Superior Resources." *Journal of Business Strategy* 1, no. 1 (Summer 1980), pp. 4–10.

Ohmae, Kenichi. *The Mind of the Strategist*. New York: Penguin Books, 1983, chaps. 10 and 12.

8

Techniques for Analyzing Diversified Companies

> If we can know where we are and something about how we got there, we might see where we are trending—and if the outcomes which lie naturally in our course are unacceptable, to make timely change.
>
> *Abraham Lincoln*

> No company can afford everything it would like to do. Resources have to be allocated. The essence of strategic planning is to allocate resources to those areas that have the greatest future potential.
>
> *Reginald Jones*

Corporate-level managers add to the value of a diversified enterprise by acting effectively upon the answers to three strategy-related questions:

- How strong is the firm's present lineup of business activities?
- If the firm continues to stay in only its present business activities, then what will its performance prospects be like for the next 5 to 10 years?
- If the answers to these questions are not fully satisfactory, then what moves need to be considered in terms of getting into new businesses, getting out of some existing businesses, and strengthening the positions of the remaining businesses?

The task of formulating and implementing action plans to improve the mix and strength of a company's business-unit portfolio is the heart of what corporate-level strategic management is all about. The procedure for evaluating the strategy of a diversified company and deciding what corporate strategy moves to make next consists of eight steps:

1. Identifying the present corporate strategy.
2. Analyzing the makeup of the company's business portfolio—usually by constructing one or more business portfolio matrixes.

3. Comparing the long-term attractiveness of each industry represented in the company's business portfolio.

4. Comparing the competitive strength of each of the company's business units.

5. Determining how well the business units have performed in comparison to each other in years past and how they rank in terms of prospects for the future.

6. Assessing each business unit's compatibility with corporate strategy and determining the value of any strategic-fit relationships among existing business units.

7. Ranking the business units in terms of priority for new capital investment and developing a general strategy direction for each business unit—grow and build, hold and maintain, overhaul and reposition, or harvest/divest. (The task of initiating *specific* business-unit strategies to improve the business unit's competitive position is usually delegated to business-level managers, with corporate-level managers offering suggestions and having authority for final approval.)

8. Choosing strategic moves to improve overall corporate performance—acquiring new businesses and/or coordinating the activities of related business units in ways which produce a $2 + 2 = 5$ type of corporate-level competitive advantage.

The rest of this chapter is devoted to exploring each of these eight steps.

IDENTIFYING THE PRESENT CORPORATE STRATEGY

Strategic analysis of a diversified company starts with a probing of the organization's present strategy and business makeup. Recall from Figure 2–2 in Chapter 2 that a diversified company's strategy can usually be deduced by looking at:

- The extent to which the firm is diversified (as measured by the proportion of total sales and total corporate profits contributed by each business unit).

- Whether a firm is pursuing a strategy of related diversification (what kind of theme and what types of strategic fit?), a strategy of unrelated diversification, or a mixed strategy involving both related and unrelated business units.

- The nature of any recent management moves to boost performance of key business units in the portfolio and/or strengthen existing business positions.

- Moves to add new businesses to the portfolio and to build positions in new industries.

- Moves to divest weak or unattractive business units.

- The internal efforts of corporate management to realize the benefits of strategic-fit relationships and to use diversification to create competitive advantage.

- The proportion of capital expenditures going to each of the different business units.

Identification of the corporate strategy lays the foundation for conducting a thoroughgoing strategy analysis and, subsequently, for reformulating the strategy as it "should be." Illustration Capsule 16 reports how one diversified company views its corporate strategy and future direction.

MATRIX TECHNIQUES FOR EVALUATING DIVERSIFIED PORTFOLIOS

The most popular analytical technique for probing the *overall makeup* of a diversified group of business units involves constructing a business portfolio matrix. A *business portfolio matrix* is a two-dimensional graphical portrait of the comparative strategic positions of different businesses. Matrixes can be constructed using any pair of strategically relevant variables; but, in practice, the most revealing variables have proved to be industry growth rate, market share, long-term industry attractiveness, competitive strength, and stage of product/market evolution. Use of two-dimensional business portfolio matrixes as a tool of corporate-strategy evaluation is based on the relative simplicity of constructing them and on the clarity of the overall picture that they produce. Three types of business portfolio matrixes have been used the most frequently—the Boston Consulting Group's growth-share matrix, the GE industry attractiveness/business strength matrix, and the Hofer-A.D. Little life-cycle matrix.

The Four-Cell BCG Growth-Share Matrix

The first business portfolio matrix to receive widespread usage was a four-square grid pioneered by the Boston Consulting Group (BCG), one of the leading management consulting firms.[1] An illustrative BCG-type matrix is depicted in Figure 8–1. The matrix is formed using *industry growth rate* and *relative market share* as the axes. Each business unit in the corporate portfolio appears as a "bubble" on the four-cell matrix, with the size of each bubble or circle being scaled to the percent of revenues it represents in the overall corporate portfolio.

BCG methodology arbitrarily places the dividing line between "high" and "low" industry growth rates at around twice the real GNP growth rate plus inflation, but the boundary percentage can be raised or lowered when it makes sense to do so. The essential criterion is to so place the line that business units in the high-growth cells can fairly be said to be in industries growing faster than the economy as a whole and those in the low-growth cells are in industries growing slower than the economywide rate and that merit labels like *mature, aging, stagnant,* or *declining.*

[1]For a readily available and more extensive treatment, see Barry Hedley, "A Fundamental Approach to Strategy Development," *Long-Range Planning,* December 1976, pp. 2–11. The original presentation is Bruce D. Henderson, "The Experience Curve—Reviewed. IV. The Growth Share Matrix of the Product Portfolio" (Boston: Boston Consulting Group, 1973), Perspectives No. 135.

For two more recent discussions of the strategic importance of the experience curve, see Pankoy Ghemawat, "Building Strategy on the Experience Curve," *Harvard Business Review* 64, no.2 (March–April, 1985), pp. 143–49; and Bruce D. Henderson, "The Application and Misapplication of the Experience Curve," *Journal of Business Strategy* 4, no. 3 (Winter 1984), pp. 3–9.

For an excellent chapter-length treatment of the use of the BCG growth-share matrix in strategic portfolio analysis, see Arnoldo C. Hax and Nicolas S. Majluf, *Strategic Management: An Integrative Perspective* (Englewood Cliffs, N.J.: Prentice-Hall, 1984), chap. 7.

Relative market share is defined as the ratio of a business's market share to the market share held by the largest rival firm in the industry, with market share being measured in terms of unit volume, not dollars. For instance, if business A has a 15 percent share of the industry's total volume and the share held by the largest rival is 30 percent, then A's relative market share is 0.5. If business B has a market-leading share of 40 percent and its largest rival has a 30 percent share,

ILLUSTRATION CAPSULE 16

Dow Chemical's Basic Corporate Strategy and Direction

In its *1985 Annual Report,* the Dow Chemical Corporation outlined the company's fundamental strategic direction:

The Dow Chemical Company is in one of the most dynamic periods in its history, for rarely has the global competitive environment for chemicals experienced such transition.

Increased participation by hydrocarbon-rich countries is creating new supply patterns for chemicals and plastics and a reordering of global competitors. Technological advancements are changing historical production and geographic relationships.

Change is also creating many new opportunities. Industrialization and urbanization in less-developed countries now call for chemically related materials and processes to produce finished products and reduce pollution. Increased food production is a high priority with most nations. Virtually everywhere there are more calls for pharmaceuticals of all types while worldwide demand for consumer conveniences continues to rise and become more homogeneous.

Important to Dow in this environment is *maximizing growth and maintaining leadership by realizing the best emerging opportunities.*

To attain superior growth in earnings per share and return on equity, Dow's strategic objective will continue to be: to grow and diversify through emphasis on specialty chemicals and services while maintaining great strength in basic chemicals and plastics. The Company will concentrate on products and services in chemistry-related technologies.

Six major priorities will be applied to each business:

- continuous improvement in the quality of Dow products and services;
- maintenance of the earning power of existing strong assets. Divestiture and de-emphasis of some products and businesses will occur where necessary;
- continuous reduction of costs through efficiency and good management;
- selective acquisitions as an added basis for further growth and diversification;
- effective administration, with a focus on productivity, not bureaucracy;
- safety in every aspect and protection of the environment.

SOURCE: 1985 Annual Report.

FIGURE 8–1
The BCG Growth-Share Business Portfolio Matrix

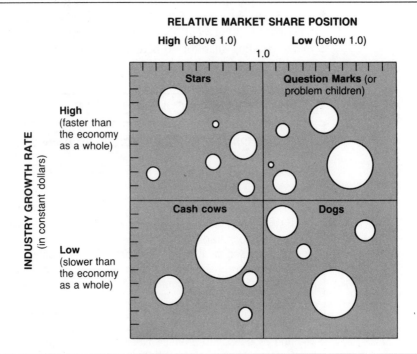

Note: Relative market share is defined by the ratio of one's own market share to the market share held by the largest *rival* firm. When the vertical dividing line is set at 1.0, the only way a firm can achieve a star or cash cow position in the growth-share matrix is to have the largest market share in the industry. Since this is a very stringent criterion, it may be "fairer" and more revealing to locate the vertical dividing line in the matrix at about 0.75 or 0.8.

then B's relative market share is 1.33. Given this definition, only business units which are market share leaders in their respective units will have relative market share values greater than 1.0; business units in the portfolio that trail rival firms in market share will have ratios below 1.0.

The most stringent BCG standard calls for the border between high and low relative market share on the grid to be set at 1.0, as shown in Figure 8–1. With 1.0 as the boundary, those circles in the two left-side cells of the matrix identify how many and which businesses in the firm's portfolio are leaders in their industry; those falling in the two right-side cells trail the leaders, with the degree to which they trail being indicated by the size of the relative market share ratio (a ratio of 0.10 indicates that the business has a market share only one tenth that of the largest firm in the market, whereas a ratio of 0.80 indicates a market share that is four fifths or 80 percent as big as the leading firm's share). A less stringent and perhaps more revealing criterion is to so place the relative market share boundary that businesses to the left enjoy positions as market leaders (though not necessarily *the* leader) and those to the right are in below-average or underdog market share positions; another possible option for locating the dividing line between high and low relative market share is to put the line at about 0.75 or 0.8.

The merit of using *relative* market share, instead of the actual market share percentage, to construct the growth-share matrix is that the former is a better indicator of comparative market strength and competitive position—a 10 percent market share is much stronger if the leader's share is 12 percent than if it is 50 percent; the use of relative market share captures this difference. An equally important consideration in using relative market share is that it is also likely to be a reflection of relative cost based on experience in producing the product and on economies of large-scale production. The potential of large businesses to operate at lower unit costs than smaller firms because of technological and efficiency gains that attach to larger size is a well-understood possibility. But personnel from the Boston Consulting Group accumulated evidence that the phenomenon of lower unit costs went beyond just the effects of economies of scale; they found that, as the cumulative volumes of production increased, the resulting knowledge and experience gained often led to the discovery of additional efficiencies and ways to reduce costs even further. The relationship between cumulative production experience and lower unit costs was labeled by BCG as *the experience curve effect*—for more details, see Illustration Capsule 10 in Chapter 3. When an important experience curve effect is present in the activity-cost chain of a particular business or industry, it places a strategic premium on market share: The firm that gains the largest market share tends to realize important cost advantages which, in turn, can be used to lower prices and gain still additional customers, sales, market share, and profit.

With these features of the BCG growth-share matrix in mind, we are ready to explore the portfolio implications for businesses falling into each cell of the matrix in Figure 8–1.

Question Marks and Problem Children. Business units falling in the upper-right quadrant of the growth-share matrix have been tagged by BCG as "question marks" or "problem children." Rapid market growth makes such business units attractive from an industry standpoint; but their low relative market share positions (and, thus, reduced access to experience curve effects) raise questions whether the profit potential associated with market growth can realistically be captured—hence, the question mark or problem children designation. Question mark businesses, moreover, are typically cash "hogs"—so labeled because their cash needs are high (owing to the investment requirements of rapid growth and product development) and their internal cash generation is low (owing to low market share, less access to experience curve effects and scale economies, and, consequently, thinner profit margins). The corporate parent of a cash hog business has to decide whether it is worthwhile to invest corporate capital to support the needs of a question mark division.

BCG has argued that the two best strategic options for a question mark business are (1) an aggressive grow-and-build strategy to capitalize on the high-growth opportunity or (2) divestiture, in the event that the costs of strengthening its market share standing via a grow-and-build strategy outweigh the potential payoff and financial risk. Pursuit of a fast-growth strategy is imperative any time an attractive question mark business is characterized by strong experience curve effects; this is because it will take major gains in market share to begin to match the lower-cost position enjoyed by firms with the greater cumulative production experience and their usually bigger market shares. The stronger the experience curve effect, the more powerful the competitive position enjoyed by the competitor that is the low-cost producer. Consequently, so the BCG thesis goes, unless a question mark/ problem child business is managed via a grow-and-build-type strategy, it will not be in a position to remain cost competitive via-à-vis large-volume firms—in which case divestiture becomes the only other viable long-run alternative. The corporate strategy prescriptions for managing question mark/problem child business units, thus, become straightforward: divest those that are weaker and less attractive and groom the attractive ones to become tomorrow's "stars."

Stars. Businesses with high relative market share positions in high-growth markets rank as "stars" in the BCG grid because they offer both excellent profit and excellent growth opportunities. As such, they are the business units that an enterprise comes to depend on for boosting overall performance of the total portfolio.

Given their dominant market share position and rapid-growth environment, stars typically require large cash investments to support expansion of production facilities and working capital needs; but they also tend to generate their own large internal cash flows, due to the low-cost advantage that attaches to economies of scale and cumulative production experience. Star-type businesses vary on whether they can support their investment needs totally from within or whether they require infusions of investment funds from corporate headquarters to support continued rapid growth and high performance. According to BCG, some stars (usually those that are well established and beginning to mature) are virtually self-sustaining in terms of cash flow and make little claim on the corporate parent's treasury. Young stars, however, often require substantial investment capital *beyond what they can generate on their own* and, thus, may be cash hogs.

Cash Cows. Businesses with a high relative market share in a low-growth market have been designated as "cash cows" by BCG, because their entrenched position tends to yield substantial cash surpluses over and above what is needed of reinvestment and growth in the business. Many of today's cash cows are yesterday's stars. Cash cows, though less attractive from a growth standpoint, are nonetheless a valuable corporate portfolio holding, because they can be "milked" for the cash to pay corporate dividends and headquarters overhead; they provide cash for financing new acquisitions; and they provide funds for investing in young stars and in those problem children that are being groomed as the next round of stars (cash cows provide the dollars to feed the cash hogs). Strong cash cows should never be harvested but, rather, should be maintained in a healthy status to sustain long-term cash flow. The idea is to preserve market position while efficiently generating dollars to reallocate to business investments elsewhere. Weak cash cows, however, may be designated as primary candidates for harvesting and eventual divestiture if their industry becomes unattractive.

Dogs. Businesses with low growth and low relative market share carry the label of "dogs" in the BCG matrix because of their weak competitive position (owing, perhaps, to high costs, low-quality products, less-effective marketing, and the like) and the low profit potential that often accompanies slow growth or impending market decline. Another characteristic of dogs is their inability to generate attractive cash flows on a long-term basis; sometimes they do not even produce enough cash to adequately fund a rear-guard hold-and-maintain strategy—especially if competition is brutal and profit margins are chronically thin. Consequently, except in unusual cases, the BCG corporate-strategy prescription is that dogs be harvested, divested, or liquidated, depending on which alternative yields the most attractive amount of cash for redeploying to other businesses or to new acquisitions.

Implications for Corporate Strategy. The chief contribution of the BCG growth-share matrix is the attention it draws to the cash flow and investment characteristics of various types of businesses and how corporate financial resources can be shifted from business unit to business unit in an effort to optimize the long-term strategic position and performance of the whole corporate portfolio. According to BCG analysis, the foundation of a sound and long-term corporate strategy is to utilize the excess cash generated by cash cow business units to finance market share increases for cash hog businesses—the young stars still unable to finance their own growth internally and those problem children that have been singled out as having the best potential to grow into stars. If successful, the cash hogs eventually become self-supporting stars and then, when the markets of the star businesses begin to mature and their growth slows down, they will become the cash cows of the future. The "success sequence" is, thus, problem child/question mark to young star (but perhaps still a cash hog) to self-supporting star to cash cow.

The weaker, less-attractive question market businesses not deemed worthy of the financial investment necessary to fund a long-term grow-and-build strategy are often a portfolio liability, because of the high-cost economics associated with a low relative market share and because they do not generate enough cash on their own to keep them abreast of fast-paced market growth. These question marks should, according to BCG prescriptions, be prime divestiture candidates *unless* they can be kept profitable and viable with their own internally generated funds (all problem child businesses are not untenable cash hogs; some may be able to generate the cash to finance a hold-and-maintain strategy and, thus, contribute enough to corporate earnings and return on investment to justify retention in the portfolio). Even so, such low-priority question marks still have a dim future in the portfolio; as market growth slows and maturity-saturation sets in, they will move vertically downward in the matrix, becoming dogs.

Dogs should be retained only as long as they can contribute positive cash flow and do not tie up assets and resources that could be more profitably redeployed. The BCG recommendation for managing a weakening or already weak dog is to employ a harvesting strategy. If and when a harvesting strategy is no longer attractive, then a weak dog business becomes a candidate for elimination from the portfolio.

There are two "disaster sequences" in the BCG scheme of things: (1) when a star's position in the matrix erodes over time to that of a problem child and then falls to become a dog and (2) when a cash cow loses market leadership to the point where it becomes a dog on the decline. Other strategic mistakes include overinvesting in a safe cash cow; underinvesting in a question mark so, instead of moving into the star category, it tumbles into a dog; and shotgunning resources thinly over many question marks, rather than concentrating them on the best question marks to boost their chances of becoming stars.

Strengths and Weaknesses in the Growth-Share Matrix Approach. The BCG business portfolio matrix makes a definite contribution to the strategist's tool kit when it comes to diagnosing the portfolio makeup and reaching broad prescriptions regarding the strategy and direction for each business unit in the portfolio. Viewing a diversified corporation as a collection of cash flows and cash requirements (present and future) is a major step forward in understanding the financial aspects of corporate strategy. The BCG matrix highlights the financial interaction within a corporate portfolio, shows the kinds of financial considerations that must be dealt with, and explains why the priorities for corporate resource allocation can legitimately be different from business to business. It also provides good rationalizations for both grow-and-build strategies and divestiture. Yet, several legitimate shortcomings exist:

1. A four-cell matrix based on high/low classifications hides the fact that many businesses (the majority?) are in markets with an average growth rate and have relative market shares that may be best characterized as neither high nor low but, rather, in between or intermediate. In which cells do these average businesses belong?

2. While viewing all businesses as being stars, cash cows, dogs, or question marks does indeed add a useful element of flavor and communicative appeal, it is a misleading simplification to neatly categorize the members of a corporate portfolio in terms of just four types of businesses. Some market leaders may be getting stronger while others are getting weaker—a few one-time stars or cash cows have encountered hard times, and some have ended up in bankruptcy as dogs. Some market share leaders have never really been stars in terms of profitability. All businesses with low relative market shares are not dogs or question marks—in many cases, runner-up firms have proven track records in terms of growth, profitability, and competitive ability, even gaining on the so-called leaders. Hence, a key characteristic to assess is the *trend* in a firm's relative market share—is it gaining ground or losing ground and why? This weakness can be solved by placing directional arrows on each of the circles in the matrix—see Figure 8-2.

3. The BCG matrix is not a reliable indicator of relative investment opportunities across business units.[2] For example, investing in a star is not necessarily more attractive than investing in a lucrative cash cow. The matrix results are silent about when a question mark business is a potential winner versus being a likely loser. It says nothing about whether shrewd investments can turn a strong dog into a star or a cash cow.

4. Being a market leader in a slow-growth industry is not a surefire guarantee of cash cow status because *(a)* the investment requirements of a hold-and-maintain

---

[2]Derek F. Abell and John S. Hammond, *Strategic Market Planning* (Englewood Cliffs, N.J.: Prentice-Hall, 1979), p. 212.

FIGURE 8–2
Present versus Future Positions in the Portfolio Matrix

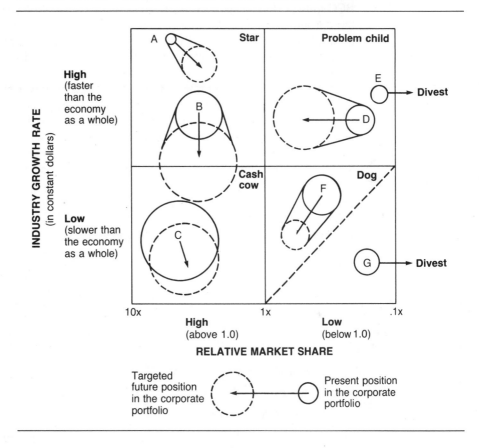

strategy, given the impact of inflation on the costs of replacing worn-out facilities and equipment, can soak up much or all of the available internal cash
flows; and *(b)* as markets mature, competitive forces often stiffen and the
ensuing vigorous battle for volume and market share can shrink profit margins
and wipe out any surplus cash flows.

5. The connection between market share and profitability is not as tight as the
experience curve effect implies. The importance of cumulative production experience in lowering unit costs varies from industry to industry. In some cases,
a larger market share can be translated into a unit-cost advantage; in others it
cannot. Hence, it is wise to be cautious in basing strategy prescriptions on the
assumption that experience curve effects are strong enough and cost differences
among competitors are big enough to totally drive competitive advantage.

6. A thorough assessment of the relative long-term attractiveness of business units
in the business portfolio requires an examination of more than just market
growth and relative market share variables.

The GE Industry Attractiveness/Business Strength Matrix

An alternative matrix approach that avoids some of the shortcomings of the BCG growth-share matrix has been pioneered by General Electric, with help from the consulting firm of McKinsey and Company. The GE effort is a nine-cell portfolio matrix based on the two dimensions of long-term product-market attractiveness and business strength/competitive position.[3] In this matrix, depicted in Figure 8–3, the area of the circles is proportional to the size of the industry, and the pie slices within the circle reflect the business's market share. The vertical axis represents each industry's long-term attractiveness, defined as a composite weighting of market growth rate, market size, historical and projected industry profitability, market structure and competitive intensity, scale economies, seasonality and cyclical influences, technological and capital requirements, emerging threats and opportunities, and social, environmental, and regulatory influences.

FIGURE 8–3
General Electric's Industry Attractiveness/Business Strength Matrix

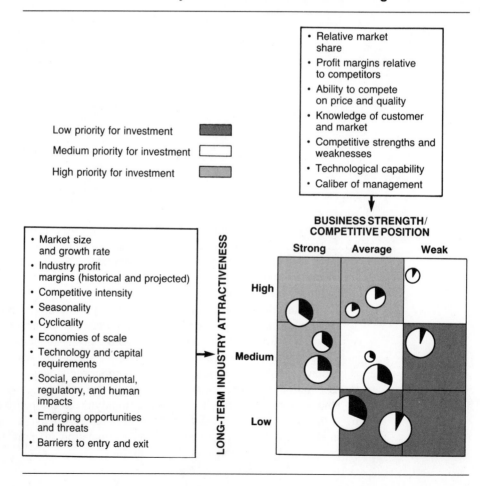

The procedure involves assigning each industry attractiveness factor a weight according to its perceived importance, assessing how the industry stacks up on each factor (using a 1-to-5 rating scale), and then obtaining a weighted composite rating as shown below:

Industry Attractiveness Factor	Weight	Rating	Value
Market size	0.15	5	0.75
Projected rate of market growth	0.20	1	0.20
Historical and projected profitability	0.10	1	1.10
Intensity of competition	0.20	5	0.10
Emerging opportunities and threats	0.15	1	0.10
Seasonality and cyclical influences	0.05	2	0.10
Technological and capital requirements	0.10	3	0.30
Environmental impact	0.05	4	0.20
Social, political, regulatory factors	Must be acceptable	—	—
	1.00		2.90

To arrive at a measure of business strength/competitive position, each business is rated, using the same approach shown above, on such aspects of business strength/competitive position as relative market share, success in increasing market share and profitability, ability to match rival firms on cost and product quality, knowledge of customers and markets, how well the firm's skills and competences in the business match the various requirements for competitive success in the industry (distribution network, promotion and marketing, access to scale economies, technological proficiency, support services, manufacturing efficiency), adequacy of production capacity, and caliber of management. The exact choice of factors on which to rate each business unit should depend entirely on what factors really determine competitive position and strength in that particular industry. The two composite values for long-term product-market attractiveness and business strength/competitive position are then used to plot each business's position in the matrix.

Corporate Strategy Implications. The most important strategic implications flowing from the attractiveness/strength matrix concern the assignment of investment priorities to each of the company's business units. Businesses in the three cells at the upper left, where long-term industry attractiveness and business strength/competitive position are favorable, are accorded top investment priority — the general strategic prescription here is grow and build, with businesses in the high-strong cell carrying the highest claim for being awarded investment funds. Next in priority come businesses positioned in the three diagonal cells stretching from the lower left to the upper right. These businesses are usually assigned medium investment priority in the portfolio and are candidates for hold-and-maintain type of strategies; if a business in one of these three cells has an unusually attractive

---

[3]For an expanded treatment, see Michael G. Allen, "Diagramming G.E.'s Planning for What's WATT," in *Corporate Planning: Techniques and Applications,* ed. Robert J. Allio and Malcolm W. Pennington (New York: AMACOM, 1979); and Hax and Majluf, *Strategic Management: An Integrative Perspective,* chap. 8.

opportunity, it can carry a higher priority and qualify for a grow-and-build strategy. The strategy prescription for businesses in the three cells in the lower right corner of the matrix is typically harvest or divest (in exceptional cases where good turnaround potential exists, it can be "rebuild and reposition" using some type of turnaround approach).[4]

The strength of the nine-cell attractiveness/strength approach is threefold. *One,* it allows for intermediate rankings between high and low and between strong and weak. *Two,* it incorporates explicit consideration of a much wider variety of strategically relevant variables. *Three,* and most important, it stresses the channeling of corporate resources to those businesses that combine medium-to-high product-market attractiveness with average-to-strong business strength/competitive position, the thesis being that it is in these combinations where the greatest probability of competitive advantage and superior performance lies. There is, of course, a powerful logic for concentrating resources in those businesses that enjoy a higher degree of attractiveness and competitive strength, being very selective in making investments in businesses with intermediate positions, and withdrawing resources from businesses that are lower in attractiveness and strength unless they offer exceptional turnaround potential.

However, the nine-cell GE matrix, like the four-cell growth-share matrix, provides no real clues or hints about the specifics of business strategy; all that the GE matrix analysis yields are *general* prescriptions: grow-and-build or hold-and-maintain or harvest-divest. Such prescriptions may occasionally suffice, insofar as corporate-level strategy formulation is concerned, but the issue of specific competitive approaches remains wide open. Another weakness has been pointed out by Professors Hofer and Schendel: The GE approach does not depict as well as it might the positions of businesses that are about to emerge as winners because the product-market is entering the takeoff stage.[5]

The Life-Cycle Matrix

To better identify a *developing-winner* type of business, Hofer developed a 15-cell matrix in which businesses are plotted in terms of stage of industry evolution and competitive position, as shown in Figure 8–4.[6] Again, the circles represent the sizes of the industries involved and pie wedges denote the business's market share. Looking at the plot in Figure 8–4, business A would appear to be a *developing winner;* business C might be classified as a *potential loser;* business E might be labeled as an *established winner;* business F could be a cash cow; and business G a loser or a dog. The power of the life-cycle matrix is the story it tells

---

[4]At General Electric, each business actually ended up in one of five types of categories: (1) *high-growth potential* businesses deserving top investment priority, (2) *stable-base* businesses deserving steady reinvestment to maintain position, (3) *support* businesses deserving periodic investment funding, (4) *selective pruning or rejuvenation* businesses deserving reduced investment funding, and (5) *venture* businesses deserving heavy R&D investment.

[5]Charles W. Hofer and Dan Schendel, *Strategy Formulation: Analytical Concepts* (St. Paul, Minn.: West Publishing, 1978), p. 33.

[6]Ibid., p. 34. This approach to business portfolio analysis was reportedly first used in actual practice by consultants at Arthur D. Little, Inc. For a full-scale review of this portfolio matrix approach, see Hax and Majluf, *Strategic Management: An Integrative Perspective,* chap. 9.

FIGURE 8–4
The Life-Cycle Portfolio Matrix

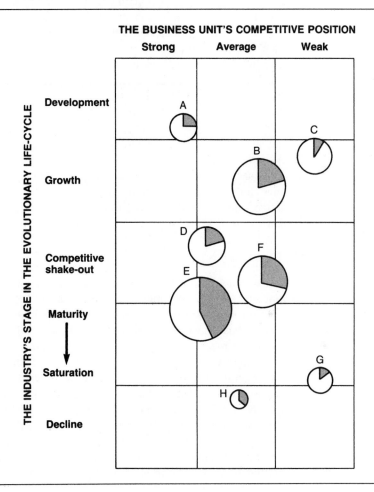

about the distribution of the firm's businesses across the stages of industry evolution.

Deciding What Type of Matrix to Construct

Actually, there is no need to force a choice about which type of portfolio matrix to use. Provided adequate data are available, all three can be constructed to gain insights from different perspectives; and each matrix type has its pros and cons. The important thing is to try to capture the overall character of the firm's business makeup in a way that provides insight into what strategic moves may be needed to boost performance of the portfolio as a whole and how to best allocate corporate resources across the portfolio.

COMPARING INDUSTRY ATTRACTIVENESS

Before corporate managers can come to a strong conclusion about the strategic roles various business units can have in the portfolio and how much the corporation should be investing in each one, they must compare the long-term attractiveness of each industry represented in the corporate portfolio. It is certain that some business units will be situated in more attractive industries than others. The question to be explored in this third analytical step is "How good an *industry* is this for the company to be in?" The methods for appraising industry attractiveness were discussed in Chapter 3 and need not be repeated here. And if the nine-cell industry attractiveness/business strength matrix has already been constructed in the preceding analytical step, then a strong basis for comparing which business units are in the most attractive industries is in place. A quantitative ranking of industry attractiveness can be obtained using the procedure described earlier in constructing the nine-cell GE portfolio matrix. A qualitative or subjective ranking from most attractive to least attractive may suffice, however, if managers have the information at their disposal to make dependable judgments.

COMPARING BUSINESS-UNIT STRENGTH

Doing an appraisal of each business unit's strength and competitive position in its industry affords corporate managers a basis for judging the business unit's chances for real success in its industry. The task here is to evaluate whether the company's business unit is well positioned in its industry and the extent to which it is a strong market contender. It can make more sense to invest in a business unit that enjoys a very strong position in an industry with only medium attractiveness than it does to invest in a weakly positioned business unit that is in a very attractive industry. The methods for assessing a business's overall strength and competitive position were presented in Chapter 4. Quantitative rankings of the strength/position of the various business units in the corporate portfolio can be calculated by using the procedure described in constructing the GE-style attractiveness/strength matrix. Subjective rankings from strongest to weakest may prove just as functional—as long as the judgments made are trustworthy.

COMPARING BUSINESS-UNIT PERFORMANCE

Step 5 in the portfolio evaluation process is to compare the different business units on the basis of both their *actual historical performance* and their *future performance prospects*. Information regarding a business unit's past performance can be gleaned from the company's financial records, and the industry attractiveness/business strength evaluations previously completed provide a basis for judging its future prospects. The most important performance yardsticks tend to be sales growth, profit growth, and return on assets employed in the business; however, cash flow generation can also be a big consideration, especially for cash cow businesses or for businesses which have potential for harvesting. Business units with weak-performance track records and little prospects for real improvement generally become candidates for divestiture. Business units with the brightest future prospects generally head the list for having their capital investment projects funded in the budget.

STRATEGIC-FIT RELATIONSHIPS

The next step is to determine how well each business unit fits in the portfolio. Fit needs to be looked at from two angles: (1) whether the business unit has strategic fit with other business units in the portfolio and the corporate value of these relationships and (2) whether the business unit meshes well with corporate strategy or otherwise adds a useful dimension to the corporate portfolio. A business is more attractive as a portfolio holding when it presents strategic-fit opportunities that can be translated into stronger competitive advantage or added profitability or both. Likewise, a business unit is more valuable when it is capable of contributing heavily to corporate-performance objectives (sales growth, profit growth, above-average return on investment, and so on), when it fits in with the strategic direction the corporation is trying to head, when it possesses the characteristics that senior management wants to build into the portfolio, and when it enhances the value of corporation's portfolio.

RANKING THE BUSINESS UNITS ON INVESTMENT PRIORITY

Using the information and results of the preceding evaluation steps, it ought to be a fairly easy task to rank the business units in terms of priority for new capital investment and to develop a general strategic direction for each business unit. The task here is to draw conclusions about where the corporation should be investing its financial resources. Which business units should have top priority for new capital investment and financial support? Which business units should carry the lowest priority for new investment? Out of this ranking comes a clearer idea of what the basic strategic approach for each business unit should be—grow and build (aggressive expansion), hold and maintain (protect current position with new investments as needed), overhaul and reposition (try to move the business into a much more desirable industry position and to a better spot in the business portfolio matrix), or harvest-divest. In deciding whether to divest a business unit, one needs to use a number of evaluating criteria: industry attractiveness, competitive strength, strategic fit with other businesses, performance potential (profit, return on capital employed, contribution to cash flow), compatibility with corporate priorities, capital requirements, and value to the overall portfolio.

As part of this evaluation step, consideration needs to be given to whether and how corporate resources and skills can be used to enhance the competitive standing of particular business units.[7] This is especially important when the firm has business units judged to be in a less than desirable competitive position and where improvement in some key success area could make a big difference to the business unit's performance. It is also important when corporate strategy is predictated on

---

[7]Hofer and Schendel, *Strategy Formulation: Analytical Concepts,* p. 80.

strategic fit and the managerial game plan calls for transferring corporate skills and strengths to recently acquired business units in an effort to give them a competitive edge and bolster their market position.[8]

OVERALL PORTFOLIO EVALUATION AND CORPORATE-STRATEGY RECOMMENDATIONS

The final evaluation phase involves judging the overall *mix* of businesses in the portfolio.[9] There are several angles from which to size up the current portfolio: Does the portfolio contain enough businesses in very attractive industries? Does it contain too many losers or question marks? Is the proportion of mature or declining businesses so great that corporate growth will be sluggish? Does the firm have enough cash cows to finance the stars and emerging winners? Are there enough businesses that generate dependable profits and cash flow? Is the portfolio overly vulnerable to inflation or recessionary influences? Does the firm have too many businesses that it really doesn't need to be in or otherwise needs to divest? Does the firm have its share of businesses with strong competitive positions or is it burdened with too many businesses in average-to-weak competitive positions? Does the makeup of the business portfolio put the corporation in good position for the future? Answers to these questions point directly to what kinds of strategic moves corporate executives have to consider in formulating a strategy to improve overall corporate performance.

Checking for Performance Gaps

The whole of corporate-level strategy analysis points toward determining whether the aggregate performance of the businesses in the portfolio can be expected to achieve corporate performance objectives, and, if not, what kinds of corporate-strategy changes can be devised to close the performance gap. If a performance gap is found to exist, then there are at least five basic types of action top management can take to reduce or close the gap between established objectives and projected performance of the present portfolio:[10]

1. *Alter the strategic plans for some (or all) of the businesses in the portfolio.* This option essentially involves renewed corporate efforts to get better performance out of its present business units. Corporate managers can push business-level managers to generate better performance out of their businesses, and, if the portfolio contains related business units with strategic-fit opportunities, corporate managers can pursue avenues to capture any untapped strategic-fit benefits. However, squeezing out better short-term performance, if pursued too zealously, can impair long-term performance of the adversely affected business units and, in any case, there are limits to how much extra performance can be squeezed out to close the gap.

---

[8]Michael E. Porter, *Competitive Advantage* (New York: Free Press, 1985), chap. 9.
[9]Barry Hedley, "Strategy and the Business Portfolio," *Long-Range Planning* 10, no. 1 (February 1977), p. 13; and Hofer and Schendel, *Strategy Formulation*, pp. 82–86.
[10]Hofer and Schendel, *Strategy Formulation*, pp. 93–100.

2. *Add new business units to the corporate portfolio.* Making new acquisitions or internal start-ups of new businesses to boost overall performance, however, raises some new strategy issues. Expanding the corporate portfolio to close a performance gap means taking a close look at *(a)* whether to acquire related or unrelated businesses, *(b)* what size acquisition(s) to try to make, *(c)* how the new units would be absorbed into or grafted onto the present corporate structure, *(d)* what specific features should be looked for in an acquisition candidate, and *(e)* if new acquisitions can be financed without shortchanging the present business units on their new investment requirements.

3. *Delete weak-performing or money-losing businesses from the corporate portfolio.* The most likely candidates for divestiture are those businesses that are in a weak competitive position or in a relatively unattractive industry or in an industry which does not fit. Funds from divestitures can, of course, be used to finance new acquisitions, pay down corporate debt, or fund new strategic thrusts in the remaining businesses.

4. *Join forces with other groups to try to alter conditions responsible for subpar performance potentials.* In some situations, concerted actions with rival firms, trade associations, suppliers, unions, customers, or other interested groups may help ameliorate adverse performance prospects. Forming or supporting a political action group may be an effective way of lobbying for solutions to import-export problems, tax disincentives, and onerous regulatory requirements.

5. *Reduce corporate performance objectives.* On occasion, adverse economic circumstances or declining fortunes in one or more big business units can render corporate objectives unreachable. Closing the gap between actual and desired performance may then require downward revision of corporate objectives to bring them more in line with reality. As a practical matter, though, this tends to be a last-resort option, being used only after other options have come up short.

USING STRATEGIC FIT TO CREATE COMPETITIVE ADVANTAGE IN DIVERSIFIED COMPANIES

One of the most important tasks of corporate-level strategy-managers is coordinating the activities of related business units in ways that produce a corporate-driven contribution to the competitive advantage of business units.[11] It is the effective performance of this task that makes the corporate-level managers of diversified companies *something more than portfolio managers* and the firm itself *something more than a holding company.* Indeed, effective performance of this task is perhaps the chief way that corporate executives can *add value* to a diversified enterprise.[12] Some other ways that corporate managers can add value to a diversified

---

[11]Porter, *Competitive Advantage,* p. 364. This point is also emphasized in Kenichi Ohmae, *The Mind of the Strategist* (New York: Penguin Books, 1983), pp. 137–40.

[12]The term *add value* is used here to mean that performance of the *corporate-level* management functions is done in a manner that causes the profit performance of a diversified firm to be *more* than the total of what its business units would earn operating as independent companies. To put it another way, unless a diversified firm turns in a better performance than its business units could earn in the aggregate on their own, corporate management adds no pecuniary value to the enterprise.

firm, besides building corporate-level competitive advantage, include:

- Doing such an especially good job of portfolio management (selecting new businesses to get into that prove to be outstanding performers, selling business units off at their peak and getting premium prices, and so on) that the enterprise consistently outperforms other firms in generating dividends and capital gains for stockholders.
- Doing such a good job of helping to manage the various business units (by providing expert problem-solving skills, innovative ideas, and improved decision-making acumen to the business-level managers) that the business units perform at a higher level than they would otherwise be able to do.
- Providing such inspirational leadership that subordinate managers and employees are motivated to perform "over their heads" on a sustained basis, thereby adding an extra measure of performance.

All three of these ways amount to better management — which is to say that for corporate management to add value to a diversified firm in some other way than through capturing strategic-fit benefits and creating competitive advantage, then corporate executives must be "managerially superior" and produce results that business-level managers cannot. That such occurs very regularly would be hard to prove (but easy to claim!).

Building competitive advantage at the corporate level is grounded in coordinating and managing the interrelationships in the activity-cost chains of a firm's business units (the concept of activity-cost chains was first discussed in Chapter 4; the remainder of this section draws heavily on the presentation of "Strategic Cost Analysis" and Figure 4–2 in Chapter 4, and also upon the material in Table 7-1 in Chapter 7).

Step 1 is to analyze the activity-cost chains of each business unit to identify opportunities for cost sharing, or differentiation enhancement, or both.[13] In searching for business-unit interrelationships to capitalize on, care has to be taken to distinguish between those opportunities where real sharing benefits can actually be achieved and those where the degree of relatedness is insignificant or else disappears when put under the microscope and nitty-gritty specifics are closely scrutinized. Moreover, there are many sources of business-unit linkages: (1) supplier or component parts interrelationships, or both; (2) technology and production process overlaps; (3) distribution channel interrelationships; (4) customer overlaps; (5) common managerial know-how requirements; and (6) competitor interrelationships (different business units may have common competitors and, often, two or more business units of one diversified firm may be in competition with two or more business units of another diversified firm—a condition that makes them *multipoint competitors).*

Once the interrelationships among business units in the corporate portfolio are identified, *step 2* is to identify important interrelationships between a firm's present

---

[13]Porter, *Competitive Advantage*, p. 368; also, see Ohmae, *The Mind of the Strategist*, pp. 137–38.
[14]Porter, *Competitive Advantage*, pp. 370–71.

business units and other industries not represented in its portfolio.[14] Looking for sharing potentials in industries outside the portfolio can turn up interesting acquisition candidates and is a fruitful way of developing stronger strategic fits. Studying the portfolios of other firms with related portfolios can yield clues about which industries may offer attractive sharing possibilities.

Step 3 is to assess the importance of the interrelationships identified in steps 1 and 2 in building an attractive corporate-based competitive advantage.[15] The size of any net gain in competitive advantage here is a function of the sharing benefits, the cost of capturing the sharing benefits, and the difficulty of matching and coordinating the business unit interrelationships. Analysis usually reveals that, while there are many actual and potential business unit interrelationships and linkages, only a few of these have enough strategic importance to generate competitive advantage.

Step 4 is to develop a corporate action plan to coordinate those targeted business-unit interrelationships where an attractive net competitive potential exists.[16] Corporate coordination of these interrelationships can be pursued in several different ways:[17]

1. Implement sharing of the related activities in the cost chain—examples include centralizing the procurement of raw materials, combining R&D and design activities into one unit, integrating manufacturing facilities wholly or partially, combining dealer networks and sales force organizations, and combining order processing and shipping (for more possibilities refer to Table 7–1 in Chapter 7).
2. Coordinating the strategies of the related business units—to unify and strengthen the firm's overall approach to customers, suppliers, and/or distribution channels, and also to present a stronger offensive or defensive front against the actions of competitors.
3. Formulating a corporate-level game plan for attacking and/or defending against multipoint competitors, the thrust of which is to strengthen the firm's overall position and to put multipoint rivals under added competitive pressure.
4. Setting up interbusiness task forces, standing committees, or project teams to transfer generic know-how, proprietary technology, and skills from one business unit to another and/or to implement sharing.
5. Diversifying into new businesses that enhance or extend strategic-fit relationships in the activity-cost chains of existing businesses.
6. Divesting units that do not have strategic-fit relationships or that make sharing and coordination more difficult.
7. Establishing incentives for business-unit managers to work together in realizing strategic-fit potentials.

Illustration Capsule 17 describes how one company pursued and achieved an attractive type of strategic fit.

---

[15]Ibid., pp. 371–72.
[16]Ibid., p. 372.
[17]Porter, *Competitive Advantage*, pp. 372–75, and Ohmae, *The Mind of the Strategist*, pp. 142–62.

Illustration Capsule 17

Harry and David: Pursuing Strategic Fit

Harry and David is a mail-order company specializing in fresh fruit and bakery goods. Headquartered at a 23-acre site south of Medford, Oregon, Harry and David grows much of its own fruit, bakes its own cakes and pastries, processes a variety of preserves, and weaves over 120,000 gift baskets for its products. The company is internationally known for its Fruit-of-the Month Club and for its Royal Riviera pears. The pears are Harry and David's most popular product and are grown at the company-owned Bear Creek Orchards near Medford. The company's hallmark is an old-fashioned concern for quality and personal attention. The fruit shipped by Harry and David is of exceptionally fine quality and meets exacting standards. Attention to detail extends to hand-tying the bows on each gift basket, and every box of fruit and gift basket contains a card identifying the packer to signal the pride and care taken with each order.

Sales at Harry and David's were highly seasonal. Over two thirds of the company's orders were received during the October–December period, following the mailing of the company's Christmas catalog. To help relieve the strong seasonal nature of its business, Harry and David elected to diversify. The company chosen for purchase was Jackson and Perkins, a New York-based firm which specialized in selling roses by mail order. Jackson and Perkins began to build a national reputation selling roses at the 1939 New York World's Fair; sales had thrived since and orders were shipped nationwide.

Shortly after Jackson and Perkins was acquired by Harry and David, it was relocated to the West Coast. Arrangements were made to grow Jackson and Perkins' roses in production fields in California and truck them to Medford for packing and shipping. The packing and shipping operations of the two businesses meshed nicely. Both are seasonal; pears are packed and shipped from October through December, and roses from mid-December through May. Both businesses, thus, are able to share the same facilities and labor for packing and shipping, to utilize common order-processing labor for packing and shipping, to utilize common order-processing personnel and procedures, and to benefit from economies in preparing and mailing their catalogs. The strategic fit between the two businesses was pivotal in Harry and David's decision to acquire Jackson and Perkins.

GUIDELINES FOR MANAGING THE CORPORATE-STRATEGY FORMATION PROCESS

Although formal analysis and entrepreneurial brainstorming are important contributors to corporate-strategy selection, there is more to where corporate strategy comes from and how it evolves. The process used to arrive at major strategic decisions is typically fragmented, incremental, and the product of a shared consensus for action among senior management.[19] Rarely is there an all-inclusive

---

[19]James Brian Quinn, *Strategies for Change: Logical Incrementalism* (Homewood, Ill.: Richard D. Irwin, 1980), p. 15.

grand formulation of the total corporate strategy. Instead, corporate strategy in major enterprises emerges incrementally from the unfolding of many different internal and external events, the result of probing the future, experimenting, gathering more information, sensing problems, building awareness of the various options, developing ad hoc responses to unexpected crises, communicating partial consensus as it emerges, and acquiring a "feel" for all the strategically relevant factors, their importance, and their interrelationships.[20]

One should not think, therefore, of corporate-strategy analysis as a time executives set aside to undertake a single comprehensive review. Such big reviews may be scheduled; but the evidence is that major strategic decisions emerge gradually, rather than from periodic full-scale analysis followed by a prompt decision. Typically, top executives approach major strategic decisions a step at a time, often starting from broad, intuitive conceptions and then embellishing, fine tuning, and modifying their original thinking as more information is gathered, as formal analysis confirms or modifies emerging judgments about the situation, and as confidence and consensus build for what strategic moves need to be made. Often, attention and resources are concentrated on a few critical strategic thrusts that illuminate and integrate corporate direction, objectives, and strategies.

ANALYTICAL CHECKLIST

Strategic analysis in diversified companies is an eight-step process. *Step one* is to identify the present corporate strategy. *Step two* is to construct business portfolio matrixes as needed to see what the overall composition of the present portfolio looks like. *Step three* is to profile the industry and competitive environment of each business unit and to draw conclusions about just how attractive each industry represented in the portfolio is. *Step four* is to probe the competitive strength of the individual businesses and how well situated each is in its respective industry. *Step five* is to compare the different business units on the basis of their actual-performance track record and their future-performance prospects. *Step six* is to determine how well each business unit fits with corporate direction and strategy and whether it has important strategic-fit relationships with other businesses in the portfolio. *Step seven* is to rank the business units from highest to lowest in investment priority, drawing conclusions about where the firm should be putting its money and about what the general strategic direction of each business unit should be (grow and build, hold and maintain, overhaul and reposition, harvest, or divest). *Step eight* is to ascertain whether the projected performance of the portfolio will meet corporate objectives; and, if a performance gap is evident, then what actions to take to close the gap. Out of this should come:

- Conclusions concerning whether to add new units to the portfolio; and, if so, whether they should be related or unrelated to those already in the portfolio.
- Decisions regarding the need to promote more strategic fit and whether and how to try to build what kind of corporate-level competitive advantage.

---

[20]Ibid., pp. 58 and 196.

SUGGESTED READINGS

Bettis, Richard A., and William K. Hall. "Strategic Portfolio Management in the Multibusiness Firm." *California Management Review* 24, Fall 1981, pp. 23–38.

————— . "The Business Portfolio Approach—Where It Falls Down in Practice." *Long Range Planning* 16, no. 2 (April 1983), pp. 95–104.

Christensen, H. Kurt; Arnold C. Cooper; and Cornelis A. Dekluyuer, "The Dog Business: A Reexamination," *Business Horizons* 25, no. 6 (November–December 1982), pp. 12–18.

Hall, William K. "SBUs: Hot, New Topic in the Management of Diversification." *Business Horizons* 21, no. 1 (February 1978), pp. 17–25.

Hamermesh, Richard G. *Making Strategy Work*. New York: John Wiley & Sons, 1986, chaps. 1, 4, and 7.

Haspeslagh, Phillippe. "Portfolio Planning: Uses and Limits." *Harvard Business Review* 60, no. 1 (January–February 1982), pp. 58–73.

Hax, Arnoldo, and Nicolas S. Majluf. *Strategic Management: An Integrative Perspective.* (Englewood Cliffs, N.J.: Prentice-Hall, 1984), chaps. 7–9.

Hedley, Barry. "A Fundamental Approach to Strategy Development." *Long Range Planning* 9, no. 6 (December 1976), pp. 2–11.

————— . "Strategy and the Business Portfolio." *Long Range Planning* 10, no. 1 (February 1977), pp. 9–15.

Henderson, Bruce D. "The Application and Misapplication of the Experience Curve." *Journal of Business Strategy* 4, no. 3 (Winter 1984), pp. 3–9.

Naugle, David G., and Garret A. Davies. "Strategic-Skill Pools and Competitive Advantage," *Business Horizons* 30, no. 6 (November–December 1987), pp. 35–42.

Porter, Michael E. *Competitive Advantage*. New York: Free Press, 1985, chap. 9–11.

————— . "From Competitive Advantage to Corporate Strategy," *Harvard Business Review* 65, no. 3 (May–June, 1987), pp. 43–59.

Quinn, James B. *Strategies for Change: Logical Incrementalism*. Homewood, Ill.: Richard D. Irwin, 1980.

Robinson, S.J.Q.; R.E. Hitchens; and D.P. Wade. "The Directional Policy Matrix: Tool for Strategic Planning," *Long Range Planning* 11, no. 3 (June 1978), pp. 8–15.

Salter, Malcolm, and Wolf Weinhold. *Diversification through Acquisition*. New York: Macmillan, 1979.

Reading 4

FROM COMPETITIVE ADVANTAGE
TO CORPORATE STRATEGY*

Michael E. Porter

Corporate strategy, the overall plan for a diversified company, is both the darling and the stepchild of contemporary management practice—the darling because CEOs have been obsessed with diversification since the early 1960s, the stepchild because almost no consensus exists about what corporate strategy is, much less about how a company should formulate it.

A diversified company has two levels of strategy: business unit (or competitive) strategy and corporate (or companywide) strategy. Competitive strategy concerns how to create competitive advantage in each of the businesses in which a company competes. Corporate strategy concerns two different questions: what businesses the corporation should be in and how the corporate office should manage the array of business units.

Corporate strategy is what makes the corporate whole add up to more than the sum of its business unit parts.

The track record of corporate strategies has been dismal. I studied the diversification records of 33 large, prestigious U.S. companies over the 1950–1986 period and found that most of them had divested many more acquisitions than they had kept. The corporate strategies of most companies have dissipated instead of created shareholder value.

The need to rethink corporate strategy could hardly be more urgent. By taking over companies and breaking them up, corporate raiders thrive on failed corporate strategy. Fueled by junk bond financing and growing acceptability, raiders can expose any company to takeover, no matter how large or blue chip.

Recognizing past diversification mistakes, some companies have initiated large-scale restructuring programs. Others have done nothing at all. Whatever the response, the strategic questions persist. Those who have restructured must decide what to do next to avoid repeating the past; those who have done nothing must awake to their vulnerability. To survive, companies must understand what good corporate strategy is.

A Sober Picture

While there is disquiet about the success of corporate strategies, none of the available evidence satisfactorily indicates the success or failure of corporate strategy. Most studies have approached the question by measuring the stock market valuation of mergers, captured in the movement of the stock prices of acquiring companies immediately before and after mergers are announced.

These studies show that the market values mergers as neutral or slightly negative, hardly cause for serious concern.[1] Yet the short-term market reaction is a highly imperfect measure of the long-term success of diversification, and no self-respecting executive would judge a corporate strategy this way.

Studying the diversification programs of a company over a long period of time is a much more telling way to determine whether a corporate strategy has succeeded or failed. My study of 33 companies,

---

[1]The studies also show that sellers of companies capture a large fraction of the gains from merger. See Michael C. Jensen and Richard S. Ruback, "The Market for Corporate Control: The Scientific Evidence," *Journal of Financial Economics*, April 1983, p. 5, and Michael C. Jensen, "Takeovers: Folklore and Science," *Harvard Business Review*, November-December 1984, p. 109.

EXHIBIT 1 Diversification Profiles of 33 Leading U.S. Companies

Company	Number Total Entries	All Entries into New Industries	Percent Acquisitions	Percent Joint Ventures	Percent Start-Ups	Entries into New Industries That Represented Entirely New Fields	Percent Acquisitions	Percent Joint Ventures	Percent Start-Ups
ALCO Standard	221	165	99%	0%	1%	56	100%	0%	0%
Allied Corporation	77	49	67	10	22	17	65	6	29
Beatrice	382	204	97	1	2	61	97	0	3
Borden	170	96	77	4	19	32	75	3	22
CBS	148	81	67	16	17	28	65	21	14
Continental Group	75	47	77	6	17	19	79	11	11
Cummins Engine	30	24	54	17	29	13	46	23	31
Du Pont	80	39	33	16	51	19	37	0	63
Exxon	79	56	34	5	61	17	29	6	65
General Electric	160	108	47	20	33	29	48	14	38
General Foods	92	53	91	4	6	22	86	5	9
General Mills	110	102	84	7	9	27	74	7	19
W. R. Grace	275	202	83	7	10	66	74	5	21
Gulf & Western	178	140	91	4	6	48	88	2	10
IBM	46	38	18	18	63	16	19	0	81
IC Industries	67	41	85	3	12	17	88	6	6
ITT	246	178	89	2	9	50	92	0	8
Johnson & Johnson	88	77	77	0	23	18	56	0	44
Mobil	41	32	53	16	31	15	60	7	33
Procter & Gamble	28	23	61	0	39	14	79	0	21
Raytheon	70	58	86	9	5	16	81	19	6
RCA	53	46	35	15	50	19	37	21	42
Rockwell	101	75	73	24	3	27	74	22	4
Sara Lee	197	141	96	1	4	41	95	2	2
Scovill	52	36	97	0	3	12	92	0	8
Signal	53	45	67	4	29	20	75	0	25
Tenneco	85	62	81	6	13	26	73	8	19
3M	144	125	54	2	45	34	71	3	56
TRW	119	82	77	10	13	28	64	11	25
United Technologies	62	49	57	18	24	17	23	17	39
Westinghouse	129	73	63	11	26	36	61	3	36
Wickes	71	47	83	0	17	22	68	0	32
Xerox	59	50	66	6	28	18	50	11	39
Total	3,788	2,644				906			
Average	114.8	80.1	70.3%	7.9%	21.8%	27.4	67.9%	7.0%	25.9%

Note: Beatrice, Continental Group, General Foods, RCA, Scovill, and Signal were taken over as the study was being completed. Their data cover the period up through takeover but not subsequent divestments.

many of which have reputations for good management, is a unique look at the track record of major corporations. (For an explanation of the research, see the insert "Where the Data Come From.") Each company entered an average of 80 new industries and 27 new fields. Just over 70 percent of the new entries were acquisitions, 22 percent were start-ups, and 8 percent were joint ventures. IBM, Exxon, Du Pont, and 3M, for example, focused on start-ups, while ALCO Standard, Beatrice, and Sara Lee diversified almost solely through acquisitions *(Exhibit 1 has a complete rundown).*

My data paint a sobering picture of the success ratio of these moves *(see Exhibit 2).* I found that, on average, corporations divested more than half their acquisitions in new industries and more than 60 percent of their acquisitions in entirely new fields. Fourteen companies left more than 70 percent of all the acquisitions they had made in new fields. The track record in unrelated acquisitions is even worse—the average divestment rate is a startling 74 percent *(see Exhibit 3).* Even a highly respected company like General Electric divested a very high percentage of its acquisitions, particularly those in new fields. Companies near the top of the list in *Exhibit 2* achieved a remarkably low rate of divestment. Some bear witness to the success of well-thought-out corporate strategies. Others, however, enjoy a lower rate simply because they have not faced up to their problem units and divested them.

I calculated total shareholder returns (stock price appreciation plus dividends) over the period of the study for each company so that I could compare them with its divestment rate. While companies near the top of the list have above-average shareholder returns, returns are not a reliable measure of diversification success. Shareholder return often depends heavily on the inherent attractiveness of companies' base industries. Companies like CBS and General Mills had extremely profitable base businesses that subsidized poor diversification track records.

I would like to make one comment on the use of shareholder value to judge performance. Linking shareholder value quantitatively to diversification performance only works if you compare the shareholder value that is with the shareholder value that might have been without diversification. Because

such a comparison is virtually impossible to make, my own measure of diversification success—the number of units retained by the company—seems to be as good an indicator as any of the contribution of diversification to corporate performance.

My data give a stark indication of the failure of corporate strategies.[2] Of the 33 companies, 6 had been taken over as my study was being completed (see the note on *Exhibit 2*). Only the lawyers, investment bankers, and original sellers have prospered in most of these acquisitions, not the shareholders.

Premises of Corporate Strategy

Any successful corporate strategy builds on a number of premises. These are facts of life about diversification. They cannot be altered, and, when ignored, they explain in part why so many corporate strategies fail.

Competition occurs at the business unit level. Diversified companies do not compete; only their business units do. Unless a corporate strategy places primary attention on nurturing the success of each unit, the strategy will fail, no matter how elegantly constructed. Successful corporate strategy must grow out of and reinforce competitive strategy.

Diversification inevitably adds costs and constraints to business units. Obvious costs, such as the corporate overhead allocated to a unit, may not be as important or subtle as the hidden costs and constraints. A business unit must explain its decisions to top management, spend time complying with planning and other corporate systems, live with parent company guidelines and personnel policies, and forgo the opportunity to motivate employees with direct equity ownership. These costs and constraints can be reduced but not entirely eliminated.

Shareholders can readily diversify themselves. Shareholders can diversify their own port-

[2] Some recent evidence also supports the conclusion that acquired companies often suffer eroding performance after acquisition. See Frederick M. Scherer, "Mergers, Sell-Offs and Managerial Behavior," in *The Economics of Strategic Planning*, ed. Lacy Glenn Thomas (Lexington, Mass.: Lexington Books, 1986), p. 143, and David A. Ravenscraft and Frederick M. Scherer, "Mergers and Managerial Performance," paper presented at the Conference on Takeovers and Contests for Corporate Control, Columbia Law School, 1985.

EXHIBIT 2
Acquisition Track Records of Leading U.S. Diversifiers Ranked by Percent Divested

Company	All Acquisitions in New Industries	Percent Made by 1980 and Then Divested	Percent Made by 1975 and Then Divested	Acquisitions in New Industries That Represented Entirely New Fields	Percent Made by 1980 and Then Divested	Percent Made by 1975 and Then Divested
Johnson & Johnson	59	17%	12%	10	33%	14%
Procter & Gamble	14	17	17	11	17	17
Raytheon	50	17	26	13	25	33
United Technologies	28	25	13	10	17	0
3M	67	26	27	24	42	45
TRW	63	27	31	18	40	38
IBM	7	33	0*	3	33	0*
Du Pont	13	38	43	7	60	75
Mobil	17	38	57	9	50	50
Borden	74	39	40	24	45	50
IC Industries	35	42	50	15	46	44
Tenneco	50	43	47	19	27	33
Beatrice	198	46	45	59	52	51
ITT	159	52	52	46	61	61
Rockwell	55	56	57	20	71	71
Allied Corporation	33	57	45	11	40	80
Exxon	19	62	20*	5	80	50*
Sara Lee	135	62	65	39	80	76
General Foods	48	63	62	19	93	93
Scovill	35	64	77	11	64	70
Signal	30	65	63	15	70	67
ALCO Standard	164	65	70	56	72	76
W. R. Grace	167	65	70	49	71	70
General Electric	51	65	78	14	100	100
Wickes	38	67	72	15	73	70
Westinghouse	46	68	69	22	61	59
Xerox	33	71	79	9	100	100
Continental Group	36	71	72	15	60	60
General Mills	86	75	73	20	65	60
Gulf & Western	127	79	78	42	75	72
Cummins Engine	13	80	80	6	83	83
RCA	16	80	92	7	86	100
CBS	54	87	89	18	88	88
Total	2,021			661		
Average per company†	61.2	53.4%	56.5%	20.0	60.0%	61.5%

Note: Beatrice, Continental Group, General Foods, RCA, Scovill, and Signal were taken over as the study was being completed. Their data cover the period up through takeover but not subsequent divestments.

*Companies with three or fewer acquisitions by the cutoff year.

†Companies with three or fewer acquisitions by the cutoff year are excluded from the average to minimize statistical distortions.

Where the Data Come From

We studied the 1950-1986 diversification histories of 33 large diversified U.S. companies. They were chosen at random from many broad sectors of the economy.

To eliminate distortions caused by World War II, we chose 1950 as the base year and then identified each business the company was in. We tracked every acquisition, joint venture, and start-up made over this period—3,788 in all. We classified each as an entry into an entirely new sector or field (financial services, for example), a new industry within a field the company was already in (insurance, for example), or a geographic extension of an existing product or service. We also classified each new field as related or unrelated to existing units. Then we tracked whether and when each entry was divested or shut down and the number of years each remained part of the corporation.

Our sources included annual reports, 10K forms, the F&S Index, and Moody's, supplemented by our judgment and general knowledge of the industries involved. In a few cases, we asked the companies specific questions.

It is difficult to determine the success of an entry without knowing the full purchase or start-up price, the profit history, the amount and timing of ongoing investments made in the unit, whether any write-offs or write-downs were taken, and the selling price and terms of sale. Instead, we employed a relatively simple way to gauge success: *whether the entry was divested or shut down*. The underlying assumption is that a company will generally not divest or close down a successful business except in a compara-

tively few special cases. Companies divested many of the entries in our sample within five years, a reflection of disappointment with performance. Of the comparatively few divestments where the company disclosed a loss or a gain, the divestment resulted in a reported loss in more than half the cases.

The data in Exhibit 1 cover the entire 1950–1986 period. However, the divestment ratios in *Exhibit 2* and *Exhibit 3* do not compare entries and divestments over the entire period because doing so would overstate the success of diversification. Companies usually do not shut down or divest new entries immediately but hold them for some time to give them an opportunity to succeed. Our data show that the average holding period is 5 to slightly more than 10 years, though many divestments occur within 5 years. To accurately gauge the success of diversification, we calculated the percentage of entries made by 1975 and by 1980 that were divested or closed down as of January 1987. If we had included more recent entries, we would have biased upward our assessment of how successful these entries had been.

As compiled, these data probably understate the rate of failure. Companies tend to announce acquisitions and other forms of new entry with a flourish but divestments and shutdowns with a whimper, if at all. We have done our best to root out every such transaction, but we have undoubtedly missed some. There may also be new entries that we did not uncover, but our best impression is that the number is not large.

folios of stocks by selecting those that best match their preferences and risk profiles.[3] Shareholders can often diversify more cheaply than a corporation because they can buy shares at the market price and avoid hefty acquisition premiums.

These premises mean that corporate strategy can-

not succeed unless it truly adds value—to business units by providing tangible benefits that off-set the inherent costs of lost independence and to shareholders by diversifying in a way they could not replicate.

Passing the Essential Tests

To understand how to formulate corporate strategy, it is necessary to specify the conditions under which diversification will truly create shareholder

---

[3]This observation has been made by a number of authors. See, for example, Malcolm S. Salter and Wolf A. Weinhold, *Diversification Through Acquisition* (New York: Free Press, 1979).

EXHIBIT 3
Diversification Performance in Joint Ventures, Start-Ups, and Unrelated Acquisitions

Company	Joint Ventures as a Percent of New Entries	Percent Made by 1980 and Then Divested	Percent Made by 1975 and Then Divested	Start-Ups as a Percent of New Entries	Percent Made by 1980 and Then Divested	Percent Made by 1975 and Then Divested	Unrelated Acquisitions as a Percent of Total Acquisitions	Percent Made by 1980 and Then Divested	Percent Made by 1975 and Then Divested
Johnson & Johnson	0%	†	†	23%	14%	20%	0%	†	†
Procter & Gamble	0	†	†	39	0	0	9	†	†
Raytheon	9	60%	60%	5	50	50	46	40%	40%
United Technologies	18	50	50	24	11	20	40	0%	0*
3M	2	100*	100*	45	2	3	33	75	86
TRW	10	20	25	13	63	71	39	71	71
IBM	18	100*	†	63	20	22	33	100*	100*
Du Pont	16	100*	†	51	61	61	43	0*	0*
Mobil	16	33	33	31	50	56	67	60	100
Borden	4	33	33	19	17	13	21	80	80
IC Industries	3	100*	100*	13	80	30	33	50	50
Tenneco	6	67	67	13	67	80	42	33	40
Beatrice	1	†	†	2	0	0	63	59	53
ITT	2	0*	†	8	38	57	61	67	64
Rockwell	24	38	42	3	0	0	35	100	100
Allied Corporation	10	100	75	22	38	29	45	50	0
Exxon	5	0	0	61	27	19	100	80	50*
Sara Lee	1	†	†	4	75	100*	41	73	73

Company									
General Goods	4	†	†	6	67	50	42	86	83
Scovill	0	†	†	3	100	100*	45	80	100
Signal	4	†	†	29	20	11	67	50	50
ALCO Standard	0	†	†	1	†	†	63	79	81
W. R. Grace	7	33	38	10	71	71	39	65	65
General Electric	20	20	33	33	33	44	36	100	100
Wickes	0	†	†	17	63	57	60	80	75
Westinghouse	11	0*	0*	26	44	44	36	57	67
Xerox	6	100*	100*	28	50	56	22	100	100
Continental Group	6	67	67	17	14	0	40	83	100
General Mills	7	71	71	9	89	80	65	77	67
Gulf & Western	4	75	50	6	100	100	74	77	74
Cummins Engine	17	50	50	29	0	0	67	100	100
RCA	15	67	67	50	99	55	36	100	100
CBS	16	71	71	17	86	80	39	100	100
Average per company‡	7.9%	50.3%	48.9%	21.8%	44.0%	40.9%	46.1%	74.0%	74.4%

Note: Beatrice, Continental Group, General Foods, RCA, Scovill, and Signal were taken over as the study was being completed. Their data cover the period up through takeover but not subsequent divestments.

*Companies with two or fewer entries.

†No entries in this category.

‡Average excludes companies with two or fewer entries to minimize statistical distortions.

value. These conditions can be summarized in three essential tests:

1. **The attractiveness test.** The industries chosen for diversification must be structurally attractive or capable of being made attractive.

2. **The cost-of-entry test.** The cost of entry must not capitalize all the future profits.

3. **The better-off test.** Either the new unit must gain competitive advantage from its link with the corporation or vice versa.

Of course, most companies will make certain that their proposed strategies pass some of these tests. But my study clearly shows that when companies ignored one or two of them, the strategic results were disastrous.

How Attractive Is the Industry?

In the long run, the rate of return available from competing in an industry is a function of its underlying structure, which I have described in another HBR article.[4] An attractive industry with a high average return on investment will be difficult to enter because entry barriers are high, suppliers and buyers have only modest bargaining power, substitute products or services are few, and the rivalry among competitors is stable. An unattractive industry like steel will have structural flaws, including a plethora of substitute materials, powerful and price-sensitive buyers, and excessive rivalry caused by high fixed costs and a large group of competitors, many of whom are state supported.

Diversification cannot create shareholder value unless new industries have favorable structures that support returns exceeding the cost of capital. If the industry doesn't have such returns, the company must be able to restructure the industry or gain a sustainable competitive advantage that leads to returns well above the industry average. An industry need not be attractive before diversification. In fact, a company might benefit from entering before the industry shows its full potential. The diversification can then transform the industry's structure.

[4]See Michael E. Porter, "How Competitive Forces Shape Strategy," *Harvard Business Review*, March-April 1979, p. 86.

In my research, I often found companies had suspended the attractiveness test because they had a vague belief that the industry "fit" very closely with their own businesses. In the hope that the corporate "comfort" they felt would lead to a happy outcome, the companies ignored fundamentally poor industry structures. Unless the close fit allows substantial competitive advantage, however, such comfort will turn into pain when diversification results in poor returns. Royal Dutch Shell and other leading oil companies have had this unhappy experience in a number of chemicals businesses, where poor industry structures overcame the benefits of vertical integration and skills in process technology.

Another common reason for ignoring the attractiveness test is a low entry cost. Sometimes the buyer has an inside track or the owner is anxious to sell. Even if the price is actually low, however, a one-shot gain will not offset a perpetually poor business. Almost always, the company finds it must reinvest in the newly acquired unit, if only to replace fixed assets and fund working capital. Diversifying companies are also prone to use rapid growth or other simple indicators as a proxy for a target industry's attractiveness. Many that rushed into fast-growing industries (personal computers, video games, and robotics, for example) were burned because they mistook early growth for long-term profit potential. Industries are profitable not because they are sexy or high tech; they are profitable only if their structures are attractive.

What Is the Cost of Entry?

Diversification cannot build shareholder value if the cost of entry into a new business eats up its expected returns. Strong market forces, however, are working to do just that. A company can enter new industries by acquisition or start-up. Acquisitions expose it to an increasingly efficient merger market. An acquirer beats the market if it pays a price not fully reflecting the prospects of the new unit. Yet multiple bidders are commonplace, information flows rapidly, and investment bankers and other intermediaries work aggressively to make the market as efficient as possible. In recent years, new financial instruments, such as junk bonds, have brought new buyers into the market and made even large companies vulnerable to takeover. Acquisition premiums are high and reflect the acquired company's future prospects—sometimes too well. Philip Morris paid more than four times book value for Seven-Up Company, for example. Simple arithmetic meant that profits had to more than quadruple to sustain the pre-acquisition ROI. Since there proved to be little Philip Morris could add in marketing prowess to the sophisticated marketing wars in the soft-drink industry, the result was the unsatisfactory financial performance of Seven-Up and ultimately the decision to divest.

In a start-up, the company must overcome entry barriers. It's a real catch-22 situation, however, since attractive industries are attractive because their entry barriers are high. Bearing the full cost of the entry barriers might well dissipate any potential profits. Otherwise, other entrants to the industry would have already eroded its profitability.

In the excitement of finding an appealing new business, companies sometimes forget to apply the cost-of-entry test. The more attractive a new industry, the more expensive it is to get into.

Will the Business Be Better Off?

A corporation must bring some significant competitive advantage to the new unit, or the new unit must offer potential for significant advantage to the corporation. Sometimes, the benefits to the new unit accrue only once, near the time of entry, when the parent instigates a major overhaul of its strategy or installs a first-rate management team. Other diversification yields ongoing competitive advantage if the new unit can market its product, through the well-developed distribution system of its sister units, for instance. This is one of the important underpinnings of the merger of Baxter Travenol and American Hospital Supply.

When the benefit to the new unit comes only once, the parent company has no rationale for holding the new unit in its portfolio over the long term. Once the results of the one-time improvement are clear, the diversified company no longer adds value to offset the inevitable costs imposed on the unit. It is best to sell the unit and free up corporate resources.

The better-off test does not imply that diversifying corporate risk creates shareholder value in and of itself. Doing something for shareholders that they can do themselves is not a basis for corporate strategy. (Only in the case of a privately held company, in which the company's and the shareholder's risk are the same, is diversification to reduce risk valuable for its own sake.) Diversification of risk should only be a by-product of corporate strategy, not a prime motivator.

Executives ignore the better-off test most of all or deal with it through arm waving or trumped-up logic rather than hard strategic analysis. One reason is that they confuse company size with shareholder value. In the drive to run a bigger company, they lose sight of their real job. They may justify the suspension of the better-off test by pointing to the way they manage diversity. By cutting corporate staff to the bone and giving business units nearly complete autonomy, they believe they avoid the pitfalls. Such thinking misses the whole point of diversification, which is to create shareholder value, rather than to avoid destroying it.

Concepts of Corporate Strategy

The three tests for successful diversification set the standards that any corporate strategy must meet; meeting them is so difficult that most diversification fails. Many companies lack a clear concept of corporate strategy to guide their diversification or pursue a concept that does not address the tests. Others fail because they implement a strategy poorly.

My study has helped me identify four concepts of corporate strategy that have been put into practice—portfolio management, restructuring, transferring skills, and sharing activities. While the concepts are not always mutually exclusive, each rests on a different mechanism by which the corporation creates shareholder value and each requires the diversified company to manage and organize itself in a different way. The first two require no connections among business units; the second two depend on them. (See Exhibit 4.) While all four concepts of strategy have succeeded under the right circumstances, today some make more sense than others. Ignoring

EXHIBIT 4
Concepts of Corporate Strategy

	Portfolio Management	Restructuring	Transferring Skills	Sharing Activities
Strategic prerequisites	• Superior insight into identifying and acquiring undervalued companies • Willingness to sell off losers quickly or to opportunistically divest good performers when buyers are willing to pay large premiums • Broad guidelines for and constraints on the types of units in the portfolio so that senior management can play the review role effectively • A private company or undeveloped capital markets • Ability to shift away from portfolio management as the capital markets get more efficient or the company gets unwieldy	• Superior insight into identifying restructuring opportunities • Willingness and capability to intervene to transform acquired units • Broad similarities among the units in the portfolio • Willingness to cut losses by selling off units where restructuring proves unfeasible • Willingness to sell units when restructuring is complete, the results are clear, and market conditions are favorable	• Proprietary skills in activities important to competitive advantage in target industries • Ability to accomplish the transfer of skills among units on an ongoing basis • Acquisitions of beachhead positions in new industries as a base	• Activities in existing units that can be shared with new business units to gain competitive advantage • Benefits of sharing that outweigh the costs • Both start-ups and acquisitions as entry vehicles • Ability to overcome organizational resistance to business unit collaboration

Organization prerequisites	• Autonomous business units • A very small, low-cost, corporate staff • Incentives based largely on business unit results	• Autonomous business units • A corporate organization with the talent and resources to oversee the turn-arounds and strategic repositionings of acquired units • Incentives based largely on acquired units' results	• Largely autonomous but collaborative business units • High-level corporate staff members who see their role primarily as integrators • Cross-business-unit committees, task forces, and other forums to serve as focal points for capturing and transferring skills • Objectives of line managers that include skills transfer • Incentives based in part on corporate results	• Strategic business units that are encouraged to share activities • An active strategic planning role at group, sector, and corporate levels • High-level corporate staff members who see their roles primarily as integrators • Incentives based heavily on group and corporate results
Common pitfalls	• Pursuing portfolio management in countries with efficient capital marketing and a developed pool of professional management talent • Ignoring the fact that industry structure is not attractive	• Mistaking rapid growth or a "hot" industry as sufficient evidence of a restructuring opportunity • Lacking the resolve or resources to take on troubled situations and to intervene in management • Ignoring the fact that industry structure is not attractive • Paying lip service to restructuring but actually practicing passive portfolio management	• Mistaking similarity or comfort with new businesses as sufficient basis for diversification • Providing no practical ways for skills transfer to occur • Ignoring the fact that industry structure is not attractive	• Sharing for its own sake, rather than because it leads to competitive advantage • Assuming sharing will occur naturally without senior management playing an active role • Ignoring the fact that industry structure is not attractive

any of the concepts is perhaps the quickest road to failure.

Portfolio Management

The concept of corporate strategy most in use is portfolio management, which is based primarily on diversification through acquisition. The corporation acquires sound, attractive companies with content managers who agree to stay on. While acquired units do not have to be in the same industries as existing units, the best portfolio managers generally limit their range of businesses in some way, in part to limit the specific expertise needed by top management.

The acquired units are autonomous, and the teams that run them are compensated according to unit results. The corporation supplies capital and works with each to infuse it with professional management techniques. At the same time, top management provides objective and dispassionate review of business unit results. Portfolio managers categorize units by potential and regularly transfer resources from units that generate cash to those with high potential and cash needs.

In a portfolio strategy, the corporation seeks to create shareholder value in a number of ways. It uses its expertise and analytical resources to spot attractive acquisition candidates that the individual shareholder could not. The company provides capital on favorable terms that reflect corporatewide fundraising ability. It introduces professional management skills and discipline. Finally, it provides high-quality review and coaching, unencumbered by conventional wisdom or emotional attachments to the business.

The logic of the portfolio management concept rests on a number of vital assumptions. If a company's diversification plan is to meet the attractiveness and cost-of-entry tests, it must find good but undervalued companies. Acquired companies must be truly undervalued because the parent does little for the new unit once it is acquired. To meet the better-off test, the benefits the corporation provides must yield a significant competitive advantage to acquired units. The style of operating through highly antonomous business units must both develop sound business strategies and motivate managers.

In most countries, the days when portfolio management was a valid concept of corporate strategy are past. In the face of increasingly well-developed capital markets, attractive companies with good managements show up on everyone's computer screen and attract top dollar in terms of acquisition premium. Simply contributing capital isn't contributing much. A sound strategy can easily be funded; small to medium-size companies don't need a munificent parent.

Other benefits have also eroded. Large companies no longer corner the market for professional management skills; in fact, more and more observers believe managers cannot necessarily run anything in the absence of industry-specific knowledge and experience. Another supposed advantage of the portfolio management concept—dispassionate review—rests on similarly shaky ground since the added value of review alone is questionable in a portfolio of sound companies.

The benefit of giving business units complete autonomy is also questionable. Increasingly, a company's business units are interrelated, drawn together by new technology, broadening distribution channels, and changing regulations. Setting strategies of units independently may well undermine unit performance. The companies in my sample that have succeeded in diversification have recognized the value of interrelationships and understood that a strong sense of corporate identity is as important as slavish adherence to parochial business unit financial results.

But it is the sheer complexity of the management task that has ultimately defeated even the best portfolio managers. As the size of the company grows, portfolio managers need to find more and more deals just to maintain growth. Supervising dozens or even hundreds of disparate units and under chain-letter pressures to add more, management begins to make mistakes. At the same time, the inevitable costs of being part of a diversified company take their toll and unit performance slides while the whole company's ROI turns downward. Eventually, a new management team is installed that initiates wholesale divestments and pares down the company to its core businesses. The experiences of Gulf & Western, Consolidated Foods (now Sara Lee), and ITT are just a few comparatively recent examples. Reflecting these realities, the U.S. capital markets today reward companies that follow the portfolio management model with a "conglomerate discount"; they value the whole less than the sum of the parts.

In developing countries, where large companies are few, capital markets are undeveloped, and professional management is scarce, portfolio management still works. But it is no longer a valid model for corporate strategy in advanced economies. Nevertheless, the technique is in the limelight today in the United Kingdom, where it is supported so far by a newly energized stock market eager for excitement. But this enthusiasm will wane—as well it should. Portfolio management is no way to conduct corporate strategy.

Restructuring

Unlike its passive role as a portfolio manager, when it serves as banker and reviewer, a company that bases its strategy on restructuring becomes an active restructurer of business units. The new businesses are not necessarily related to existing units. All that is necessary is unrealized potential.

The restructuring strategy seeks out undeveloped, sick, or threatened organizations or industries on the threshold of significant change. The parent intervenes, frequently changing the unit management team, shifting strategy, or infusing the company with new technology. Then it may make follow-up acquisitions to build a critical mass and sell off unneeded or unconnected parts and thereby reduce the effective acquisition cost. The result is a strengthened company or a transformed industry. As a coda, the parent sells off the stronger unit once results are clear because the parent is no longer adding value and top management decides that its attention should be directed elsewhere.

When well implemented, the restructuring concept is sound, for it passes the three tests of successful diversification. The restructurer meets the cost-of-entry test through the types of company it acquires. It limits acquisition premiums by buying companies with problems and lackluster images or by buying into industries with as yet unforeseen potential. Intervention by the corporation clearly meets the better-off test. Provided that the target industries are structurally attractive, the restructuring model can create enormous shareholder value. Some restructuring companies are Loew's, BTR, and General Cinema. Ironically, many of today's restructurers are profiting from yesterday's portfolio management strategies.

To work, the restructuring strategy requires a corporate management team with the insight to spot undervalued companies or positions in industries ripe for transformation. The same insight is necessary to actually turn the units around even though they are in new and unfamiliar businesses.

These requirements expose the restructurer to considerable risk and usually limit the time in which the company can succeed at the strategy. The most skillful proponents understand this problem, recognize their mistakes, and move decisively to dispose of them. The best companies realize they are not just acquiring companies but restructuring an industry. Unless they can integrate the acquisitions to create a whole new strategic position, they are just portfolio managers in disguise. Another important difficulty surfaces if so many other companies join the action that they deplete the pool of suitable candidates and bid their prices up.

Perhaps the greatest pitfall, however, is that companies find it very hard to dispose of business units once they are restructured and performing well. Human nature fights economic rationale. Size supplants shareholder value as the corporate goal. The company does not sell a unit even though the company no longer adds value to the unit. While the transformed units would be better off in another company that had related businesses, the restructuring company instead retains them. Gradually, it becomes a portfolio manager. The parent company's ROI declines as the need for reinvestment in the units and normal business risks eventually offset restructuring's one-shot gain. The perceived need to keep growing intensifies the pace of acquisition; errors result and standards fall. The restructuring company turns into a conglomerate with returns that only equal the average of all industries at best.

Transferring Skills

The purpose of the first two concepts of corporate strategy is to create value through a company's relationship with each autonomous unit. The corporation's role is to be a selector, a banker, and an intervenor.

The last two concepts exploit the inter-relationships between businesses. In articulating them, however, one comes face to face with the often ill-defined concept of synergy. If you believe the text of the countless corporate annual reports, just about anything is related to just about anything else! But imagined synergy is much more common than real synergy. GM's purchase of Hughes Aircraft simply because cars were going electronic and Hughes was an electronics concern demonstrates the folly of paper synergy. Such corporate relatedness is an ex post facto rationalization of a diversification undertaken for other reasons.

Even synergy that is clearly defined often fails to materialize. Instead of cooperating, business units often compete. A company that can define the synergies it is pursuing still faces significant organizational impediments in achieving them.

But the need to capture the benefits of relationships between businesses has never been more important. Technological and competitive developments already link many businesses and are creating new possibilities for competitive advantage. In such sectors as financial services, computing, office equipment, entertainment, and health care, interrelationships among previously distinct businesses are perhaps the central concern of strategy.

To understand the role of relatedness in corporate strategy, we must give new meaning to this often ill-defined idea. I have identified a good way to start—the value chain.[5] Every business unit is a collection of discrete activities ranging from sales to accounting that allow it to compete. I call them value activities. It is at this level, not in the company as a whole, that the unit achieves competitive advantage.

I group these activities in nine categories. *Primary* activities create the product or service, deliver and market it, and provide after-sale support. The categories of primary activities are inbound logistics, operations, outbound logistics, marketing and sales,

and service. *Support* activities provide the input and infrastructure that allow the primary activities to take place. The categories are company infrastructure, human resource management, technology development, and procurement.

The value chain defines the two types of inter-relationships that may create synergy. The first is a company's ability to transfer skills or expertise among similar value chains. The second is the ability to share activities. Two business units, for example, can share the same sales force or logistics network.

The value chain helps expose the last two (and most important) concepts of corporate strategy. The transfer of skills among business units in the diversified company is the basis for one concept. While each business unit has a separate value chain, knowledge about how to perform activities is transferred among the units. For example, a toiletries business unit, expert in the marketing of convenience products, transmits ideas on new positioning concepts, promotional techniques, and packaging possibilities to a newly acquired unit that sells cough syrup. Newly entered industries can benefit from the expertise of existing units and vice versa.

These opportunities arise when business units have similar buyers or channels, similar value activities like government relations or procurement, similarities in the broad configuration of the value chain (for example, managing a multisite service organization), or the same strategic concept (for example, low cost). Even though the units operate separately, such similarities allow the sharing of knowledge.

Of course, some similarities are common; one can imagine them at some level between almost any pair of businesses. Countless companies have fallen into the trap of diversifying too readily because of similarities; mere similarity is not enough.

Transferring skills leads to competitive advantage only if the similarities among businesses meet three conditions:

1. The activities involved in the businesses are similar enough that sharing expertise is meaningful. Broad similarities (marketing intensiveness, for example, or a common core process technology, such as bending metal) are not a sufficient basis for di-

---

[5]Michael E. Porter, *Competitive Advantage* (New York: Free Press, 1985).

versification. The resulting ability to transfer skills is likely to have little impact on competitive advantage.

2. The transfer of skills involves activities important to competitive advantage. Transferring skills in peripheral activities such as government relations or real estate in consumer goods units may be beneficial but is not a basis for diversification.

3. The skills transferred represent a significant source of competitive advantage for the receiving unit. The expertise or skills to be transferred are both advanced and proprietary enough to be beyond the capabilities of competitors.

The transfer of skills is an active process that significantly changes the strategy or operations of the receiving unit. The prospect for change must be specific and identifiable. Almost guaranteeing that no shareholder value will be created, too many companies are satisfied with vague prospects or faint hopes that skills will transfer. The transfer of skills does not happen by accident or by osmosis. The company will have to reassign critical personnel, even on a permanent basis, and the participation and support of high-level management in skills transfer is essential. Many companies have been defeated at skills transfer because they have not provided their business units with any incentives to participate.

Transferring skills meets the tests of diversification if the company truly mobilizes proprietary expertise across units. This makes certain the company can offset the acquisition premium or lower the cost of overcoming entry barriers.

The industries the company chooses for diversification must pass the attractiveness test. Even a close fit that reflects opportunities to transfer skills may not overcome poor industry structure. Opportunities to transfer skills, however, may help the company transform the structures of newly entered industries and send them in favorable directions.

The transfer of skills can be one-time or ongoing. If the company exhausts opportunities to infuse new expertise into a unit after the initial post-acquisition period, the unit should ultimately be sold. The corporation is no longer creating shareholder value. Few companies have grasped this point, however, and many gradually suffer mediocre returns. Yet a company diversified into well-chosen businesses can transfer skills eventually in many directions. If corporate management conceives of its role in this way and creates appropriate organizational mechanisms to facilitate cross-unit interchange, the opportunities to share expertise will be meaningful.

By using both acquisitions and internal development, companies can build a transfer-of-skills strategy. The presence of a strong base of skills sometimes creates the possibility for internal entry instead of the acquisition of a going concern. Successful diversifiers that employ the concept of skills transfer may, however, often acquire a company in the target industry as a beachhead and then build on it with their internal expertise. By doing so, they can reduce some of the risks of internal entry and speed up the process. Two companies that have diversified using the transfer-of-skills concept are 3M and PepsiCo.

Sharing Activities

The fourth concept of corporate strategy is based on sharing activities in the value chains among business units. Procter & Gamble, for example, employs a common physical distribution system and sales force in both paper towels and disposable diapers. McKesson, a leading distribution company, will handle such diverse lines as pharmaceuticals and liquor through superwarehouses.

The ability to share activities is a potent basis for corporate strategy because sharing often enhances competitive advantage by lowering cost or raising differentiation. But not all sharing leads to competitive advantage, and companies can encounter deep organizational resistance to even beneficial sharing possibilities. These hard truths have led many companies to reject synergy prematurely and retreat to the false simplicity of portfolio management.

A cost-benefit analysis of prospective sharing opportunities can determine whether synergy is possible. Sharing can lower costs if it achieves economies of scale, boosts the efficiency of utilization, or helps a company move more rapidly down the learning curve. The costs of General Electric's advertising, sales, and after-sales service activities in major appliances are low because they are spread over a wide range of appliance products. Sharing can also enhance the potential for differentiation. A shared order-processing system, for instance, may allow new features and services that a buyer will value. Sharing can also reduce the cost of differentiation. A shared service network, for example, may make more advanced, remote servicing technology economically feasible. Often, sharing will allow an activity to be wholly reconfigured in ways that can dramatically raise competitive advantage.

Sharing must involve activities that are significant to competitive advantage, not just any activity. P&G's distribution system is such an instance in the diaper and paper towel business, where products are bulky and costly to ship. Conversely, diversification based on the opportunities to share only corporate overhead is rarely, if ever, appropriate.

Sharing activities inevitably involves costs that the benefits must outweigh. One cost is the greater coordination required to manage a shared activity. More important is the need to compromise the design or performance of an activity so that it can be shared. A salesperson handling the products of two business units, for example, must operate in a way that is usually not what either unit would choose were it independent. And if compromise greatly erodes the unit's effectiveness, then sharing may reduce rather than enhance competitive advantage.

Many companies have only superficially identified their potential for sharing. Companies also merge activities without consideration of whether they are sensitive to economies of scale. When they are not, the coordination costs kill the benefits. Companies compound such errors by not identifying costs of sharing in advance, when steps can be taken to minimize them. Costs of compromise can frequently be mitigated by redesigning the activity for sharing. The shared salesperson, for example, can be provided with a remote computer terminal to boost productivity and provide more customer information. Jamming business units together without such thinking exacerbates the costs of sharing.

Despite such pitfalls, opportunities to gain advantage from sharing activities have proliferated because of momentous developments in technology, deregulation, and competition. The infusion of electronics and information systems into many industries creates new opportunities to link businesses. The corporate strategy of sharing can involve both ac-

quisition and internal development. Internal development is often possible because the corporation can bring to bear clear resources in launching a new unit. Start-ups are less difficult to integrate than acquisitions. Companies using the shared-activities concept can also make acquisitions as beachhead landings into a new industry and then integrate the units through sharing with other units. Prime examples of companies that have diversified via using shared activities include P&G, Du Pont, and IBM. The fields into which each has diversified are a cluster of tightly related units. Marriott illustrates both successes and failures in sharing activities over time.

Following the shared-activities model requires an organizational context in which business unit collaboration is encouraged and reinforced. Highly autonomous business units are inimical to such collaboration. The company must put into place a variety of what I call horizontal mechanisms—a strong sense of corporate identity, a clear corporate mission statement that emphasizes the importance of integrating business unit strategies, an incentive system that rewards more than just business unit results, cross-business-unit task forces, and other methods of integrating.

A corporate strategy based on shared activities clearly meets the better-off test because business units gain ongoing tangible advantages from others within the corporation. It also meets the cost-of-entry test by reducing the expense of surmounting the barriers to internal entry. Other bids for acquisitions that do not share opportunities will have lower reservation prices. Even widespread opportunities for sharing activities do not allow a company to suspend the attractiveness test, however. Many diversifiers have made the critical mistake of equating the close fit of a target industry with attractive diversification. Target industries must pass the strict requirement test of having an attractive structure as well as a close fit in opportunities if diversification is to ultimately succeed.

Choosing a Corporate Strategy

Each concept of corporate strategy allows the diversified company to create shareholder value in a different way. Companies can succeed with any of the concepts if they clearly define the corporation's role and objectives, have the skills necessary for meeting the concept's prerequisites, organize themselves to manage diversity in a way that fits the strategy, and find themselves in an appropriate capital market environment. The caveat is that portfolio management is only sensible in limited circumstances.

A company's choice of corporate strategy is partly a legacy of its past. If its business units are in unattractive industries, the company must start from scratch. If the company has few truly proprietary skills or activities it can share in related diversification, then its initial diversification must rely on other concepts. Yet corporate strategy should not be a once-and-for-all choice but a vision that can evolve. A company should choose its long-term preferred concept and then proceed pragmatically toward it from its initial starting point.

Both the strategic logic and the experience of the companies I studied over the last decade suggest that a company will create shareholder value through diversification to a greater and greater extent as its strategy moves from portfolio management toward sharing activities. Because they do not rely on superior insight or other questionable assumptions about the company's capabilities, sharing activities and transferring skills offer the best avenues for value creation.

Each concept of corporate strategy is not mutually exclusive of those that come before, a potent advantage of the third and fourth concepts. A company can employ a restructuring strategy at the same time it transfers skills or shares activities. A strategy based on shared activities becomes more powerful if business units can also exchange skills. As the Marriott case illustrates, a company can often pursue the two strategies together and even incorporate some of the principles of restructuring with them. When it chooses industries in which to transfer skills or share activities, the company can also investigate the possibility of transforming the industry structure. When a company bases its strategy on interrelationships, it has a broader basis on which to create shareholder value than if it rests its entire strategy on transforming companies in unfamiliar industries.

My study supports the soundness of basing a cor-

porate strategy on the transfer of skills or shared activities. The data on the sample companies' diversification programs illustrate some important characteristics of successful diversifiers. They have made a disproportionately low percentage of unrelated acquisitions, *unrelated* being defined as having no clear opportunity to transfer skills or share important activities (see Exhibit 3). Even successful diversifiers such as 3M, IBM, and TRW have terrible records when they have strayed into unrelated acquisitions. Successful acquirers diversify into fields, each of which is related to many others. Procter & Gamble and IBM, for example, operate in 18 and 19 interrelated fields respectively and so enjoy numerous opportunities to transfer skills and share activities.

Companies with the best acquisition records tend to make heavier-than-average use of start-ups and joint ventures. Most companies shy away from modes of entry besides acquisition. My results cast doubt on the conventional wisdom regarding start-ups. *Exhibit 3* demonstrates that, while joint ventures are about as risky as acquisitions, start-ups are not. Moreover, successful companies often have very good records with start-up units, as 3M, P&G, Johnson & Johnson, IBM, and United Technologies illustrate. When a company has the internal strength to start up a unit, it can be safer and less costly to launch a company than to rely solely on an acquisition and then have to deal with the problem of integration. Japanese diversification histories support the soundness of start-up as an entry alternative.

My data also illustrate that none of the concepts of corporate strategy works when industry structure is poor or implementation is bad, no matter how related the industries are. Xerox acquired companies in related industries, but the businesses had poor structures and its skills were insufficient to provide enough competitive advantage to offset implementation problems.

An Action Program

To translate the principles of corporate strategy into successful diversification, a company must first take an objective look at its existing businesses and the value added by the corporation. Only through such an assessment can an understanding of good corporate strategy grow. That understanding should guide future diversification as well as the development of skills and activities with which to select further new businesses. The following action program provides a concrete approach to conducting such a review. A company can choose a corporate strategy by:

1. Identifying the interrelationships among already existing business units.

A company should begin to develop a corporate strategy by identifying all the opportunities it has to share activities or transfer skills in its existing portfolio of business units. The company will not only find ways to enhance the competitive advantage of existing units but also come upon several possible diversification avenues. The lack of meaningful interrelationships in the portfolio is an equally important finding, suggesting the need to justify the value added by the corporation or, alternately, a fundamental restructuring.

2. Selecting the core businesses that will be the foundation of the corporate strategy.

Successful diversification starts with an understanding of the core businesses that will serve as the basis for corporate strategy. Core businesses are those that are in an attractive industry, have the potential to achieve sustainable competitive advantage, have important interrelationships with other business units, and provide skills or activities that represent a base from which to diversify.

The company must first make certain its core businesses are on sound footing by upgrading management, internationalizing strategy, or improving technology. My study shows that geographic extensions of existing units, whether by acquisition, joint venture, or start-up, had a substantially lower divestment rate than diversification.

The company must then patiently dispose of the units that are not core businesses. Selling them will free resources that could be better deployed elsewhere. In some cases disposal implies immediate liquidation, while in others the company should dress up the units and wait for a propitious market or a particularly eager buyer.

3. Creating horizontal organizational mechanisms to facilitate interrelationships among the core businesses and lay the groundwork for future related diversification.

Top management can facilitate interrelationships by emphasizing cross-unit collaboration, grouping units organizationally and modifying incentives, and taking steps to build a strong sense of corporate identity.

4. Pursuing diversification opportunities that allow shared activities.

This concept of corporate strategy is the most compelling, provided a company's strategy passes all three tests. A company should inventory activities in existing business units that represent the strongest foundation for sharing, such as strong distribution channels or world-class technical facilities. These will in turn lead to potential new business areas. A company can use acquisitions as a beachhead or employ start-ups to exploit internal capabilities and minimize integrating problems.

5. Pursuing diversification through the transfer of skills if opportunities for sharing activities are limited or exhausted.

Companies can pursue this strategy through acquisition, although they may be able to use start-ups if their existing units have important skills they can readily transfer.

Such diversification is often riskier because of the tough conditions necessary for it to work. Given the uncertainties, a company should avoid diversifying on the basis of skills transfer alone. Rather it should also be viewed as a stepping-stone to subsequent diversification using shared activities. New industries should be chosen that will lead naturally to other businesses. The goal is to build a cluster of related and mutually reinforcing business units. The strategy's logic implies that the company should not set the rate of return standards for the initial foray into a new sector too high.

6. Pursuing a strategy of restructuring if this fits the skills of management or no good opportunities exist for forging corporate interrelationships.

When a company uncovers undermanaged companies and can deploy adequate management talent and resources to the acquired units, then it can use a restructuring strategy. The more developed the capital markets and the more active the market for companies, the more restructuring will require a patient search for that special opportunity rather than a head-long race to acquire as many bad apples as possible. Restructuring can be a permanent strategy, as it is with Loew's, or a way to build a group of businesses that supports a shift to another corporate strategy.

7. Paying dividends so that the shareholders can be the portfolio managers.

Paying dividends is better than destroying share-holder value through diversification based on shaky underpinnings. Tax considerations, which some companies cite to avoid dividends, are hardly legit-imate reason to diversify if a company cannot dem-onstrate the capacity to do it profitably.

Creating a Corporate Theme

Defining a corporate theme is a good way to ensure that the corporation will create shareholder value. Having the right theme helps unite the efforts of business units and reinforces the ways they inter-relate as well as guides the choice of new businesses to enter. NEC Corporation, with its "C&C" theme, provides a good example. NEC integrates its com-puter, semiconductor, telecommunications, and con-sumer electronics businesses by merging computers and communication.

It is all too easy to create a shallow corporate theme. CBS wanted to be an "entertainment com-pany," for example, and built a group of businesses related to leisure time. It entered such industries as toys, crafts, musical instruments, sports teams, and hi-fi retailing. While this corporate theme sounded good, close listening revealed its hollow ring. None of these businesses had any significant opportunity to share activities or transfer skills among themselves or with CBS's traditional broadcasting and record businesses. They were all sold, often at significant losses, except for a few of CBS's publishing-related units. Saddled with the worst acquisition record in my study, CBS has eroded the shareholder value created through its strong performance in broad-casting and records.

Moving from competitive strategy to corporate strategy is the business equivalent of passing through the Bermuda Triangle. The failure of corporate strat-egy reflects the fact that most diversified companies have failed to think in terms of how they really add value. A corporate strategy that truly enhances the competitive advantage of each business unit is the best defense against the corporate raider. With a sharper focus on the tests of diversification and the explicit choice of a clear concept of corporate strat-egy, companies' diversification track records from now on can look a lot different.

Author's note: The research for this article was done with the able assistance of my research associate Cheng G. Ong. Malcolm S. Salter, Andrall E. Pearson, A. Michael Kechner, and the Monitor Company also provided helpful comments.

PART IV

Strategy Implementation: The Key Administrative Tasks

9

Implementing Strategy: Organization-Building, Budgets, and Work Assignments

Just being able to conceive bold new strategies is not enough. The general manager must also be able to translate his or her strategic vision into concrete steps that "get things done."

Richard G. Hamermesh

You've got to put your heart in the business and the business in your heart.

Thomas Watson

Once the course of strategy has been charted, the manager's priorities swing to converting the chosen strategic plan into actions and good results. Putting the strategy into effect and getting the organization moving in the direction of strategy accomplishment calls for a fundamentally different set of managerial tasks and skills. Whereas crafting strategy is largely an *entrepreneurial* activity, implementing strategy is primarily an internal *administrative* activity. Whereas strategy formulation entails heavy doses of vision, analysis, and entrepreneurial judgment, successful strategy implementation depends upon the skills of working through others, organizing, motivating, culture-building, and creating strong fits between strategy and how the organization does things. Ingrained behavior does not change just because a new strategy has been announced.

In comparison, implementing strategy poses the tougher, more time-consuming management challenge. Practitioners are emphatic in saying that it is a whole lot easier to develop a sound strategic plan than it is to "make it happen." To see why, let's look at what strategy implementation involves.

A GENERAL FRAMEWORK FOR STRATEGY IMPLEMENTATION

What makes the job of the strategy-implementer so complicated is the multiplicity of tasks combined with the variety of ways to approach each task. Strategy implementation has to be custom-tailored to the organization's overall condition and setting, to the nature of the strategy and the amount of strategic change involved (shifting to a bold new strategy poses different implementation problems than fine tuning a strategy already in place), and to the manager's own skills, style, and ways of getting things done. Figure 9–1 illustrates the six principal administrative tasks that shape a manager's action agenda for implementing strategy.

In general, every unit of an organization, from headquarters down to each operating department, has to ask, "What is required for us to implement our part of the overall strategic plan and how can we best get it done?" A thorough answer to this question entails scrutinizing the whole internal organization to diagnose what strategy-supportive changes are needed and how to accomplish them.

The specific components of each of the six strategy-implementation tasks are highlighted in Figure 9–2. The strategy-implementer's job is to bring the organization's conduct of its internal operations into good alignment with strategy and to unite the total organization behind strategy accomplishment. The challenge is one of building such determined enthusiasm and commitment up and down the ranks that a virtual organizationwide crusade emerges to carry out the chosen

FIGURE 9–1
Implementing Strategy: The Key Tasks

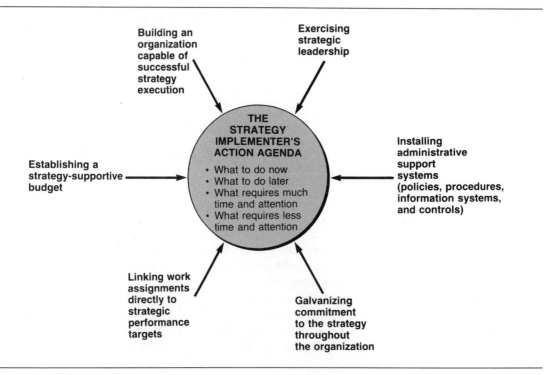

strategy. The stronger the strategy-supportive "fits" that are created, the greater the chances of successful strategy implementation. Strategy-supportive matchups are needed with organizational skills and capabilities, with organization structure, with reward systems and incentives, with policies and procedures, with information systems and operating controls, with budgets and resource allocation, and with the workplace culture. Making these fits strong prevents internal activities from being at cross-purposes with strategy and brings the organization's work effort into closer harmony with the strategic plan.

The Manager's Role in Leading the Implementation Process

The chief executive officer and the heads of major organizational subunits are obviously the persons most responsible for leading and keynoting the tone, pace, and style of strategy implementation. There are many ways to proceed. A strategy-implementer can opt for an active, visible role or a low-key, behind-the-scenes role. He or she can elect to make decisions authoritatively or on the basis of consensus, to delegate much or little, to be personally involved in the details of implementation or to stand on the sidelines and coach others carrying the day-to-day burden. It is up to the strategy-implementer to decide whether to proceed swiftly (launching implementation initiatives on many fronts) or to move deliberately, content with gradual progress over a long time frame. Moreover, work on all six strategy-implementing tasks (Figure 9–1) has to be launched and supervised, and decisions made regarding which of the several strategy-supportive fits to work on first and what steps to take to create the fits.

How a manager goes about the implementation task is, in addition, a function of his or her experience and accumulated knowledge about the business: whether the manager is new to the job or a secure incumbent; the manager's network of personal relationships with others in the organization; the manager's own diagnostic, administrative, interpersonal, and problem-solving skills; the authority which the manager has been given; and the manager's own leadership preferences for how to proceed. The remaining determinant of the manager's approach to strategy implementation is the context of the organization's situation—the seriousness of the firm's strategic difficulties, the nature and extent of the strategic change involved, the type of strategy being implemented, the strength of the ingrained behavior patterns, the financial and organizational resources available to work with, the configuration of personal and organizational relationships that have permeated the firm's history, the pressures for short-term performance, and other such factors that make up the firm's "culture" and overall work climate.

Each company's internal situation is unique enough to require the strategy-implementer to custom-tailor his or her action agenda to fit the specific organizational environment at hand. This forces the manager to carefully consider all that strategy implementation involves and to diagnose carefully the action priorities and in what sequence things need to be done. The strategy-implementer's role is, thus, all important. His or her agenda for action and his or her conclusions about how hard and how fast to push for change are decisive in shaping the character of the implementation and moving the process along.

In the remainder of this chapter and in Chapter 10, we shall survey the ins and outs of the manager's role as chief strategy-implementer. For convenience, the discussion will be organized around the six administrative components of the strategy-implementation process and the recurring administrative issues associated with each—as displayed in Figure 9–2. This chapter will explore the management tasks of organization-building, budget allocations, and work assignments. Chapter 10 deals with galvanizing organizationwide commitment to the chosen strategy, installing administrative support systems to fit strategy, and exercising strategic leadership.

BUILDING A CAPABLE ORGANIZATION

Successful strategy execution depends greatly on good internal organization and competent personnel. Building a capable organization is, thus, always a top strategy-implementation priority. Three organizational issues stand out as dominant:

1. Developing an internal organization structure that is responsive to the needs of strategy.
2. Building and nurturing the skills and distinctive competences in which the strategy is grounded and to see, generally, that the organization has the managerial talents, technical know-how, and competitive capabilities it needs.
3. Selecting people for key positions.

Matching Organization Structure to Strategy

There are very few hard and fast rules for designing a strategy-supportive organization structure. Every firm's internal organization is partly idiosyncratic, the result of many organizational decisions and historical circumstances. Moreover, every strategy is grounded in its own set of key success factors and critical tasks. The only real ironclad imperative is to design the internal organization structure around the key success factors and critical tasks inherent in the firm's strategy. The following five-sequence procedure serves as a useful guideline for fitting structure to strategy:[1]

1. Pinpoint the key functions and tasks requisite for successful strategy execution.
2. Reflect on how the strategy-critical functions and organizational units relate to those that are routine and to those that provide staff support.
3. Make strategy-critical business units and functions the main organizational building blocks.
4. Determine the degrees of authority needed to manage each organizational unit, bearing in mind both the benefits and costs of decentralized decision making.
5. Provide for coordination among the various organizational units.

---

[1]LaRue T. Hosmer, *Strategic Management: Text and Cases on Business Policy* (Englewood Cliffs, N.J.: Prentice-Hall, 1982), chap. 10; and J. Thomas Cannon, *Business Strategy and Policy* (New York: Harcourt Brace Jovanovich, 1968), p. 316.

FIGURE 9–2
The Administrative Components of Strategy Implementation

BUILDING AN ORGANIZATION CAPABLE OF CARRYING OUT THE STRATEGIC PLAN		ESTABLISHING A STRATEGY SUPPORTIVE BUDGET		LINKING WORK ASSIGNMENTS DIRECTLY TO STRATEGIC PERFORMANCE TARGETS		GALVANIZING ORGANIZATION-WIDE COMMITMENT TO THE CHOSEN STRATEGIC PLAN		INSTALLING INTERNAL ADMINISTRATIVE SUPPORT SYSTEMS		EXERCISING STRATEGIC LEADERSHIP
Specific Tasks: 1. Developing a strategy-supportive organization structure. 2. Building and nurturing the skills and distinctive competence upon which strategy is grounded. 3. Selecting people for key positions.	+	**Specific Tasks:** 1. Seeing that each organizational unit has the budget to carry out its part of the strategic plan. 2. Ensuring that resources are used efficiently to get "the biggest bang for the buck."	+	**Specific Tasks:** 1. Defining work assignments in terms of what is to be accomplished, not just in terms of what duties are to be performed. 2. Insisting that "doing a good job" means "achieving the target objectives."	+	**Specific Tasks:** 1. Motivating organizational units and individuals to accomplish strategy. 2. Creating a strategy-supportive work environment and corporate culture. 3. Promoting a results orientation and a spirit of high performance. 4. Keeping the reward structure tightly linked to strategic performance and the achievement of target objectives.	+	**Specific Tasks:** 1. Establishing and administering strategy-facilitating policies and procedures. 2. Generating the right strategic information on a timely basis. 3. Instituting internal "controls" to keep the organization on its strategic course. 4. Creating "fits" between strategy and the various internal ways of doing things.	+	**Specific Tasks:** 1. Leading the process of shaping values, molding culture, and energizing strategy accomplishment. 2. Keeping the organization innovative, responsive, and opportunistic. 3. Dealing with the politics of strategy coping with power struggles and of building consensus. 4. Initiating corrective actions to improve strategy execution.

Pinpointing the Strategy-Critical Activities.   In any organization, some activities and skills are always more critical to strategic success than others. From a strategy perspective, much of an organization's total work effort is routine and falls under the rubric of administrative good housekeeping and necessary detail (handling payrolls, managing cash flows, controlling inventories, processing grievances, taking care of normal maintenance, processing customer payments, and complying with regulations). Other activities are primarily support functions (data processing, accounting, training, public relations, market research, and purchasing). Yet there are usually certain crucial tasks and functions which have to be exceedingly well done for the strategy to be successful. For instance, tight cost control is essential for a firm trying to be the low-cost producer in a commodity business where margins are low and price-cutting is a widely used competitive weapon. For a luxury goods manufacturer, the critical skills may be quality craftsmanship, distinctive design, and sophisticated promotional appeal. The strategy-critical activities vary according to the particulars of a firm's strategy and competitive requirements.

Two questions help identify what an organization's strategy-critical activities are: "What functions have to be performed extra well and on time for the strategy to succeed?" and "In what areas would malperformance seriously endanger strategic success?"[2] The answers generally point squarely at what activities and skills are crucial and indicate where to concentrate organization-building efforts.

Understanding the Relationships among Activities.   Before the various critical, supportive, and routine activities are grouped into organizational units, the strategic relationships that prevail among them need to be scrutinized thoughtfully. Activities can be related by the flow of material through the production process, by the type of customer served, by the distribution channels used, by the technical skills and know-how needed to perform them, by a strong need to centralize authority over them for purposes of coordination, by the sequence in which tasks must be performed, and by geographic location, to mention some of the most obvious ways. Such relationships are important because one (or more) of the interrelationships usually becomes the basis for grouping activities into organizational units. If the needs of strategy are to drive organization design, then the relationships to look for are those that link one piece of the strategy to another.

Grouping Activities into Organization Units.   The chief guideline here is to make strategy-critical activities the main building blocks in the organization structure. The rationale is compelling: *If activities crucial to strategic success are to get the attention and visibility they merit, then they have to be a prominent part of the organizational scheme.* When key functions and critical tasks take a backseat to less-important activities, the politics of organizational budget-making usually leads to them being given fewer resources and accorded less significance than they actually have. On the other hand, when they form the core of the whole organization structure, their role and power in the overall scheme of things is highlighted and institutionalized. Senior managers can seldom give a stronger signal about what is strategically important than by making key functions and critical skills the most

---

[2]Peter F. Drucker, *Management: Tasks, Responsibilities, Practices* (New York: Harper & Row, 1974), pp. 530, 535.

prominent organizational building blocks and, further, assigning them a high position in the organizational pecking order.

Determining the Degree of Authority and Independence to Give Each Unit. How much authority and decision-making latitude to give each organization unit, especially line-of-business units, is important. In the case of line-of-business units, one polar alternative is to centralize authority for the big strategy and policy decisions at the corporate level and delegate only operating decisions to business-level managers. At the other extreme, line-of-business units can be delegated enough autonomy to function independently, with little direct authority being exerted by corporate headquarters staff.

Several guidelines for parceling out authority across the various units can be offered. Activities and organizational units with a key role in strategy execution should not be made subordinate to routine and non-key activities. Revenue-producing and results-producing activities should not be made subordinate to internal support or staff functions. With few exceptions, decisions should be delegated to those managers closest to the scene of the action. Corporate-level authority over operating decisions at the business-unit level and below should be held to a minimum. The crucial administrative skill is in selecting strong managers to head each unit and delegating them enough authority to formulate and execute an appropriate strategy for their unit; if the results such managers produce prove unsatisfactory, then those with a poor track record of right and wrong decisions should be weeded out.

Providing for Coordination among the Units. Providing for coordination of the activities or organizational units is accomplished mainly through positioning them in the hierarchy of authority. Managers higher up in the pecking order, generally, have authority over more organizational units and, thus, the clout to coordinate, integrate, and otherwise arrange for the cooperation of the units under their supervision. The chief executive officer, the chief operating officer, and business-level managers are, of course, central points of coordination, because of their position of authority over the whole unit. Besides positioning organizational units along the vertical scale of managerial authority, coordination of strategic efforts can also be achieved through informal meetings, project teams, special task forces, standing committees, formal strategy reviews, and annual strategic planning and budgeting cycles. And, additionally, the formulation of the strategic plan itself serves a coordinating role; the whole process of negotiating and deciding upon the objectives and strategies of each organizational unit and making sure that related activities mesh suitably together help coordinate operations across organization units.

The Structure-Follows-Strategy Thesis. The practice of *consciously* matching organization design and structure to the particular needs and requirements of strategy is a fairly recent management development, and it springs from research evidence about the actual experiences of firms. The landmark study is Alfred Chandler's *Strategy and Structure*.[3] Chandler found that changes in an organiza-

---

[3]Cambridge, Mass.: MIT Press, 1962. Although the stress here is on matching structure to strategy, it is worth noting that structure can and does influence the choice of strategy. A "good" strategy must be doable. When an organization's present structure is so far out line with the requirements of a particular

tion's strategy bring about new administrative problems, which, in turn, require a new or refashioned structure if the new strategy is to be successfully implemented. His study of 70 large corporations revealed that structure tends to follow the growth strategy of the firm—but often not until inefficiency and internal operating problems provoke a structural adjustment. The experience of these firms followed a consistent sequential pattern: new strategy creation, emergence of new administrative problems, a decline in profitability and performance, a shift to a more appropriate organizational structure, and then recovery to more profitable levels and improved strategy execution. Chandler found this sequence to be oft-repeated as firms grew and modified their corporate strategies. The lesson of Chandler's research is that the choice of organization structure *does make a difference* in how an organization performs. All forms of organization structure are not equally supportive in implementing a given strategy.

The *structure-follows-strategy* thesis is undergirded with powerful logic: How the work of an organization is structured is just a means to an end—not an end in itself. Structure is no more than a managerial device for facilitating the implementation and execution of the organization's strategy and, ultimately, for achieving the intended performance and results. Toward this end, the structural design of an organization acts both as a harness that helps people pull together in their performance of diverse tasks and as a means of tying the organizational building blocks together in ways that promote strategy accomplishment and improved performance. Without *deliberately* organizing responsibilities and activities to produce linkages between structure and strategy, the outcomes are likely to be disorder, friction, and inefficiency.[4]

How Structure Evolves as Strategy Evolves: The Stages Model

In a number of respects, the strategist's approach to organization-building is governed by the size and growth stage of the enterprise, as well as by the key success factors inherent in the organization's business. For instance, the type of organization structure that suits a small specialty steel firm relying upon a concentration strategy in a regional market is not likely to be suitable for a large, vertically integrated steel producer doing business in geographically diverse areas. The organization form that works best in a corporation pursuing unrelated diversification is, understandably, likely to be different yet again. Recognition of this characteristic has prompted several attempts to formulate a model linking changes in organizational structure to stages in an organization's strategic development.[5]

---

strategy that the organization would have to be turned upside down and inside out to implement it, then the strategy may, as a practical matter, not be doable and ought not to be given further consideration. In such cases, structure shapes the choice of strategy. The point here, however, is that, once strategy is chosen, structure must be made to fit the strategy if, in fact, an approximate fit does not already exist. Any influences of structure on strategy should, logically, come before the point of strategy selection, rather than after it.

[4]Drucker, *Management*, p. 523.

[5]See, for example, Malcolm S. Salter, "Stages of Corporate Development," *Journal of Business Policy* 1, no. 1 (Spring 1970), pp. 23–27; Donald H. Thain, "Stages of Corporate Development," *The Business Quarterly*, Winter 1969, pp. 32–45; Bruce R. Scott, "The Industrial State: Old Myths and New Realities," *Harvard Business Review* 51, no. 2 (March –April 1973), pp. 133–48; and Alfred D. Chandler, *Strategy and Structure*, chap. 1.

The underpinning of the stages concept is that enterprises can be arrayed along a continuum running from very simple to very complex organizational forms and that there is a tendency for an organization to move along this continuum toward more complex forms as it grows in size, market coverage, and product-line scope and as the strategic aspects of its customer-technology-business portfolio become more intricate. Four distinct stages of strategy-related organization structure have been singled out.

Stage I. Stage I organizations are small, single-business enterprises managed by one person. The owner-entrepreneur has close daily contact with employees and with each phase of operations. Most employees report directly to the owner, who makes all the pertinent decisions regarding mission, objectives, strategy, and daily operations.

Stage II. Stage II organizations differ from Stage I enterprises in one essential respect: An increased scale and scope of operations force a transition from one-person management to group management. However, a Stage II enterprise, although run by a team of managers with functionally specialized responsibilities, remains fundamentally a single-business operation. Some Stage II organizations prefer to divide strategic responsibilities along classic functional lines—marketing, production, finance, human resources, engineering, public relations, procurement, shipping, and so on. In vertically integrated Stage II companies, the main organization units often relate to the distinct production stages in the industry chain; for example, the organizational building blocks of a large oil company usually consist of exploration, drilling, pipelines, refining, wholesale distribution, and retail sales. In practice, there is wide variation in how Stage II firms define the functional area building blocks.

Stage III. Stage III consists of organizations whose operations, though concentrated in a single field or product line, are large enough and scattered over a wide geographic area to justify having geographically decentralized operating units. These units all report to corporate headquarters and conform to corporate policies, but they are given the flexibility to tailor their unit's strategic plan to meet the specific needs of each respective geographic area. Ordinarily, each of the semiautonomous operating units of a Stage III organization is structured along functional lines.

The key difference between Stage II and Stage III, however, is that, while the functional units of a Stage II organization stand or fall together (in that they are built around one business and one end-market), the operating units of a Stage III firm can stand alone (or nearly so) in the sense that the operations in each geographic unit are not rigidly tied to or dependent on those in other areas. Characteristic firms in this category would be breweries, cement companies, and steel mills having production capacity and sales organizations in several geographically separate market areas. Corey and Star cite Pfizer International as being a good example of a company whose strategic requirements made geographic decentralization propitious:

> With sales of $223 million in 1964, Pfizer International operated plants in 27 countries and marketed in more than 100 countries. Its product lines included pharmaceuticals (antibiotics and other ethical prescription drugs), agriculture and

veterinary products (such as animal feed supplements and vaccines and pesticides), chemicals (fine chemicals, bulk pharmaceuticals, petrochemicals, and plastics), and consumer products (cosmetics and toiletries).

Ten geographic Area Managers reported directly to the President of Pfizer International and exercised line supervision over Country Managers. According to a company position description, it was "the responsibility of each Area Manager to plan, develop, and carry out Pfizer International's business in the assigned foreign area in keeping with company policies and goals."

Country Managers had profit responsibility. In most cases a single Country Manager managed all Pfizer activities in his country. In some of the larger, well-developed countries of Europe there were separate Country Managers for pharmaceutical and agricultural products and for consumer lines.

Except for the fact that New York headquarters exercised control over the to-the-market prices of certain products, especially prices of widely used pharmaceuticals, Area and Country Managers had considerable autonomy in planning and managing the Pfizer International business in their respective geographic areas. This was appropriate because each area, and some countries within areas, provided unique market and regulatory environments. In the case of pharmaceuticals and agriculture and veterinary products (Pfizer International's most important lines), national laws affected formulations, dosages, labeling, distribution, and often price. Trade restrictions affected the flow of bulk pharmaceuticals and chemicals and packaged products, and might in effect require the establishment of manufacturing plants to supply local markets. Competition, too, varied significantly from area to area.[6]

Stage IV. Stage IV includes large, diversified firms decentralized by line of business. Typically, each separate business unit is headed by a general manager who has profit-and-loss responsibility and whose authority extends across all of the unit's functional areas except, perhaps, accounting and capital investment (both of which are traditionally subject to corporate approval). Both business-strategy decisions and operating decisions are concentrated at the line-of-business level, rather than at the corporate level. The organizational structure within the line-of-business unit may be along the lines of Stage II or III types of organizations. Characteristic Stage IV companies include General Electric, ITT, Procter & Gamble, PepsiCo, Du Pont, United Technologies, R. J. Reynolds, and Litton Industries.

Movement through the Stages. The stages model provides useful insights into why organization structure tends to change. As firms progress from small, entrepreneurial enterprises following a basic concentration strategy to more complex strategic phases of volume expansion, vertical integration, geographic expansion, and line-of-business diversification, their organizational structures tend to evolve from unifunctional to functionally centralized to multidivisional decentralized organizational forms. Firms that remain single-line businesses almost always have some form of a centralized functional structure. Enterprises predominantly in one industry but slightly diversified typically have a hybrid structure; the dominant business is managed via functional organization, and the diversified activities are handled through a decentralized divisionalized form. The more diversified an organization becomes, irrespective of whether the diversification is along related or unrelated lines, the more it moves toward some form of decentralized business unit structure. In short, as a company's strategic direction shifts from a small, single-product business to a large, dominant-product business and then on to broad diversification, its organizational structure evolves from one-man management to large-group functional management to decentralized, line-of-business management. About 90 percent of the Fortune 500 firms (nearly all of which are diversified to one degree or another) have a divisionalized organizational structure with the primary basis for decentralization being line-of-business considerations.

One final lesson that the stages model teaches is that a reassessment of organization structure and authority is always useful whenever strategy is changed.[7] A new strategy is likely to entail new or different skills and key activities. If these changes go unrecognized, especially the subtle ones, the resulting mismatch between strategy and organization can pose implementation problems and curtail performance.

The Strategy-Related Pros and Cons of Alternative Organization Forms

There are essentially five strategy-related approaches to organization: (1) functional specialization, (2) geographic organization, (3) decentralized business divisions, (4) strategic business units, and (5) matrix structures featuring dual lines of authority and strategic priority. Each form relates structure to strategy in a different way and, consequently, has its own set of strategy-related pros and cons.

The Functional Organization Structures.   A functional organization structure tends to be effective in single-business units where key activities revolve around well-defined skills and areas of specialization. In such cases, in-depth specialization and focused concentration on performing functional-area tasks and activities can enhance both operating efficiency and the development of a distinctive competence. Generally, organizing by functional specialties promotes full utilization of the most up-to-date technical skills and helps a business capitalize on the efficiency gains to be had from using specialized manpower, facilities, and equipment. These are strategically important considerations for single-business organizations, dominant-product enterprises, and vertically integrated firms and account for why they usually have some kind of centralized, functionally specialized structure.

However, just what form the functional specialization will take varies according to customer-product-technology considerations. For instance, a technical instruments manufacturer may be organized around research and development, engineering, production, technical services, quality control, marketing, personnel, and finance and accounting. A municipal government may, on the other hand, be

---

[7]For an excellent documentation of how a number of well-known corporations revised their organization structures to meet the needs of strategy changes and specific product/market developments, see Corey and Star, *Organization Strategy,* chap. 3.

departmentalized according to purposeful function—fire, public safety, health services, water and sewer, streets, parks and recreation, and education. A university may divide its organizational units into academic affairs, student services, alumni relations, athletics, buildings and grounds, institutional services, and budget control. Two types of functional organizational approaches are diagrammed in Figure 9–3.

FIGURE 9–3
Functional Organizational Structures

A. **The building blocks of a "typical" functional organization structure:**

B. **The building blocks of a process-oriented functional structure:**

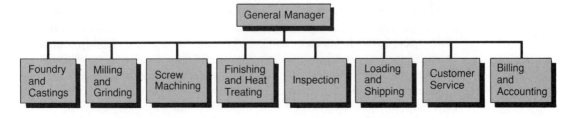

Strategic Advantages	Strategic Disadvantages
• Permits centralized control of strategic results.	• Poses problems of functional coordination.
• Very well-suited for structuring a single business.	• Can lead to interfunctional rivalry, conflict, and empire-building.
• Structure is linked tightly to strategy by designating key activities as functional units.	• May promote overspecialization and narrow management viewpoints.
• Promotes in-depth functional expertise.	• Hinders development of managers with cross-functional experience because the ladder of advancement is up the ranks within the same functional area.
• Well suited to developing a functional-based distinctive competence.	• Forces profit responsibility to the top.
• Conducive to exploiting learning/experience curve effects associated with functional specialization.	• Functional specialists often attach more importance to what's best for the functional area than to what's best for the whole business.
• Enhances operating efficiency where tasks are routine and repetitive.	• May lead to uneconomically small units or underutilization of specialized facilities and manpower.
	• Functional myopia often works against creative entrepreneurship, adapting to change, and attempts to restructure the activity-cost chain.

The Achilles' heel of a functional structure is getting and keeping tight strategic coordination across the separated functional units. Functional specialists, partly because of how they were trained and the technical "mystique" of their jobs, tend to develop their own mindset and ways of doing things. The more that functional specialists differ in their perspectives and their approaches to task accomplishment, the more difficult it becomes to achieve both strategic and operating coordination between them. They neither talk the same language nor have adequate understanding and appreciation for one another's strategic role, problems, and changed circumstances. Each functional group is more interested in its own empire and promoting its own strategic interest and importance (despite the lip service given to cooperation and "what's best for the company"). Tunnel vision and empire-building in functional departments impose a time-consuming administrative burden on a business-level manager in terms of resolving cross-functional differences, enforcing joint cooperation, and opening lines of communication across departments. In addition, a purely functional organization tends to be myopic when it comes to promoting entrepreneurial creativity, adapting quickly to major customer-market-technological changes, and pursuing opportunities that go beyond the conventional boundaries of the industry.

Geographic Forms of Organization. Organizing according to geographic areas or territories is a rather common structural form for large-scale enterprises whose strategies need to be tailored to fit the particular needs and features of different geographical areas. As indicated in Figure 9–4, geographic organization has its advantages and disadvantages; but the chief reason for its popularity is that, for one reason or another, it promotes improved performance.

In the private sector, a territorial structure is typically utilized by chain store retailers, power companies, cement firms, restaurant chains, and dairy products enterprises. In the public sector, such organizations as the Internal Revenue Service, the Social Security Administration, the federal courts, the U.S. Postal Service, the state troopers, and the Red Cross have adopted territorial structures to be directly accessible to geographically dispersed clienteles.

Decentralized Business Units. Grouping activities along business and product lines has been a clear-cut trend among diversified enterprises for the past half century, beginning with the pioneering efforts of Du Pont and General Motors in the 1920s. Separate business/product divisions emerged because diversification made a functionally specialized manager's job incredibly complex. Imagine the problems a manufacturing executive and his or her staff would have if put in charge of, say, 50 different plants using 20 different technologies to produce 30 different products in 8 different businesses/industries. In a multibusiness enterprise, the needs of strategy virtually dictate that the organizational sequence be corporate to line of business to functional area within a business, rather than corporate to functional area (aggregated for all businesses). The latter produces a nightmare in making sense out of business strategy and achieving functional-area coordination for a given business.

Strategy implementation is facilitated by grouping key activities belonging to the same business under one organizational roof, thereby creating line-of-business units (which then can be subdivided into whatever functional subunits that suits the key activities/critical tasks makeup of the business.) The outcome not only is a structure which fits strategy but also a structure which makes the jobs of managers

FIGURE 9–4
A Geographic Organizational Structure

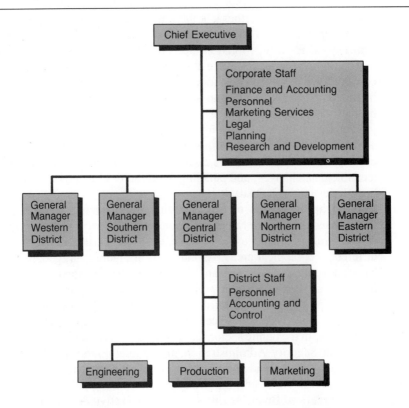

Strategic Advantages	Strategic Disadvantages

Strategic Advantages

- Allows tailoring of strategy to needs of each geographic market.
- Delegates profit/loss responsibility to lowest strategic level.
- Improves functional coordination within the target market.
- Takes advantage of economies of local operations.
- Area units make an excellent training ground for higher-level general managers.

Strategic Disadvantages

- Poses a problem of how much geographic uniformity headquarters should impose versus how much geographic diversity should be allowed.
- Greater difficulty in maintaining consistent company image/reputation from area to area when area managers exercise much strategic freedom.
- Adds another layer of management to run the geographic units.
- Can result in duplication of staff services at headquarters and district levels, creating a relative-cost disadvantage.

more doable. The creation of separate business units is then accomplished by decentralizing authority over the unit to the business-level manager. The approach, very simply, is to put entrepreneurially oriented general managers in charge of the business unit, giving them enough authority to formulate and implement the business strategy that they deem appropriate, motivating them with incentives, and then holding them accountable for the results they produce. Each business unit then operates as a stand-alone profit center. However, when strong strategic fit exists across related business units, it can be tough to get autonomy-conscious business-unit managers to cooperate in coordinating and sharing the related activities; they are prone to argue long and hard about turf and about being held accountable for activities not totally under their control.

A typical line-of-business organizational structure is shown in Figure 9–5, along with the strategy-related pros and cons of this type of organizational form.

Strategic Business Units.   In the really large, diversified companies, the number of decentralized business units can be so great that the span of control is too much for a single chief executive. Then it may be useful to group those that are related and to delegate authority over them to a senior executive who reports directly to the chief executive officer. While this imposes a layer of management between business-level managers and the chief executive, it may nonetheless improve strategic planning and top-management coordination of diverse business interests. This explains both the popularity of the group vice president concept among broadly diversified firms and the recent trend toward the formation of *strategic business units*.

A strategic business unit (SBU) is a grouping of business units based on some important strategic elements common to each; the possible elements of relatedness include an overlapping set of competitors, a closely related strategic mission, a common need to compete globally, an ability to accomplish integrated strategic planning, common key success factors, and technologically related growth opportunities. At General Electric, a pioneer in the concept of SBUs, 190 units were grouped into 43 SBUs and then aggregated further into 6 "sectors."[8] At Union Carbide, 15 groups and divisions were decomposed into 150 "strategic planning units" and then regrouped and combined into 9 new "aggregate planning units." At General Foods (now a division of Philip Morris), SBUs were originally defined on a product-line basis but were later redefined according to menu segments (breakfast foods, beverages, main meal products, desserts, and pet foods).

The managerial value of the SBU concept is that it provides diversified companies with a way to rationalize the organization of many different businesses and a way to give separate but related areas within the total enterprise some cohesive direction. SBUs are particularly helpful in reducing the complexity of dovetailing corporate strategy and business strategy and in cross-pollinating the growth opportunities in different industries, perhaps to create altogether new industries. SBUs also make headquarters' reviews of the strategies of lower-level units less imposing

---

[8]William K. Hall, "SBUs: Hot New Topic in the Management of Diversification," *Business Horizons* 21, no. 1 (February 1978), p. 19. For an excellent discussion of the problems of implementing the SBU concept at 13 companies, see Richard A. Bettis and William K. Hall, "The Business Portfolio Approach—Where It Falls Down in Practice," *Long Range Planning* 16, no. 2 (April 1983), pp. 95–104.

FIGURE 9–5
A Decentralized Line-of-Business Type of Organization Structure

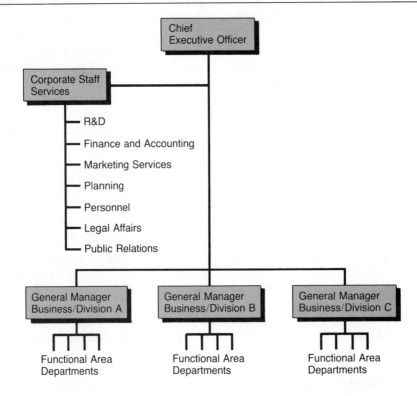

Strategic Advantages

- Offers a logical and workable means of decentralizing responsibility and delegating authority in diversified organizations.

- Puts responsibility for business strategy in closer proximity to each business's unique environment.

- Allows each business unit to organize around its own set of key activities and functional-area requirements.

- Frees CEO to handle corporate strategy issues.

- Puts clear profit/loss accountability on shoulders of business-unit managers.

Strategic Disadvantages

- May lead to costly duplication of staff functions at corporate and business-unit levels, thus raising administrative overhead costs.

- Poses a problem of what decisions to centralize and what decisions to decentralize (business managers need enough authority to get the job done, but not so much that corporate management loses control of key business-level decisions).

- May lead to excessive division rivalry for corporate resources and attention.

- Business/division autonomy works against achieving coordination of related activities in different business units, thus blocking to some extent the capture of strategic-fit benefits.

- Corporate management becomes heavily dependent on business-unit managers.

- Corporate managers can lose touch with business-unit situations, end up surprised when problems arise, and not know much about how to fix such problems.

(there is no practical way for a CEO to conduct in-depth reviews of a hundred or more different businesses). Figure 9–6 illustrates the SBU form of organization, along with its strategy-related pros and cons.

Matrix Forms of Organization. A matrix organization is a structure with two (or more) channels of command, two lines of budget authority, and two sources of performance and reward. The key feature of the matrix is that product (or business) and functional lines of authority are overlaid to form a matrix or grid, and managerial authority over the activities in each unit/cell of the matrix is shared between the product manager and functional manager—as shown in Figure 9–7. In a matrix structure, subordinates have a continuing dual assignment: to the business/product line/project and to their home base function.[9] The outcome is a compromise between functional specialization (engineering, R&D, manufacturing, marketing, finance) and product line or project or line-of-business specialization (where all of the specialized talent needed for the product line/project line of business are assigned to the same organizational unit).

A matrix-type organization is a genuinely different structural form and represents a "new way of life." One reason is that the unity-of-command principle is broken; two reporting channels, two bosses, and shared authority create a new kind of organizational climate. In essence, the matrix is a conflict-resolution system through which strategic and operating priorities are negotiated, power is shared, and resources are allocated internally on a "strongest case for what is best overall for the unit" basis.[10]

The impetus for matrix organizations stems from growing use of strategies that add new sources of diversity (products, customer groups, technology, lines of business) to a firm's range of activities. Out of this diversity are coming product managers, functional managers, geographic area managers, new-venture managers, and business-level managers—all of whom have important strategic responsibilities. When at least two of several variables (product, customer, technology, geography, functional area, and market segment) have roughly equal strategic priorities, then a matrix organization can be an effective structural form. A matrix arrangement promotes internal checks and balances among competing viewpoints and perspectives, with separate managers for different dimensions of strategic initiative. A matrix approach, thus, allows each of several strategic considerations to be managed directly and to be formally represented in the organization structure. In this sense, it helps middle managers make trade-off decisions from an organizationwide perspective.[11]

Companies using matrix structures include General Electric, Texas Instruments, Citibank, Shell Oil, TRW, Bechtel, Boeing, and Dow Chemical. However, most applications of matrix organization are limited to a portion of what the firm does (certain important functions), rather than spanning the whole of a large-scale diversified enterprise.

---

[9]A more thorough treatment of matrix organizational forms can be found in Jay R. Galbraith, "Matrix Organization Designs," *Business Horizons* 15, no. 1 (February 1971), pp. 29–40.

[10]An excellent critique of matrix organizations is presented in Stanley M. Davis and Paul R. Lawrence, "Problems of Matrix Organizations," *Harvard Business Review* 56, no. 3 (May–June 1978), pp. 131–42.

[11]Ibid., p. 132.

FIGURE 9–6
An SBU Type of Organization Structure

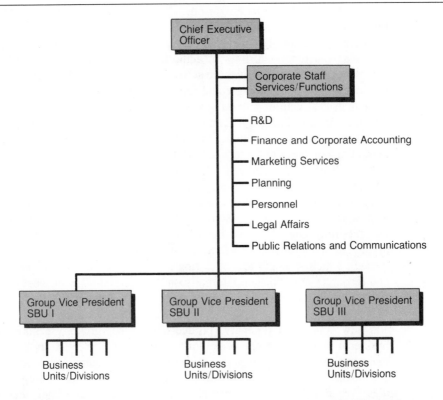

Strategic Advantages

- Provides a strategically relevant way to organize large numbers of different business units.

- Improves coordination between the role and authority of the businesses with similar strategies, markets, and growth opportunities.

- Allows strategic planning to be done at the most relevant level within the total enterprise.

- Makes the task of strategic review by top executives more objective and more effective.

- Helps allocate corporate resources to areas with greatest growth opportunities.

- Promotes more cohesiveness among the new inititatives of separate but related businesses.

- Facilitates the coordination of related activities *within* an SBU, thus helping to capture the benefits of strategic fits in the SBU.

Strategic Disadvantages

- It is easy for the definition and grouping of businesses into SBUs to be so arbitrary that the SBU serves no other purpose than administrative convenience. If the criteria for defining SBUs are rationalizations and have little to do with the nitty-gritty of strategy coordination, then the groupings lose real strategic significance.

- The SBUs can still be myopic in charting their future direction.

- Adds another layer to top management.

- The roles and authority of the CEO, the group vice president, and the business-unit manager have to be carefully worked out or the group vice president gets trapped in the middle with ill-defined authority.

- Unless the SBU head is strong willed, very little strategy coordination is likely to occur across business units in the SBU.

- Performance recognition gets blurred; credit for successful business units tends to go to corporate CEO, then to business-unit head, last to group vice president.

FIGURE 9–7
A Matrix Organization Structure*

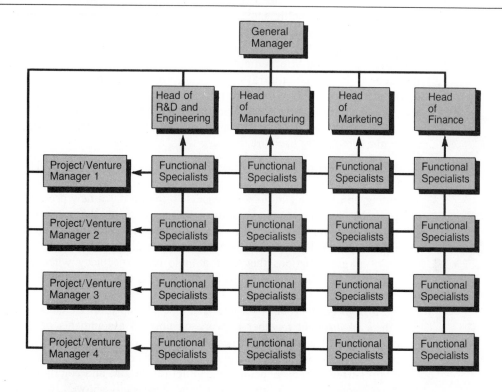

Strategic Advantages

- Permits more attention to each dimension of strategic priority.
- Creates checks and balances among competing viewpoints.
- Facilitates simultaneous pursuit of different types of strategic initiative.
- Promotes making trade-off decisions on the basis of "what's best for the organization as a whole."
- Encourages cooperation, consensus-building, conflict resolution, and coordination of related activities.

Strategic Disadvantages

- Very complex to manage.
- Hard to maintain "balance" between the two lines of authority.
- So much shared authority can result in a transactions logjam and disproportionate amounts of time being spent on communications.
- It is hard to move quickly and decisively without getting clearance from many other people.
- Promotes an organizational bureaucracy and hamstrings creative entrepreneurship.

*Arrows indicate reporting channels.

A number of companies shun matrix organization because of its chief weaknesses.[12] It is a complex structure to manage; people often end up confused over whom to report to for what. Moreover, because the matrix signals that everything is important and, further, that everybody needs to communicate with everybody else, a transactions logjam can emerge. Action turns into paralysis since, with shared authority, it is hard to move decisively without first considering many points of view and getting clearance from many other people. Sizable transactions costs and communications inefficiency can arise, as well as delays in responding. Even so, there are situations where the benefits of conflict resolution and consensus-building outweigh these weaknesses.

Combination and Supplemental Methods of Organization. A single type of structural design is not always sufficient to meet the requirements of strategy. When this occurs, one option is to mix and blend the basic organization forms, matching structure to strategy requirement by requirement and unit by unit. Another is to supplement a basic organization design with special-situation devices. Three of the most frequently used are:

1. The *project manager* or *project staff approach*—where a separate, largely self-sufficient subunit is created to oversee the completion of a special activity (setting up a new technological process, bringing out a new product, starting up a new venture, consummating a merger with another company, seeing through the completion of a government contract, supervising the construction of a new plant). Project management is a relatively popular means of handling one-of-a-kind situations that have a finite life expectancy when the normal organization is ill-equipped to achieve the same results in addition to regular duties.

2. The *task force approach*—where a number of top-level executives and specialists are brought together to work on unusual assignments of a problem-solving or innovative nature. Special task forces provide increased opportunity for: creativity, open communication across lines of authority, tight integration of specialized talents, expeditious conflict resolution, and common identification for coping with the problem at hand. One study showed that task forces were most effective when they had less than 10 members, membership was voluntary, the seniority of the members was proportional to the importance of the problem, the task force moved swiftly to deal with its assignment, the task force was pulled together only on an as-needed basis, no staff was assigned, and documentation was scant.[13] In these companies, the prevailing philosophy about task forces is to use them to solve real problems, produce some solution efficiently, and then disband them. At the other extreme, Peters and Waterman report one instance where a company had formed 325 task forces, none of which had completed its charge in three years and none of which had been disbanded.

3. The *venture team approach*—whereby a group of individuals is formed for the

---

[12]Thomas J. Peters and Robert H. Waterman, Jr., *In Search of Excellence* (New York: Harper & Row, 1982), pp. 306–7.
[13]Peters and Waterman, *In Search of Excellence*, pp. 127–32.

purpose of bringing a specific product to market or a specific new business into being. Dow, General Mills, Westinghouse, General Electric, and Monsanto have used the venture team approach as a regenesis of the entrepreneurial spirit. The difficulties with venture teams include deciding to whom the venture manager should report; whether funding for ventures should come from corporate, business, or departmental budgets; how to keep the venture clear of bureaucratic and vested interests; and how to coordinate large numbers of different ventures.

Perspectives on Matching Strategy and Structure

The foregoing discussion brings out two points: (1) there is no such thing as a perfect or ideal organization design and (2) there are no universally applicable rules for matching strategy and structure. All of the basic organizational forms have their strategy-related strengths and weaknesses. Moreover, use of one of the basic organizational forms does not preclude simultaneous use of others; many organizations are large enough and diverse enough to have subunits organized by functional specialty, by geographical area, by market segment, by line of business, by SBU, and by matrix principles—there is no need to adhere slavishly to one basic organization type. In a very real sense, *the best organizational arrangement is the one that best fits the firm's situation at the moment.* Experience shows that firms have a habit of regularly outgrowing their prevailing organizational arrangement—either an internal shakeup is deemed periodically desirable or else changes in the size and scope of customer-product-technology relationships make the firm's structure strategically obsolete. An organization's structure, thus, is dynamic; changes are not only inevitable but typical.

There is room to quibble over whether organization design should commence with a strategy-structure framework or with a pragmatic consideration of the realities of the situation at hand—the corporate culture, the constraints imposed by the personalities involved, and the way things have been done before. By and large, agonizing over where to begin is unnecessary; both considerations have to be taken into account. However, strategy-structure factors usually have to take precedence if structure is to be firmly built around the organization's strategy-critical tasks, key success factors, and high-priority business units. Adapting structure to the peculiar circumstances of the organization's internal situation and personalities is usually done to modify the strategy-structure match in "minor" ways.

Drucker has summed up the intricacies of organization design thusly:

> The simplest organization structure that will do the job is the best one. What makes an organization structure "good" are the problems it does not create. The simpler the structure, the less that can go wrong.
>
> Some design principles are more difficult and problematic than others. But none is without difficulties and problems. None is primarily people-focused rather than task-focused; none is more "creative," "free," or "more democratic." Design principles are tools; and tools are neither good nor bad in themselves. They can be used properly or improperly; and that is all. To obtain both the greatest possible simplicity and the greatest "fit," organization design has to start out with a clear focus on *key activities* needed to produce *key results.* They have to

be structured and positioned in the simplest possible design. Above all, the architect of organization needs to keep in mind the purpose of the structure he is designing.[14]

Peters and Waterman, in their study of excellently managed companies, confirm what Drucker says; their organization prescription is "simple form, lean staff."[15] Illustration Capsule 18 explains some of the organizational principles and approaches being used at these companies.

Building a Distinctive Competence

A good match between structure and strategy is plainly one key facet of a strategically capable organization. But an equally dominant organization-building concern is that of staffing the chosen structure with the requisite managerial talent and technical skills—and, most particularly, staffing in a manner calculated to give the firm a distinctive competence in performing one or more critical tasks. The strategic importance of deliberately trying to develop a distinctive competence within an organization stems from the extra contribution which special expertise and a competitive edge make both to performance and to strategic success. To the extent that an organization can build an astutely conceived distinctive competence in its chosen business domains, it creates a golden opportunity for achieving a competitive advantage and posting a superior record of performance. As indicated in prior chapters, a distinctive competence can take the form of greater proficiency in product development or quality of manufacture or caliber of technical services offered to customers or speed of response to changing customer requirements or being the low-cost producer or any other strategically relevant factor.

However, distinctive competences do not just naturally appear. They have to be consciously developed and nurtured. Consequently, for a distinctive competence to emerge from organization-building actions, strategy implementers have to push aggressively to secure an inventory of technical skills and capabilities in those few select subunits where superior performance of strategically critical tasks can make a real difference to greater strategic success. Usually, this means (1) giving above-average operating budget support to strategy-critical tasks and activities, (2) seeing that these tasks and activities are staffed with high-caliber managerial and technical talent, and (3) insisting upon high performance standards from these subunits, backed up with a policy of rewarding superior performance. In effect, strategy-implementers must take premeditated actions to see that the organization is staffed with enough of the right kinds of people, and that these people have the budgetary and administrative support needed to generate a distinctive competence.

Once developed, the strengths and capabilities that attach to distinctive competences become logical cornerstones for successful strategy implementation as well as for the actual strategy itself. Moreover, really distinctive internal skills and capabilities are not easily duplicated by other firms; this means that any differential advantage so gained is likely to have a lasting strategic impact and,

---

[14]Drucker, *Management*, pp. 601–2.
[15]Peters and Waterman, *In Search of Excellence*, chap. 11.

ILLUSTRATION CAPSULE 18

Organization Lessons from the "Excellently Managed" Companies

Peters and Waterman's study of America's best-managed corporations provides some important lessons in building a strategically capable organization:

1. The organizational underpinning of most of the excellently managed companies is a fairly stable, unchanging form—usually a decentralized business/product division—that provides the structural building block which everyone in the enterprise understands and that serves as the base for approaching day-to-day issues and complexities.

2. Beyond the crystal-clear primacy of this basic and simple organizational building block, the rest of the organization structure is deliberately kept fluid and flexible to permit response to changing environmental conditions. Much use is made of task forces, project teams, and the creation of new, small divisions to address emerging issues and opportunities.

3. New divisions are created to pursue budding business opportunities, as opposed to letting them remain a part of the originating division. Often, there are established guidelines when a new product or product line automatically becomes an independent division.

4. People and even products and product lines are frequently shifted from one division to another—so as to improve efficiency, promote shared costs, enhance competitive strength, and adapt to changing market conditions.

5. Many excellently managed companies have comparatively few people at the corporate level, and many of these are out in the field frequently, rather than in the home office all the time. Emerson Electric with 54,000 employees had a headquarters staff of fewer than 100 people. Dana Corporation employed 35,000 people and had a corporate staff numbering about 100. Schlumberger Ltd., a $56 billion diversified oil service company, ran its worldwide organization with a corporate staff of 90 people. At Intel (sales of over $1 billion), all staff assignments were temporary ones given to line officers. Rolm managed a $200 million business with about 15 people in corporate headquarters. In addition, corporate planners were few and far between. Hewlett-Packard Company, Johnson & Johnson, and 3M had no planners at the corporate level; Fluor Corporation ran a $6 billion operation with three corporate planners. At IBM, management rotated staff assignments every three years. Few IBM staff jobs were manned by "career staffers"; most were manned temporarily by managers with line jobs in the divisions who will rotate back to line jobs.

6. Functional organization forms are efficient and get the basic activities performed well; yet they are not particularly creative or entrepreneurial, they do not adapt quickly, and they are apt to ignore important changes.

7. The key to maintaining an entrepreneurial, adaptive organization is *small size*—and the way to keep units small is to spin off new or expanded activities into independent units. Division sizes often run no bigger than $50 to $100 million in sales, with a maximum of 1,000 or so employees. At Emerson Electric, plants rarely employed more than 600 workers, so that management could maintain personal contact with employees. (Emerson, by the way, has

ILLUSTRATION CAPSULE 18 *(concluded)*

a good track record on efficiency; its strategy of being the low-cost producer has worked beautifully in chain saws and several other products.) At Blue Bell, a leading apparel firm, manufacturing units usually employ under 300 people. The lesson seems to be that small units are both more cost-effective and more innovative.

8. To prevent "calcification" and stodginess, it helps to rely on such "habitbreaking" techniques as *(a)* reorganizing regularly; *(b)* putting top talent on project teams and giving them a "charter" to move quickly to solve a key problem or execute a central strategic thrust (i.e., the creation of the General Motors Project Center to lead the downsizing effort); *(c)* shifting products or product lines among divisions to take advantage of special management talents or the need for market realignments; *(d)* breaking up big, bureaucratic divisions into several new, smaller divisions; and *(e)* being flexible enough to try experimental organization approaches and support the pursuit of new opportunities.

9. It is useful to adopt a simultaneous "loose-tight" structure that on the one hand fosters autonomy, entrepreneurship, and innovation from rank-and-file managers yet, on the other hand, allows for strong central direction from the top. Such things as regular reorganization, flexible form (the use of teams and task forces), lots of decentralized autonomy for lower-level general managers, and extensive experimentation all focus on the excitement of trying things out in a slightly "loose" fashion. Yet, regular communication, quick feedback, concise paperwork, strong adherence to a few core values, and self-discipline can impose "tight" central control so that nothing gets far out of line.

Application of these "principles" in the best-managed companies tends to produce an environment that fosters entrepreneurial pursuit of new opportunities and adaptation to change. A fluid, flexible structure is the norm—the basic form is stable, but there is frequent reorganization "around the edges." The aim is to keep structure matched to the changing needs of an evolving strategy and to avoid letting the current organization structure become so ingrained and political that it becomes a major obstacle to be hurdled.

SOURCE: Drawn from Thomas J. Peters and Robert H. Waterman, Jr., *In Search of Excellence* (New York: Harper & Row, 1982), especially chaps. 11 and 12.

thus, help pave the way for above-average performance over the long term. Conscious management attention to the task of building strategically relevant internal skills and strengths into the overall organizational scheme is, therefore, one of the central tasks of organizational building and effective strategy implementation.

Selecting People for Key Positions

Assembling a capable management team is an obvious part of the strategy-implementation task. The recurring administrative issues here center around what kind of core management team is needed to carry out the strategy and finding the people to fill each slot. Sometimes the existing management team is suitable and sometimes the core executive group needs to be strengthened or expanded, or both, either by promoting qualified people from within or by bringing in skilled managerial talent from the outside to help infuse fresh ideas and fresh approaches into the organization's management. In turnaround situations, in rapid-growth situations, and in those cases where the right kinds of managerial experience and skills are not present in-house, recruiting outsiders to fill key management slots is a fairly standard part of the organization-building process.

The important dimension of assembling a core executive group is discerning what mix of backgrounds, experiences, know-how, values, beliefs, styles of managing, and personalities will reinforce and contribute to successful strategy execution. As with any kind of team-building exercise, it is important to put together a compatible group of managers who possess a full set of skills; and to get things done—the personal chemistry needs to be right and the talent base needs to match the managerial requirements of the chosen strategy. Picking good lieutenants and consciously molding a solid management team is always an essential strategy-implementing function.[16]

LINKING THE BUDGET WITH STRATEGY

Keeping an organization on the strategy-implementation path thrusts a manager squarely into the budgeting process. Not only must a strategy-implementer oversee "who gets how much" but the budget must also be put together with an equal concern for "getting the biggest bang for the buck."

There is little need to belabor the role of budgets and programs in the strategy-implementation process. Obviously, organizational units must have the resources needed to carry out their part of the strategic plan. This includes having enough of the right kinds of people and having enough operating funds for them to carry out their work. Moreover, each subunit must program its activities to meet its objectives, establish schedules and deadlines for accomplishment, and parcel out assignments for exactly who is responsible for what by when. Budgets and programs go hand in hand. Programs lay out detailed, step-by-step action plans, and budgets specify the costs of the planned activities.

How well a strategy-implementer ties the organization's budget directly to the needs of strategy can, quite clearly, either promote or impede the process of strategy implementation and execution. Too little funding deprives subunits of the capability to carry out their pieces of the strategic plan. Too much funding is a waste of organizational resources and reduces financial performance. Both outcomes argue for the strategy-implementer to be deeply involved in the budgeting process, closely reviewing the programs and proposals of strategy-critical subunits within the organization.

A ready willingness to shift resources in support of strategic change is especially

---

[16]For an analytical framework in top-management team analysis, see Donald C. Hambrick, "The Top Management Team: Key to Strategic Success," *California Management Review* 30, no. 1 (Fall 1987), pp. 88–108.

critical. For example, at Harris Corporation, where one element of strategy is to diffuse research ideas into areas that are commercially viable, top management regularly shifts groups of engineers out of government projects and moves them (as a group) into new commercial-venture divisions. Boeing has a similar approach to reallocating ideas and talent; according to one Boeing officer, "We can do it [create a big new unit] in two weeks. We couldn't do it in two years at International Harvester."[17] A fluid, flexible approach to reorganization and reallocation of people and budgets is characteristic of implementing strategic change successfully.

Fine tuning existing strategy usually involves less reallocation and more of an extrapolation approach. Big movements of people and money from one area to another are seldom necessary. Fine tuning can usually be accomplished by incrementally increasing or decreasing the budgets and staffing of existing organization units. The chief exception occurs where a prime ingredient of corporate/business strategy is to generate fresh, new products and business opportunities from within; then, as attractive ventures "bubble up" from below, major decisions have to be made regarding budgets and staffing. Companies like 3M, GE, Boeing, IBM, and Digital Equipment all shift resources and people from area to area on an as-needed basis to support budding ideas and ventures; they empower "product champions" and small bands of would-be entrepreneurs by giving them financial and technical support and by setting up organizational units and programs to facilitate moving things along.

LINKING WORK ASSIGNMENTS TO PERFORMANCE TARGETS

As previously indicated, successful strategy implementation and execution is assisted when critical tasks and key activities are linked directly and clearly to accomplishing the strategic plan. Defining jobs and assignments in terms of the strategic results to be accomplished (not just in terms of the duties and functions to be performed) adds an equally important linkage.

The value of defining jobs and assignments in terms of what is to be accomplished is that it makes the work environment results-oriented and performance-oriented. From a strategy perspective, what is to be accomplished is (1) carrying out the strategy and (2) achieving the target levels of organization performance. When an organization's attention and its energies are kept firmly trained on executing strategy and achieving the agreed-upon objectives, the chances for accomplishing the strategic plan are decidedly greater.

The question, then, is how to keep the organization trained on achieving the right strategic results, as opposed to routinely carrying out duties and functions in hopes that the by-product will be the desired levels of performance. Making the right things happen, rather than hoping they will happen, is, of course, what "managing with objectives" is all about. For the tool of managing with objectives to be of real assistance in implementing and executing the strategic plan, two things must happen. One, the strategy manager must insist that jobs and assignments be defined *primarily* in terms of the results to be accomplished and *sec-*

---

[17]Peters and Waterman, *In Search of Excellence*, p. 125.

ondarily in terms of descriptions of the duties and functions to be performed. The danger of the latter is that it is very easy for people and organization subunits to become so engrossed in doing their duties and performing their functions that they lose sight of what it is the functions and duties are intended to accomplish in the first place. By defining jobs and activities in terms of what strategic results and objectives are to be achieved, the spotlight is kept on accomplishment of the strategic plan. Two, the strategy-manager must not waver far from the standard that "doing a good job" *equals* "achieving the agreed-upon strategic objectives and performance." Any other standard simply serves to undermine strategy implementation and to condone the diversion of time and money into activities that don't really matter much.

Using performance objectives as the ultimate results for work and job assignments, therefore, begins with the question, "What are our objectives and what results do we want to show for our efforts?" If the details of strategy have been fleshed out thoroughly from the corporate level on down to the operating level, the answers to this question are explicit in the strategic plan itself or, at least, are reasonably unambiguous in the minds of the managers of each organizational unit. Otherwise, the answers are suggested by the role and contribution expected of the organization unit in achieving financial-performance targets and in carrying out day-to-day operations. Keep in mind that strategy-making involves establishing specific objectives and performance targets not only for the organization as a whole but also for each organizational subunit. While there is ample room for the agreed-upon objectives and results to reflect both top-down and bottom-up considerations, the key is to promote understanding and emphasis on what each organizational unit's part is in achieving the target levels of strategic performance. This makes clearer the kind of work and effort that can be strategically productive. It relates departments and functional areas to the strategic needs of the organization as a whole. But most important, it lets people know what is expected of them—*from a results perspective,* instead of from an activity and effort perspective. The pressure to perform should be nothing short of brutal. A "no excuses" environment has to prevail.[18]

Next, it must be asked, "What specific activities, work assignments, and jobs are needed to produce the target levels of performance?" The answers here should suggest the skills, technical expertise, staffing, and funding needed to reach the established objectives.

Finally, managers have to address "How can jobs and work efforts in my unit be designed around the unit's strategy-related objectives?" Placing the emphasis of job design and work assignments on "what to accomplish" instead of "what to do" is an important difference. As any student knows, just because an instructor conducts his or her classes regularly, it cannot be safely assumed that students are learning what they are being taught—teaching and learning are different things. The first is an activity and the second is a result.

In any job, doing an activity is not equivalent to achieving the intended objective. Working hard, staying busy, and diligently attending to one's duties do not guar-

---

[18]Tom Peters and Nancy Austin, *A Passion for Excellence* (New York: Random House, 1985), p. xix.

antee results. Hence, the creativity of managers in drawing attention to the right things to shoot for (accomplishing our part of the strategic plan) and creating a results-oriented work environment (where work efforts are aimed squarely at reaching the unit's target-performance objectives) is more than incidental. Indeed, figuring out how to make the achievement of strategy-related objectives a way of life up and down the whole organization is central to the task of strategy implementation. *The more that organization energies and resources flow in the direction of strategy execution, the more that strategy implementation stays on track.*

ANALYTICAL CHECKLIST

Linking daily activities and work efforts directly and clearly to accomplishing the organization's strategic plan is critical to successful strategy implementation. The three strategy-implementing tasks of a manager which aim at creating this linkage are (1) building a capable organization, (2) creating a strategy-supportive budget, and (3) focusing work efforts on performance objectives. The first task centers around the strategy-critical components of matching of structure to fit the requirements of strategy and of staffing each organizational unit with the skills, expertise, and competences it needs to carry out its assigned role in the strategic plan. The second task involves providing organizational units with the budgetary resources and priorities requisite for accomplishing their piece of the overall strategy. The third task entails keeping organizationwide attention focused on "what to achieve" (the targeted strategic objectives) and not letting work efforts aim simply at "what to do."

All three tasks are an integral part of the foundation for strategy implementation. In the next chapter, we shall examine the rest of the strategy-implementers' job of converting strategy into action and then into results.

SUGGESTED READINGS

Bettis, Richard A. and William K. Hall. "The Business Portfolio Approach—Where It Falls Down in Practice." *Long Range Planning* 16, no. 2 (April 1983), pp. 95–104.

Chandler, Alfred D. *Strategy and Structure.* Cambridge, Mass.: MIT Press, 1962.

Corey, Raymond E., and Steven H. Star. *Organization Strategy: A Marketing Approach.* Boston: Division of Research, Harvard University Graduate School of Business Administration, 1971, chaps. 2, 3, 4, and 5.

Davis, Stanley M., and Paul R. Lawrence. "Problems of Matrix Organizations." *Harvard Business Review* 56, no. 3 (May–June 1978), pp. 131–42.

Drucker, Peter. *Management: Tasks, Responsibilities, Practices.* New York: Harper & Row, 1974, chaps. 41–48.

Hall, William K. "SBUs: Hot, New Topic in the Management of Diversification." *Business Horizons* 21, no. 1 (February 1978), pp. 17–25.

Hambrick, Donald C. "The Top Management Team: Key to Strategic Success." *California Management Review* 30, no. 1 (Fall 1987), pp. 88–108.

Larson, Erik W., and David H. Gobeli. "Matrix Management: Contradictions and Insights." *California Management Review* 29, no. 4 (Summer 1987), pp. 126–38.

Leontiades, Milton. "Choosing the Right Manager to Fit the Strategy." *Journal of Business Strategy* 3, no. 2 (Fall 1981), pp. 58–69.

Lorsch, Jay W., and Arthur H. Walker. "Organizational Choice: Product vs. Function." *Harvard Business Review* 46, no. 6 (November–December 1968), pp. 129–38.

Mintzberg, Henry. "Organization Design: Fashion or Fit." *Harvard Business Review* 59, no. 1 (January–February 1981), pp. 103–116.

Paulson, Robert D. "Making It Happen: The Real Strategic Challenge." *The McKinsey Quarterly*, Winter 1982, pp. 58–66.

Peters, Thomas J. "Beyond the Matrix Organization." *Business Horizons* 22, no. 5 (October 1979), pp. 15–27.

Peters, Thomas J., and Robert H. Waterman, Jr. *In Search of Excellence*. New York: Harper & Row, 1982.

Powell, Walter W. "Hybrid Organizational Arrangements: New Form or Transitional Development?" *California Management Review* 30, no. 1 (Fall 1987), pp. 67–87.

Rumelt, Richard. *Strategy, Structure, and Economic Performance*. Cambridge, Mass.: Harvard University Press, 1974.

Salter, Malcolm S. "Stages of Corporate Development." *Journal of Business Policy* 1, no. 1 (1970), pp. 23–37.

Waterman, Robert H.; Thomas J. Peters; and Julien R. Phillips. "Structure Is Not Organization." *Business Horizons* 23, no. 3 (June 1980), pp. 14–26.

10

Implementing Strategy: Commitment, Culture, Support Systems, and Leadership

Weak leadership can wreck the soundest strategy; forceful execution of even a poor plan can often bring victory.

Sun Zi

What gets measured gets done.

Mason Haire

In the previous chapter we examined three of the strategy-implementer's tasks—building a capable organization, steering resources into strategy-critical programs and activities, and creating a tight fit between work assignments and strategic-performance targets. In this chapter we explore the three remaining implementation tasks: galvanizing organizationwide commitment to strategic accomplishment, installing internal administrative support systems, and exercising strategic leadership. These last three tasks touch upon the day-to-day aspects of strategy execution, involving such things as motivation and reward, building a strategy-supportive corporate culture, instituting strategy-related policies and procedures, implementing strategic controls, gathering information about strategic progress, and exercising whatever leadership is needed to keep strategy implementation on course.

GALVANIZING ORGANIZATIONWIDE COMMITMENT TO THE STRATEGIC PLAN

The task of generating, maintaining, and otherwise orchestrating organizationwide commitment to strategy implementation and execution has four pieces:

1. Motivating organizational units and individuals to execute the strategic plan and achieve the targeted results.
2. Building a strategy-supportive corporate culture.

3. Creating a strong results orientation and a spirit of high performance.

4. Linking the reward structure to actual strategic performance.

Motivating People to Execute the Strategy

Obviously, it is important for organizational subunits and individuals to be committed to implementing and accomplishing strategy. Solidifying organization-wide commitment to putting the strategic plan in place, as with anything else that needs doing, is typically achieved via motivation, incentives, and the rewarding of good performance. The range of options for getting people and organizational subunits to push hard for successful strategy implementation involves creatively using the standard reward/punishment mechanisms—salary raises, bonuses, stock options, fringe benefits, promotions (or fear of demotions), assurance of not being sidelined and ignored, praise, recognition, constructive criticism, tension, peer pressure, more (or less) responsibility, increased (or decreased) job control and decision-making autonomy, the promise of attractive locational assignments, and the bonds of group acceptance. The skill is to inspire employees to do their best and to be winners, giving them in the process a sense of ownership in the strategy and a commitment to make it work.

Some actual examples of strategy-supportive motivational approaches indicate the range of options:[1]

- At Mars, Inc. (best known for its candy bars), every employee, including the president, gets a weekly 10 percent bonus by coming to work on time each day that week. This on-time incentive is based on minimizing absenteeism and tardiness so as to boost worker productivity and to produce the greatest number of candy bars during each available minute of machine time.

- In a number of Japanese companies, employees meet regularly to hear inspirational speeches, sing company songs, and chant the corporate litany. In the United States, Tupperware conducts a weekly Monday night rally to honor, applaud, and fire up its salespeople who conduct Tupperware parties. Amway and Mary Kay Cosmetics hold similar inspirational get-togethers for their sales force organizations.

- A San Diego area company assembles its 2,000 employees at its six plants the first thing every workday to listen to a management talk about the state of the company. Then they engage in brisk calisthenics. This company's management believes "that by doing one thing together each day, it reinforces the unity of the company. It's also fun. It gets the blood up." Managers take turns making the presentations. Many of the speeches "are very personal and emotional, not approved beforehand or screened by anybody."

- Texas Instruments and Dana Corporation insist that teams and divisions set their own goals and have regular peer reviews.

- Procter & Gamble's brand managers are asked to compete fiercely against each

---

[1]The list that follows is abstracted from Thomas J. Peters and Robert H. Waterman, Jr., *In Search of Excellence* (New York: Harper & Row, 1982), pp. xx, 213–14, 276, and 285.

other; the official policy is "a free-for-all among brands with no holds barred." P&G's system of purposeful internal competition breeds people who love to compete and excel. Those who "win" become corporate "heroes," and around them emerges a folklore of "war stories" of valiant brand managers who waged uphill struggles against great odds and made a market success out of their assigned brands.

Whereas the above motivational approaches accentuate the positive, others blend positive and negative features. Consider the way Harold Geneen, former president and chief executive officer of ITT, allegedly combined the use of money, tension, and fear:

> Geneen provides his managers with enough incentives to make them tolerate the system. Salaries all the way through ITT are higher than average—Geneen reckons 10 percent higher—so that few people can leave without taking a drop. As one employee put it: "We're all paid just a bit more than we think we're worth." At the very top, where the demands are greatest, the salaries and stock options are sufficient to compensate for the rigors. As some said, "He's got them by their limousines."
>
>   Having bound his men to him with chains of gold, Geneen can induce the tension that drives the machine. "The key to the system," one of his men explains, "is the profit forecast. Once the forecast has been gone over, revised, and agreed on, the managing director has a personal commitment to Geneen to carry it out. That's how he produces the tension on which the success depends." The tension goes through the company, inducing ambition, perhaps exhilaration, but always with some sense of fear: what happens if the target is missed?[2]

It goes without saying that if and when a strategy-implementer's use of rewards and punishments induces too much tension, anxiety, and job insecurity, the results can be counter-productive. Yet, it is doubtful whether it is ever useful to completely eliminate tension, pressure for performance, and anxiety from the strategy-implementation process; there is, for example, no evidence that the quiet life is highly correlated with superior strategy implementation. On the contrary, high-performing organizations need a cadre of ambitious people who relish the opportunity to climb the ladder of success, who love a challenge, who thrive in a performance-oriented environment, and, thus, who find some degree of competition and pressure useful to satisfy their own drives for personal recognition, accomplishment, and self-satisfaction. There almost has to be some meaningful incentive and career consequence associated with implementation, else few people will attach much significance to the strategic plan.

The conventional view is that a manager's push for strategy implementation should incorporate more positive than negative motivational elements because, when cooperation is positively enlisted, rather than negatively strong-armed, people tend to respond with more enthusiasm and more effort. Nevertheless, how much of which incentives to use depends on how hard the task of strategy implementation

---

[2]Anthony Sampson, *The Sovereign State of ITT* (New York: Stein and Day, Publishers, 1973), p. 132.

will be in light of all the obstacles to be overcome. Suffice it to say that a manager has to do more than just talk to everyone about how important strategy implementation is to the organization's future well-being. Talk, no matter how inspiring, seldom commands people's best efforts for long. Ensuring sustained, energetic commitment to strategy virtually always requires resourceful use of incentives. The more that a manager understands what motivates subordinates and the more that motivational incentives are relied upon to implement and execute strategy, the greater will be the commitment to carrying out the strategic plan.

Building a Strategy-Supportive Corporate Culture

Every organization is a unique culture. It has its own special history of how the organization has been managed, its own set ways of approaching problems and conducting activities, its own mix of managerial personalities and styles, its own established patterns of "how we do things around here," its own legendary set of war stories and heroes, its own experiences of how changes have been instituted—in other words, its own climate, folklore, and organization personality. This says something important about the leadership task of orchestrating strategy implementation: *Anything so fundamental as implementing and executing the chosen strategic plan involves moving the whole organizational culture into alignment with strategy.* The optimal condition is a climate so in tune with strategy that execution of the game plan can be truly powerful. As one observer noted:

> It has not been just strategy that led to big Japanese wins in the American auto market. It is a culture that enspirits workers to excel at fits and finishes, to produce moldings that match and doors that don't sag. It is a culture in which Toyota can use that most sophisticated of management tools, the suggestion box, and in two years increase the number of worker suggestions from under 10,000 to over 1 million with resultant savings of $250 million.[3]

The taproot of corporate culture is the philosophy, the attitudes, the beliefs, and the shared values upon and around which the organization operates. Such things in a company's activities can be hard to pin down, even harder to characterize accurately—in a sense, they are intangible and "soft." They manifest in people's attitudes, their feelings, the stories they tell about happenings in the organization, and the "chemistry" and the "vibrations" which emanate from the work environment. What we are beginning to learn and appreciate is that an organization's culture is an important contributor (or obstacle) to successful strategy execution.

The best way to understand corporate culture is by example. Illustration Capsule 19 on the culture at Tandem Computers provides one good example.

Peters and Waterman, in their study of America's best-managed companies, provide some additional insights on what culture is, where to look for it, and why it is relevant:[4]

---

[3]Robert H. Waterman, Jr., "The Seven Elements of Strategic Fit," *Journal of Business Strategy* 2, no. 3 (Winter 1982), p. 70.

[4]Peters and Waterman, *In Search of Excellence*, pp. xxi, 75–77, and 280–85; see also, Thomas J. Peters and Nancy Austin, *A Passion for Excellence* (New York: Random House, 1985), pp. 282–83, and 334.

ILLUSTRATION CAPSULE 19

The Corporate Culture at Tandem Computers

Tandem Computers is a leading producer of modular, expandable, multiple-processor computing systems designed so that failure of no one module can substantially affect system operations—Tandem calls it "the fail-safe nonstop computing system." Tandem's success is tied to offering customers the assurance that they will always have computer power available—if one processing unit breaks down, the backup unit carries on. Tandem's nonstop computer system can support thousands of terminals in online, nonstop conditions, thus preserving data integrity, reliability, and system flexibility. According to Tandem, "no one else has this capability." Key applications are in businesses in which computer "down time" can have serious consequences: electric power monitoring, emergency vehicle dispatching, back office transaction processing for financial institutions, online order entry, credit verification, and inventory control.

Tandem's main operations are in California's famous Silicon Valley where many other electronics firms are located. The Silicon Valley is noted for the fierceness with which area companies compete for talent; demand for talented employees is so high that assembly people, operators, and engineers can literally walk across the street and get a job with another company the next day. The Valley's high-technology companies are constantly "pirating" employees from each other's staffs. Moreover, many of the most creative people are unique personality types, sometimes labeled as "semifreakies" and "pseudohippies," and are products of the California culture of the 1960s and early 1970s, with a preference for openness, spontaneity, nonjudgmental acceptance, brotherhood, freedom, and expressiveness.

The Tandem Gospel

As conceived largely by cofounder-president James G. Treybig, pronounced Try-big, Tandem Computers' approach to dealing with its high-technology employees in the Silicon Valley culture represents "the convergence of capitalism and humanism, and incorporates a blend of ideology and incentives." The ideology centers around Treybig's five cardinal principles for running a company:

1. All people are good.
2. People workers, management, and company are all the same thing.
3. Every single person in a company must understand the essence of the business.
4. Every employee must benefit from the company's success.
5. You must create an environment where all the above can happen.

These principles are pushed in a continual stream of orientation lectures, breakfast meetings, newsletters, a company magazine, and periodic communications with employees—the content of which is predicated on and inspired by a company manual entitled *Understanding Our Philosophy*. All employees are given a copy of the manual and are put through a two-day indoctrination course.

As an example of how conventional platitudes are instilled with new meaning, Treybig took the oft-said phrase "All employees should be treated with respect"

ILLUSTRATION CAPSULE 19 *(continued)*

and translated it at Tandem into "You never have the right at Tandem to screw a person or to mistreat him. It's not allowed. . . . No manager mistreats a human without a fear of his job." This statement is given teeth by giving any aggrieved employee ready access to anyone in the company—"guilty" managers have been fired.

In indoctrinating employees to the Tandem philosophy, pains are taken to explain the essence of the company's business, to give them a companywide perspective, and to go through the company's five-year plan. *Understanding Our Philosophy,* a road map-size chart which took Treybig two weeks to draw up, shows how a performance breakdown in one area spills over into lower performance in other parts of the company. While the main purpose of the big picture approach is to explain what various groups in the company are doing and how it all fits together and, thus, to point people in the direction of strategy accomplishment. It also helps to boost employee enthusiasm and loyalty. As one of the company founders put it, "People really get a great kick out of being part of the team and trusted with the corporate jewels."

Another key part of Tandem's philosophy is that companies can be overmanaged. According to Treybig, "most people need less management than you think." At Tandem, top-management control is not accomplished with numerous reviews, meetings, and reports but rather with giving employees a full understanding and appreciation of the company's business concepts and managerial philosophy. Supervision is loose and flexible. There is no formal organization chart and there are few formal rules. Employees are encouraged to exercise freedom and creativity. They speak in glowing terms about how the company has helped them grow. The importance of people and personal growth is emphasized in Tandem's corporate philosophy, which states: "Tandem's greatest resource—its people, creative action, and fun." T-shirts and bulletin boards proclaim:

Get the job done no matter what it takes.

Tandemize it—means make it work.

It takes two to Tandem.

It's so nice, it's so nice, we do it twice.

Company literature speaks of efforts to foster not just the welfare of employees but also their spouses and "spouse equivalents." Most employees respond positively to all this, describing Tandem's management as "people oriented."

Tandem's Incentive Package

Undergirding the ideology and philosophy is a package of reinforcing incentives and practices. *Every* employee participates in the company's stock option plans. As of mid-1982, an employee who had been with the company since its stock began to be traded publicly in 1977 had received stock options worth almost $100,000. At the company's 1981 Halloween costume party (which was so well attended that the crowd filled most of the large warehouse), the company announced the granting of a 100-share stock option to each of 3,000-plus employees.

ILLUSTRATION CAPSULE 19 *(continued)*

Even with Tandem's rapid growth, three out of five new managers have risen from within the company's ranks.

An abundance of attention is paid to employee working conditions and amenities. Working hours are kept flexible and no one punches a time clock, the philosophy being, "We don't want to pay people for attendance but for output." The company has built a swimming pool, jogging trails, spaces for yoga classes and dance exercise, and a basketball court. There are periodic company-supplied weekend barbecues for employees working overtime. Employees get six-week sabbatical leaves every four years. On Friday afternoons at 4:30, the company conducts its weekly beer bust (attended by about 60 percent of the employees).

Treybig is seen regularly at the beer busts, once coming in a cowboy hat and boots. Associates note that Treybig deliberately does and says things for their shock value. The result, says one vice president, is that "a lot of people when they meet Jim for the first time think he's a bullshitter, just shuckin' and jivin'." Yet, beneath the rhetoric and philosophy are some hardnosed policies.

Enhanced Loyalty and Commitment

Managers are pushed to hire new employees who are smarter and more qualified than they are. Normally, only experienced and proven applicants are seriously considered (to help Tandem gain access to new ideas and the best talent available). Interviews are very thorough, sometimes running 20 hours. Managers, not the personnel department, do the hiring, and prospective co-workers play a big role in the selection process. One employee observed, "A manager will never hire somebody his people don't think is good. Basically, he says will you work with this person, and you say yes or no." Employees are paid a $500 bonus for referring prospective candidates who subsequently are employed over 90 days. The hiring system exposes new employees to the Tandem culture before their first day on the job and endeavors to convey the feeling that they have been chosen by an exacting process. Tandem believes that such an initiation builds dedication because, by being ordeals, people tend to place a higher value on what has cost them a lot.

The results have been impressive. Tandem's productivity figures are among the highest in the industry. The work culture is one of commitment, hard work, loyalty, self-esteem, creativity, learning, personal growth, light supervision, and self-discipline. Tandem's turnover rate is about one third the average for the U.S. computer industry. Many employees are convinced that their jobs are filling their innermost goals of self-realization. Several employee comments about the company's approach and its effects are telling:

I feel like putting a lot of time in. There is a real kind of loyalty here. We are all working in this together—working a process together. I'm not a workaholic—it's just the place. I love the place.

I don't think someone who thought Tandem was just a job would work out because Tandem expects commitment.

I feel like I'm accomplishing something with myself.

ILLUSTRATION CAPSULE 19 *(concluded)*

I speak to my manager about once a month—that's how often my manager manages me.

It's progressive. It's ahead of the times. I don't know what's right or wrong. I know that it's very unique. It sure feels right to me; it fits in with the way I like to see people treated.

Why Does Tandem's Corporate Culture Work?

Part of what makes the corporate culture at Tandem Computers successful, however, is its close fit with the situation. Tandem has one basic product and one clearly defined market. Most of its parts and components are supplied by subcontractors. Everything is cleaned by a contract janitorial service. What manufacturing Tandem does itself is skilled assembly and massive testing—activities that are conducted in quiet, airy rooms more like labs than factories. Most employees are well trained, highly skilled, self-disciplined, and intelligent enough to work well without close supervision. Much of Tandem's work activity is creative and highly technical, and workers need freedom and solitude to perform well. Good performance is handsomely rewarded (although some of the stock options are carefully calibrated to make leaving the company before four years very expensive). Rapid growth and financial success have funded the payment of generous benefits, created numerous promotion opportunities, and otherwise helped to make Tandem's unique blend of ideology and incentive work well up to this point. In addition, Tandem's management is strong, and the company dominates its market niche via careful product engineering, attention to manufacturing and skill in marketing—aspects that are also critical in the computer business.

Irrespective of whether the Tandem approach could be successful in other companies (and it may not continue to work as well at Tandem if growth slows and the company's fortunes slacken), the Tandem experience does spotlight the value of deliberately creating a corporate culture that is in close alignment with strategy.

SOURCE: Based on information reported in Myron Magnet, "Managing by Mystique at Tandem Computers" *Fortune*, June 28, 1982, pp. 84–91; and Terence E. Deal and Allen A. Kennedy, *Corporate Cultures* (Reading, Mass: Addison-Wesley Publishing, 1982), pp. 8–13.

● At Frito-Lay, stories abound about potato chip route salesmen slogging through sleet, mud, hail, snow, and rain to uphold the 99.5 percent service level to customers in which the entire organization takes such great pride. At IBM, the key themes are respect for the individual and services to the customer. At Procter & Gamble, the overarching value is product quality. At McDonald's, the dominant factors are quality, service, cleanliness, and value, and the emphasis is on attention to detail and perfecting every fundamental of the business. At Delta Airlines, the culture is driven by "Delta's family feeling" that builds a team spirit and nurtures each employee's cooperative attitude toward others, cheerful outlook toward life, and pride in a job well done. At Johnson &

Johnson, the credo is that customers come first, employees second, the community third, and shareholders fourth and last. At Du Pont, there is a fixation on safety—a report of every accident must be on the chairman's desk within 24 hours (Du Pont's safety record is 17 times better than the chemical industry average and 68 times better than the all-manufacturing average).

- Companies with strong cultures are unashamed collectors and tellers of stories, anecdotes, and legends in support of basic beliefs. L. L. Bean tells customer service stories. 3M tells innovation stories. P&G, Johnson & Johnson, Perdue Farms, and Maytag tell quality stories. From an organizational standpoint, such tales are very important because people in the organization take pride in identifying strongly with the stories, and they start to share in the traditions and values which the stories relate.

- The most typical values and beliefs which shape culture include (1) a belief in being the best (or, as at GE, "better than the best"), (2) a belief in superior quality and service, (3) a belief in the importance of people as individuals and a faith in their ability to make a strong, positive contribution, (4) a belief in the importance of the details of execution, the nuts and bolts of doing the job well, (5) a belief that customers should reign supreme, (6) a belief in inspiring the best of people whatever their ability, (7) a belief in the importance of informality to enhance communication, and (8) a recognition that growth and profits are essential to a company's well-being. While the themes are common, however, every company implements them differently (to fit their particular situations), and every company's values are the articulated handiwork of one or two legendary figures in leadership positions. Accordingly, each company has its own distinct culture which, they believe, no one can copy successfully.

- In companies with strong cultures, managers and workers either "buy in" to the culture and accept its norms or else they opt out and leave the company.

- The stronger the corporate culture and the more it is directed toward customers and markets, the less a company uses policy manuals, organization charts, and detailed rules and procedures to enforce discipline and norms. The reason is that the guiding values inherent in the culture convey in crystal-clear fashion what everybody is supposed to do in most situations. Often, poorly performing companies have strong cultures, too. The difference is that their cultures are dysfunctional, being focused on internal politics or operating by the numbers as opposed to emphasizing customers and the people who make and sell the product.

- Companies with strong cultures are clear on what they stand for, and they take the process of shaping values and reinforcing cultural norms. Significantly, the values these companies espouse undergird the strategies they employ.

While one can become impressed quickly with the contribution culture can have on "keeping the herd moving roughly West" (as Professor Terry Deal puts it), the strategy-implementer's concern is with how the values get laid down and instilled in an organization's norms and activities. Building a strategy-supportive culture hinges directly on the abilities and actions of the strategy manager. The value-shaping, culture-building task of the manager is concerned, on the one hand, with specifying lofty, inspirational visions that will generate enthusiasm organization-wide—not just among a few top-level subordinates—and, on the other hand, with instilling these values mainly through actions and deeds, rather than emotional rhetoric.[5] Words alone don't work. Instead, value-building and culture-shaping hinge on scores of actions at the most mundane levels of detail. No ceremonial function and no conversation is too insignificant. Implanting the desired values derives from obvious, sincere, sustained commitment by the chief executive, coupled with extraordinary persistence in reinforcing those values at every opportunity through both word and deed. Neither charisma nor personal magnetism are necessary. However, being highly visible around and about the organization on a regular basis is essential; the job cannot be done from one's office through written pronouncements.

Creating a Fit between Strategy and Culture. It is the strategy-maker's responsibility to choose a strategy that is compatible with the "sacred" or unchangeable parts of the prevailing corporate culture. It is the strategy-implementer's task, once strategy is chosen, to bring the corporate culture into alignment with strategy and keep it there.

Creating an organizational culture which is fully harmonized with the strategic plan offers a strong challenge to the strategy-implementer's administrative leadership abilities. *Step 1* is to diagnose which facets of the present culture are in line with strategy and which are not. *Step 2* is to develop ways to make the needed changes in culture and to recognize how long it will take for the new culture, once culture-changing actions are initiated, to take hold (an overnight transformation is seldom possible!). In fact, it is usually a tougher task to reshape a deeply ingrained culture that is not strategy-supportive than it is to instill a strategy-supportive culture from scratch in a brand new organization.

Step 3 is to use the available opportunities to make incremental changes that improve the alignment of culture and strategy. Such opportunities crop up regularly: New and vacant positions can be filled with people who are willing and able to refashion the old ways of doing things; the appearance of a new problem can pave the way for making a desirable policy change; those proposals of subordinates which have positive culture impacts can be strongly supported; individuals and subunits that "get with the program" can be visibly rewarded and singled out for praise; and the annual budgetary process can be used as a vehicle to steer resources into activities and events that promote the desired culture.

Step 4 is to insist that subordinate managers take actions of their own to set an example and to do things which will further instill organizational values and reinforce the culture. *Step 5* is to proactively build and nurture the emotional commitment that managers and employees have to the strategy—to produce a temperamental fit between culture and the overall strategic plan.

Normally, managerial *actions taken to modify corporate culture need to be both symbolic and substantive*. The strategy-manager's leadership role is essential here. In addition to being out front, personally keynoting the push for new attitudes and communicating widely and often the reasons for new approaches, the manager has

---

[5]Peters and Waterman, *In Search of Excellence*, pp. 287–88. The leadership role of the strategy manager is discussed in considerably more detail in Peters and Austin, *A Passion for Excellence*, chaps. 16–19.

to convince the organization that more than cosmetics is involved. Talk has to be backed up by substance and real movement. The actions taken have to be credible, highly visible, and serve as unmistakable signals to the whole organization of the seriousness of management's commitment to a new climate and culture. Some quick successes in reorienting the way some things are done help to highlight the value of the new order, thus making enthusiasm for the changes contagious. However, figuring out how to get some instant results is usually not as important as having the will and patience to mold the parts of the organization into a solid, competent team which is psychologically committed to carrying out the strategy in a superior fashion.

Creating a Results Orientation and a Spirit of High Performance

The degree to which an organization's culture is results-oriented hinges directly on defining and enforcing performance standards at each organization level. The most relevant strategy-related performance measures to use are those stated or implied in the strategic plan. If the strategic plan does not contain a full set of explicit objectives for the organization as a whole, for each line of business, for each functional area within a business, and for each operating-level unit, then specific performance measures need to be agreed upon early in the strategy-implementation phase.

Usually a number of performance measures are needed at each level; rarely will a single measure suffice. At the corporate and line-of-business levels, the typical performance measures include profitability (measured in terms of total profit, return on equity investment, return on total assets, return on sales, operating profit, and so on), market share, growth rates in sales and profits, and hard evidence that competitive position and future prospects have improved. In the manufacturing area, the strategy-relevant performance measures may focus on unit manufacturing costs, productivity increases, meeting production and shipping schedules, quality control, the number and extent of work stoppages due to labor disagreements and equipment breakdowns, and so on. In the marketing area, the measures may include unit selling costs, the increases in dollar sales and unit volume, the degree of sales penetration of each target customer group, increases in market share, the success of newly introduced products, the severity of customer complaints, advertising effectiveness, and the number of new accounts acquired. While most performance measures are quantitative in nature, there are always several which have elements of subjectivity—improvements in labor-management relations, whether employee morale is up or down, whether customers are more or less satisfied with the quality of the firm's products, what impact advertising is having, and how far the firm is ahead or behind rivals on quality, service, technological capability, and other key success factors.

The Importance of a Results Orientation and a Spirit of High Performance. An ability to instill high levels of commitment to strategic success and to create an atmosphere where there is constructive pressure to perform is one of the most valuable strategy-implementing skills. When an organization performs consistently at or near peak capability, the outcome is not only improved strategic success but also an organizational climate where the emphasis is on excellence and achievement—a spirit of high performance pervades. Such a spirit of performance should not be confused with whether employees are "happy" or "satisfied" or whether they "get along well together." For an organization to be instilled with and sustain a spirit of performance, it must maintain a focus on achievement and on excellence. It must strive at developing a consistent ability to produce results over prolonged periods. It must succeed in utilizing the full range of rewards and punishment to establish and enforce standards of excellence.

The successful approaches to creating a spirit of high performance involve an intense people-orientation, reinforced at every conceivable occasion in every conceivable way and mirrored to down-the-line people in every activity. The goal is to get everybody in the organization involved and emotionally committed. The idea is to try to generate contagious enthusiasm at all levels and among all employees, utilizing a tough-minded respect for the individual employee, a willingness to train each employee thoroughly, a belief in setting reasonable and clear performance expectations, and a painstaking effort to grant employees enough autonomy to stand out, excel, and contribute. An important aspect of creating a results-oriented organizational culture is making champions out of the people who turn in winning performances; examples of how this is done are cited below:[6]

- At Boeing, IBM, General Electric, and 3M Corporation, top executives deliberately make "champions" out of individuals who believe so strongly in their ideas that they take it on themselves to hurdle the bureaucracy, maneuver their projects through the system, and turn them into improved services, new products, or even new businesses. In these companies, "product champions" are given high visibility, room to push their ideas, and strong executive support. Champions whose ideas prove out are usually handsomely rewarded; those whose ideas don't pan out still have secure jobs and are given chances to try again.

- The manager of a New York area sales office rented the Meadowlands Stadium (home field of the New York Giants) for an evening. After work, the salesmen were all assembled at the stadium and then asked to run one at a time through the player's tunnel onto the field. As each one emerged, the electronic scoreboard flashed his name to those gathered specially in the stands—executives from corporate headquarters, employees from the office, family, and friends. Their role was to cheer loudly in honor of the individual's sales accomplishments. The company involved was IBM. The occasion for this action was to reaffirm IBM's commitment to be part of something great and to reiterate IBM's concern for championing individual accomplishment.

- Some companies upgrade the importance and status of individual employees by referring to them as Cast Members (Disney), Crew Members (McDonald's), or Associates (Wal-Mart and J. C. Penney). Companies like IBM, Tupperware, and McDonald's actively seek out reasons and opportunities to give pins,

---

[6]Peters and Waterman, *In Search of Excellence*, pp. xviii, 240, and 269; and Peters and Austin, *A Passion for Excellence*, pp. 304–07.

buttons, badges, and medals to good showings by average performers—the idea being to show appreciation and help give a boost to the "middle 60 percent" of the work force.

* McDonald's has a contest to determine the best hamburger cooker in its entire chain. It begins with a competition to determine the best hamburger cooker in each store. Store winners go on to compete in regional championships, and regional winners go on to the "All-American" contest. The winners get trophies and an All-American patch to wear on their shirts.

* Milliken & Company holds Corporate Sharing Rallies once every three months at which teams come from all over the company to swap success stories and ideas. A hundred or more teams make five-minute presentations over a two-day period. Each rally has a major theme—quality, cost reduction, and so on. No criticisms and negatives are allowed, and there is no such thing as a big idea or a small one. Quantitative measures of success are used to gauge improvement. All those present vote on the best presentation and several ascending grades of awards are handed out. Everyone, however, receives a framed certificate for participating.

What makes a spirit of high performance come alive is more than a belief or statement or philosophy or program. It is a complex network of practices, words, symbols, styles, values, and policies pulling together to form a system that produces an ability to achieve extraordinary results with ordinary people. The drivers of the system are a belief in the worth of the individual, attention to detail, and an effort to do the "itty-bitty, teeny-tiny things" right.

While emphasizing a spirit of high performance nearly always accentuates the positive, there are negative aspects, too. Managers whose units consistently rank poor on performance have to be removed. Aside from the organizational benefits, weak-performing managers should be reassigned for their own good—people who find themselves in a job they cannot handle are usually frustrated, anxiety ridden, harassed, and unhappy.[7] Moreover, subordinates have a right to be managed with competence, dedication, and achievement; unless their boss performs well, they themselves cannot perform well.

Linking Rewards to Performance

If strategy accomplishment is to be a really top-priority activity, then the reward structure must be linked explicitly and tightly to actual strategic performance. *Decisions on salary increases, on promotions, on who gets which key assignments, and on the ways and means of awarding praise and recognition are the strategy-implementer's foremost attention-getting, commitment-generating devices.* How a manager parcels out the rewards signals who is perceived as doing a good job and what sort of behavior and performance management wants. Such matters seldom escape the closest scrunity of every member of the organization. If anything, people will overreact to the system of incentives and how rewards are handed out—

---

[7]Drucker, *Management*, p. 457.

indeed, pursuit of rewards sometimes becomes so zealous that abuses of the system creep in.

Creating a tight fit between strategy and the reward structure is generally best accomplished by agreeing upon strategic objectives, fixing responsibility and deadlines for achieving them, and then treating their achievement as a *contract*. Next, the contracted-for strategic performance has to be the *real* basis for designing incentives, evaluating individual efforts, and handing out rewards. To prevent undermining and undoing the whole managing-with-objectives approach to strategy implementation, a manager must insist that actual performance be judiciously compared against the contracted-for target objectives. The reasons for any deviations have to be explored fully to determine whether the causes are attributable to poor individual performance or to circumstances beyond the individual's control. All managers need to understand clearly how their rewards have been calculated. In short, managers at all levels have to be held accountable for carrying out their assigned part of the strategic plan, and they have to know their rewards are based on the caliber of their strategic accomplishments (allowing for both the favorable and unfavorable impacts of uncontrollable, unforseeable, and unknowable circumstances).

INSTALLING INTERNAL ADMINISTRATIVE SUPPORT SYSTEMS: CREATING MORE FITS

The fifth key task of strategy implementation concerns installing internal administrative support systems which fit the needs of strategy. The specific strategy-implementing considerations here are:

1. What kinds of strategy-facilitating policies and procedures to establish.
2. How to get the right strategy-critical information on a timely basis.
3. What controls are needed to keep the organization on its strategic course.

Implementing Strategy-Supportive Policies and Procedures

Changes in strategy generally call for some changes in how internal activities are conducted and administered. The process of changing from the old ways to the new ways has to be initiated and managed. Asking people to alter actions and practices always upsets the internal order of things somewhat. It is normal for pockets of resistance to emerge and, certainly, questions will be raised about the *hows* as well as the whys of change. The role of new and revised policies is to promulgate standard operating procedures that will (1) facilitate strategy implementation and (2) counteract any tendencies for parts of the organization to resist or reject the chosen strategy. Policies and procedures help enforce strategy implementation in several noteworthy respects:

1. Policy acts as a lever for institutionalizing strategy-supportive practices and operating procedures on an organizationwide basis, thus pushing day-to-day activities in the direction of efficient strategy execution.
2. Policy places limits on independent action and sets boundaries on the kinds and directions of action that can be taken. By making a statement about how

things are now to be done, policy communicates what is expected, guides strategy-related activities in particular directions, and places bounds on unwanted variations.

3. Policy acts to align actions and behavior with strategy throughout the organization, thereby minimizing zigzag decisions and conflicting practices and establishing some degree of regularity, stability, and dependability in how the organization is attempting to make the strategy work.

4. Policy helps to shape the character of the internal work climate and to translate the corporate philosophy into how things are done, how people are treated, and what the corporate beliefs and attitudes mean in terms of everyday activities. Policy operationalizes the corporate philosophy, thus potentially playing a key role in establishing a fit between corporate culture and strategy.

From a strategy-implementation perspective, managers need to be inventive in establishing policies that can provide vital support to an organization's strategic plan. IBM's policy of trying to offer the best service of any company in the world undergirds its whole competitive strategy and corporate philosophy. McDonald's policy manual, in an attempt to channel "crew members" into stronger quality and service behavior patterns, spells out such detailed procedures as: "Cooks must turn, never flip, hamburgers. If they haven't been purchased, Big Macs must be discarded in 10 minutes after being cooked and french fries in 7 minutes. Cashiers must make eye contact with and smile at every customer." At Delta Airlines, it is corporate policy to check out all stewardess applicants thoroughly regarding their aptitudes for friendliness, cooperativeness, and teamwork. Caterpillar Tractor has a policy of giving its customers 48-hour guaranteed parts delivery anywhere in the world, and, if it fails to fulfill the promise, the part is supplied free of charge. Hewlett-Packard has a policy requiring R&D people to make regular visits to customer premises to learn of their problems, to talk about new product applications, and, in general, to keep the company's R&D programs customer-oriented.

Thus, there is a definite role for policies and procedures in the strategy-implementation process. Wisely constructed policies and procedures help enforce strategy implementation by channeling actions, behavior, decisions, and practices in directions which promote strategy accomplishment. Management failure to check out the alignment between existing policies and strategy runs the risk that some existing policies will act as burdensome obstacles to overcome and that people who disagree with the strategy will utilize certain policies to thwart or even defeat the strategic plan. On the other hand, consciously instituting policies and procedures that promote strategy-supportive behavior builds organization commitment to the strategic plan and creates a tighter fit between corporate culture and strategy.

None of this is meant to imply, however, that a fat, omnibus manual of policies is called for. Too much policy can be as stifling as wrong policy or as chaotic as no policy. Sometimes, the best policy for implementing strategy is a willingness to let subordinates do it any way they want if it makes sense and works. A little structured chaos can be a good thing where individual creativity is more essential to strategy than standardization and strict conformity. When Rene McPherson became CEO at Dana Corporation, he dramatically threw out 22.5 inches of policy manuals and replaced them with a one-page statement of philosophy focusing on "productive people."[8] Creating a strong supportive fit between strategy and policy can mean more policies, less policies, or different policies. It can mean policies that require things to be done a certain way or policies that give the person performing a job the autonomy to do it the way he or she thinks best.

Gathering Strategy-Critical Information—The MBWA Approach

To stay on top of how well the strategy-implementation process is going, a manager needs to develop a broad network of contacts and sources of information, both formal and informal. The regular channels include talking with key subordinates, reading written reports, gleaning statistics from the latest operating results, getting feedback from customers, watching the competitive reactions of rival firms, tapping into the flow of gossip through the grapevine, listening to what is on the minds of rank-and-file employees, and firsthand observation. However, some of this information tends to be more trustworthy than others. The content of formal written reports may represent the truth but not the whole truth. Bad news may be covered up, minimized, or not reported at all. Sometimes subordinates delay conveying failures and problems in hopes that more time will give them room to turn things around. As information flows up an organization, there is a tendency for it to get censored and sterilized to the point that it may fail to reveal strategy-critical information. Hence, there is reason for strategy-managers to guard against major surprises by making sure that they have accurate information and a "feel" for the existing situation. The chief way this is done is by regular visits to the field and talking with many different people at many different levels. The technique of *managing by wandering around* (MBWA) is practiced in a variety of styles:[9]

- At Hewlett-Packard, there are weekly beer busts in each division, attended by both executives and employees, to create a regular opportunity to keep in touch. Tidbits of information flow freely between down-the-line employees and executives—facilitated in part because "the H-P Way" is for people at all ranks to be addressed by their first names. Bill Hewlett, one of HP's co-founders, had a companywide reputation for getting out of his office and "wandering around" the plant greeting people, listening to what was on their minds, and asking questions. He found this so valuable that he made MBWA a standard practice for all H-P managers. Furthermore, ad hoc meetings of people from different departments spontaneously arise; they gather in rooms with blackboards and work out solutions informally.

- McDonald's founder Ray Kroc regularly visited store units and did his own personal inspection on Q.S.C.& V. (Quality, Service, Cleanliness, and Value)—the themes he preached regularly. There are stories of him pulling

---

[8]Peters and Waterman, *In Search of Excellence*, p. 65.

[9]*Ibid.*, pp. xx, 15, 120–23, 191, 242–43, 246–47, 287–90. For an extensive report on the benefits of MBWA, see Thomas J. Peters and Nancy Austin, *A Passion for Excellence* (New York: Random House, 1985), chaps. 2, 3, and 19.

into a unit's parking lot, seeing litter lying on the pavement, getting out of his limousine to pick it up himself, and then lecturing the store staff at length on the subject of cleanliness.

- The CEO of a firm making titanium products, spends much of his time riding around the factory in a golf cart, waving and joking with workers, listening to them, and calling all 2,000 employees by their first names. In addition, he spends a lot of time with union officials, inviting them to meetings and keeping them well informed about what is going on.

- Sam Walton, Wal-Mart's founder, insists "The key is to get out into the store and listen to what the associates have to say. Our best ideas come from clerks and stockboys." Walton himself visits every one of Wal-Mart's 700-plus stores every year (a policy he has followed since 1962 when there were just 18 stores). On one occasion he flew the company plane to a Texas town, got out, and instructed the copilot to meet him 100 miles down the road. Then he flagged a Wal-Mart truck and rode the rest of the way to "chat with the driver—it seemed like so much fun." Walton makes a practice of greeting store managers and their spouses by name at annual meetings and has been known to go to the company's distribution centers at 2 A.M. (carrying boxes of doughnuts to share with all those on duty) to have a chance to find out what was on their minds.

- When Ed Carlson became CEO at United Airlines, he traveled about 200,000 miles a year talking with United's employees. He observed, "I wanted these people to identify me and to feel sufficiently comfortable to make suggestions or even argue with me if that's what they felt like doing. . . . Whenever I picked up some information, I would call the senior officer of the division and say that I had just gotten back from visiting Oakland, Reno, and Las Vegas, and here is what I found." Carlson insisted that his top 15 executives travel 200,000 miles yearly, too; all 15 spent 65 percent or more of their time in the field.

- At Marriott Corporation, Bill Marriott not only personally inspects all Marriott hotels at least once a year but he also invites all Marriott guests to send him their evaluations of Marriott's facilities and services. He personally reads every customer complaint and has been known to telephone hotel managers about them.

Managers at many companies attach great importance to informal communications. They report that it is essential to have a "feel" for situations and to gain quick, easy access to information. When executives stay in their offices, they tend to become isolated and often surround themselves with people who are not likely to offer criticisms and different perspectives; then, prompt, flexible, timely solutions to problems go by the wayside.

Instituting Formal Reporting of Strategic Information

Naturally, more than informal communications and personal contacts with field operations are called for. A formal effort to gather and report strategy-critical information is necessary. The work of individuals and subunits has to be monitored beyond just the controls of budgets, the reward structure, established policies and procedures, cultural norms, and networks of personal contacts.

In designing formal reports to monitor strategic progress, five guidelines can be recommended:[10]

1. Information and reporting systems should involve no more data and reporting than is really needed to give a reliable picture of what is going on. The information gathered should emphasize strategically meaningful variables and symptoms of potentially significant developments. Temptations to supplement "what managers need to know" with other "interesting" but marginally useful information should be avoided.
2. Reports and statistical data gathering have to be timely—not come too late to take corrective action nor generated so often as to overburden.
3. The flow of information and statistics should be kept simple. Complicated reports are likely to confound and obscure because of the attention that has to be paid to mechanics, procedures, and interpretive guidelines, instead of measuring and reporting the really critical variables.
4. Information and reporting systems should aim at "no surprises" and generating "early-warning signs," rather than just producing information. It is debatable whether reports should receive wide distribution ("for your information"), but they should, without fail, be put directly in the hands of managers who are in a position to act when trouble signs appear.
5. Statistical reports should make it easy to flag big or unusual variances from plan and the "exceptions," thus directing management attention to significant departures from targeted performance.

Statistical information gives the strategy-implementer a feel for the numbers; reports and meetings provide a feel for new developments and the problems that exist; and personal contacts and conversations add a feel for the people dimension. All are good barometers of the overall tempo of performance and which things are on and off track. Identifying deviations from plan and problems areas to be addressed are prerequisites for initiating actions to either improve implementation or fine tune strategy.

BONDING THE ADMINISTRATIVE FITS: THE ROLE OF SHARED VALUES AND BELIEFS

As emphasized earlier, "fits" with strategy need to be created in many areas, including structure, staffing (both managerial and technical), organizational skills and distinctive competence, budgets, work assignments, rewards and incentives, policies and procedures, shared values and culture, information systems, and controls. The better the "goodness of fit" among these administrative activities and characteristics, the more powerful strategy execution is likely to be.

---

[10]Drucker, *Management,* pp. 498–504; Harold Koontz, "Management Control: A Suggested Formulation of Principles," *California Management Review* 2, no. 2 (Winter 1959), pp. 50–55; and William H. Sihler, "Toward Better Management Control Systems," *California Management Review* 14, no. 2 (Winter 1971), pp. 33–39.

McKinsey & Company, a leading consulting firm with wide-ranging experiences in strategic analysis, has developed a framework for examining the fits in seven broad areas: (1) strategy; (2) structure; (3) shared values, attitudes, and philosophy; (4) approach to staffing the organization and its overall "people orientation"; (5) administrative systems, practice, and procedures used to run the organization on a day-to-day basis, including the reward structure, formal and informal policies, budgeting and programs, training, cost accounting, and financial controls; (6) the organization's skills, capabilities, and distinctive competence; and (7) style of top management (how they allocate their time and attention, symbolic actions, their leadership skills, the way the top-management team comes across to the rest of the organization).[11] McKinsey has diagramed these seven elements into what it calls the McKinsey 7-S Framework (the seven S's are strategy, structure, shared values, staff, systems, skills, and style—so labeled to promote recall), shown in Figure 10–1. Shared values are the central core of the framework because they are the heart-and-soul themes around which an organization rallies; they define its main beliefs and aspirations, its guiding concepts of "who we are, what we do, where we are headed, and what principles we will stand for in getting there." They drive the corporate culture.

The virtue of the McKinsey 7-S Framework is that it draws attention to some important organizational interconnections and why these interconnections are relevant in trying to effect change. In orchestrating a major shift in strategy and gathering full momentum for implementation, the pace of real change will be governed by all seven S's. The 7-S framework is a simple way to illustrate that the job of implementing strategy is one of bringing all seven S's into harmony. When the seven S's are in good alignment, an organization is poised and energized to execute strategy to the best of its ability.

EXERTING STRATEGIC LEADERSHIP

The litany of good strategic management is simple: formulate a sound strategic plan, implement it, execute it to the fullest, win! It's clearly something that's easier said than done. Exerting take-charge leadership, being a spark plug, ramrodding things through, and getting things done by coaching others to do them are not simple tasks to execute. Moreover, a strategy-manager has many different leadership roles to play: chief entrepreneur, chief administrator, crisis solver, taskmaster, figurehead, spokesman, resource allocator, negotiator, motivator, advisor, inspirationist, consensus builder, policymaker, and so on. Sometimes it is useful to be authoritarian and hardnosed; at other times being a perceptive listener and a compromising decision maker works best; and at still other times a strongly participative, collegial approach is called for. Many occasions call for a highly visible role and extensive time commitments, while others entail a brief ceremonial performance with the details being mostly delegated to subordinates.

---

[11]For a more extended discussion, see Robert H. Waterman, Jr., Thomas J. Peters, and Julien R. Phillips, "Structure Is Not Organization," *Business Horizons* 23, no. 3 (June 1980), pp. 14–26; and Robert H. Waterman, Jr., "The Seven Elements of Strategic Fit," *Journal of Business Strategy* 2, no. 3 (Winter 1982), pp. 68–72.

FIGURE 10–1
Bonding the Administrative Fits: The McKinsey 7-S Framework

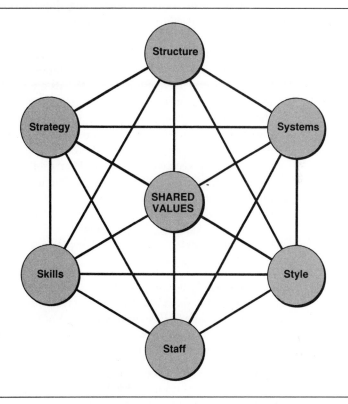

SOURCE: Thomas J. Peters and Robert H. Waterman, Jr., *In Search of Excellence* (New York: Harper & Row, 1982), p. 10.

In general, the problem of strategic leadership is one of diagnosing the situation at hand and choosing from any of several ways to handle it. Four leadership issues dominate the manager's action agenda:

1. What actions to take in promoting a climate and culture in which the organization is "energized" to accomplish strategy and perform at a high level.
2. How to keep the organization responsive to changing conditions, alert for new opportunities, and bubbling with innovative ideas.
3. How to deal with the politics of strategy formulation and implementation, cope with power struggles, and build consensus.
4. When and how to push corrective actions to improve strategy execution and overall strategic performance.

Fostering a Strategy-Supportive Climate and Culture

Strategy-implementers have to be out front in promoting a strategy-supportive organizational climate. When major strategic changes are being implemented, scarcely anything else is likely to constitute a better use of the manager's time than personally leading the way on creating a more strategy-supportive work environment. When only strategic fine tuning is being implemented, less generally needs to be done in bringing values and culture into better alignment with strategy; but there is still a lead role for the manager to play in pushing ahead. As organizational commander-in-chief, the manager always stands squarely in the center ring of attention, keynoting the belief that the chosen strategy is right and that implementing it to the best of the organization's ability is top priority.

Both words and deeds play a part. Words are needed to inspire accomplishment of the strategy, to infuse spirit and drive, to define strategy-supportive cultural norms and values, to articulate the reasons for strategic organizational change, to legitimize new viewpoints and new priorities, to urge and reinforce commitment to the course being charted, and to arouse confidence in the new strategy being implemented. Deeds are essential to add credibility to the words, to create strategy-supportive symbols, to set examples, to give meaning and content to the language, and to teach the organization what sort of behavior is needed and expected.

Highly visible symbols and imagery are needed to complement substantive actions. As an example of the value of symbolic actions, consider the explanation one General Motors manager gave for the striking difference in performance between two large plants:[12]

> At the poorly performing plant, the plant manager probably ventured out on the floor once a week, always in a suit. His comments were distant and perfunctory. At South Gate, the better plant, the plant manager was on the floor all the time. He wore a baseball cap and a UAW jacket. By the way, whose plant do you think was spotless? Whose looked like a junk yard?

At General Electric, a company consistently rated by other CEOs as one of the best-managed industrial corporations in the United States, the chief executive officer, John Welch, has tried to install a new cultural norm by challenging GE's 250-plus business-level managers to "be better than the best." He has translated this theme into a single, overarching performance standard: They must establish their business as number 1 or number 2 in their industries or else achieve a competitive advantage by virtue of decided technological superiority. All business-unit managers are asked to visit the corporate R&D labs for brainstorming sessions that might produce ideas for developing "clear technological edge businesses." Welch's plan calls for divesting businesses that are unable to meet these standards, his belief being that future economic and competitive conditions will leave "no room for the mediocre suppliers of products and services."

As a rule, the greater the degree of strategic change being implemented or the greater the shift in cultural norms needed to accommodate a new strategy, or both, the more visible the strategy-implementer's words and deeds need to be. The lesson from the well-managed companies is that what the manager says and does has a significant bearing on down-the-line strategy implementation and execution.[13] According to one view, "It is not so much the articulation . . . about what an [organization] should be doing that creates new practice. It's the imagery that

---

[12]As quoted in Peters and Waterman, *In Search of Excellence*, p. 262.
[13]Peters and Waterman, *In Search of Excellence*, chap. 9.

creates the understanding, the compelling moral necessity that the new way is right."[14] Moreover, the actions and images, both substantive and symbolic, have to be hammered out regularly, not just restricted to ceremonial speeches and special occasions. This is where a high profile and managing by wandering around comes heavily into play. As a Hewlett-Packard official expresses it in the company publication *The HP Way:*

> Once a division or department has developed a plan of its own—a set of working objectives—it's important for managers and supervisors to keep it in operating condition. This is where observation, measurement, feedback, and guidance come in. It's our "management by wandering around." That's how you find out whether you're on track and heading at the right speed and in the right direction. If you don't constantly monitor how people are operating, not only will they tend to wander off track but also they will begin to believe you weren't serious about the plan in the first place. It has the extra benefit of getting you off your chair and moving around your area. By wandering around, I literally mean moving around and talking to people. It's all done on a very informal and spontaneous basis, but it's important in the course of time to cover the whole territory. You start out by being accessible and approachable, but the main thing is to realize you're there to listen. The second reason for MBWA is that it is vital to keep people informed about what's going on in the company, especially those things that are important to them. The third reason for doing this is because it is just plain fun.

Such contacts give the manager a feel for how things are progressing, and they provide opportunity to speak with encouragement, to uplift spirits, to shift attention from the old to the new priorities, to create some excitement, and to project an atmosphere of informality and fun—all of which drive implementation along in a positive fashion and intensify the organizational energy behind strategy execution. John Welch of General Electric sums up the hands-on role and motivational approach well: "I'm here every day, or out into a factory, smelling it, feeling it, touching it, challenging the people."[15]

Keeping the Internal Organization Responsive and Innovative

While formulating and implementing strategy is very much a manager's responsibility, the task of generating fresh ideas, identifying new opportunities, and being responsive to changing conditions cannot be accomplished by a single person. It is an organizationwide task, particularly in large corporations. One of the toughest parts of exerting strategic leadership is generating a dependable supply of fresh ideas from the rank and file, managers and employees alike, and promoting an entrepreneurial, opportunistic spirit that permits continuous adaptation to changing conditions. A flexible, responsive, innovative internal environment is critical in fast-moving high-technology industries, in businesses where products have short

---

[14]Warren Bennis, *The Unconscious Conspiracy: Why Leaders Can't Lead* (New York: AMACOM, 1987), p. 93.

[15]As quoted in Ann M. Morrison, "Trying to Bring GE to Life," *Fortune,* January 25, 1982, p. 52.

life cycles and growth depends on new product innovation, in managing widely diversified business portfolios (where opportunities are varied and scattered), in industries where successful product differentiation is key, and in businesses where the strategy of being the low-cost producer hinges on productivity improvement and cost reduction. One cannot mandate such an environment by simply exhorting people to be "creative."

One useful leadership approach is to take special pains to foster, nourish, and support people who are willing to champion new ideas, better services, new products and product applications and are eager for a chance to try to turn their ideas into new divisions, new businesses, and even new industries. When Texas Instruments recently reviewed its last 50 or so successful and unsuccessful new-product introductions, one factor marked every failure: "Without exception we found we hadn't had a volunteer champion. There was someone we had cajoled into taking on the task. When we take a look at a product and decide whether to push it or not these days, we've got a new set of criteria. Number one is the presence of a zealous, volunteer champion. After that comes market potential and project economics in a distant second and third."[16] The rule seems to be that the idea of something new or something better either finds a champion or it dies. And the champion is usually persistent, competitive, tenacious, committed, and more than a bit fanatic about the idea and seeing it through to success. An example of a typical champion is presented in Illustration Capsule 20.

Empowering Champions

To promote an organizational climate where champion innovators can blossom and thrive, strategy management needs to do several things. *One,* individuals and groups have to be encouraged to bring their ideas forward. *Two,* the maverick style of the champion has to be tolerated and given room to operate. People's imaginations need to be encouraged to fly in all directions. Autonomy to experiment

---

ILLUSTRATION CAPSULE 20

How the Product Champion Thinks and Works: The Case of Howard Head

Product champions seem to be different types of people. Oftentimes they appear to be obsessed with their ideas, slightly fanatic, bullheaded, willing to battle the status quo and struggle against heavy odds. Nearly always they have the know-how, energy, daring, and staying power to see their ideas through to implementation. A well-known case of a champion at work and what the process is like comes from *Sports Illustrated's* story of Howard Head's invention of the metal snow ski:[1]

---

[16]As quoted in Peters and Waterman, *In Search of Excellence,* pp. 203–4.

ILLUSTRATION CAPSULE 20 *(concluded)*

In 1946 Head went off to Stowe, Vermont, for his first attempt at skiing. "I was humiliated and disgusted by how badly I skied," he recalls, "and, characteristically, I was inclined to blame it on the equipment, those long, clumsy, hickory skis. On my way home I heard myself boasting to an Army officer beside me that I could make a better ski out of aircraft materials than could be made from wood."

Back at Martin [Head's workplace], the cryptic doodles that began appearing on Head's drawing board inspired him to scavenge some aluminum from the plant scrap pile. In his off-hours he set up shop on the second floor of a converted stable in an alley near his one-room basement flat. His idea was to make a "metal sandwich" ski consisting of two layers of aluminum with plywood sidewalls and a center filling of honeycombed plastic.

Needing pressure and heat to fuse the materials together, Head concocted a process that would have made Rube Goldberg proud. To achieve the necessary pressure of 15 pounds per square inch, he put the ski mold into a huge rubber bag and then pumped the air out through a tube attached to an old refrigerator compressor that was hooked up backward to produce suction. For heat, he welded together an iron, coffinlike tank, filled it with motor oil drained from automobile crankcases and, using two Sears Roebuck camp burners, cooked up a smelly 350-degree brew. Then he dumped the rubber bag with the ski mold inside into the tank of boiling oil and sat back like Julia Child waiting for her potato puffs to brown.

Six weeks later, out of the stench and smoke, Head produced his first six pairs of skis and raced off to Stowe to have them tested by pros. To gauge the ski's chamber, an instructor stuck the end of one into the snow and flexed it. It broke. So, eventually, did all six pairs. "Each time one of them broke," says Head, "something inside me snapped with it."

Instead of hanging up his rubber bag, Head quit Martin the day after New Year's 1948, took $6,000 in poker winnings he had stashed under his bed, and went to work in earnest. Each week he would send a new and improved pair of skis to Neil Robinson, a ski instructor in Bromley, Vermont, for testing, and each design would take 40 versions before the ski was any good. "I might have given it up," says Head, "but fortunately, you get trapped into thinking the next design will be it."

Head wrestled with his obsession through three agonizing winters. The refinements were several: steel edges for necessary bite, a plywood core for added strength, and a plastic running surface for smoother, ice-free runs. One crisp day in 1950, Head stood in the bowl of Tuckerman's Ravine in New Hampshire and watched ski instructor Clif Taylor come skimming over the lip of the headwall, do a fishtail on the fall line, and sweep into a long, graceful curve, swooshing to a stop in front of the beaming inventor.

"They're great, Mr. Head, just great," Taylor exclaimed. At that moment, Head says, "I knew deep inside I had it."

[1]The following excerpts are reprinted courtesy of *Sports Illustrated* from the September 29, 1980, issue (pp. 68–70). © 1980 Time. "Howard Head says, 'I'm giving up the thing world'" by Ray Kennedy.

and informal brainstorming sessions need to become ingrained behavior. Above all, people with creative ideas must not be looked upon as disruptive or troublesome. *Three,* managers have to induce and promote lots of "tries" and be willing to tolerate mistakes and failures. Most ideas will not pan out, yet it is likely that a good try results in learning even when it fails. *Four,* strategy-managers should demonstrate a willingness to use all kinds of ad hoc organizational forms to support ideas and experimentation—venture teams, task forces, internal competition among different groups working on the same project (IBM calls the showdown between the competing approaches a "performance shootout"), informal "boot-legged" projects composed of volunteers, and so on. *Five,* strategy-managers have to see that the rewards for a successful champion are large and visible and that people who champion an unsuccessful idea are encouraged to try again, rather than being punished or sidetracked. In effect, the leadership task here is one of putting internal support systems for entrepreneurial innovation into place.

Dealing with Company Politics

It would be naive to presume that a manager can effectively formulate and implement strategy without being perceptive about company politics and being adept at political maneuvering.[17] Politics virtually always comes into play in formulating the strategic plan. Inevitably, key individuals and groups will form coalitions around the issues of which direction the organization should be headed, with each group pressing the benefits and potential of its own ideas and vested interests. Political considerations enter into which strategic objectives will take precedence and which lines of business in the corporate portfolio will have top priority in resource allocation. Internal politics is a factor in building a consensus for which business strategy alternative to employ and in settling upon the role and contribution of each functional area in supporting line of business strategy.

Likewise, there is politics in implementing strategy. Typically, internal political considerations enter into decisions affecting organization structure (whose areas of responsibility need to be reorganized, who reports to whom, who has how much authority over subunits), the choice of individuals to fill key positions and head up strategy-critical activities, and which organizational units get the biggest budget increases. As a case in point, Quinn cites a situation where three strong managers who fought each other constantly formed a potent coalition to resist a reorganization scheme to coordinate the very things that caused their function.[18]

In short, political considerations and the forming of alliances are an integral part of building organizationwide support for the strategic plan and in gaining consensus on the various mechanics of how to implement strategy. Indeed, having astute political skills is a definite, and maybe even a necessary, asset for a manager to have in orchestrating the whole strategic process.

---

[17]For further discussion of this point, see Abraham Zaleznik, "Power and Politics in Organizational Life," *Harvard Business Review* 48, no. 3 (May–June 1970), pp. 47–60; R. M. Cyert, H. A. Simon, and D. B. Trow, "Observation of a Business Decision," *Journal of Business,* October 1956, pp. 237–48; and James Brian Quinn, *Strategies for Change: Logical Incrementalism* (Homewood, Ill.: Richard D. Irwin, 1980).

[18]Quinn, *Strategies for Change,* p. 68.

There is a clear-cut imperative for a strategy-manager to understand how an organization's power structure works, who wields influence in the executive ranks, which groups and individuals are activists and which are defenders of the status quo, who can be helpful in a showdown on key decisions, and which direction the political winds are blowing on a given issue. On those occasions where major decisions have to be made, strategy-managers need to be especially sensitive to the politics of managing coalitions and reaching some consensus on which way to go. As the chairman of a major British corporation expressed it:

> I've never taken a major decision without consulting my colleagues. It would be unimaginable to me, unimaginable. First, they help me make a better decision in most cases. Second, if they know about it and agree with it, they'll back it. Otherwise, they might challenge it, not openly, but subconsciously.[19]

The politics of strategy centers chiefly around stimulating options, nurturing support for strong proposals and killing the weak ones, guiding the formation of coalitions on particular issues, and achieving consensus and commitment. A recent study of strategy management in nine large corporations showed that the political tactics of successful executives included:[20]

- Letting weakly supported ideas and proposals die through inaction.
- Establishing additional hurdles or tests for strongly supported ideas which the manager views as unacceptable but which are best not opposed openly.
- Keeping a low political profile on unacceptable proposals by getting subordinate managers to say "no."
- Letting most negative decisions come from a group consensus that a manager merely confirms, thereby reserving one's own personal vetoes for big issues and crucial moments.
- Leading the strategy but not dictating it—giving few orders, announcing few decisions, depending heavily on informal questioning, and seeking to probe and clarify until a consensus emerges.
- Staying alert to the symbolic impact of one's actions and statements, lest a false signal stimulate proposals and movements in unwanted directions.
- Ensuring that all major power bases within the organization have representation in or access to top management.
- Injecting new faces and new views into considerations of major changes, so as to preclude those who are primarily involved from coming to see the world the same way and then acting as systematic screens against other views.
- Minimizing one's own political exposure on issues which are highly controversial and in circumstances where opposition from major power centers can trigger a shootout.

---

[19]This statement was made by Sir Alastair Pilkington, chairman, Pilkington Brothers, Ltd.; the quote appears in Quinn, *Strategies for Change,* p. 65.

[20]Quinn, *Strategies for Change,* pp. 128–45.

The politics of strategy implementation is especially critical in attempting to introduce a new strategy against the support enjoyed by the old strategy. Except for crisis situations where the old strategy is plainly revealed as out of date, it is usually bad politics to push the new strategy via attacks on the old strategy.[21] Bad-mouthing old strategy can easily be interpreted as an attack on those who formulated it and those who supported it in the enterprise's climb to its present success. Besides, the former strategy and the judgments behind it may have been well suited to the organization's earlier circumstances, and the people who made these judgments may still be in positions where support for the new strategy is important.

In addition, a wise strategy-manager will recognize that there are a variety of legitimate views about what can and should be done in the present circumstances; the new strategy and the plans for implementing it may not have been the first choices of others and lingering doubts may remain. Consequently, in trying to surmount resistance, nothing is gained by knocking the views of those who argued for alternative approaches. Such attacks are likely to produce alienation instead of cooperation.

In short, to bring the full force of an organization behind a strategic plan calls for the strategy-manager to assess and deal with the most important centers of potential support and opposition to new strategic thrusts.[22] One needs to secure the support of key people, co-opt or neutralize serious opposition and resistance when and where necessary, and learn where the zones of indifference are.

Leading the Process of Making Corrective Adjustments

No strategic plan and no scheme for strategy implementation can foresee all the events and problems that will arise. Making adjustments and mid-course corrections are, therefore, a normal and necessary part of strategic management.

Consider, first, the case of reacting and responding to new conditions involving either the strategy or its implementation. The process of what to do starts with an evaluation of whether immediate action needs to be taken or whether time permits a more deliberate response. In a crisis, the typical approach is to wield a heavy hand in pushing key subordinates to gather as much information as time permits and to formulate recommendations for consideration, personally presiding over extended discussions of the pros and cons of proposed responses, and trying to build a quick consensus among members of the executive inner circle. If no consensus emerges, or if several key subordinates remain divided in their views, the burden falls on the strategy-manager to choose the response and urge best-efforts support of it.

In cases where time permits a full-fledged evaluation, strategy-managers seem to prefer a process of incrementally solidifying commitment to a response.[23] The approach seems to be one of consciously:

1. Staying flexible and keeping a number of options open.

---

[21]Ibid., pp. 118–19.
[22]Ibid., p. 205.
[23]Ibid., pp. 20–22.

2. Asking a lot of questions.
3. Gaining in-depth information from specialists.
4. Encouraging subordinates to participate in developing alternatives and proposing solutions.
5. Getting the reactions of many different people to proposed solutions, as a test of their potential and political acceptability.
6. Seeking to build commitment to a response by gradually moving toward a consensus solution.

The governing principle seems to be to make a final decision as late as possible, and thus (1) bring as much information to bear as is needed, (2) let the situation clarify enough to know what to do, and (3) allow the various political constituencies and power bases within the organization to move toward a consensus solution. Executives are often wary of committing themselves to a major change too soon, because it discourages others from asking questions that need to be raised.

Corrective adjustments to strategy need not be just reactive, however. Proactive adjustments constitute a second approach to improving strategy or its implementation. The distinctive feature of a proactive posture is that adjusting actions arise out of management's own drives and initiatives for better performance, as opposed to forced reactions. Successful strategy-managers have been observed to employ a variety of proactive tactics.[24]

1. Commissioning studies to explore and amplify areas where they have a "gut feeling" or sense a need exists.
2. Shopping ideas among trusted colleagues and putting forth trial concepts.
3. Teaming people with different skills, interests, and experiences and letting them push and tug on interesting ideas to expand the variety of approaches considered.
4. Contacting a variety of people inside and outside of organization to sample viewpoints, to probe, and to listen, thereby trying to get early warning signals of impending problems/issues and deliberating short-circuiting all the careful screens of information flowing up from below.
5. Stimulating proposals for improvement from lower levels, encouraging the development of competing ideas and approaches, and letting the momentum for change come from below, with final choices being postponed until it is apparent which option best matches the organization's situation.
6. Seeking options and solutions that go beyond just extrapolations from the status quo.
7. Accepting and committing to partial steps forward as a way of building up comfort levels before going on ahead.
8. Managing the politics of change, to thereby promote managerial consensus and to solidify management's commitment to whatever course of action is chosen.

Both the reactive and proactive approaches exhibit commonality in the process of deciding what adjusting actions to take; the leadership sequence seems to be one of sensing needs, gathering information, amplifying understanding and awareness, putting forth trial concepts, developing options, exploring the pros and cons,

---

[24]Ibid., chap. 4.

testing proposals, generating partial solutions, empowering champions, building a managerial consensus, and formally adopting an agreed-upon course of action.[25] The ultimate managerial prescription may have been given by Rene McPherson, former CEO at Dana Corporation. In speaking to a class of students at Stanford, he said, "You just keep pushing. You just keep pushing. I made every mistake that could be made. But I just kept pushing."[26]

This points to a key feature of strategic management: The job of formulating and implementing strategy is not one of steering a clear-cut, linear course of carrying out the original strategy intact in accordance with some preconceived and highly detailed implementation plan. Rather, it is one of creatively (1) adapting and reshaping strategy to unfolding events and (2) employing analytical-behavioral-political techniques to bring internal activities and attitudes into alignment with strategy. The process is iterative, with much looping and recycling to fine tune and adjust in a continuously evolving process, whereby the conceptually separate acts of strategy formulation and strategy implementation blur and join together.

ANALYTICAL CHECKLIST

The action menu for implementing strategy is expansive. Virtually every aspect of administrative work comes into play; the checklist of what is involved includes:

- Building a capable organization—choosing an appropriate structure, establishing a distinctive competence, and selecting people for key positions.
- Formulating strategy-supportive budget allocations and programs.
- Linking work assignments closely to the achievement of strategic performance targets.
- Galvanizing commitment to strategy execution via creative use of reward systems and recognition of high performance.
- Devising policies, information and reporting networks, and internal support systems to facilitate strategy execution.
- Trying to build a strategy-supportive culture and work climate.
- Taking into account the overall organizational situation in which implementation must take place—the degree of strategic change called for, the type of strategy being implemented, and the nature and seriousness of existing internal problems.
- Deciding upon a leadership approach—whether to push hard for rapid change or accept gradual adjustments, whether to be authoritative or seek consensus and broad participation, and whether to adopt a high profile or a low profile.

Because the organizational circumstances of strategy implementation are so idiosyncratic, a manager's action agenda for implementing a given strategy is always a function of the specifics of the situation at hand. Thus, the challenge to "make it happen" is big, varied, and interesting, with lots of room for managerial creativity.

---

[25]Quinn, *Strategies for Change*, p. 146.
[26]As quoted in Peters and Waterman, *In Search of Excellence*, p. 319.

SUGGESTED READINGS

Adizes, Ichak. "Mismanagement Styles." *California Management Review* 19, no. 2 (Winter 1976), pp. 5–20.

Bower, Joseph L., and Martha W. Weinberg. "Statecraft, Strategy, and Corporate Leadership." *California Management Review* 30, no. 2 (Winter 1988), pp. 39–56.

Deal, Terence E., and Allen A. Kennedy. *Corporate Cultures*. Reading, Mass.: Addison-Wesley Publishing, 1982, especially chaps. 1 and 2.

Drucker, Peter F. *Management: Tasks, Responsibilities, Practices*. New York: Harper & Row, 1974, chaps. 16–19 and 33–39.

Gabarro, J. J. "When a New Manager Takes Charge." *Harvard Business Review* 64, no. 3 (May–June 1985), pp. 110–23.

Hall, Jay. "To Achieve or Not: The Manager's Choice." *California Management Review* 18, no. 4 (Summer 1976), pp. 5–18.

Herzberg, Frederick. "One More Time: How Do You Motivate Employees." *Harvard Business Review* 65, no. 4 (September–October 1987), pp. 109–20.

Hosmer, LaRue T. "The Importance of Strategic Leadership." *Journal of Business Strategy* 3, no. 2 (Fall 1982), pp. 47–57.

Machiavelli, N. *The Prince*. New York: Washington Square Press, 1963.

McClelland, David C., and David H. Burnham. "Power Is the Great Motivator." *Harvard Business Review* 54, no. 2 (March–April 1976), pp. 100–10.

Oliver, Alex R., and Joseph R. Garber. "Implementing Strategic Planning: Ten Sure-Fire Ways to Do It Wrong." *Business Horizons* 16, no. 2 (March–April 1983), pp. 49–51.

O'Toole, James. "Employee Practices at the Best-Managed Companies." *California Management Review* 28, no. 1 (Fall 1985), pp. 35–66.

Pascale, Richard. "The Paradox of 'Corporate Culture': Reconciling Ourselves to Socialization." *California Management Review* 27, no. 2 (Winter 1985), pp. 26–41.

Peters, Thomas J., and Robert H. Waterman. *In Search of Excellence*. New York: Harper & Row, 1982, chaps. 4, 5, and 9.

Peters, Thomas J., and Nancy Austin. *A Passion for Excellence*. New York: Random House, 1985, especially chaps. 11, 12, 15–19.

Quinn, James Brian. *Strategies for Change: Logical Incrementalism*. Homewood, Ill.: Richard D. Irwin, 1980, chap. 4.

———. "Managing Innovation: Controlled Chaos." *Harvard Business Review* 64, no. 3 (May–June 1985), pp. 73–84.

Reimann, Bernard C., and Yoash Wiener. "Corporate Culture: Avoiding the Elitest Trap." *Business Horizons* 31, no. 2 (March–April 1988), pp. 36–44.

Scholz, Christian. "Corporate Culture and Strategy—The Problem of Strategic Fit." *Long Range Planning* 20 (August 1987), pp. 78–87.

Schwartz, Howard, and Stanley H. Davis. "Matching Corporate Culture and Business Strategy." *Organizational Dynamics*, Summer 1981, pp. 30–48.

Tannenbaum, Robert, and Warren H. Schmidt. "How to Choose a Leadership Pattern." *Harvard Business Review* 51, no. 3 (May–June 1973), pp. 162–80.

Vancil, Richard F. *Implementing Strategy: The Role of Top Management*. Boston: Division of Research, Harvard Business School, 1985.

Zaleznik, Abraham. "Power and Politics in Organizational Life." *Harvard Business Review* 48, no. 3 (May–June 1970), pp. 47–60.

Reading 5

MANAGING CULTURE: THE INVISIBLE BARRIER TO STRATEGIC CHANGE*

Jay W. Lorsch

Culture affects not only the way managers believe within the organization, but also the decisions they make about the organization's relationships with its environment and its strategy. In fact, my central argument is that culture has a major impact on corporate strategy. To clarify what I mean, let me define two key concepts: *culture* and *strategy.*

* By culture I mean the shared beliefs top managers in a company have about how they should manage themselves and other employees, and how they should conduct their business(es). These beliefs are often invisible to the top managers but have a major impact on their thoughts and actions.

* By strategy I mean the stream of decisions taken over time by top managers, which, when understood as a whole, reveal the goals they are seeking and the means used to reach these goals. Such a definition of strategy is different from common business use of the term in that it does not refer to an explicit plan. In fact, by my definition strategy may be implicit as well as explicit.

I define these two terms at the outset because culture and strategy are concepts widely used by scholars and managers, often without being clear about their precise meaning. My purpose is not to take issue with others' definitions. I only want to be sure the reader understands mine.

Focusing on the connection between culture and strategy is critical because at no time in recent history have American top managers been confronted with such a wide array of challenges to the traditional strategies of their companies:

* Regulatory changes have revolutionized the competitive game in industries as diverse as airlines, trucking, banking, insurance, and telecommunications.

* Advancing electronic technology has spurred competition in the computer industry and also has made the computer a key weapon for financial services, retailing, and telecommunication companies.

* The cost of technological and product development has caused even the giants of the aircraft industry to undertake joint ventures with foreign partners, formerly their competitors.

* Automotive companies facing changing consumer tastes and intense foreign competition are restructuring product lines, improving quality and productivity, and adopting foreign sources and joint ventures.

* Similarly, managers in a wide range of mature industries from steel to consumer durables are reexamining and changing traditional manufacturing and distribution policies to remain competitive in the world market.

There is considerable evidence that such pressures will accelerate in the years ahead, given the rapid rate of technological change, the increasing inter-

*This article is an adapted version of an essay appearing in Ralph H. Kilmann, Mary J. Saxton, Roy Serpa and Associates, editors, *Gaining Control of the Corporate Culture,* copyright © 1985, by the Regents of the University of California. Reprinted/Condensed from the *California Management Review,* Vol. 28, No. 2. By permission of the Regents.

dependence of global markets, and continuing regulatory change in the United States. This means that many top managers will increasingly find that they are confronted with major questions of how to position their companies in a new business and how to change fundamentally their firm's strategy in their existing business.

In the face of such pressures for strategic change, a major concern for managers must be to avoid missteps and to shorten the time required to develop effective new strategic approaches. Unfortunately, strategic repositioning has historically been a complex and long-term process (even in highly successful companies) and one that is heavily influenced by the company's culture. The following examples illustrate the point:

- A consumer food company recognized in the late 1950s that changing consumer tastes were obsoleting its major products. It took over 15 years and two generations of top management to successfully reposition the company into growing businesses which built on its strengths in consumer marketing.

- A manufacturer of industrial supplies became aware in the late 1960s that the market for their major product was shrinking due to the development of alternate processing technologies. Top management needed almost a decade to develop and implement a strategy which today makes the company again a successful source of supplies to its customers.

- In the early 1970s, the top management of a growing electronics firm turned down a proposal from engineering and middle-managers who wanted to manufacture and market a mainframe computer with innovative new features. The reason—the project seemed too risky. It was almost 10 years before this top management found a suitable way to squarely position itself in the computer industry.

And these are successful top managers, those who are able to pull off major strategic changes that allowed their companies to remain financially healthy and growing in changing times.

The Difficulties of Strategic Change

Some might argue that the long time required to achieve strategic change is a direct result of management's inadequacies in logical analysis or their failure to use the latest tools for strategic planning. But the facts of the matter are quite different.

Obviously, strategic changes necessarily involve many actions, which require months and years to accomplish. Old businesses may have to be divested or shut down. New products may have to be developed by scientists and engineers. Market tests may be required. Manufacturing facilities may have to be built or modified. An alternative approach to internally developing new businesses may involve acquisitions, which require time to locate, to negotiate, and to integrate successfully with the parent.

In a more subtle but equally important way, strategic change requires a basic rethinking of the beliefs by which the company defines and carries on its businesses. In a study of 12 successful companies, we found that there exists among top managers a system of beliefs (a culture) which underlies these strategic choices. These beliefs have been developed over many years of successful operation. As a top manager in one firm stated:

> It is a closed loop. You make the argument that in the beginning of the company, the founders wanted to make certain products, which in turn led to our way of managing, which reinforced our products. It all hangs together. It isn't the result of any intellectual process, but it evolves. The pattern of principles which emerge out of a lot of individual decisions is totally consistent, and it is a fabric which hangs together and leads to success.

As this executive also points out, the beliefs in each successful company truly have a systemic quality. Each individual premise fits into a pattern or cultural whole which had guided managers' decisions to many years of corporate success.

Managers learn to be guided by these beliefs because they have worked successfully in the past. As one CEO said:

> If you have a way that's working, you want to stay

with it. . . . This is not the only way to run a company, but it has sure worked for us.

Executives in successful companies become emotionally committed to these beliefs because, having usually spent their entire careers in their companies, they have learned them from valued mentors and have had them reinforced by success at various stages of their career. This longevity was not only true of the CEOs in the 12 companies studied, but of most Fortune 500 companies. The president of another company provided a specific example:

My predecessor became president about 1947. In our staff meetings he'd say, "We're caught between two giants—the retailers and our suppliers." We're the little unit in between. We need to grow so we can exercise power on both sides. I can't remember a staff meeting in the early 1950s when an officer didn't make some mention of this point. It led directly to our concern with growth.

These beliefs cover a range of topics: what the firm's financial goals should be; in what businesses it can succeed; how marketing should be done in these businesses; what types of risks are acceptable, which are not. But at the core of each system of beliefs is top management's particular vision of its company's distinctive competence. This vision is management's own assessment of the capabilities and limits of the company's employees, its market position, and its financial resources and technological base. In sum, it is management's core beliefs about what the company is capable of accomplishing. (Table 1 illustrates the system of beliefs in a typical company.)

These beliefs can inhibit strategic change in two ways. First, they can produce a strategic myopia. Because managers hold a set of beliefs, they see events through this prism. Frequently, they miss the significance of changing external conditions because they are blinded by strongly held beliefs. For example, the management of the industrial supply manufacturer mentioned earlier was rudely awakened to the decline of its major product by a dramatic market study. The current CEO of the company recalled:

Back in the 1950s, a member of the finance department made a study of the industry which showed that it was in a mature phase. This was the first time that the company had done such a study and management was shocked by its implications that the industry and the company would stop growing. From that point on, everyone became concerned about the problem and what they were going to do about it.

In retrospect they recognized that they could have seen the decline several years earlier.

Second, even when managers can overcome such myopia, they respond to changing events in terms of their culture. Because the beliefs have been effective guides in the past, the natural response is to stick with them. For example, the food processing company mentioned earlier studiously avoided opportunities to grow internationally. Why? An early international failure convinced its top managers that such expansion was outside of the company's distinctive competence. Their vision was that: "We can succeed with products which are marketed to consumers in the United States. We understand them." While top managers are usually able to recognize the practical difficulties involved in accomplishing a major strategic change, they are much less likely to recognize that their deeply held beliefs represent an invisible barrier to strategic change which must be penetrated.

The Process of Strategic Change

An examination of strategic change (as we learned about it in our study of the 12 successful companies) illustrates how the invisible barrier of culture can be overcome. In those companies where major strategic change was a necessity because of changing product market conditions, managers for a time did suffer from strategic myopia. The severity of this ailment depended upon for how long and how well the old culture continued to achieve top management's cherished financial goals. Persistent problems in achieving the desired financial goals was, in each case, the trigger that made managers aware that something was wrong with their beliefs. The pattern of principles which had worked well no longer did so.

TABLE 1
Commodity Products Company—Top Management Culture

BELIEFS ABOUT CAPITAL MARKET EXPECTATIONS

- Have a return on equity of "x" %, which places us among the upper ⅓ of all manufacturing companies.
- Have a steady improvement in market share.
- Dividends should *never* be cut and should be "x" % of earnings.
- Maintain "x" credit rating and keep debt less than "x" % of capital.

STRATEGIC VISION

We can be the strongest and top ranked company in our industry, but will not diversify outside it.

BELIEFS ABOUT INTERNAL ORGANIZATION

- We must have the strongest management structure in the industry.
- Foster harmony and preserve the family feeling within the company through all levels of employees including those in the union.
- We must keep employees who believe in the industry happy because the industry is what we are good at.
- Preserve the drama and emotion of the industry.
- We want to keep management open door and participating.
- Top management must always include at least one person who understands manufacturing process and operations.
- Good coordination between sales and manufacturing gives us the ability to serve customers better than competition.

BELIEFS ABOUT PRODUCT MARKET COMPETITION

- Our geographic location provides us with a cost advantage.
- We must offer better service than competitors to our customers.
- Major customers like big suppliers committed to the industry.
- We must improve profit position through lower costs, not higher prices.
- Market share is important, but not through low prices.
- We must compete on innovation in processes and basic products not in rice.
- We must expand and modernize plants for the long haul.

In sum: Beliefs about capital market expectations reflect management's convictions about what is necessary to keep investors and lenders satisfied given their strategic vision of staying in a mature industry. Beliefs about product market competition reflect their conviction about why and how they can succeed in a highly competitive mature industry. Their beliefs about internal management reflect what management approaches will lead to competitive success and, therefore, will meet capital market expectations.

Incremental Change—The initial response to this discovery was a period of questioning various individual premises. Could the problem be fixed with minor modifications? In some instances, these attempts at incremental change succeeded. For example, in one of these companies, adverse financial results in 1974 and 1975 alarmed top management because they were simultaneously investing heavily in a major new product. They either had to undertake more long-term debt or abandon the new product. Either option meant departing from an important belief. Two executives recalled the dilemma:

We were using our debt capacity too fast. The momentum of our capital expenditures program was carrying us out too fast, especially in one business where the outlook had been changing negatively. We had to decide what was useful to the future of the company.

Well, in 1974–75, survival was the name of the game. The first thing we had to do was perpetuate the company and not let it get away from us, but [the new product] represented the future and we couldn't let that go. It was a technological breakthrough. It was a big chip to bet on.

In the end, this company's top management altered their beliefs about what was an acceptable level of long-term debt so that they could continue the development of the major new product. In the past, such new products had fueled the company's profitable growth. To depart from the principle that major new products assured the future health of the company would have shattered their central cultural vision of the company's distinctive competence. It was far easier to bend one less central principle than those at the core of top management's culture.

Such incremental changes in top management's beliefs occur periodically in most successful companies. One belief or another is altered, but the basic fabric of their culture remains the same. However, in the rapidly changing world of the 1980s, changing events are likely to require even more fundamental changes. This had also been the case in the history of several of the companies we examined. While their top managers had tried initially to adjust to external market change through incremental actions, they found such small steps did not achieve the desired results. This led to much more serious departures from past strategic beliefs and practices, which changed the fundamental nature of their belief system.

Fundamental Change—Top managers went through several distinct but interrelated stages in their thoughts and actions as they led their companies in fundamentally new directions.

Awareness—The first stage grew directly out of earlier attempts at incremental changes. Top managers gradually developed a *shared* awareness that fundamental changes in their culture would be necessary to assure corporate survival. Because top managers were so emotionally committed to their beliefs, an awareness of the need for fundamental

change did not come easily. During this early phase, top managers would engage in months of what psychiatrists label *denial*. They chose to ignore the possibility that key beliefs could and should be modified. But gradually, in each firm, an awareness did develop among the top group that external events had changed permanently. Incremental steps were not solving their problems. Drastic changes in the whole pattern of beliefs were needed.

Confusion—This recognition was followed by a period of confusion. While all the top managers could agree that the old beliefs were not working, there were often as many ideas as top managers about what to do next. No one idea attracted wide support. Strategic planners and their concepts offered little help, because the confusion went to the heart of top managers' own judgments about such matters as what the firm's distinctive competence had been and could be in the future.

As long as the firm's financial viability is not seriously in question, the period of confusion can continue for many months or even years. One executive described such a period in his company's past:

We acquired business after business. There was no real support, so it failed. We flubbed around. People said we should be in a [particular business] because it had growth, but we never picked out what segment, and the president and chairman weren't comfortable with the program.

While aware of the need for major change in strategic direction, but confused about what to do, top management was ready for new leadership, and the boards of directors apparently shared that view. In these companies, the board turned to new leadership to find a path out of the period of confusion. In all but one instance, the new CEO was promoted from within. However, he always represented a new generation of management with fresh ideas. Because these CEOs were generally insiders, they also had an understanding and an appreciation of the old pattern of strategic beliefs. This, too, was important because their major task was to bring a clear new direction out of the existing confusion, while building as much as possible on existing strengths.

Developing a Strategic Vision—The first steps out of the confusion took place inside the heads of the new CEOs and may have even predated their ascension to corporate leadership. They developed a personal set of ideas about what their company could become. Their next task was to elaborate and clarify this strategic vision and to rally other top managers and the larger management organization to it. For a while, their activities in this regard were largely mental and verbal—thinking and talking and listening to their subordinates.

A company executive described this phase:

What we did in the mid-sixties was to assess the management group. We stepped back. There were several sessions with top management out of the office. It was a self-assessment. It was top management assessing itself and saying we didn't see the good prospects for technology in [a basic consumer products business] we had hoped for. If we had anything to bring to new industries, it was our ability to think about customers, how to do market research, market planning, etc.

Out of such discussions evolved a vision shared among the top managers about what the company's distinctive capabilities could be in the future. In the instance of this executive's company, it was to be a manufacturer and marketer of a wide range of nondurable branded products to United States consumers; and to do this in such a way that the company would be an "all weather company"—one that would do well in all phases of the business cycle.

In each company, the CEO and his associates developed a unique vision. What these strategic visions had in common, however, was that they took fundamentally new ideas and meshed them with some old beliefs about how to compete effectively, how to manage their employees, and about corporate finances. Such a fusion of old and new is realistic because it reflects the best assessment these executives could make about their own and their company's capabilities. Psychologically it made sense because it enabled them to retain as many beliefs from their cherished culture as possible, even as they fashioned new directions. Because the new CEO and his colleagues were almost all career-long managers in their companies, adherence to old beliefs was comfortable and minimized resistance to strategic change.

In fact, one of the two major accomplishments of this phase was to overcome the persistent doubts among the executives about departing too far from established beliefs. The other accomplishment was a refinement and clarification of the direction that was to carry the firm forward. While this clarification was achieved, initially by thought and discussion, at some point the ideas had to be converted into concrete decisions. Such decisions signalled the final stage of the process—experimentation.

Experimentation—Like scientists in a laboratory, executives in these successful companies experimented with their new ideas. Gradually and incrementally they committed money and people to the new direction.

An executive in a consumer products company described this phase:

During the 1960s, we had four out of every five capital investment dollars going into acquisitions. There were many new venture teams going and we got into quite a number of businesses. We were searching for new business.

In this particular company, experimentation took the form of both acquisitions and internal development. For example, part of their vision was to open retail shops, so they could sell directly to the consumer. A number of different types of stores were opened. Results were evaluated, new ideas tried. But none of the ideas really caught fire. Frustrated but not discouraged by several years of trying, these executives discovered a small chain of outlets which they could acquire and which already embodied many of the ideas they had concluded were important as a result of their own internal development. These four stores were acquired and today have been expanded into a nationwide network of 300 outlets. Success with this acquisition led to additional acquisitions repeating the pattern with other products.

The top managers in the industrial supply company went through a similar process. They began a search for products which could build upon the strengths of their sales force and distribution network. A number of small acquisitions were made.

Some were kept and others divested. Gradually, again over several years, they learned what products fit their vision and which did not. For example, it became clear to them that consumable supplies were desirable and that there was an upper limit on the technological content of the businesses they could enter.

In some of these companies, top managers also learned through experimentation that their new vision wouldn't work. A forest products company provides an example. Even though their company was a good performer in its industry, these top managers, frustrated by slow growth and low profitability in the base business, concluded that diversification into unrelated businesses would solve these problems. Several acquisitions were made and the company operated them for several years. The results were only mediocre and the top management concluded that their vision of the company as a diversified "conglomerate" was not viable. Instead, they began experimenting with new products more closely related to their core business.

These examples illustrated one reason why fundamental strategic change can consume years. It simply takes that long for top managers to convert abstract ideas into concrete realities. As they do so, they are learning new beliefs which combine with the old ones they retain to shape the pattern of their culture and their corporate strategy for the future. As their predecessors before them, they become committed to a system of beliefs which work. Experimentation gradually subsides and top management finds itself with a stable pattern of beliefs which have created new corporate success, but which are fundamentally different from those with which they started the process of strategic change.

Breaking through the Invisible Barrier

If this is the reality of fundamental strategic change—what can managers do to speed up the process in an era which demands more rapid adaptation to constantly changing realities? Is it possible to reduce the time required, which—as we have seen even in successful firms—could be as long as a decade? Of course, part of the answer rests in the speed with which top managers and their organizations can deal with the pragmatics of strategic change—acquisitions, diversification, new product development, test markets, building new facilities, and so on. And there are obviously real limits here, particularly if one agrees that experimentation (which is so characteristic of strategic change in successful companies) is important to minimize major missteps in defining new direction. But, as we have seen, there is another major reason for the long time required. This is the invisible barrier of the top manager's culture. Is it possible for managers to retain the benefits of strong beliefs, while still being capable of changing them more rapidly? I believe the answer is yes.

One key is for top managers to accept as a major premise in any company's culture the importance of flexibility and innovation. Whatever else they hold sacred, they must recognize that in the world of the eighties and beyond, the need for strategic change will be a constant. However else top managers define their unique strategic vision, it must recognize this fact. But such a commitment will only be meaningless words unless it can be converted into activities and actions which cause managers to use this conviction to examine and challenge their other strategic premises. Several ways of assuring that this happens are suggested by the experience of these successful companies.

Making Beliefs Visible—In a few of these companies, top managers had put their major beliefs into writing. In one, for example, the central beliefs were available for employees, customers, and visitors to read in a printed brochure distributed widely throughout the company's offices, visitors' waiting rooms, etc. Similarly, at Johnson & Johnson (which, while certainly a highly successful company, was not included in our study) the company's "credo" hangs on the wall of most executives' offices. Such formalized statements, while they may not capture all aspects of a company's culture, do remind managers that their decisions are guided by such principles.

The important lesson to be drawn from these attempts to develop formal statements of beliefs is that the invisible beliefs can be made more visible in this way. Of course, displaying these beliefs publicly may or may not be a sound idea depending upon whether managers feel they contain proprietary ideas. But that is not the critical point. What is more important is that top managers can and should make their implicit beliefs explicit, at least to each other. If managers are aware of the beliefs they share, they are less likely to be blinded by them and are apt to understand more rapidly when changing events obsolete aspects of their culture.

In companies which, like the vast majority of those we studied, do not have such explicit statements, top managers should undertake a *cultural audit* so that they are aware of their beliefs prior to having to deal with changing events. A culture audit involves the top management group developing a consensus about their shared beliefs. The process starts with each member of the top group answering questions such as those listed in Table 2. Then, individual answers to these questions are compared and provide a basis for discussion among top managers. Through this process, the beliefs which are shared can be identified and codified. In answering these questions, it is critical that the emphasis be on what top managers believe as evidenced by their practices, not on some idealized view of their company.

This is important to emphasize in the wake of the current management obsession with excellence and corporate culture, a by-product of which has been a spate of statements of corporate philosophy. While these may be admirable statements of top management's intentions, they may have little to do with the strategic beliefs top managers actually operate upon, which is what the culture audit is intended to identify.

An effective culture audit cannot be delegated. It must involve the company's major decision makers, including the CEO. They must be willing to commit the thought and time, probably several days, to answer such questions individually and then to collectively compare and discuss their individual responses until they reach a consensus.

As they go through this process, top managers should be able gradually to identify the consistent pattern of their culture and how beliefs are related one to the other. If the audit is successful, top managers will have made the once invisible barrier of the culture visible. Then they can deal with it more rapidly in the face of change, retaining beliefs which still are valid and discarding those which are not.

Assuring Flexibility

Making culture explicit is one way to facilitate more rapid strategic change. Also required, however, are other ways to stimulate top managers to maintain a commitment to flexibility, whatever else they believe. Successful companies use a variety of means to accomplish this.

Top Managers without Portfolio—One device is the presence of a very senior and experienced top manager whose role is to raise questions, challenge beliefs, and suggest new ideas. Such managers, we found, generally had few other responsibilities. They often have the title of "Vice Chairman." At first glance, it might seem that they have been shunted out of the line management. But a more careful examination indicates that these managers without portfolio are valued members of the top-management group. Always highly intelligent with long experience, often skeptical and inquiring, they interact constantly with other top managers, challenging their beliefs and suggesting new ideas. While they understand and are committed to the existing culture, they keep it fluid and dynamic through their presence in the management group.

The qualifications for such positions may seem unique, and there may be no way to assure that such a person is available to every top-management group. Yet the presence of such managers in several of these successful companies suggests that the CEOs understood the value of intelligent dissent and creativity in their top management.

The Role of Outside Directors—Outside directors can also play an important part in assuring strategic flexibility. While they usually are affiliated with companies for long periods of time and may, therefore, fall prey to sharing many of top-management's beliefs, they are also far enough removed to provide objectivity and raise important questions about the appropriateness of these beliefs in changing times. While many top managers hold to the view that strategic decisions are the sole purview of manage-

**TABLE 2
Culture Audit**

	Questions	Examples
Beliefs about Goals	● About what financial objectives do we have strong beliefs based on traditions and history?	● Return on assets. ● Rate of growth. ● Debt/equity ratio. ● Bond rating. ● Dividend policies.
	● How, if at all, are those beliefs about financial goals related to each other? ● What other goals do we believe to be important?	● Growth should be financed internally, which means no long-term debt and limited dividends. ● To be in the top quartile of Fortune 500 companies. ● To be the best in our country. ● To be a responsible corporate citizen. ● To be an "all-weather" company.
Beliefs about Distinctive Competences	● What do we believe to be the appropriate scope of our competitive activity?	● We can manage any business. ● We can succeed in domestic consumer products. ● We can succeed with products based upon our technological expertise. ● We can only succeed in the paper industry. ● We can manage our business worldwide.
	● To what earlier experience can we trace these beliefs? ● Do they reflect a realistic assessment of the competence of management and the company?	
Beliefs about Product Market Guidelines	● What broad guidelines do we believe should guide our managers in competing in product markets?	● Have one or two share in each market. ● Provide the best quality product. ● Compete on service not on price.
	● Can these principles be traced to earlier historical events? ● Are these guildelines valid today in our various businesses?	
Key Beliefs about Management Employees*	● What do we believe employees want and/or deserve in exchange for their effort?	● Safe working conditions. ● Stable employment. ● High wages. ● Share of profits. ● Equity ownership.
	● What beliefs do we hold about the importance of employees to company success?	● Our scientists are key to innovation. ● We want managers and employees to work as one big team. ● Committed employees lead to satisfied customers.

*While these are not strategic beliefs, strictly speaking, they are important to understand because they are so closely related to strategic premises.

ment, outside directors can, even with limited time and information, play an important role in keeping top managers alert to their culture and to changing external events. Such activities may be conducted in informal contacts or may, as in some companies, be formally assigned to a Strategy Committee of the board.

Bringing in New Blood—Another way to assure cultural flexibility is to bring in an outside manager at a very senior level. Such an individual brings a new perspective and objectivity. But to be successful, he or she must deal effectively with two problems. First, any newcomer comes with a set of beliefs from his or her prior experience. What worked with the previous employer can become a dearly held set of principles for each individual. To be effective in a new setting, the newcomer needs to develop an awareness of these personal beliefs. Second, the new executive needs to develop an awareness of the culture of the new company. If these beliefs have been explicitly stated, the transition is easier; but if not, the newcomer will have to be an effective detective. Not understanding the existing beliefs can cause the newcomer to unwittingly step on too many sensitive toes and to be rejected before the objectivity and new ideas for which the newcomer was hired can be tried out.

Flexibility Down the Line—Another way to assure flexibility at the top is to encourage flexibility of thinking at subordinate levels of management. This can assure that succeeding generations of top management will be less blindly rigid in their adherence to cultural traditions. It can also provide a source of new perspective to the present top managers as new ideas bubble up from subordinate levels.

Two different routes can be used to encourage flexibility among middle managers. One is to stimulate new ideas within the organization. An in-company education program for middle managers, with outside experts as instructors, is one frequently employed means. Another is to encourage systematic rotation of managers among functions and businesses. In this way, their perspectives can be broad-

ened. Such inside activities always have the inherent limitation that new ideas are learned with company colleagues in the context of the company's culture.

There is a way to avoid this pitfall. High potential subordinate managers are provided an opportunity to broaden their perspectives outside the company. University executive education programs are one vehicle for achieving this. Whatever else they achieve, they do broaden the perspective of participants through contact with peers from other companies. Business and government exchange programs, like the White House Exchange Fellowships, can accomplish the same objective. Another possibility used successfully is to encourage travel to other companies in other countries to learn new methods and gain broadened perspective. Such programs have been used recently by several companies to challenge the beliefs and broaden the perspectives of manufacturing executives. The result has been improved manufacturing practices which depart from strong traditions.

Change and Stability

Our focus has been on how top managers can overcome the invisible barrier of culture to speed up the process of strategic change. As necessary as this will be in the future, we must not lose sight of the positive value of a strong culture. In the successful companies studied, these belief systems were critical components in corporate success, providing guidance to managers as they made complex decisions. As long as external conditions do not change dramatically, culture is an invaluable aid to speedy and coherent strategic choices. Even when conditions change dramatically, many old beliefs describe the essence of the company's character and competence. They cannot be abandoned without a high cost.

Thus, the real challenge for top managers is to encourage flexibility while still respecting and valuing their culture. Awareness of these beliefs is a prerequisite to achieving this balance, which will be critical to corporate survival in the dynamic decades ahead.

Reading 6

LINKING COMPETITIVE STRATEGIES WITH HUMAN RESOURCE MANAGEMENT PRACTICES*

Randall S. Schuler and Susan E. Jackson

Over the past several years there has been increased recognition that there is a need to match the characteristics of top managers with the nature of the business. According to Reginald H. Jones, former chairman and CEO of the General Electric Company:

> When we classified . . . [our] . . . businesses, and when we realized that they were going to have quite different missions, we also realized we had to have quite different people running them.[1]

Within academia there has been similar growing awareness of this need. Although this awareness is being articulated in several ways, one of the most frequent involves the conceptualization and investigation of the relationship between business strategy and the personal characteristics of top managers.[2] Here, particular manager characteristics such as personality, skills, abilities, values, and perspectives are matched with particular types of business strategies. For example, a recently released study conducted by Hay Group Incorporated, in conjunction with the University of Michigan and the Strategic Planning Institute, reports that when a business is pursuing a growth strategy it needs top managers who are likely to abandon the status quo and adapt their strategies and goals to the marketplace. According to the study, insiders are slow to recognize the onset of decline and tend to persevere in strategies that are no longer effective; so, top managers need to be recruited from the outside.

Recruiting outsiders as a part of strategy has been successful for Stroh Brewing Company, once a small, family-run brewery in Detroit. Some 20 percent of its senior management team of 25 executives, including President Roger T. Fridholm, have been brought into Stroh since 1978. They've been instrumental in transforming it into the third-largest U.S. brewer.[3]

The result of such human resource staffing practices has been rather significant:

> Growth companies that staffed 20 percent of their top three levels with outsiders exceeded their expected return on investment by 10 percent. Those that relied on inside talent fell short of their goals by 20 percent. The same holds true for companies in declining industries: companies with outsiders in one out of every five top-management jobs exceeded expected returns by 20 percent; those with a low proportion of outsiders fell 5 percent short.[4]

*Reprinted with permission from *The Academy of Management EXECUTIVE* 1, no. 3 (August 1987), pp. 207–219.

[1]C. Fombrun, "An Interview with Reginald Jones," *Organizational Dynamics*, Winter 1982, p. 46.

[2]D.C. Hambrick and P.A. Mason, "Upper Echelons: The Organization as a Reflection of Its Top Managers," *Academy of Management Review* 9, (1984), pp. 193–206; A.K. Gupta, "Contingency Linkages Between Strategy and General Manager Characteristics: A Conceptual Examination," *Academy of Management Review* 9 (1984), pp. 399–412; A.K. Gupta and V. Govindarajan, "Build, Hold, Harvest: Converting Strategic Intentions into Reality," *Journal of Business Strategy* 4 (1984a), pp. 34–47; A.K. Gupta and Govindarajan, "Business Unit Strategy, Managerial Characteristics, and Business Unit Effectiveness at Strategy Implementation," *Academy of Management Journal* 9 (1984b), pp. 25–41; M. Gerstein and H. Reisman, "Strategic Selection: Matching Executives to Business Conditions," *Sloan Management Review*, Winter 1983, pp. 33–49; D. Miller, M.F.R. Kets de Vries, and J.M. Toulouse, "Top Executives' Locus of Control and Its Relationship to Strategy-Making, Structure, and Environment," *Academy of Management Journal* 25 (1982), pp. 237–53; A.D. Szilagyi and D.M. Schweiger, "Matching Managers to Strategies: A Review and Suggested Framework," *Academy of Management Review* 9 (1984), pp. 626–37; and J.D. Olian and S.L. Rynes, "Organizational Staffing: Integrating Practice with Strategy," *Industrial Relations* 23 (1984), pp. 170–83.

[3]Lee J.A. Byrne and A. Leigh Cowan, "Should Companies Groom New Leaders or Buy Them?" *Business Week*, September 22, 1986, pp. 94–95.

[4]Ibid.

Outsiders, of course, are not always helpful. When a business is pursuing a mature strategy, what is needed is a stable group of insiders who know the intricacies of the business.

The results of the Hay study suggest that the staffing practices of top management be tied to the nature of the business because different aspects of business demand different behaviors from the individuals running them. The implication, then, is that selecting the right top manager is an important staffing decision.

Another perspective holds that top managers are capable of exhibiting a wide range of behavior, and all that is needed is to match compensation and performance appraisal practices with the nature of the business. Peter Drucker, commenting on the relationship between compensation and a strategy of innovation, observed that:

> I myself made this mistake [thinking that you can truly innovate within the existing operating unit] 30 years ago when I was a consultant on the first major organizational change in American history, the General Electric reorganization of the early 1950s. I advised top management, and they accepted it, that the general managers would be responsible for current operations as well as for managing tomorrow. At the same time, we worked out one of the first systematic compensation plans, and the whole idea of paying people on the basis of their performance in the preceding year came out of that.
>
> The result of it was that for 10 years General Electric totally lost its capacity to innovate, simply because tomorrow produces costs for 10 years and no return. So, the general manager—not only out of concern for himself but also out of concern for his group—postponed spending any money for innovation. It was only when the company dropped this compensation plan and at the same time organized the search for the truly new, not just for improvement outside the existing business, that GE recovered its innovative capacity, and brilliantly. Many companies go after this new and slight today and soon find they have neither.[5]

Similar results illustrating the power of performance appraisal and compensation to affect individ-

ual behavior have been reported in the areas of reinforcement, behavior modification, and motivation theories.[6] However, while there has been much written on matching the behavior of top managers with the nature of the business, less attention has been given to the other employees in the organization. Nevertheless, it seemed reasonable to assume that the rest of the work force would also have to be managed differently, depending on the business. This, then, became our focus of attention.

A critical choice we had to make in our study concerned which aspects of the business we were going to use. Consistent with previous studies, we decided to use the general notion of organizational strategy.[7] On the basis of previous studies that looked at strategy and human resource practices, we decided to adapt Porter's framework of competitive strategy.[8] Using the competitive strategy framework, we developed three archetypes of competitive strategy—PHRM practices combinations. These were derived from the literature, secondary sources, and our previous research. We then examined each of the three archetypes in depth, using additional secondary data and field results, and addressed issues regarding implementation and revision of the archetypes. All are presented in this article.

First, we shall review the nature and importance of competitive strategy, and then we shall describe the concept of needed role behavior that enabled

---

[5]A.J. Rutigliano, "Managing the New: An Interview with Peter Drucker," *Management Review,* January 1986, pp. 38–41.

[6]D.Q. Mills, *The New Competitors* (New York: Free Press, 1985); and M. Beer, B. Spector, P.R. Lawrence, D.Q. Mills, and R.E. Walton, *Managing Human Assets* (New York: Macmillan, 1984); R.M. Kanter, "Change Masters and the Intricate Architecture of Corporate Culture Change," *Management Review,* October 1983, pp. 18–28; and R.M. Kanter, *The Change Masters* (New York: Simon & Schuster, 1983).

[7]J.L. Kerr, "Diversification Strategies and Managerial Rewards: An Empirical Study," *Academy of Management Journal* 28 (1985), pp. 155–79; J.W. Slocum, W.L. Cron, R.W. Hansen, and S. Rawlings, "Business Strategy and the Management of Plateaued Employees," *Academy of Management Journal* 28 (1985), pp. 133–54; D.C. Hambrick and C.C. Snow, "Strategic Reward Systems," in C.C. Snow (ed.), *Strategy, Organization Design and Human Resources Management* (Greenwich, Conn.: JAI Press, 1987).

[8]For detailed examples of how firms use their human resource practices to gain competitive advantage, see R.S. Schuler and I.C. MacMillan, "Gaining Competitive Advantage through Human Resource Management Practices," *Human Resource Management,* Autumn 1984, pp. 241–55; R.S. Schuler, "Fostering and Facilitating Entrepreneurship in Organizations: Implications for Organization Structure and Human Resource Management Practices," *Human Resource Management,* Winter 1986, pp. 607–29; and M.E. Porter, *Competitive Strategy* (New York: Free Press, 1980); and M.E. Porter, *Competitive Advantage* (New York: Free Press, 1985).

us to link competitive strategies and HRM practices.

Competitive Strategies

Crucial to a firm's growth and prosperity is the ability to gain and retain competitive advantage. One way to do this is through strategic initiative. MacMillan defines "strategic initiative" as the ability to capture control of strategic behavior in the industries in which a firm competes.[9] To the extent one company gains the initiative, competitors are obliged to respond and thereby play a *reactive* rather than proactive role. MacMillan argues that firms that gain a strategic advantage control their own destinies. To the extent a firm gains an advantage difficult for competitors to remove, it stays in control longer and therefore should be more effective.

The concept of competitive advantage is described by Porter as the essence of competitive strategy.[10] Emerging from his discussion are three competitive strategies that organizations can use to gain competitive advantage: innovation, quality enhancement, and cost reduction. The *innovation strategy* is used to develop products or services different from those of competitors; the primary focus here is on offering something new and different. Enhancing product and/or service quality is the primary focus of the *quality-enhancement strategy*. In the *cost-reduction strategy,* firms typically attempt to gain competitive advantage by being the lowest cost producer. Although we shall describe these three competitive strategies as pure types applied to single-business units or even single plants or functional areas, some overlap can occur. That is, it is plausible to find business units, plants, or functional areas pursuing two or more competitive strategies simultaneously. This, and how to manage it, are discussed later.

Competitive Strategy: Needed Role Behaviors

Before developing a linkage between competitive strategy and HRM practices, there must be a *rationale* for that linkage. This rationale gives us a basis for predicting, studying, refining, and modifying both strategy and practices in specific circumstances.

Consistent with previous research, the rationale developed is based on what is needed from employees apart from the specific technical skills, knowledges, and abilities (SKAs) required to perform a specific task.[11] Rather than thinking about task-specific SKAs, then, it is more useful to think about what is needed from an employee who works with other employees in a social environment.[12] These needed employee behaviors are actually best thought of as needed role behaviors.[13] The importance of roles and their potential dysfunction in organizations, particularly role conflict and ambiguity, is well documented.[14]

Based on an extensive review of the literature and secondary data, several role behaviors are assumed to be instrumental in the implementation of the competitive strategies. Exhibit 1 shows several dimensions along which employees' role behaviors can vary. The dimensions shown are the ones for which there are likely to be major differences across competitive strategies. This can be illustrated by describing the various competitive strategies and their necessary organizational conditions in more detail, along with the needed role behaviors from the employees.

Innovation Strategy and Needed Role Behaviors

Because the imperative for an organization pursuing an innovation strategy is to be the most unique producer, conditions for innovation must be created.

[9]For an extensive discussion of competitive initiative, competitive strategy, and competitive advantage see I.C. MacMillan's "Seizing Competitive Initiative," *Journal of Business Strategy*, 1983, pp. 43–57.

[10]See note 18, Porter, 1980, 1985.

[11]B. Schneider, "Organizational Behavior," *Annual Review of Psychology* (1985), 36, pp. 573–611.

[12]D. Katz and R.L. Kahn, *The Social Psychology of Organizations,* 2nd ed. (New York: John Wiley & Sons, 1978).

[13]J.C. Naylor, R.D. Pritchard, and D.R. Ilgen, *A Theory of Behavior in Organizations* (New York: Academic Press, 1980); T.W. Dougherty and R.D. Pritchard, "The Measurement of Role Variables: Exploratory Examination of a New Approach," *Organizational Behavior and Human Decision Processes* 35 (1985), pp. 141–55.

[14]J.R. Rizzo, R.J. Hose, and S.I. Lirtzman, "Role Conflict and Ambiguity in Complex Organizations," *Administrative Science Quarterly* 14 (1970), pp. 150–63; S.E. Jackson and R.S. Schuler, "A Meta-Analysis and Conceptual Critique of Research on Role Ambiguity and Role Conflict in Work Settings," *Organizational Behavior and Human Decision Processes* 36 (1985), pp. 16–78.

EXHIBIT 1
Employee Role Behaviors for Competitive Strategies

1. Highly repetitive, predictable behavior	— Highly creative, innovative behavior
2. Very short-term focus	— Very long-term behavior
3. Highly cooperative, interdependent behavior	— Highly independent, autonomous behavior
4. Very low concern for quality	— Very high concern for quality
5. Very low concern for quantity	— Very high concern for quantity
6. Very low risk taking	— Very high risk taking
7. Very high concern for process	— Very high concern for results
8. High preference to avoid responsibility	— High preference to assume responsibility
9. Very inflexible to change	— Very flexible to change
10. Very comfortable with stability	— Very tolerant of ambiguity and unpredictability
11. Narrow skill application	— Broad skill application
12. Low job (firm) involvement	— High job (firm) involvement

Adapted from R. S. Schuler, "Human Resource Management Practice Choices," in R. S. Schuler, S. A. Youngblood, and V. L. Huber (eds.), *Readings in Personnel and Human Resource Management*, 3rd ed. (St. Paul, Minn.: West Publishing, 1988).

These conditions can be rather varied. They can be created either formally through official corporate policy or more informally. According to Rosabeth Moss Kanter:

> Innovation [and new venture development] may originate as a deliberate and official decision of the highest levels of management or there may be the more-or-less "spontaneous" creation of mid-level people who take the initiative to solve a problem in new ways or to develop a proposal for change. Of course, highly successful companies allow both, and even official top-management decisions to undertake a development effort benefit from the spontaneous creativity of those below.[15]

To encourage as many employees as possible to be innovative, 3M has developed an informal doctrine of allowing employees to "bootleg" 15 percent of their time on their own projects. A less-systematic approach to innovation is encouraging employees to offer suggestions for new and improved ways of doing their own job or manufacturing products.

Overall, then, for firms pursuing a competitive strategy of innovation, the profile of employee role behaviors includes (1) a high degree of creative be-havior, (2) a longer-term focus, (3) a relatively high level of cooperative, interdependent behavior, (4) a moderate degree of concern for quality, (5) a moderate concern for quantity, (6) an equal degree of concern for process and results, (7) a greater degree of risk taking, and (8) a high tolerance of ambiguity and unpredictability.[16]

The implications of pursuing a competitive strategy of innovation for managing people may include selecting highly skilled individuals, giving employees more discretion, using minimal controls, making a greater investment in human resources, providing more resources for experimentation, allowing and even rewarding occasional failure, and appraising performance for its long-run implications. As a consequence of these conditions, pursuing an innovation strategy may result in feelings of enhanced personal control and morale, and, thus, a greater commitment to self and profession, rather than to the employing organization. Nevertheless, benefits may accrue to the firm as well as the employee, as evidenced by the success of such innovative firms as Hewlett-Packard, the Raytheon Corporation, 3M, Johnson & Johnson, and PepsiCo.

Thus, the innovation strategy has significant implications for human resource management. Rather

---

[15]R.M. Kanter, "Supporting Innovation and Venture Development in Established Companies," *Journal of Business Venturing*, Winter 1985, pp. 47–60.

[16]H. DePree, *Business as Unusual* (Zeeland, Mich.: Herman Miller, 1986).

than emphasizing managing people so they work *harder* (cost-reduction strategy) or *smarter* (quality strategy) on the same products or services, the innovation strategy requires people to work *differently*. This, then, is the necessary ingredient.[17]

Quality-Enhancement Strategy and Needed Role Behaviors

At Xerox, CEO David Kearns defines quality as "being right the first time every time." The implications for managing people are significant. According to James Houghton, chairman of Corning Glass Works, his company's "total quality approach" is about people. At Corning, good ideas for product improvement often come from employees, and in order to carry through on their ideas Corning workers form short-lived "corrective action teams" to solve specific problems.

> Employees [also] give their supervisors written "method improvement requests," which differ from ideas tossed into the traditional suggestion box in that they get a prompt formal review so the employees aren't left wondering about their fate. In the company's Erwin Ceramics plant, a maintenance employee suggested substituting one flexible tin mold for an array of fixed molds that shape the wet ceramic product baked into catalytic converters for auto exhausts.[18]

At Corning, then, quality improvement involves getting employees committed to quality and continual improvement. While policy statements emphasizing the "total quality approach" are valuable, they are also followed up with specific human resources practices: feedback systems are in place, team work is permitted and facilitated, decision making and responsibility are a part of each employee's job description, and job classifications are flexible.

Quality improvement often means changing the processes of production in ways that require workers to be more involved and more flexible. As jobs change, so must job classification systems. At Brunswick's Mercury Marine division, the number of job classifications was reduced from 126 to 12. This has permitted greater flexibility in the use of production processes and employees. Machine operators have gained greater opportunities to learn new skills. They inspect their own work and do preventive maintenance in addition to running the machines.[19] It is because of human resource practices such as these that employees become committed to the firm and, hence, willing to give more. Not only is the level of quality likely to improve under these conditions, but sheer volume of output is likely to increase as well. For example, in pursuing a competitive strategy involving quality improvement, L.L. Bean's sales have increased tenfold while the number of permanent employees has grown only fivefold.[20]

The profile of employee behaviors necessary for firms pursuing a strategy of quality enhancement is (1) relatively repetitive and predictable behaviors, (2) a more long-term or intermediate focus, (3) a modest amount of cooperative, interdependent behavior, (4) a high concern for quality, (5) a modest concern for quantity of output, (6) high concern for process (*how* the goods or services are made or delivered), (7) low risk-taking activity, and (8) commitment to the goals of the organization.

Because quality enhancement typically involves greater employee commitment and utilization, fewer employees are needed to produce the same level of output. As quality rises, so does demand, yet this demand can be met with proportionately fewer employees than previously. Thanks to automation and a cooperative workforce, Toyota is producing about 3.5 million vehicles a year with 25,000 production workers—about the same number as in 1966 when it was producing 1 million vehicles. In addition to having more productive workers, fewer are needed to repair the rejects caused by poor quality. This phenomenon has also occurred at Corning Glass, Honda, and L.L. Bean.

---

[17]The following discussion is based on our survey and observations, and on findings reported on by others. For a review of what others have reported, see R.S. Schuler's "Human Resource Management Practice Choices," *Human Resource Planning,* March 1987, pp. 1–19.

[18]M. McComas, "Cutting Costs without Killing the Business," *Fortune,* October 13, 1986, p. 76.

[19]For a detailed presentation of Mercury Marine's program to improve quality, see Endnote 18 above.

[20]S.E. Prokesch, "Bean Meshes Man, Machine," *The New York Times,* December 23, 1985, pp. 19, 21.

Cost-Reduction Strategy and Needed Role Behaviors

Often, the characteristics of a firm pursuing the cost-reduction strategy are tight controls, overhead minimization, and pursuit of economies of scale. The primary focus of these measures is to increase productivity, that is, output cost per person. This can mean a reduction in the number of employees and/or a reduction in wage levels. Since 1980, the textile industry's labor force decreased by 17 percent, primary metals almost 30 percent, and steel, 40 percent. The result has been that, over the past four years, productivity growth in manufacturing has averaged 4.1 percent per year, versus 1.2 percent for the rest of the economy.[21] Similar measures have been taken at Chrysler and Ford and now are being proposed at GM and AT&T. Reflecting on these trends, Federal Reserve Governor Wayne D. Angell states, "We are invigorating the manufacturing sector. The period of adjustment has made us more competitive."[22]

In addition to reducing the number of employees, firms are also reducing wage levels. For example, in the household appliance industry where GE, Whirlpool, Electrolux, and Maytag account for 80 percent of all production, labor costs have been cut by shifting plants from states where labor is expensive to less-costly sites. The result of this is that a new breed of cost-effective firms is putting U.S. manufacturing back on the road to profitability.[23]

Cost reduction can also be pursued through increased use of part-time employees, subcontractors, work simplification and measurement procedures, automation, work rule changes, and job assignment flexibility. Thus, there are several methods for reducing costs. Although the details are vastly different, they all share the goal of reducing output cost per employee.

In summary, the profile of employee role behav-iors necessary for firms seeking to gain competitive advantage by pursuing the competitive strategy of cost reduction is as follows: (1) relatively repetitive and predictable behaviors, (2) a rather short-term focus, (3) primarily autonomous or individual activity, (4) modest concern for quality, (5) high concern for quantity of output (goods or services), (6) primary concern for results, (7) low risk-taking activity, and (8) a relatively high degree of comfort with stability.

Given these competitive strategies and the needed role behaviors, what HRM practices need to be linked with each of the three strategies?

Typology of HRM Practices

When deciding what human resource practices to use to link with competitive strategy, organizations can choose from six human resource practice "menus." Each of the six menus concerns a different aspect of human resource management. These aspects are planning, staffing, appraising, compensating, and training and development.

A summary of these menus is shown in Exhibit 2. Notice that each of the choices runs along a continuum. Most of the options are self-explanatory, but a rundown of the staffing menu will illustrate how the process works. A more detailed description of all menus is provided elsewhere.[24]

Recruitment

In each of these areas, a business unit (or a plant) must make a number of decisions; the first choice involving where to recruit employees. Companies can rely on the internal labor market, for example, other departments in the firm and other levels in the organizational hierarchy, or they can rely on the external labor market exclusively. Although this decision may not be significant for entry-level jobs, it is very important for most other jobs. Recruiting internally essentially means a policy of promotion from within. While this policy can serve as an effective reward, it commits a firm to providing train-

[21]S.E. Prokesch, "Are America's Manufacturers Finally Back on the Map?" *Business Week,* November 17, 1986, pp. 92, 97.

[22]Ibid., p. 92.

[23]Ibid., p. 97. For more on Electrolux's human resource practices, see B.J. Feder's "The Man Who Modernized Electrolux," *The New York Times,* December 31, 1986, p. 24.

[24]Schuler, 1987, in footnote 17.

EXHIBIT 2
Human Resource Management Practice Menus

Planning Choices

Informal	_____	Formal
Short term	_____	Long term
Explicit job analysis	_____	Implicit job analysis
Job simplification	_____	Job enrichment
Low employee involvement	_____	High employee involvement

Staffing Choices

Internal sources	_____	External sources
Narrow paths	_____	Broad paths
Single ladder	_____	Multiple ladders
Explicit criteria	_____	Implicit criteria
Limited socialization	_____	Extensive socialization
Closed procedures	_____	Open procedures

Appraising Choices

Behavioral Criteria	_____	Results criteria
Purposes: Development, Remedial, Maintenance		
Low employee participation	_____	High employee participation
Short-term criteria	_____	Long-term criteria
Individual criteria	_____	Group criteria

Compensating Choices

Low base salaries	_____	High base salaries
Internal equity	_____	External equity
Few perks	_____	Many perks
Standard, fixed package	_____	Flexible package
Low participation	_____	High participation
No incentives	_____	Many incentives
Short-term incentives	_____	Long-term incentives
No employment security	_____	High employment security
Hierarchical	_____	High participation

Training and Development

Short term	_____	Long term
Narrow application	_____	Broad application
Productivity emphasis	_____	Quality of work life emphasis
Spontaneous, unplanned	_____	Planned, systematic
Individual orientation	_____	Group orientation
Low participation	_____	High participation

Adapted from R. S. Schuler, "Human Resource Management Practice Choices," in R. S. Schuler, S. A. Youngblood, and V. L. Huber (eds.), *Readings in Personnel and Human Resource Management,* 3rd ed., (St. Paul, Minn.: West Publishing, 1988).

ing and career development opportunities if the promoted employees are to perform well.

Career Paths

Here, the company must decide whether to establish broad or narrow career paths for its employees. The broader the paths, the greater the opportunity for employees to acquire skills that are relevant to many functional areas and to gain exposure and visibility within the firm. Either a broad or a narrow career path may enhance an employee's acquisition of skills and opportunities for promotion, but the time frame is likely to be much longer for broad skill acquisition than for the acquisition of a more limited skill base. Although promotion may be quicker under a policy of narrow career paths, an employee's career opportunities may be more limited over the long run.

Promotions

Another staffing decision to be made is whether to establish one or several promotion ladders. Establishing several ladders enlarges the opportunities for employees to be promoted and yet stay within a given technical specialty without having to assume managerial responsibilities. Establishing just one promotion ladder enhances the relative value of a promotion and increases the competition for it.

Part and parcel of a promotion system are the criteria used in deciding who to promote. The criteria can vary from the very explicit to the very implicit. The more explicit the criteria, the less adaptable the promotion system is to exceptions and changing circumstances. What the firm loses in flexibility, the employee may gain in clarity. This clarity, however, may benefit only those who fulfill the criteria exactly. On the other hand, the more implicit the criteria, the greater the flexibility to move employees around to develop them more broadly.

Socialization

After an employee is hired or promoted, he or she is next socialized. With minimal socialization, firms convey few informal rules and establish new procedures to immerse employees in the culture and practices of the organization. Although it is probably easier and cheaper to do this than to provide maximum socialization, the result is likely to be a more restricted psychological attachment and commitment by the employee to the firm, and perhaps less predictable behavior from the employee.

Openness

A final choice to be made in the staffing menu is the degree of openness in the staffing procedures. The more open the procedures, the more likely there is to be job posting for internal recruitment and self-nomination for promotion. To facilitate a policy of openness, firms need to make the relevant information available to employees. Such a policy is worthwhile; since it allows employees to select themselves into jobs, it is a critical aspect of attaining successful job-person fit. The more secret the procedures, the more limited the involvement of employees in selection decisions, but the faster the decision can be made.

A key aspect of the choices within the staffing activity or any other HRM activity is that different choices stimulate and reinforce different role behaviors. Because these have been described in detail elsewhere, their impact is summarized below.

Hypotheses of Competitive Strategy-HRM Archetypes

Based on the above descriptions of competitive strategies and the role behaviors necessary for each, and the brief typology of HRM practices, we offer three summary hypotheses.

Innovation Strategy

Firms pursuing the innovation strategy are likely to have the following characteristics: (1) jobs that require close interaction and coordination among groups of individuals, (2) performance appraisals that are more likely to reflect longer-term and group-based achievements, (3) jobs that allow employees to develop skills that can be used in other positions in the firm, (4) compensation systems that emphasize internal equity, rather than external or market-based equity, (5) pay rates that tend to be low, but that allow employees to be stockholders and have more freedom to choose the mix of components (salary, bonus, stock options) that make up their pay package, and (6) broad career paths to reinforce the development of a broad range of skills. These practices facilitate cooperative, interdependent behavior that is oriented toward the longer term, and foster exchange of ideas and risk taking.[25]

---

[25]E.E. Lawler III, "The Strategic Design of Reward Systems," in R.S. Scholer and S.A. Youngblood (eds.), *Readings in Personnel and Human Resource Management*, 2nd ed. (St. Paul, Minn.: West Publishing, 1984), pp. 253–69; and R.S. Schuler, "Human Resource Management Practice Choices," in R.S. Schuler, S.A. Youngblood, and V.L. Huber (eds.), *Readings in Personnel and Human Resource Management*, 3rd ed. (St. Paul, Minn.: West Publishing, 1988.) Other factors that can influence the human resource practices are top management, hierarchical considerations, what other firms are doing, what the firm has done in the past, the type of technology, size and age of firm, unionization status, and the legal environment and its structure (see R.K. Kazanjian and R. Drazin, " Implementing Manufacturing Innovations: Critical Choices of Structure and Staffing Roles," *Human Resource Management*, Fall 1986, pp. 385–404).

Quality-Enhancement Strategy

In an attempt to gain competitive advantage through the quality-enhancement strategy, the key HRM practices include (1) relatively fixed and explicit job descriptions, (2) high levels of employee participation in decisions relevant to immediate work conditions and the job itself, (3) a mix of individual and group criteria for performance appraisal that is mostly short-term and results-oriented, (4) relatively egalitarian treatment of employees and some guarantees of employment security, and (5) extensive and continuous training and development of employees. These practices facilitate quality enhancement by helping to ensure highly reliable behavior from individuals who can identify with the goals of the organization and, when necessary, be flexible and adaptable to new job assignments and technological change.[26]

Cost-Reduction Strategy

In attempting to gain competitive advantage by pursuing a strategy of cost reduction, key human resource practice choices include (1) relatively fixed (stable) and explicit job descriptions that allow little room for ambiguity, (2) narrowly designed jobs and narrowly defined career paths that encourage specialization, expertise, and efficiency, (3) short-term, results-oriented performance appraisals, (4) close monitoring of market pay levels for use in making compensation decisions, and (5) minimal levels of employee training and development. These practices maximize efficiency by providing means for management to monitor and control closely the activities of employees.[27]

An Innovative Strategy: One Company's Experience

Frost, Inc., is one company that has made a conscious effort to match competitive strategy with human resource management practices. Located in Grand Rapids, Michigan, Frost is a manufacturer of overhead conveyor trolleys used primarily in the auto industry, with sales of $20 million.[28] Concerned about depending too heavily on one cyclical industry, President Charles D. "Chad" Frost made several attempts to diversify the business, first into manufacturing lawn mower components and later into material-handling systems, such as floor conveyors and hoists. These attempts failed. The engineers didn't know how to design unfamiliar components, production people didn't know how to make them, and sales people didn't know how to sell them. Chad Frost diagnosed the problem as inflexibility. "We had single-purpose machines and single-purpose people," he said, "including single-purpose managers."

Frost decided that automating production was the key to flexibility. Twenty-six old-fashioned screw machines on the factory floor were replaced with 11 numerical-controlled machines paired within 18 industrial robots. Frost decided to design and build an automated storage-and-retrieval inventory control system, which would later be sold as a proprietary product, and to automate completely the front office to reduce indirect labor costs. The new program was formally launched in late 1983.

What at first glance appeared to be a hardware-oriented strategy turned out to be an exercise in human resource management. "If you're going to reap a real benefit in renovating a small to medium-size company, the machinery is just one part, perhaps the easiest part, of the renovation process," says Robert McIntyre, head of Amprotech, Inc., an affiliated consulting company Frost formed early in the automation project to provide an objective, "outside" view. "The hardest part is getting people to change."

Frost was clearly embarking on a strategy of innovation. As it turns out, many of the choices the company made about human resource practices were intended to support the employee role behaviors identified as being crucial to the success of an innovation strategy.

[26]P.F. Drucker, *Innovation and Entrepreneurship* (New York: Harper & Row, 1985); K. Albrecht and S. Albrecht, *The Creative Corporation* (Homewood, Ill.: Dow Jones-Irwin, 1987).

[27]P.F. Drucker, "Quality Means a Whole New Approach to Manufacturing," *Business Week*, June 8, 1987, pp. 131–43; P.F. Drucker, "Puleeze! Will Somebody Help Me?" *Time*, February 2, 1987, pp. 48–57; and R.L. Desatnick, *Managing to Keep the Customer* (San Francisco: Jossey-Bass, 1987).

[28]This description is expanded upon in detail in S. Galante, "Frost, Inc.," *Human Resource Planning*, March 1987, pp. 57–67.

For example, the company immediately set out to increase employee identification with the company by giving each worker 10 shares of the closely held company and by referring to them henceforth as "shareholder-employees." The share ownership, which employees can increase by making additional purchases through a 401(d) plan, are also intended to give employees a long-term focus, which is another behavior important for an innovation strategy to succeed. Additional long-term incentives consist of a standard corporate profit-sharing plan and a discretionary profit-sharing plan administered by Chad Frost.

Frost's compensation package was also restructured to strike a balance between results (productivity) and process (manufacturing). In Frost's case, the latter is a significant consideration, since the production process is at the heart of the company's innovation strategy. Frost instituted a quarterly bonus that is based on companywide productivity, and established a "celebration fund" that managers can tap at their discretion to reward significant employee contributions. The bonuses serve to foster other needed employee role behaviors. By making the quarterly bonus dependent on companywide productivity, the company is encouraging cooperative, interdependent behavior. The "celebration fund" meanwhile, can be used to reward and reinforce innovative behavior. (Even the form of the celebration can be creative. Rewards can range from dinner with Chad Frost to a weekend for an employee and spouse at a local hotel, to a belly dancing performance in the office.)

Frost encourages cooperative behavior in a number of other ways as well. Most offices (including Chad Frost's) lack doors, which is intended to foster openness of communication. Most executive perks have been eliminated, and all employees have access to the company's mainframe computer (with the exception of payroll information) by way of more than 40 terminals scattered around the front office and factory floor.

In our view, a vital component of any innovation strategy is getting employees to broaden their skills, assume more responsibilities, and take risks. Frost encourages employees to learn new skills by paying for extensive training programs, both at the company and at local colleges. It even goes further, identifying the development of additional skills as a prerequisite for advancement. This is partly out of necessity, since Frost has compressed its 11 previous levels of hierarchy into 4. Because this has made it harder to reward employees through traditional methods of promotion, employees are challenged to advance by adding skills, assuming more responsibilities, and taking risks.

Honda's Quality-Enhancement Strategy

We can identify those human resource practices that facilitate product quality by examining Honda of America's Marysville, Ohio, plant.[29] With a current work force of approximately 4,500, this plant produces cars of quality comparable to those produced by Honda plants in Japan. Although pay rates (independent of bonuses) may be as much as 30–40 percent lower than rates at other Midwest auto plants, Honda has fewer layoffs and lower inventory rates of new cars than its competitors. How is this possible?

One possible explanation is that Honda knows that the delivery of quality products depends on predictable and reliable behavior from its employees. In the initial employee-orientation session, which may last between three and four hours, job security is emphasized. Employees' spouses are encouraged to attend these sessions, because Honda believes that spouse awareness of the company and its demands on employees can help minimize absenteeism, tardiness, and turnover. Of course, something so critical to quality as reliable behavior is not stimulated and reinforced by only one human resource practice. For example, associates who have perfect attendance for four straight weeks receive a bonus of $56. Attendance also influences the size of the semiannual bonus (typically paid in spring and autumn). Impressive attendance figures also enhance an employee's chances for promotion. (Honda of America has a policy of promotion from within.)

In addition to getting and reinforcing reliable and

---

[29]For additional collaborating information, see J. Merwin, "A Tale of Two Worlds," *Forbes,* June 16, 1986, pp. 101–105; and S. Chira, "At 80, Honda's Founder Is Still a Fiery Maverick," *New York Times,* January 12, 1987, p. 35.

predictable behavior, Honda's HRM practices encourage a longer-term employee orientation and a flexibility to change. Employment security, along with constant informal and formal training programs, facilitate these role behaviors. Training programs are tailored to the needs of the associates (employees) through the formal performance-appraisal process, which is developmental rather than evaluational. Team leaders (not supervisors) are trained in spotting and removing performance deficiencies as they occur. To help speed communication and remove any organizational sources of performance deficiencies, the structure of the organization is such that there are only four levels between associates and the plant manager.

At Honda, cooperative, interdependent behavior is fostered by egalitarian HRM practices. All associates wear identical uniforms with their first names embossed; parking spaces are unmarked, and there is only one cafeteria. All entry-level associates receive the same rate of pay except for a 60-cents-an-hour shift differential. The modern health center adjacent to the main plant is open to all. These practices, in turn, encourage all associates to regard themselves collectively as "us" rather than "us" versus "them." Without this underlying attitude, the flexible work rules, air-conditioned plant, and automation wouldn't be enough to sustain associate commitment and identification with the organization's goal of high quality.

The success of Honda's quality enhancement strategy goes beyond concern for its own HRM practices. It is also concerned with the human resource practices of other organizations, such as its suppliers. For example, Delco-Remy's practice of participative management style, as well as its reputation of producing quality products at competitive prices, was the reason why Delco was selected by Honda as its sole supplier of batteries.[30]

A Cost-Reduction Strategy at United Parcel Service

Through meticulous human engineering and close scrutiny of its 152,000 employees, United Parcel Service (UPS) has grown highly profitable despite stiff competition. According to Larry P. Breakiron, the company's senior vice president of engineering,

"Our ability to manage labor and hold it accountable is the key to success."[31] In other words, in an industry where "a package is a package," UPS succeeds by its cost-reduction strategy.

Of all paths that can be taken to pursue a cost-reduction strategy, the one taken by UPS is the work standard/simplification method. This method has been the key to gains in efficiency and productivity increases. UPS's founder, James E. Casey, put a premium on efficiency. In the 1920s, Casey hired pioneers of time and motion study, such as Frank Gilbreth and Fredrick Taylor, to measure the time each UPS driver spent each day on specific tasks. UPS engineers cut away the sides of UPS trucks to study how the drivers performed, and then made changes in techniques to enhance worker effectiveness. The establishment of effective work standards has led not only to enormous gains in efficiency and cost reduction; it actually makes employees less tired at the end of the day. During the day, the employees engage in short-term, highly repetitive role behaviors that involve little risk taking. Because specialists identify the best way to accomplish tasks, employee participation in job decisions is unnecessary.

Through the use of time and motion studies, UPS has established very specific ways for workers to perform their jobs. The company also monitors closely the performance of the workers. More than 1,000 industrial engineers use time and motion study to set standards for a variety of closely supervised tasks. In return, the UPS drivers, all of whom are Teamsters, earn approximately $15 per hour—a dollar or so more than the drivers at other companies. In addition, employees who perform at acceptable levels enjoy job security.

Implementation Issues

These descriptions of Frost, Honda, and UPS illustrate how a few organizations systematically match their HRM practices not only with their articulated competitive strategies but also with their

---

[30]As reported in Schuler and MacMillan, "Gaining Competitive Advantage through Human Resource Management Practices," *Human Resource Management*, Autumn 1984, pp. 249–250.

[31]D. Machalaba, "United Parcel Service Gets Deliveries Done by Driving Its Workers," *The Wall Street Journal*, April 22, 1986, pp. 1 and 23.

perceptions of needed role behavior from their employees. Although only a beginning, the success of these firms suggests that HRM practices for all levels of employees are affected by strategic considerations. Thus, while it may be important to match the characteristics of top management with the strategy of the organization, it may be *as* important to do this for *all* employees.

Although the results of these examples generally support the three major hypotheses, they also raise several central issues: Which competitive strategy is best? Is it best to have one competitive strategy or several? What are the implications of a change of competitive strategy?

Which Competitive Strategy Is Best?

Of the three competitive strategies described here, deciding which is best depends on several factors. Certainly customer wants and the nature of the competition are key factors. If customers are demanding quality, a cost-reduction strategy may not be as fruitful as quality-improvement strategy. At the Mercury Marine division of Brunswick and at Corning Glass Works, the issues seem to be quality. According to McComas, "Customers, particularly industrial trial buyers, would have been no more inclined to buy their products even if the manufacturer could have passed along savings of, say, 10 percent or even 20 percent."[32]

If, however, the product or service is relatively undifferentiated, such as the overnight parcel delivery industry, a cost-reduction strategy may be the best way to gain competitive advantage. Even here, though, there is a choice. United Parcel Service, for example, is pursuing the cost-reduction strategy through work process refinements, such as work clarification, standardization, measurement, and feedback. Roadway, in contrast, pursues the same strategy by combining employee independence and ownership (drivers own their own trucks, of various colors; UPS drivers do not own their brown trucks) with as much automation as possible.[33] The advantage of these latter approaches to cost reduction,

compared with such approaches as wage concessions or work-force reductions, is the amount of time required to implement them. Cost reduction through wage concessions or employee reductions, though painful, can be relatively straightforward to implement. As a consequence, it can be duplicated by others, essentially eliminating the competitive advantage gained by being able to offer lower prices. The adoption of two-tiered wage contracts within the airline industry is a good example: Soon after American Airlines installed a two-tier wage system for its pilots, Eastern, United, and Frontier Airlines negotiated similar contracts with their employees.

There may, however, be some external conditions that might permit the success of a strategy of cost reduction to last. After four straight years of losses and a shrinkage in the number of stores from nearly 3,500 in 1974 to a little more than 1,000 in 1982, the Great Atlantic & Pacific Tea Company (A&P) and the United Food and Commercial Workers (UFCW) saw the handwriting on the wall: Either reduce costs and be competitive, or go out of business. According to a *Business Week* article:

> In an experimental arrangement negotiated with the . . . UFCW at 60 stores in the Philadelphia area, workers took a 25 percent pay cut in exchange for an unusual promise: If a store's employees could keep labor costs at 10 percent of sales—by working more efficiently or by boosting store traffic—they'd get a cash bonus equal to 1 percent of the store's sales. They'd get a 0.5 percent bonus at 11 percent of sales or 1.5% at 9.5 percent of sales. It was a gamble in the low-margin supermarket business, but it worked.[35]

The result? An 81 percent increase in operating profits in 1984 and a doubling of A&P's stock price. Although the UFCW agreed with the incentive compensation scheme at A&P, the union appears unwilling to see this practice spread. Consequently, competitors of A&P, such as Giant Food, Inc., would

---

[32]M. McComas, "Cutting Costs without Killing the Business," *Fortune*, October 13, 1986, p. 77.
   [33]Ibid.

[34]M. McComas, "How A&P Fattens Profits by Sharing Them," *Business Week*, December 22, 1986, p. 44. For an excellent discussion of the difficulties to be overcome in dealing with changing from human resource practices based on hierarchy or status to those based on performance or what's needed, see R.M. Kanter, "The New Workforce Meets the Changing Workplace: Strains, Dilemmas, and Contradictions in Attempts to Implement Participative and Entrepreneurial Management," *Human Resource Management*, Winter 1986, pp. 515–538.

have difficulty implementing the same scheme.[35]

By contrast, a quality-improvement strategy, whether by automation or quality teams, is more time consuming and difficult to implement. As the U.S. auto industry has experienced, it is taking a long time to overcome the competitive advantage gained by the Japanese auto industry through quality improvement. The J.D. Powers 1986 Consumer Satisfaction Index of automobiles suggests, however, that Ford's dedicated approach to quality enhancement may be reaping benefits.

One Competitive Strategy or Several?

Although we focused on the pursuit of a common competitive strategy in our examples, this may be oversimplifying reality. For example, at Honda in Marysville, associates are encouraged to be innovative. Each year the group of associates that designs the most unique or unusual transportation vehicle is awarded a trip to Japan. At UPS, teamwork and cooperation are valued and at Frost, Inc., product and service quality are of paramount importance. Lincoln Electric is recognized as one of the lowest-cost *and* highest-quality producers of arc welders. While these examples indicate that organizations may pursue more than one competitive strategy at a time, it may be that organizations actually need to have multiple and concurrent competitive strategies. Using multiple strategies results in the challenge of stimulating and rewarding different role behaviors while at the same time trying to manage the conflicts and tensions that may arise as a consequence. This may be the very essence of the top manager's job. According to Mitchell Kapor of Lotus Development Corporation:

> To be a successful enterprise, we have to do two apparently contradictory things quite well: We have to stay innovative and creative, but at the same time we have to be tightly controlled about certain aspects of our corporate behavior. But I think that what you have to do about paradox is embrace it. So we have the kind of company where certain things are very

loose and other things are very tight. The whole art of management is sorting things into the loose pile or the tight pile and then watching them carefully.[36]

Perhaps, then, the top manager's job is facilitated by separating business units or functional areas that have different competitive strategies. To the extent that this separation is limited or that a single-business unit has multiple strategies, effective means of confrontation and collaboration need to exist. However, even with this issue under control, there is another equally significant challenge.

Change of Competitive Strategy

By implication, changes in strategy should be accompanied by changes in human resources practices. As the products of firms change, as their customers' demands change, and, as the competition changes, the competitive strategies of firms will change. Consequently, employees will face an ever-changing employment relationship. A significant implication of this is that employees of a single firm may be exposed to different sets of human resource practices during the course of employment. Thus, employees may be asked to exhibit different role behaviors over time and they may be exposed to several different conditions of employment. Although it remains to be seen whether all employees can adjust to such changes, it appears that many can and have. For those who wish not to, firms may offer outplacement assistance to another firm, or even to another division in the company. For those who have problems changing, firms may offer training programs to facilitate the acquisition of necessary skills and abilities as well as needed role behaviors.

Another implication is that all components of a system of human resource practices need to be changed and implemented simultaneously. The key human resource practices work together to stimulate and reinforce particular needed employee behaviors. Not to invoke a particular practice (e.g., high participation) implies invoking another (e.g., low participation) that is less likely to stimulate and reinforce the necessary employee behaviors. The likely

---

[35]For a discussion of relevant issues, see D.Q. Mills, "When Employees Make Concessions," *Harvard Business Review*, May–June 1983, pp. 103–113; and R.R. Rehder and M.M. Smith, "Kaizen and the Art of Labor Relations," *Personnel Journal*, December 1986, pp. 83–94.

[36]*Boston Globe*, January 27, 1985.

result is that employees will experience conflict, ambiguity, and frustration.

Conclusion

The recent attack on U.S. firms for failing to keep costs down, not maintaining quality, and ignoring innovation are misdirected, given what many firms like Frost, Honda-Marysville, UPS, Corning Glass, A&P, 3M, and Brunswick are doing.[37] These firms and others are pursuing competitive strategies aimed at cost reduction, quality improvement, and innovation. The aim in implementing these strategies is to gain competitive advantage and beat the competition—both domestically and internationally. While cost and market conditions tend to constrain somewhat the choice of competitive strategy, the constraint appears to be one of degree, rather than of kind. Consequently, we can find firms pursuing these three competitive strategies regardless of industry.

All firms are not seeking to gain competitive strategy. Not doing so, however, is becoming more of a luxury. For those attempting to do so, the experiences of other firms suggest that effectiveness can be increased by systematically melding human resource practices with the selected competitive strategy. Certainly, the success or failure of a firm is not likely to turn entirely on its human resource management practices, but the HRM practices are likely to be critical.[38]

---

[37]Recent attacks on public and private firms have been summarized by the use of the word *corpocracy*. A description of corpocracy is found in M. Green and J.F. Berry's "Takeovers, a Symptom of Corpocracy," *New York Times*, December 3, 1986.

---

[38]The application of these human resource practices to strategy can be done by a firm on itself and even upon other firms that may be upstream or downstream of the local firm. For a further description, see Schuler and MacMillan (footnote 30).

ENDNOTE: The authors wish to thank John W. Slocum, Jr., C.K. Prahalad, and John Dutton for their many helpful suggestions, and the Human Resource Planning Society, the Center for Entrepreneurial Studies, New York University, and the University of Michigan for their financial support of this project.

APPENDIX

Preparing a Case for Class Discussion or for Written Assignments

I keep six honest serving men
(They taught me all I knew);
Their names are What and Why and When;
And How and Where and Who.
Rudyard Kipling

In most courses in strategic management, students practice at being strategy-managers via case analysis. A case sets forth, in a factual manner, the events and organizational circumstances surrounding a particular managerial situation. It puts readers at the scene of the action and familiarizes them with the situation as it prevailed. A case on strategic management can concern a whole industry, a single organization, or some part of an organization; the organization involved can be either profit seeking or not-for-profit. The essence of the student's role in case analysis is to *diagnose* and *size up* the situation described in the case and *recommend* what, if any, actions need to be taken.

WHY USE CASES TO PRACTICE STRATEGIC MANAGEMENT

A student of business with tact
Absorbed many answers he lacked.
But acquiring a job,
He said with a sob,
"How *does* one fit answer to fact?"

The foregoing limerick was offered some years ago by Charles I. Gragg in a classic article, "Because Wisdom Can't Be Told," to characterize the plight of business students who had no exposure to cases.[1] Gragg observed that the mere act of listening to lectures and sound advice about managing does little for anyone's

---

[1]Charles I. Gragg, "Because Wisdom Can't Be Told," in *The Case Method at the Harvard Business School*, ed. M.P. McNair (New York: McGraw-Hill, 1954), p. 11.

management skills and that the accumulated managerial experience and wisdom cannot effectively be passed on by lectures and readings alone. Gragg suggested that if anything has been learned about the practice of management, it is that a storehouse of ready-made textbook answers does not exist. Each managerial situation has unique aspects, requiring its own diagnosis, judgment, and tailor-made actions. Cases provide would-be managers with a valuable way to practice wrestling with the actual problems of actual managers in actual companies.

The case approach to strategic analysis is, first and foremost, an exercise in learning by doing. Since cases provide you with detailed information about conditions and problems of different industries and companies, your task of analyzing company after company and situation after situation has the twin benefit of boosting your analytical skills and giving you some "experience" in the ways companies and managers actually do things. Few college students have much direct personal contact with different kinds of companies and real-life strategic situations. Cases offer a viable substitute for actual on-the-job experience by (1) bringing you into close contact with a variety of industries, organizations, and strategic problems; (2) forcing you to assume a managerial role (as opposed to that of just an onlooker); (3) providing a test of how to apply the tools and techniques of strategic management; and (4) asking you to come up with pragmatic managerial action plans to deal with the issues at hand.

OBJECTIVES OF CASE ANALYSIS

Using cases to learn about strategic management is beneficial to you the student in five specific ways:[2]

1. Increasing your understanding of what managers must do and not do to make a business succeed over the long haul.
2. Building your skills in conducting strategic analysis in a variety of industries, competitive situations, and company circumstances.
3. Giving you valuable practice in diagnosing strategic issues, evaluating strategic alternatives, and formulating workable plans of action.
4. Enhancing your sense of business judgment, as opposed to uncritically accepting the authoritative crutch of the professor or "back-of-the-book" answers.
5. Providing you with in-depth exposure to the conditions and problems of different industries and companies in ways that give you something close to actual business experience.

If you understand that these are the objectives of case analysis, then you are less likely to be consumed with curiosity about "the answer to the case." Students who have grown comfortable with and accustomed to textbook statements of fact and definitive lecture notes are often frustrated when discussions about a case do not produce concrete answers. Usually, case discussions produce good arguments for more than one course of action. Differences of opinion nearly always exist. Thus, should a class discussion conclude without a strong, unambiguous consensus

---

[2]Ibid., pp. 12–14; and D.R. Schoen and Philip A. Sprague, "What Is the Case Method?" in *The Case Method at the Harvard Business School*, ed. M.P. McNair, pp. 78–79.

on what to do, don't grumble too much when you are *not* told what the answer is or what the company actually did. Just remember that in the business world answers don't come in conclusive black-and-white terms. There are nearly always several feasible courses of action and approaches, each of which may work out satisfactorily. Moreover, in the business world when one elects a particular course of action, there is no peeking at the back of a book to see if you have chosen the best thing to do and no one to turn to for a provably correct answer. The only valid test of management action is *results*. If the results of an action turn out to be "good," the decision to take it may be presumed "right." If not, then the action chosen was "wrong" in the sense that it "didn't work out."

Hence, the important thing for a student to understand in case analysis is that it is the managerial exercise of identifying, diagnosing, and recommending that builds your skills; discovering the right answer or finding out what actually happened is no more than frosting on the cake. Even if you learn what the company did, you can't conclude that it was necessarily right or best. All that can be said is "here is what they did . . ."

The point is this: *The purpose of giving you a case assignment is not to cause you to run to the library to look up what the company actually did but, rather, to enhance your skills in sizing up situations and developing your managerial judgment about what needs to be done and how to do it.* The aim of case analysis is for *you* to bear the strains of thinking actively, of offering your analysis, of proposing action plans, and of explaining and defending your assessments—this is how cases provide you with meaningful practice at being a manager.

PREPARING A CASE FOR CLASS DISCUSSION

If this is your first experience with the case method, you may have to reorient your study habits. Unlike lecture courses where you can get by without preparing intensively for each class and where you have latitude to work assigned readings and reviews of lecture notes into your schedule, *a case assignment requires conscientious preparation before class*. You will not get much out of hearing the class discuss a case you haven't read, and you certainly won't be able to contribute anything yourself to the discussion. What you have got to do to get ready for class discussion of a case is to study the case, reflect carefully on the situation presented, and develop some reasoned thoughts. Your goal in preparing the case should be to end up with what you think is a sound, well-supported analysis of the situation and a sound, defensible set of recommendations about what managerial actions need to be taken.

To prepare a case for class discussion, we suggest the following approach:

1. *Read the case through rather quickly for familiarity.* The initial reading should give you the general flavor of the situation and indicate what issue or issues are involved. If your instructor has provided you with study questions for the case, now is the time to read them carefully.
2. *Read the case a second time.* On this reading, try to gain full command of the facts. Begin to develop some tentative answers to the study questions your instructor has provided. If your instructor has elected not to give you assignment

questions, then now is the time to decide whether there's one big issue, several big issues, or a bunch of lesser issues, some related and some not; get a handle on how serious the issues posed in the case are.

3. *Study all the exhibits carefully.* Often, the real story is in the numbers contained in the exhibits. Expect the information in the case exhibits to be crucial enough to materially affect your diagnosis of the situation.

4. *Decide what the strategic issues are.* Until you have identified the strategic issues and problems in the case, you don't know what to analyze, what tools and analytical techniques are called for, or otherwise how to proceed. At times the strategic issues are clear—either being stated in the case or else obvious from reading the case. At other times you will have to dig them out from all the information given.

5. *Start your analysis of the issues with some number crunching.* A big majority of strategy cases call for some kind of number crunching on your part. This means calculating assorted financial ratios to check out the company's financial condition and recent performance, calculating growth rates of sales or profits or unit volume, checking out profit margins and the makeup of the cost structure, and understanding whatever revenue-cost-profit relationships are present. See Table 1 for a summary of key financial ratios, how they are calculated, and what they show.

6. *Use whatever tools and techniques of strategic analysis are called for.* Strategic analysis is not just a collection of opinions; rather, it entails application of a growing number of powerful tools and techniques that cut beneath the surface and produce important insight and understanding of strategic situations. Every case assigned is strategy related and contains opportunity to usefully apply the weapons of strategic analysis. Your instructor will be looking for you to demonstrate that you know *how* and *when* to use the strategic-management concepts that have been presented and covered earlier in the course. Furthermore, expect to have to draw regularly on what you have learned in your finance, economics, production, marketing, and human resources management courses.

7. *Check out conflicting opinions and make some judgments about the validity of all the data and information provided.* Many times cases will report views and opinions that are contradictory (after all, people don't always agree on things, and different people see the same things in different ways). Forcing you to evaluate the validity of the data and information presented in the case helps you develop your powers of inference and judgment. Asking you to resolve conflicting information "comes with the territory" because a great many managerial situations entail opposing points of view, conflicting trends, and inaccurate information.

8. *Support your diagnosis and opinions with reasons and evidence.* The most important thing to prepare for are your answers to the question "Why?" For instance, if after studying the case you are of the opinion that the company's managers are "doing a poor job," then it is your answer to "Why?" that establishes just how good your analysis of the situation is. If your instructor has provided you with specific study questions for the case, then by all means prepare answers that include all the reasons and number-crunching evidence

TABLE 1
A Summary of Key Financial Ratios, How They Are Calculated, and What They Show

Ratio	How Calculated	What It Shows
Profitability ratios:		
1. Gross profit margin	$\dfrac{\text{Sales} - \text{Cost of goods sold}}{\text{Sales}}$	An indication of the total margin available to cover operating expenses and yield a profit.
2. Operating profit margin (or return on sales)	$\dfrac{\text{Profits before taxes and before interest}}{\text{Sales}}$	An indication of the firm's profitability from current operations without regard to the interest charges accruing from the capital structure.
3. Net profit margin (or net return on sales)	$\dfrac{\text{Profits after taxes}}{\text{Sales}}$	Shows aftertax profits per dollar of sales. Subpar-profit margins indicate that the firm's sales prices are relatively low or that its costs are relatively high, or both.
4. Return on total assets	$\dfrac{\text{Profits after taxes}}{\text{Total assets}}$ or $\dfrac{\text{Profits after taxes} + \text{Interest}}{\text{Total assets}}$	A measure of the return on total investment in the enterprise. It is sometimes desirable to add interest to aftertax profits to form the numerator of the ratio since total assets are financed by creditors as well as by stockholders; hence, it is accurate to measure the productivity of assets by the returns provided to both classes of investors.
5. Return on stockholder's equity (or return on net worth)	$\dfrac{\text{Profits after taxes}}{\text{Total stockholders' equity}}$	A measure of the rate of return on stockholders' investment in the enterprise.
6. Return on common equity	$\dfrac{\text{Profits after taxes} - \text{Preferred stock dividends}}{\text{Total stockholders equity} - \text{Par value of preferred stock}}$	A measure of the rate of return on the investment which the owners of the common stock have made in the enterprise.
7. Earnings per share	$\dfrac{\text{Profits after taxes} - \text{Preferred stock dividends}}{\text{Number of shares of common stock outstanding}}$	Shows the earnings available to the owners of each share of common stock.
Liquidity ratios:		
1. Current ratio	$\dfrac{\text{Current assets}}{\text{Current liabilities}}$	Indicates the extent to which the claims of short-term creditors are covered by assets that are expected to be converted to cash in a period roughly corresponding to the maturity of the liabilities.
2. Quick ratio (or acid-test ratio)	$\dfrac{\text{Current assets} - \text{Inventory}}{\text{Current liabilities}}$	A measure of the firm's ability to pay off short-term obligations without relying on the sale of its inventories.
3. Inventory to net working capital	$\dfrac{\text{Inventory}}{\text{Current assets} - \text{Current liabilities}}$	A measure of the extent to which the firm's working capital is tied up in inventory.
Leverage ratios:		
1. Debt-to-assets ratio	$\dfrac{\text{Total debt}}{\text{Total assets}}$	Measures the extent to which borrowed funds have been used to finance the firm's operations.
2. Debt-to-equity ratio	$\dfrac{\text{Total debt}}{\text{Total stockholders' equity}}$	Provides another measure of the funds provided by creditors versus the funds provided by owners.

TABLE 1 *(concluded)*

Ratio	How Calculated	What It Shows
3. Long-term debt-to-equity ratio	$$\frac{\text{Long-term debt}}{\text{Total stockholders' equity}}$$	A widely used measure of the balance between debt and equity in the firm's long-term capital structure.
4. Times-interest-earned (or coverage) ratio	$$\frac{\text{Profits before interest and taxes}}{\text{Total interest charges}}$$	Measures the extent to which earnings can decline without the firm becoming unable to meet its annual interest costs.
5. Fixed-charge coverage	$$\frac{\text{Profits before taxes and interest} + \text{Lease obligations}}{\text{Total interest charges} + \text{Lease obligations}}$$	A more inclusive indication of the firm's ability to meet all of its fixed-charge obligations.
Activity ratios:		
1. Inventory turnover	$$\frac{\text{Sales}}{\text{Inventory of finished goods}}$$	When compared to industry averages, it provides an indication of whether a company has excessive or perhaps inadequate finished goods inventory.
2. Fixed assets turnover	$$\frac{\text{Sales}}{\text{Fixed assets}}$$	A measure of the sales productivity and utilization of plant and equipment.
3. Total assets turnover	$$\frac{\text{Sales}}{\text{Total assets}}$$	A measure of the utilization of all the firm's assets; a ratio below the industry average indicates the company is not generating a sufficient volume of business, given the size of its asset investment.
4. Accounts receivable turnover	$$\frac{\text{Annual credit sales}}{\text{Accounts receivable}}$$	A measure of the average length of time it takes the firm to collect the sales made on credit.
5. Average collection period	$$\frac{\text{Accounts receivable}}{\text{Total sales} \div 365}$$ or $$\frac{\text{Accounts receivable}}{\text{Average daily sales}}$$	Indicates the average length of time the firm must wait after making a sale before it receives payment.
Other ratios:		
1. Dividend yield on common stock	$$\frac{\text{Annual dividends per share}}{\text{Current market price per share}}$$	A measure of the return to owners received in the form of dividends.
2. Price-earnings ratio	$$\frac{\text{Current market price per share}}{\text{Aftertax earnings per share}}$$	Faster growing or less risky firms tend to have higher price-earnings ratios than slower growing or more risky firms.
3. Dividend payout ratio	$$\frac{\text{Annual dividends per share}}{\text{Aftertax earnings per share}}$$	Indicates the percentage of profits paid out as dividends.
4. Cash flow per share	$$\frac{\text{Aftertax profits} + \text{Depreciation}}{\text{Number of common shares outstanding}}$$	A measure of the discretionary funds over and above expenses available for use by the firm.

Note: Industry-average ratios against which a particular company's ratios may be judged are available in *Modern Industry* and *Dun's Reviews* published by Dun & Bradstreet (14 ratios for 125 lines of business activities), Robert Morris Associates' *Annual Statement Studies* (11 ratios for 156 lines of business), and the FTC–SEC's *Quarterly Financial Report* for manufacturing corporations.

you can muster to support your diagnosis. *Generate at least two pages of notes!*

9. *Develop an appropriate action plan and set of recommendations.* Diagnosis divorced from corrective action is sterile. The test of a manager is always to convert sound analysis into sound actions—actions that will produce the desired results. Hence, the final and most telling step in preparing a case is to develop an "action agenda" for management that lays out a set of specific recommendations on what to do. Bear in mind that proposing realistic, workable solutions is far preferable to casually tossing out off-the-top-of-your-head suggestions. Be prepared to argue why your recommendations are more attractive than other courses of action that are open.

As long as you are conscientious in preparing your analysis and recommendations, and as long as you have ample reasons, evidence, and arguments to support your views, then you shouldn't fret unduly about whether what you've prepared is the right answer to the case. In case analysis there is rarely just one right approach or one right set of recommendations. Managing companies and devising and implementing strategies are not such exact sciences that there exists a single, provably correct analysis and action plan for each strategic situation. Of course, some analyses and action plans are better than others; but, in truth, there's nearly always more than one good way to analyze a situation and more than one good plan of action. So, if you have done a careful and thoughtful job of preparing the case, then don't waste your time worrying about the correctness of your work and judgment.

PARTICIPATING IN CLASS DISCUSSION OF A CASE

Classroom discussions of cases are sharply different from attending a lecture class. In a case class students do most of the talking. The instructor's role is to solicit student participation, keep the discussion on track, ask "Why?" often, offer alternative views, play the devil's advocate (if no students jump in to offer opposing views), and otherwise lead the discussion. It is the students in the class who carry the burden for analyzing the situation and for being prepared to present and defend their diagnoses and recommendations. Expect a classroom environment, therefore, that calls for *your* size up of the situation, *your* analysis, what actions *you* would take, and why *you* would take them. Do not be dismayed if, as the class discussion unfolds, some insightful things are said by your fellow classmates that you did not think of. It is normal for views and analyses to differ and for the comments of others in the class to expand your own thinking about the case. As the old adage goes, "Two heads are better than one." So it is to be expected that the class as a whole will do a more penetrating and searching job of case analysis than will any one person working alone. This is the power of group effort, and its virtues are that it will help you see more analytical applications, let you test your analyses and judgments against those of your peers, and force you to wrestle with differences of opinion and approaches.

To orient you to the classroom environment on the days a case discussion is scheduled, we compiled the following list of things to expect:

1. Expect students to dominate the discussion and do most of the talking. The case method enlists a maximum of individual participation in class discussion. It is not enough to be present as a silent observer; if every student took this approach, then there would be no discussion. (Thus, expect a portion of your grade to be based on your participation in case discussions.)
2. Expect the instructor to assume the role of extensive questioner and listener.
3. Expect to be cross-examined for evidence and reasons by your instructor or by others in the class.
4. Expect and tolerate challenges to the views expressed. All students have to be willing to submit their conclusions for scrutiny and rebuttal. Each student needs to learn to state his or her views without fear of disapproval and to overcome the hesitation of speaking out. Learning respect for the views and approaches of others is an integral part of case analysis exercises. But there are times when it is OK to swim against the tide of majority opinion. In the practice of management, there is always room for originality and unorthodox approaches. So, while discussion of a case is a group process, there is no compulsion for you or anyone else to cave in and conform to group opinions and group consensus.
5. Don't be surprised if you change your mind about some things as the discussion unfolds. Be alert to how these changes affect your analysis and recommendations (in case you get called on).
6. Expect to learn a lot from each case discussion; use what you learn to be better prepared for the next case discussion.

There are several things you can do on your own to be good and look good as a participant in class discussions:

- Although you should do your own independent work and independent thinking, don't hesitate before (and after) class to discuss the case with other students. In real life, managers often discuss the company's problems and situation with other people to refine their own thinking.
- In participating in the discussion, make a conscious effort to contribute, rather than just talk. There is a big difference between saying something that builds the discussion and offering a long-winded, off-the-cuff remark that leaves the class wondering what the point was.
- Avoid the use of "I think . . . ," "I believe . . . ," and "I feel . . . "; instead, say, "My analysis shows . . ." and "The company should do . . . because . . ." Always give supporting evidence for your views; then your instructor won't have to ask you "Why?" every time you make a comment.
- In making your points, assume that everyone has read and knows what the case says; avoid reciting and rehashing information in the case—instead, use the data and information to explain your assessment of the situation and to support your position.
- Always prepare good notes (usually two or three pages worth) for each case and use them extensively when you speak. There's no way you can remember everything off the top of your head—especially the results of

your number-crunching. To reel off the numbers or to present all five reasons why, instead of one, you will need good notes. When you have prepared good notes to the study questions and use them as the basis for your comments, *everybody* in the room will know you are well prepared, and your contribution to the case discussion will stand out.

PREPARING A WRITTEN CASE ANALYSIS

Preparing a written case analysis is much like preparing a case for class discussion, except that your analysis must be more complete and reduced to writing. Unfortunately, though, *there is no ironclad procedure for doing a written case analysis*. All we can offer are some general guidelines and words of wisdom—this is because company situations and management problems are so diverse that no one mechanical way to approach a written case assignment always works.

Your instructor may assign you a specific topic around which to prepare your written report. Or, alternatively, you may be asked to do a comprehensive written case analysis, where the expectation is that you will (1) *identify* all the pertinent issues that management needs to address, (2) perform whatever *analysis* and *evaluation* is appropriate, and (3) propose an *action plan* and set of *recommendations* addressing the issues you have identified. In going through the exercise of identify, evaluate, and recommend, you should keep the following pointers in mind:[3]

Identification.   It is essential early on in your paper that you provide a sharply focused diagnosis of strategic issues and key problems and that you demonstrate a good grasp of the company's present situation. Make sure you can identify the firm's strategy (use the concept material in Chapters 1–8 as diagnostic aids) and that you can pinpoint whatever strategy implementation issues may exist (again, consult the concept material in Chapters 9 and 10 for diagnostic help). Consult the analytical checklists we have provided at the end of each chapter for further diagnostic suggestions. Consider beginning your paper by sizing up the company's situation, its strategy, and the significant problems and issues that confront management. State problems/issues as clearly and precisely as you can. Unless it is necessary to do so for emphasis, avoid recounting facts and history about the company (assume your professor has read the case and is familiar with the organization).

Analysis and Evaluation.   This is usually the hardest part of the report. Analysis is hard work! Check out the firm's financial ratios, its profit margins and rates of return, and its capital structure, and decide how strong the firm is financially. Table 1 contains a summary of various financial ratios and how they are calculated. Use it to assist in your financial diagnosis. Similarly, look at marketing, production, managerial competence, and other factors underlying the organization's strategic successes and failures. Decide whether it has a distinctive competence and, if so, whether it is capitalizing on it.

Check to see if the firm's strategy is working and determine the reasons why or why not. Probe the nature and strength of the competitive forces confronting

---

[3]For some additional ideas and viewpoints, you may wish to consult Thomas J. Raymond, "Written Analysis of Cases," in *The Case Method at the Harvard Business School*, ed. M.P. McNair, pp. 139–63. In Raymond's article is an actual case, a sample analysis of the case, and a sample of a student's written report on the case.

the company. Decide whether and why the firm's competitive position is getting stronger or weaker. Use the tools and concepts presented by the instructor (or in an accompanying text) to perform whether analysis and evaluation is appropriate.

In writing your analysis and evaluation, bear in mind four things:

1. You are obliged to offer supporting evidence for your views and judgments. Do not rely on unsupported opinions, overgeneralizations, and platitudes as a substitute for tight, logical argument backed up with facts and figures.
2. If your analysis involves some important quantitative calculations, then use tables and charts to present the calculations clearly and efficiently. Don't just tack the exhibits on at the end of your report and let the reader figure out what they mean and why they were included. Instead, in the body of your report cite some of the key numbers, highlight the conclusions to be drawn from the exhibits, and refer the reader to your charts and exhibits for more details.
3. Demonstrate that you have command of the strategic concepts and analytical tools to which you have been exposed. Use them in your report.
4. Your interpretation of the evidence should be reasonable and objective. Be wary of preparing a one-sided argument that omits all aspects not favorable to your conclusions. Likewise, try not to exaggerate or overdramatize. Endeavor to inject balance into your analysis and to avoid emotional rhetoric. Strike phrases like "I think," "I feel," and "I believe" when you edit your first draft and write in "My analysis shows," instead.

Recommendations. The final section of the written case analysis should consist of a set of definite recommendations and a plan of action. Your set of recommendations should address all of the problems/issues you identified and analyzed. If the recommendations come as a surprise or do not follow logically from the analysis, the effect is to weaken greatly your suggestions of what to do. Obviously, your recommendations for action should offer a reasonable prospect of success. High-risk, bet-the-company recommendations should be made with caution. State how your recommendations will solve the problems you identified. Be sure the company is financially able to carry out what your recommend; also check to see if your recommendations are workable in terms of acceptance by the persons involved, the organization's competence to impelement them, and prevailing market and environmental constraints. Try not to hedge or weasel on the actions you believe should be taken.

By all means state your recommendations in sufficient detail to be meaningful— get down to some definite nitty-gritty specifics. Avoid such unhelpful statements as "the organization should do more planning" or "the company should be more aggressive in marketing its product." For instance, do not stop with saying "the firm should improve its market position" but continue on what exactly how you think this should be done. Offer a definite agenda for action, stipulating a timetable and sequence for initiating actions, indicating priorities, and suggesting who should be responsible for doing what.

In proposing an action plan, remember there is a great deal of difference between being responsible, on the one hand, for a decision that may be costly if it proves in error and, on the other hand, casually suggesting courses of action that might be taken when you do not have to bear the responsibility for any of the consequences. A good rule to follow in making your recommendations is: *Avoid rec-*

ommending anything you would not yourself be willing to do if you were in management's shoes. The importance of learning to develop good judgment in a managerial situation is indicated by the fact that, while the same information and operating data may be available to every manager or executive in an organization, the quality of the judgments about what the information means and what actions need to be taken do vary from person to person.[4]

It goes without saying that your report should be well organized and well written. Great ideas amount to little unless others can be convinced of their merit—this takes tight logic, the presentation of convincing evidence, and persuasively written arguments.

THE TEN COMMANDMENTS OF CASE ANALYSIS

As a way of summarizing our suggestions about how to approach the task of case analysis, we have compiled what we like to call "The Ten Commandments of Case Analysis." They are shown in Table 2. If you observe all or even most of these commandments faithfully as you prepare a case either for class discussion or for a written report, then your chances of doing a good job on the assigned cases will be much improved. Hang in there, give it your best shot, and have some fun exploring what the real world of strategic management is all about.

TABLE 2
The Ten Commandments of Case Analysis

(To be observed in written reports, oral presentations, and participating in class discussions.)

1. Read the case twice, once for an overview and once to gain full command of the facts; then take care to explore every one of the exhibits.
2. Make a list of the problems and issues that have to be confronted.
3. Do enough number crunching to discover the story told by the data presented in the case. (To help you comply with this commandment, consult Table 1 to guide your probing of a company's financial condition and financial performance.)
4. Look for opportunities to use the concepts and analytical tools you have learned earlier.
5. Be thorough in your diagnosis of the situation and make at least a one- or two-page outline of your assessment.
6. Support any and all opinions with well-reasoned arguments and numerical evidence; don't stop until you can purge "I think" and "I feel" from your assessment and, instead, are able to reply completely on "My analysis shows . . ."
7. Develop charts, tables, and graphs to expose more clearly the main points of your analysis.
8. Prioritize your recommendations and make sure they can be carried out in an acceptable time frame with the available skills and financial resources.
9. Review your recommended action plan to see if it addresses all of the problems and issues you identified.
10. Avoid recommending any course of action that could have disastrous consequences if it doesn't work out as planned; be, therefore, as alert to the downside risks or your recommendations as you are to their upside potential and appeal.

---

[4]Gragg, "Because Wisdom Can't Be Told," p.10.

Index

X–Z